Slavonic and
Western Music
Essays for Gerald Abraham

Russian Music Studies, No. 12

Malcolm Hamrick Brown, Series Editor

Professor of Music
Indiana University

Other Titles in This Series

ng/812   £16.50

£4=95

Gerard McBurney
London   1st Aug 92

Slavonic and Western Music
Essays for Gerald Abraham

Edited by
Malcolm Hamrick Brown
Professor of Music
Indiana University
Bloomington, Indiana
and
Roland John Wiley
Associate Professor of Music
The University of Michigan
Ann Arbor, Michigan

UMI RESEARCH PRESS
Ann Arbor, Michigan

Oxford University Press
Oxford, England

Produced and distributed in the
U.S., Canada, Mexico, Japan,
China, and Central and South America by
UMI Research Press
an imprint of
University Microfilms International
A Xerox Information Resources Company
Ann Arbor, Michigan 48106

Library of Congress Cataloging in Publication Data

Slavonic and western music.

(Russian music studies ; no. 12)
Includes index.
Bibliography: p.
1. Abraham, Gerald, 1904-   . 2. Music—Addresses,
essays, lectures. 3. Music—Russia—Addresses, essays,
lectures. I. Brown, Malcolm Hamrick. II. Wiley,
Roland John.
ML55.A18 1984   780   84-2625
ISBN 0-8357-1594-9

Distributed in the United Kingdom,
Middle East, Continental Europe,
Africa, Australia, New Zealand, and
The Far East, with the exception of
Japan and China by
Oxford University Press
Walton Street,
Oxford OX2 6DP

British Library Cataloguing in Publication Data

**Slavonic and Western music : essays for
Gerald Abraham.**
1. Music—Soviet Union—19th century—
History and criticism
I. Brown, Malcolm Hamrick   II. Abraham, Gerald
III. Wiley, Roland John
781.747   ML300.4
ISBN 0-19-311209-4

Frontispiece: Gerald Ernest Heal Abraham

Contents

Introduction

This collection of essays is presented to honor Gerald Ernest Heal Abraham on the occasion of his eightieth birthday, which occurred on 9 March 1984. DA ZDRAVSTVUET! VIVAT! LONG LIVE!

The trilingual acclamation and the title of our volume as well fall shy of suggesting the range of Gerald Abraham's scholarly interests and demonstrated expertise. He has written authoritatively on both medieval and modern music, on Nietzsche and Tolstoy, on Handel and Janáček. Moreover, he has harbored a lively, lifelong passion for naval and military history, which prompted his first foray into scholarship at about age ten, when he began (but soon abandoned) a history of the Boer War—with sketch-maps! On the eve of the 1918 Armistice, young Abraham, then fourteen, was reading about Lee's surrender at Appomattox, and eight years later, his first visit to France took him to Alsace and Lorraine to explore the 1870 battlefields. (His diary records that he spent 6 August 1926 rambling over the field of Gravelotte.) A few years later, he would complete an account (still unpublished) of the Serbo-Bulgarian War of 1885, and as recently as the early 1960s, he began gathering materials for what was to have been his *opus ultimum,* a book on the last of the Russo-Turkish Wars. But except for becoming a respectable rifle-shot and serving in the BBC Home Guard during World War II, Abraham's militarism has remained all "in the head."

It might not have been so. He had actually prepared at Portsmouth for a career in the navy, but ill-health intervened. Recuperating at his family home on the Isle of Wight, Abraham sought diversion in the practical application of a long-time interest in music: he began scoring arrangements and, on occasion, composing original music for the band of the Argyll and Sutherland Highlanders at the local garrison. Like some of the nineteenth-century Russians about whom he would one day write, Abraham taught himself by doing. Starting as a rank amateur gifted with innate musicality—as a boy, he had piano lessons—he relied on an alert, inquiring, and disciplined mind to train himself, first as a competent arranger and composer, eventually as the learned musicologist we celebrate.

The article on Abraham in the *New Grove* provides a good and mostly accurate account of our honoree's life and activity in the world of music, though a few corrections and some up-dating are in order. *This Modern Stuff* (1933), which Abraham prefers to count as his first book, was renamed *This Modern Music* at the time of its third edition (1952; reprint, 1955). He not only completed and edited M.D. Calvocoressi's unfinished study of Musorgsky for the Master Musicians series (1946), he also edited his deceased colleague's *magnum opus* on the composer—*Modest Mussorgsky: His Life and Works* (1956). In 1967, Abraham was chief, not deputy, music critic of the *Daily Telegraph,* and in 1968-69, he was named Ernest Bloch Professor of Music at the University of California, Berkeley, where he delivered the Ernest Bloch Lectures during April and May 1969 (published as *The Tradition of Western Music,* 1974). Abraham served as secretary of the editorial board of the *New Oxford History of Music* only until 1975, when he became General Editor; he has also chaired the committee for the publication of *Early English Church Music* (1973-83).

Abraham is an honorary Doctor of Music not only of Durham University (1961) but also of the universities in Liverpool (1978) and Southampton (1979), and in 1982 he was elected to Corresponding Membership in the American Musicological Society.

Let it be remembered that this brief account of Abraham's professional activities does not duplicate but merely revises and supplements the detailed survey found in the *New Grove*—a process that we foresee to be on-going! Abraham has been known sometimes of late to quote Haydn about himself, "Hin ist alle meine Kraft, alt und schwach bin ich," but those of us his junior by many years can only marvel at the *Kraft* Abraham continues to command. His *Concise Oxford History of Music* was published in 1979 (German ed., 1983), and volume 8 of the *New Oxford History of Music—The Age of Beethoven, 1790-1830*—which he both edited and contributed to, appeared in 1982.

Our appreciation of Abraham the scholar may not be increased, but our sense of him as a personality is enhanced by knowing how deeply he has loved the English countryside and felt its lasting influence in his life. Though he was born in a small town on the edge of country, his eyes were really opened to it as a boy, he remembers, by the writings of Richard Jefferies—"not so much his mystical pantheism (very like Rimsky-Korsakov's at about the same time!) as his accurate, beautifully written observation of nature." It never made Abraham a natural historian (he leaves that to his wife and daughter); identification of an unfamiliar flower interferes, he says, with his pleasure in the flower. But he feels really happy only when he is in the country. When he lived in London (1935-47), it was fortunately in Hampstead Village, on the edge of the Heath; Liverpool (1947-62) would have been intolerable, he declares, if he and his wife could not have escaped into Cheshire and North Wales during weekends. For twenty years now, he and his wife have lived in a small house— The Old School House—in a hamlet, surrounded by trees, five or six miles from the nearest small town. Visitors have loved it, too: Friedrich Blume, also a great walker and nature-lover *and* an amateur naturalist, spent happy hours there, and Donald Grout, another fancier of rural isolation, has enjoyed visiting this remote country retreat. (Abraham recalls a time when he had Grout and Oliver Strunk sitting side by side in the garden.)

The measure of a man and his achievement can be taken in part from the measure of those whom he felt fortunate enough to number among his friends (to number his colleagues and acquaintances would be nigh impossible for Abraham!): among the scholars, in addition to Blume and Grout, have been Edward Dent, Jack Westrup, Egon Wellesz, Joseph Kerman, David Boyden, and Vincent Duckles; among the composers, Zoltan Kodály, William Walton, Constant Lambert, and Edmund Rubbra; and such non-musicians as the dramatist and novelist, J.B. Priestley, and the Irish poet, Louis MacNeice.

Our honoree's advancement to the status of septuagenarian was warmly acknowledged in a special editorial section entitled, "A Birthday Greeting to Gerald Abraham," in the April 1974 issue of *Music and Letters*. (Abraham's very first contribution to that journal was written when he was but a lad of eighteen—"Burns and the Scottish Folk Song," *ML* 4 [January 1923]—and it was that journal's founder and then editor, A.H. Fox Strangways, who facilitated young Abraham's early introduction into an ever-widening circle of scholars and critics.)

Abraham's advancement to the still more rarefied status of octogenarian mandated a festschrift as the only tribute appropriate to marking the occasion. From the beginning, the project at hand moved forward with unwavering support and enthusiasm from our honoree's colleagues. Regrettably, some of them were prevented by circumstance from contributing essays of their own. Others would no doubt gladly have contributed had it been possible to invite them.

When it was learned that Roland John Wiley had earlier taken the initiative to speak with a publisher about sponsoring an Abraham festschrift, but without success because of prevailing economic stringencies, Wiley was immediately asked to join our enterprise as co-editor, to share equally in the preparation of the contributions for publication. His help has been invaluable and his editorial diligence exemplary. As the senior editor, I am obliged to acknowledge that without his willing and energetic participation in the editorial process, this volume could not have been accomplished so soon or so successfully.

To the authors represented here, without whom there would have been no editorial process, most sincere thanks.

To Gerald Ernest Heal Abraham, on behalf of us all, may our token of respect and scholarly affection bring grist aplenty to your ready and waiting mill!

Malcolm Hamrick Brown
Bloomington, November 1982

Gerald Abraham in his garden on 20 June 1983 (photo by Roland John Wiley).

A Recollection of 20 June 1983

Roland John Wiley

It is midday; the 10:30 train from London stops for a moment at the small town of Haslemere. A dozen steps, the front of the station facing the street, a few minutes—was there some confusion about the arrival time? A bright green car turns into the street and hurries up to the curb. Its white-maned driver shouts a greeting; we drive through the lovely Sussex countryside to his home.

After lunch, in the garden, there is talk of a life in music. He describes his extraordinary career as the combination of happenstance and the good offices of other people; his own labor and musicality have played only a small part. "It has always been accidents," he claims. "Everything that has happened to me has been good fortune and the kindness of friends." Modesty this perhaps, but not patronizing, for here is a man who has always backed up his words with facts.

His anecdotes are no less authoritative than his scholarly observations. Was it to have been music from the beginning? "I had piano lessons when I was a child, . . . but I wasn't very interested in music. I intended to go into the navy, curiously enough, and I went to what we call a 'crammer,' a man who pushes you through the naval examinations and that sort of thing. There was a chap who played the piano better than I did and he . . . oh he used to play things like *Finlandia*. . . . And I didn't go into the navy, as you can see. Like Rimsky-Korsakov I was a failed sailor; I failed even quicker than Rimsky."

The Royal Navy having lost an excellent prospect, it was time for new experiences abroad, to Germany, life with a German family, and fresh musical impressions. "I had my first introduction to Wagner, *Walküre* at the Cologne Opera, and then I heard Mahler for the first time—I never heard of Mahler and Bruckner until I went to Germany. And also Russian music, . . . it must have been the Borodin B-minor Symphony which was my real introduction to Russian music. I thought, 'Ah! He's the chap for me!' And then at about the same time the Russian Ballet—it was no longer Diaghilev, it was called the Ballets Russes de Monte Carlo—gave a season at the Alhambra Theatre in London, and they did the dances from *Igor*. And I thought, 'My, this is the stuff!'"

He decides on a career in writing and criticism, his subjects at the outset including Nietzsche and Tolstoy. Soon, however, music takes precedence over literature and imposes new demands: whence the necessary technical knowledge? "I've never been educated," he quips. "I taught myself! This is the only thing to do. Everything really, I suppose, I taught myself as it became necessary to know it." Self-taught? Drawn to the music of Borodin? A failed sailor, like Rimsky-Korsakov? Such affinities with the inspired amateurs of an earlier time make it fitting that essays on the Russian nationalists should establish his reputation.

In the fifty years marked approximately by *Borodin* and *The Concise Oxford History of Music* he builds and justifies that reputation. Through his work with the British Broadcasting Corporation and through writings and editorial work so prolific as to confound bibliographers, this "terribly uneducated" man brings delight to a nation and illumination to generations of scholars. Two thoughts cross one's mind: in his great diversity narrow specialty is soon abandoned, and in his career university teaching has played so small a part.

This day he speaks little of the whole career, but tells many stories of experiences it produced. A gift for vignette is revealed as the conversation ranges over the vast spectrum of his acquaintances: one luminary was "a wonderful tester, he didn't believe easily"; another told stories over a cup of tea and two digestive biscuits at the National Liberal Club; and of a third, "... if you turned over a stone in the garden, he was sort of like the creature you'd find under it." One realizes that his perspective, vignettes aside, has been seasoned by contact with some of the most distinguished musicians of our time: Boult, Calvocoressi, Shostakovich, Britten—to him these are not just names.

"I am indirectly responsible for *Peter Grimes*," he says with undisguised pleasure:

> "I was deputy editor of *The Listener* for a time. E.M. Forster gave a talk about George Crabbe. The editor came into my office who had got the script of Forster's talk, and he said, 'You don't think we want to print this, do you?' I read it and said, 'This is rather interesting. I never knew anything about Crabbe; I think we might print it; other people probably don't know much more about him than I do.' 'All right, we'll print it.'
>
> It so happened that someone was sending *Listeners* to Ben in America, and he also, although he came from that part of the country, didn't know anything about Crabbe. He was interested. And that's what drew him to *Peter Grimes* as a subject, and he composed it.
>
> I had my revenge on Forster later. At Liverpool, he was to give a talk. ... He was invited by the English Department, but as he was going to talk about musical subjects, they asked me to go along and take the chair. Among the points he made was that creative work gives rise to criticism, but criticism never repays the debt. In thanking him I remarked: 'In one regard I think Mr. Forster has made a remarkable error. He says that criticism has never led to any creative work.' And then I told him the story about his broadcast talk, and how this had led to the composition of *Peter Grimes*. ..."

And so it continued—Walton, Kodály, A.H. Fox Strangways, Yury Shaporin, the state of musicology—and too soon it is time to go. Again the rolling hills, again the town, and then farewells. As the train leaves for Waterloo Station there comes a feeling of enrichment, a feeling the reader no doubt will know who has ever encounted so rare a man as Gerald Abraham.

Observation, Elucidation, Utilization: Western Attitudes to Eastern Musics, ca. 1600-ca. 1830

Frank Ll. Harrison

Attitudes determine, or at least influence, behavior. For the present purpose, distinctions will be made between three categories of behavior, arising from the different attitudes that westerners, during the period indicated, have taken to eastern musics. These are: (1) written observation and documentation; (2) exposition of musical systems and practices; and (3) incorporation of eastern musical materials into western music situations. The aim of this paper is to exemplify these attitudes and the procedures arising from them in the context of the cultural impacts involving music that occurred when west met east.

Though an attitude of total dismissal lies outside this topic, two late instances may be cited. Berlioz, open-minded and progressive in his views on musical practices in Europe, descended to cultural xenophobia in reacting to his experience at the World Exhibition of 1851 in London. This is a sample:

> Finally, I come to the conclusion that the Chinese and Indians would have a music similar to ours if they were to have one, but that they are still in this respect plunged into the deepest shades of barbarism, and into a childish ignorance, in which some vague and weak instincts barely show their existence. I conclude moreover that the orientals call music what we term *charivari*, and that for them, like the witches in *Macbeth*, the horrible is the beautiful.[1]

Fifteen years later, a similar attitude, using the same derogatory terms *"charivari"* and "barbarism," was printed by Félix Clément in his *Dictionnaire Lyrique* of 1869. Clément praised Boieldieu for not using exotic music material in his opera *Le Calife de Bagdad* (1800). "It is a delicious fantasy, this opera," Clément wrote; "people have extolled for a long time pretensions to local colour... Boieldieu had too much sense and good taste to introduce into the theater the frightful *charivari* known by the name of oriental music—that barbarous, degenerate and almost unrecognizable relic of ancient tune repertories. He has sought to express the images that can produce in our spirit the ideal concept: that of an Orient glimpsed through the prism of our European civilization."[2]

Clément's kind of "Orientalism" (the title, incidentally, of a relevant book by Edward W. Said[3]) was implicit in many cases of observation, whether original or derived. Marin Mersenne, for example, provided, in his *Harmonie Universelle* (1636-37), drawings and morphological discussion of an Indian *bin sitar,* a Turkish *tambur* and a Chinese *sheng* (though he called the last an Indian instrument).[4] His drawing and description of the *sitar* were obtained from England by Claude Hardy, lawyer, linguist and mathematician. Mersenne was not in a position to discuss the sound of these instruments. His object, however, as stated in the heading of Proposition II in the section, "Concerning the genres of music," was to prove the diatonic system, i.e., the western system, to be more "natural" than others. His conclusion of the discussion of this proposition was cautious: "... if experience had shown us," he wrote, "that a child were to sing the enharmonic degrees, or other degrees smaller or larger, as easily as the diatonic, after having taken as much trouble as the others who learn to sing in the ordinary way, it would have to be admitted that there are no degrees or intervals, neither the one kind nor the other, easier to sing or more natural. But since all experiences and observations conspire to persuade us that the diatonic is more natural than the other kinds of music, one must align oneself with that affirmative view."[5]

Fourteen years later Athanasius Kircher gave, in his *Musurgia* of 1650, notations of a Turkish and of a Chinese tune. His comment on the former was: "I hear that some Turkish priests, whenever they intone solemnly that *alla alla* of theirs, use this kind of musical phrase—filled with extraordinary, unusual, congested and abhorrent intervals":[6]

Ex. 1

On the Chinese tune, Kircher merely noted that "the Chinese, as Father Samedius of our Society, who has been conversant with them for many years, has informed me, use this musical phrase while they are adoring Confucius":[7]

Ex. 2

Kircher's conclusion, less cautious than Mersenne's, revealed the same motivation, that of asserting the superiority of the diatonic system of the West on the ground of "nature"; he insisted moreover that all the world's peoples prefer it. "I declare," he wrote, "the diatonic above the rest to be the natural one, because I see that all the peoples of the whole world prefer it naturally in their songs. This appears from various examples that I have obtained from the mouths of Fathers of our Society gathered here in Rome from the whole world in the year 1645."

To the long Jesuit presence in China the West owed the greater part of its knowledge of the elements of Chinese civilization, including music. Possibly the earliest Jesuit report from that country to be printed was sent by Diego de Pantoya to his Provincial in March 1602. This was translated into German by Egidius Albertinus and printed in Munich in 1608. A paragraph mentions music and other arts:[8]

> The Chinese like poetry... In the same way they like painting, music and playing on instruments so much that even people of high rank and distinction use them. Although they understand very little about painting, and do not paint anything with shadows or paint in oils, they are very outstanding and artful in music, and play on an instrument seriously and slowly. I have heard various kinds of music in the King's palace... which, although it did not displease me, yet is not to be compared to the music of our country. Nonetheless, the Chinese believe that it is much superior to ours. They have only one single species of instrument for distinguished persons, by whom it is held in high esteem. This is rather similar to our harp; the form and style of the instrument, however, as well as the manner of playing it, do not in the least agree with ours.

In 1723 the Jesuit Filippo Bonanni published in Rome his *Gabinetto Armonico pieno de stromenti sonori.*[9] Among its 177 depictions were seven Chinese instruments (though one of these seems to represent an Indian female dancer with cup-shaped cymbals). Doubtless Bonanni's information was derived from reports from Jesuits; in a note preceding some additions at the end of the volume Bonanni mentioned "Father Giampriano our missionary, sent by the Emperor of China to Italy for secret negotiations." He gave as his source for a depiction of a Chinese bell actuated by a cylinder *L'Istoria dell' Ambasceria all Cina degl' Olandesi.*[10] Bonanni copied Mersenne's drawing of the Indian *bin sitar,* and gave depictions of Turkish, Persian, Armenian and Indonesian instruments.

In 1735 the Jesuit priest Jean-Baptiste Du Halde (1674-1743), who was secretary to Louis XIV's confessor and had not been to China, published a five-volume work based on Jesuit reports from that country since the sixteenth century. A two-volume translation into English was printed in London in 1738 and 1741,[11] and Du Halde's compilation became the main source of information about China for eighteenth-century Europeans. Du Halde gave no sources for the five tunes he printed, merely presenting them as evidence of the "imperfection" of Chinese music. Du Halde detailed an interchange in 1679 between the Chinese Emperor's musicians and two Jesuit fathers, Grimaldi and Pereira, who played for the Emperor on organ and harpsichord. The Emperor was astonished at Pereira's ability to transcribe a Chinese tune during its performance and to play it immediately. Pereira subsequently produced a work on the elements of European music for use in an Academy of Music founded by the same Emperor. In 1713 there was printed a book entitled *Lŭ Lŭ Dscheng I* by the Emperor Kang H'si, with an appendix on western music theory by Thomas Pereira and Theodorico Pedrini. There seems no evidence, however, that such instruction became a part of the Academy's curriculum.

With the *Mémoire sur la musique des Chinois* (Paris, 1779), by the Jesuit Jean-Joseph-Marie Amiot (born 1718; died in Peking 1794), we come to the first work of elucidation, as well as observation, of Chinese music by a European. Amiot tells in the Introduction to his *Mémoire* (which he protested was not a treatise) that during his first years in Peking, where he arrived in 1750, he played *Les Sauvages* and *Les Cyclopes* by Rameau and pieces for flute by Blavet to learned Chinese persons. Their reaction was: "The tunes of our music go from the ear to the heart, and from the heart to the soul; we feel them, we understand them. Those you have just played do not have that effect upon us."[12] Amiot decided to study the Chinese science of music, as well as their religious and civil ceremonies. In 1754 he sent back to Father Latour, Procurer in France of the Jesuit mission to China, a translation of a contemporary treatise on ancient and current Chinese music. He sent two copies, one for the Procurer, for the information of prospective missionaries, and one for the secretary of the *Académie Royale des Inscriptions et Belles Lettres,* for the information of interested *savants.* Latour was apparently uninterested, while the manuscript in the *Académie* remained unnoticed by any to whom it might have been of interest until six years later, when it came to the attention of Jean-Philippe Rameau. It was not until twenty-five years later that Amiot's subsequent summary of his studies of Chinese music, the *Mémoire,* was printed, with additional notes and observations by l'Abbé Pierre-Joseph Roussier, Canon of Ecuis and Correspondent of the *Académie.*

Amiot's account of his motivation in undertaking his studies may be quoted from the manuscript of his Preface to the 1754 translation, as this was given by Jean-Benjamin de La Borde (1734—guillotined 1794) in his *Essai sur la musique ancienne et moderne* (Paris, 1780). This ran: "Father Gaubil was the first to suggest that I acquire a knowledge of an art about which there were hitherto only very imperfect notions. He helped me when I was hesitant, and encouraged me to pursue an enterprise which could have the greatest success. He put it to me that since music had gained for me the advantage of being a missionary in this capital, entry to which is strictly forbidden to anyone who is not officially in the Emperor's service, I should not fail to acquire a profound knowledge of the music that the Chinese cultivated of old, and of that in use under the present dynasty."

The circumstances surrounding the printing of Amiot's *Mémoire* are informative about eighteenth-century thought about music, as well as about the impact, upon learned persons at that time of information about oriental music. Jean-Philippe Rameau (1683-1764) added to the end of one of his last theoretical works, the *Code de musique pratique, ou méthodes pour apprendre la musique, même à des aveugles* (Paris, 1760), a section unrelated to the book's subject, under the heading *Nouvelles refléxions sur le principe sonore.*[13] "The principle of everything is one," he wrote. "Convinced of the necessity of this universal principle, the earliest philosophers sought it in music. Pythagoras, following the Egyptians, applied the laws of harmony to the movements of the planets. Plato made it preside over the composition of the soul. Aristotle, his disciple, having said that music is a celestial and divine thing, added that one finds in it the rationale of the system of the world." Here Rameau added a footnote, which may be summarized. A few days before, there had fallen into his hands the *Académie* copy of Amiot's translation of the treatise by Ly-koang-ty, which had reposed there for six years. This expounded the source of the ancient Chinese music system as a geometrical progression with the factor nine up to the thirteenth term. This Rameau explained thus: the Chinese take their systems from the triple progression, as did Pythagoras. They aim to have five tones only in their *Lu,* a term signifying system, scale, gamut or mode. Ly-koang-ty gives it in this order: *sol,* 3; *la,* 27; *si,* 243; *ut dièze,* 2187; *ré dièze,* 19683; *mi dièze,* 177147. This, observed Rameau, is the most defective order one could imagine; these five tones give false intervals, except for the major whole tone. Another Chinese authority, he continued, gives the following: *sol dièze,* 6561; *la dièze,* 59049; *ut dièze,* 2187; *ré dièze,* 13683 (*recte* 19683, as Roussier pointed out in his *Mémoire*—see the following paragraph); *mi dièze,* 177147. This, Rameau noted, is equivalent to *sol, la, ut, ré, mi,* to which the octave *sol* is joined to begin another *Lu.* It is also equivalent, he added, to the sequence of tones in an organ from Barbary, (clearly meaning a Chinese *sheng*) that was brought from the Cape of Good Hope by a M. Dupleix and kindly presented to Rameau. On it he could execute all the Chinese tunes given in notation in the third volume of Father Du Halde (also found on page 380 of the twenty-second volume of *L'Histoire des voyages* by the Abbé Prevôt). This proves well enough, Rameau concluded, that this latter *Lu* has been predominant in China for a long time.

Rameau left the subject at that, with the comment that the difference of a comma, imperceptible to the ear, was chiefly what made the Greek and Chinese music systems so very imperfect. An opposite view was arrived at by Roussier, who, as Fétis noted, did not know a note of music till he was twenty-five.[14] In the year that Rameau died, Roussier, then forty-eight, published a *Traité des accords,* and in the following year *L'Harmonie pratique.* He dogged Rameau's footsteps in both works, criticizing him only in details. After four years' further study Roussier published his final manifesto, entitled: *Mémoire sur la musique*

*des anciens, où l'on expose le principe des proportions authentiques, dites de
Pythagore, & de divers systèmes de musique chez les grecs, les chinois & les
égyptiens* (Paris, 1770). This was intended as a demonstration that the
proportions of musical intervals given by Ptolemy and adopted by Zarlino and
all following geometricians were false, while those of Pythagoras were true.
The Chinese element in Roussier's discussion was admittedly derived from
Rameau's in the *Code*. Roussier concurred with Rameau's description of the
current Chinese system as "un ordre des plus vicieux qu'on puisse imaginer."
He considered this Chinese evidence to prove that the systems of the ancient
Greeks and Chinese formed one and the same system. It was therefore evident
that "this whole was the system of some people more ancient than the Greeks
and Chinese, and that it was the dismemberings of this primitive system that
formed different systems among various nations."[15]

We return to Amiot, who meanwhile had been unaware of the fate of his
translation of the Chinese treatise. He received from M. Bignon, the King's
Librarian, a copy of Roussier's *Mémoire* four years after that book was
published. Two years later, in 1776, Amiot signed his name in Peking to the
Introduction and to the last page of his *Mémoire sur la musique des Chinois*.
He sent two copies of the manuscript to Paris, one to M. Bignon and one to M.
Bertin, Minister and Secretary of State. The latter was the posessor of a
"cabinet de curiosités chinoises," to whom Amiot had earlier sent a *kin (ch'in)*.
Three years later Amiot's *Mémoire* was printed, lavishly farced with verbose
footnotes by Roussier.

The manner in which this was arranged was explained by La Borde in his
Essai, printed one year after Amiot's *Mémoire*. La Borde had a manuscript of
the *Mémoire,* and used it for an extensive chapter, *De la musique des Chinois,*
and for a chapter on modern Chinese instruments. In a footnote to the former
chapter he noted that while his *Essai* was in the press he learned with great
pleasure that a minister known for his attachment to the arts (this must have
been M. Bertin) had charged the Abbé Roussier with directing the printing of
Amiot's precious *Mémoire*. It would include observations and a quantity of
notes that Roussier wished to add to it. It appears that La Borde also possessed
a manuscript of Amiot's translation of the Chinese treatise.[16]

In the Introduction to his *Mémoire* Amiot praised Roussier's book, while
Roussier seized the opportunity of propagating his theories about musical
systems and their history (ideas which Fétis unkindly called *"rêveries"*).
Roussier objected to the current fusion of the chromatic and diatonic
semitones (as *la dièze* with *si bémol*). He found proof of the importance of the
Chinese distinction between them in Amiot's translation of the Chinese
treatise. From it proceeded the fundamental principles of music. These should
at every possible opportunity be put before Europeans, among whom many
"températeurs &... joueurs d'instruments à touches" persistently taught the
contrary. Amiot agreed with Roussier's belief in the identity of the

Pythagorean system with that of the ancient Chinese. Some of Amiot's conclusions were: that the Chinese system had almost all the elements of those of the Greeks and Egyptians; that since the Chinese is the oldest, the others must have been derived from it; and that Pythagoras must have visited China.

Whereas Kircher in the previous century believed on his geographical evidence that the western system was universally preferred, and must therefore be the basis for the unity of all systems, Roussier viewed this supposed unity as the initial stage of a historical process of decline from past perfection to present imperfection. A similar obsession about the degeneration of European music as compared with ancient Greek had been the lifetime preoccupation of Giovanni Battista Doni (1595-1647), a contemporary of Mersenne who invented instruments to prove his doctrines. Doni wrote in a letter to Mersenne in 1633: "I hope to have begun to illustrate the ancient music, and by that means to bring back ours to its ancient splendour from the barbarism in which it lies since the German and Arabic inundations".[17]

While Amiot's main interest was in theory, he also made a notable contribution to documentation, in the form of the text and music notation of a "Chinese Hymn in Honour of the Ancestors," together with a description of the ceremonial, including dance and instrument playing, involved in its performance.[18] Having shed his initial prejudices, he was able to write revealingly about the effect upon him of this experience:

> When the Emperor had arrived before the representation of his ancestors, and the musicians began to intone the hymn, I was convinced that the first sounds that one hears penetrate to the soul, and awaken in the heart the most delicious feelings by which it can be affected. It is thus that one can explain how music was able to work such great marvels among ancient peoples, while ours, with all its harmony, is barely able to scratch the surface of the soul, so to speak.[19]

This statement may be compared with the reaction of Johann Hüttner to a comparable experience on the Emperor's birthday in 1793, during the Earl of Macartney's embassy to China.[20]

As has been noted, Amiot's material was used by La Borde, with re-engravings of fine quality, a year after the *Mémoire* was printed. A summary of the *Mémoire* was published anonymously in the *Musikalischer Almanach für Deutschland* five years after its appearance.[21] Amiot's work and one of Roussier's assertions were referred to by John Barrow when he wrote his account of the Earl of Macartney's embassy.[22]

During the period under discussion, western interest in what was referred to in France as *"les curiosités chinoises"* amounted to a movement that acquired the name *chinoiserie*. Was there a musical *chinoiserie?* Did observation and elucidation, of the sort that have been discussed, have some concomitant utilization? Richard Engländer, in his study of Gluck's opera *Le Cinesi* and the ballet *L'Orfano della China* (then thought to be Gluck's, later shown to be by Grétry), discussed the appearance of Chinese figures in stage works involving music, and also in balls, from the late seventeenth century onwards.[23] He noted that Du Halde was drawn upon for information about Chinese costumes and drama, and also for a description of a Festival of Lanterns.[24] The latter was put on the Paris Opéra stage in Grétry's opera *Panurge dans l'Isle des Lanternes* (1785). Engländer mentioned Du Halde's music notations in this context. Nevertheless, there seems not to have been any utilization, in these spheres of entertainment, of the tune material available in Du Halde or elsewhere. On the other hand, certain instrumental timbres were accepted as an exotic element within the normal (or slightly eccentricized) musical language of the time. François Castil-Blaze observed in a section on instrumental usages in his largely retrospective *De l'Opéra en France* (Paris, 1820):

> Les cimbales, les tambours, le triangle, les clochettes, le sistre . . . sont placés convenablement dans les marches militaires, les airs de danse d'un caractère fier ou sauvage, quelques choeurs, et tout ce qui doit avoir la couleur asiatique.[25]

In fact, the overture to Gluck's *Le Cinesi* had in performance a battery of such instruments, though they are not shown in the score. Their sound made a strong impression on the composer Karl Ditters von Dittersdorf at the performance in the Schlosshof in Vienna on 24 September, 1754. He wrote:

> I have still in my memory the extremely beautiful performance of the short opera *La Danza* [actually *Le Cinesi*] which Metastasio had made out of his piece *Il Ballo Cinese* and for which Gluck had written music. The decor by Quaglio was completely in Chinese style, and translucent. Lacquer painters, sculptors and gilders had decorated it lavishly with everything their art made possible. What gave the decor the greatest glamour were the prismatic tubes of glass which were ground in Bohemian glass-factories, and which were placed precisely in the empty spaces, which moreover were made multi-colored with oil paint. The beautiful and astonishing sight produced by the innumerable lights of the lighted prism, which even simply in the light of the sun have a great effect—this sight is undescribable . . . And the divine music of Gluck! Not only did the sweet sound of the brilliant *sinfonia*, which at times was accompanied by small bells, triangles, small hand drums, jingles and the like . . . enchant the audience already at the beginning, even before the curtain was raised, but all the music was from beginning to end a work of magic.[26]

In giving a notated quotation from the last movement of *L'Orfano della China,* Richard Engländer commented on the following technical points (I follow his terminology): rondo design, sixteenth-notes by the triangle, *pizzicato* of the *murkibassartig geführten*[27] violas, repeated notes of horns and divided bassoons, supporting of the violins' tune by oboes or flutes, "exotic" flattened leading note, and "specifically Chinese" manifold repetition of a short phrase. While the use of such percussion as Dittersdorf and Castil-Blaze described, which may often have been added without notation in the score, is perhaps an instance of utilization in the sense of our title, the pseudo-orientalisms in music sound distinguished by Engländer do not come in that category.

The fact that such Chinese music material as that printed by Du Halde, Amiot, John Barrow and perhaps others was not used by these composers may be ascribed to three factors: the nature of music transmission; the restrictive conventions of music genres; and the corresponding expectations of particular groups of music users. Since music, unlike most cultural possessions of a society, is not a material object, its utilization, in the present context, involved processes different from those concerned with, say, literature or *objets d'art*. (A musical instrument, however, may be totally abstracted from its soundmaking use, and become solely an *objet d'art*.) Though music has been termed a "universal language," its meaning is not such as may be "translated" in the same sense as verbal language. Its semiotic element lies primarily in its use, and only secondarily, in a derived sense, in its structure.[28] Aside from exceptional cases, a specific music in its original form is not meaningfully transferable without some transference of its contexts of occasion and their social significance. It has been observed that "music, learned or popular is the most widespread and unsuspected contraband commodity."[29] This percipient comment is truly valid only of differing genres within a particular culture. It is in general true of music, though not of most other cultural commodities, that in the absence of some convergence between two or more types of social system, or of conscious incorporation of both music and its context from one society into another, simple transmission of music structure *in toto* almost never occurs. Moreover, the expectations of music users tend to ensure that availability of music material cross-culturally, in whatever form, does not of itself stimulate its use.

In the situations that have been considered so far, liaison between composers and those intellectually concerned with oriental music was not expected, although those who provided the visual and story elements of a ballet or *Singspiel* on a Chinese subject drew upon works like Du Halde's for ideas. Du Halde's first notated tune is a case in point; the people who took notice of it during the hundred years after its publication were those who may be called disseminators. Jean-Jacques Rousseau, for example, printed at the end of his *Dictionnaire de Musique* (Paris, 1768) some non-European tunes; among them were Du Halde's first tune and a *Chanson Persane* taken from Jean Chardin's *Voyages en Perse* (Amsterdam, 1711).[30] In the body of the *Dictionnaire* Rousseau made a comment that suggests he was aware of the inadequacy of notating non-European tunes in European symbols. Their apparent degree of conformity to our system, he felt, might cause some people to admire our system's universality; it might equally cause others to doubt the intelligence or accuracy of those who transmitted the tunes.[31] But in the case of Du Halde's first tune Rousseau's own accuracy comes into question. Du Halde had this:

Ex. 3

etc.

Rousseau printed this:

Ex. 4

etc.

La Borde, in the chapter already referred to, printed this tune and its Chinese notation, attributing both to Amiot and giving a translation of its title *Lieou yé Kin* as *"Le Satin à feuilles de Saule,"* i.e., "The Silk Material with Leaves of Willow."[32] It seems he took these from Amiot's manuscript of the *Mémoire,* for they do not appear in the print. La Borde described Rousseau's version as "étrangement défiguré"[33] on the ground that it was notated in a quarter note unit (as in Du Halde), suggesting a sort of *air de danse,* whereas Amiot's notation was in a half note unit, appropriate to a slow and serious tune—La Borde marked it *grave.* He also observed that Rousseau's third measure, containing *f* twice, was false, since the Chinese used only five pitches. Amiot's form of the tune, as given by La Borde, also differed from Du Halde's in six points of detail. This tune appeared a second time in La Borde's *Essai,* in a separately numbered section at the end of his second volume entitled *Choix de Chansons Françaises . . .* There the tune, headed *Air Chinois mal noté dans le Père Du Halde,*[34] has all Du Halde's even eighth notes in dotted eighth-plus-sixteenth rhythm, and has other slighter changes. In addition, La Borde printed Du Halde's fourth tune with its rhythm completely changed.[35]

This writer has examined two undated offprints of an article on music written by Jean-le-Rond D'Alembert, mathematician, collaborator with Diderot in the *Encyclopédie,* and supporter of Rameau's theories, for a *Dictionnaire raisoné [sic] des Arts.* The one that appears to be the earlier has Du Halde's first tune unchanged, but the dotted eighth and sixteenth notes in the third measure are even eighth notes. The other offprint has this and other tunes as in Rousseau's *Dictionnaire,* clearly printed from the same engraving. Both offprints have a short section headed *Système de Musique des Orientaux,* explained as meaning Turks, Arabs and Persians, and also a discussion of the

Chinese tune and the Chinese music system, with acknowledgment to Du Halde, but no mention of Amiot.[36]

The Welsh harper Edward Jones (1752-1824), "bard" to the Prince of Wales, later George IV (from 1820), and best known for his *Musical and Poetical Relicks of the Welsh Bards* (London, 1784), published in 1804, also in London, a collection of tunes, with basses for harp or pianoforte, entitled *Lyric Airs: Consisting of Specimens of Greek, Albanian, Wallachian, Turkish, Arabian, Chinese and Moorish National Songs and Melodies (being the first selection of the kind ever yet offered to the public)*. Jones gave little information about his sources. He included in his anthology, whose claim to primacy may well be justified, an item headed *"Chin-Chin-Joss—A Hymn Sung by the Chinese to their Deity, Joss,"* acknowledging it as the contribution of "a Gentleman, who resided some time in the English factory, at CANTON."[37] It is probable that this was the Mr. Matthew Roper who sent to Charles Burney "two Gongs and oriental instruments in Chests" and may have provided drawings of Chinese instruments and some notated tunes for John Barrow's *Travels in China.*[38] The tune in question has an unmistakable resemblance to Du Halde's tune in its first five measures, thereafter diverging in a manner unique to this version, that smacks of westernization:

Ex. 5

Jones's publication also has a "Hindostanee Song" with the footnote: "The above Song was written down from the natives singing it."[39] There seems no evidence that Jones visited India, and the manner of this song's transmission remains unexplained. One wonders if Jones actually played any of these non-European tunes at the Prince's gatherings.

The latest transmitter of Du Halde's first tune to come under notice here is Dr. William Crotch (1775-1847), the musical prodigy who at twenty-two became Professor of Music at Oxford. About 1807 Crotch published three volumes of *Specimens of Various Styles of Music referred to in a Course of Lectures read at Oxford and London and Adapted to Keyed Instruments.* The first volume contains exclusively material that would now be called "ethnomusicological," with 354 numbered items, of which about 44 are oriental. The work shows extraordinary assiduity in collecting exotic material for pedagogical use. The tune under discussion is the first of five Chinese tunes,[40] three of which are acknowledged in the Preface to Du Halde. The other two are from John Barrow's book. In the former of those Crotch compromised with authenticity by adopting a version devised and published by Karl Kambra (who is unknown to *MGG* or *New Grove*), though keeping the pentatonic pitch choice. The three forms are shown in example 6:[41]

Ex. 6

The latter of the two songs taken from Barrow was the "Chinese Boatmen's Song,"[42] which Crotch correctly but academically labelled "Canon 2 in 1 Unison". He commented on four of the Chinese tunes that they "are in the same scale as the Irish and Scotch music, which seems to prove that they had one common origin". A similar observation was made by Sir George Staunton, second-in-command of the Earl of Macartney's embassy, and its official chronicler, when he wrote: "The musicians affected mostly slow and plaintive airs, not unlike those of the Highlanders of Scotland."

With Karl Kambra's arrangements of the two songs we are in the category of utilization, though at the level of salon music. In arranging the "Boatmens' Song," Kambra made of it a classical binary design, with the boatmens' tune as refrain.

An example of more drastic westernization of Chinese music material is a *"Mélodie Chinoise: Hymne des dix* [sic] *mille ans"* by Friedrich Wilhelm Michael Kalkbrenner (1785-1849). This travesty perpetrated by one of the best known composers of his time was based on the second of Du Halde's tunes, which is also the first of the group of ten tunes in La Borde. Pitch choice, tune contour, rhythm and unit design were all deformed into something still capable of being accepted as ancient Chinese, while the whole was provided with a piano accompaniment in a harmony exercise style conceived to be appropriate.[43] It was clearly produced to flatter Napoleon, and seems to have been devised for his birthday. Its date must be between 1804, when

Kalkbrenner returned to Paris, and 1814, the fall of the Emperor. In example 7 the tune is shown as notated by Du Halde and La Borde and as transformed by Kalkbrenner.

Ex. 7

An instance, on the other hand, of a Chinese tune virtually uninterfered with occurred in the light opera *The Travellers,* music by Domenico Corri (1744-1825), produced in London in 1806 and printed there in keyboard score in the same year. The work, which Crotch referred to in his Preface, does not belie its title, which reads: *The Travellers, or Music's Fascination; a dramatic opera in five acts, the first in Pekin, the second in Constantinople, the third in Naples, the fourth in Caserta, the fifth in Portsmouth.* The time taken to mount and change the elaborate decor caused some music to be omitted in performance. The foot of the title-page has this statement:

> The Music of the Opera is published as originally intended to be performed, but on account of the great number of decorations, etc., several pieces are omitted in the presentation.

The first scene of act 1 is a Chinese garden; scene 3 is the Emperor of China's hall. Here there is performed a "Chinese Chorus—Unison and accompanied by wind instruments only" with the indication: "NB This melody is a Chinese Hymn, 2000 years old." The tune is Amiot's Hymn to the Ancestors, with one note changed and with punctuating strokes on a large gong:

Ex. 8

1. Amiot has

While no date is indicated on Crotch's publication, this has been put at ca. 1807. It seems a remarkable coincidence that Carl Maria von Weber composed in 1804-5 an *Overtura Chinesa* using as its main theme the first of Du Halde's tunes. However, Weber used Rousseau's version of the third measure; Crotch was true to Du Halde. Weber revised the first form of his overture (which is lost) to become the overture of his incidental music to Schiller's *Turandot,* with which the first form had had no connection. Four of the movements of the incidental music have the Chinese tune in various rhythms and orchestrations.[44]

The latest stage in the European history of this tune is its use by Hindemith in his *Symphonic Metamorphoses on Themes of Weber* (1945). Hindemith broke the tune into two sections, put its beginning a tone lower, and metamorphosed it from the third measure onward into terms of a twentieth-century use of western tonality:

Ex. 9

Two further instances of the presentation of oriental music material to the west during the period under discussion may be noted here. La Borde included in the first volume of his *Essai* two paragraphs on *Musique des Siamois,* with a song in the form of tune with western style bass. And the seventh issue of *Allgemeine musikalische Zeitung,* published at Leipzig in 1804-5, had a discussion of music in the Marquezas Islands, with a notated tune and an illustration.[45]

In the case of Japan, whose Buddhist chant and court music were derived from China, the initial impact was of West upon East. Eva Harich-Schneider has documented the intriguing story of the first contact in the sixteenth century, with the presence in Japan of St. Francis Xavier, and Japanese acceptance of the musical apparatus of the Christian West, including plainsong, mystery plays and secular chamber music.[46] Following the policy reversal of 1635 the only continuing link with western culture for the next two hundred years was a Dutch male colony who were permitted the occupation of the tiny island of Deshima, now part of Nagasaki. With the reintroduction of western usages, military bands in Dutch style were formed between 1830 and 1844, though Japanese interest in other genres of music remained slight until after 1874. All this may serve to explain why the serious study of Japanese music in the West belongs to the second half of the twentieth century.

Early instances of observation of Indian music seem rare: Mersenne's drawing and description of a *bin sitar* have been mentioned,[47] but there appears to be little evidence of western interest in the subject until the British occupation and domination began in 1758. First in time and importance was the monograph *On the Musical Modes of the Hindoos* which the pioneer and pre-eminent scholar of the Orient Sir William Jones wrote in 1784 and published in 1792.[48] Jones had mastered Arabic, Hebrew and Persian before leaving England in 1783 to take up a post in Calcutta with the East India Company. Among the "Objects of Enquiry During My Residence in Asia" that he listed at that point were "Poetry, Rhetoric and Morality of Asia" and "Music of the Eastern Nations." His first official task was to assist in the translation of the Sanskrit code of laws that Warren Hastings had decided in 1776 should be the laws of India. In January 1784 Jones convened the inaugural meeting of the Asiatic Society of Bengal, which was to be for India what the Royal Society was for England. After Jones, it has been said, "Sanskrit, Indian religion and Indian history acquired the status of scientific knowledge."[49] It was to the Asiatic Society that Jones's music monograph was initially presented; its aim should therefore be seen in the larger framework of his particular kind of "scientific" orientalism. "Music belongs, as a science," it began, "to an interesting part of natural philosophy, which, by mathematical deductions from constant phenomena, explains the causes and properties of sound."[50] Following some comparative discussion, it continued: "Let us proceed to the Indian system, which is minutely explained in a great number of Sanskrit books, by authors, who leave arithmetic and geometry to their astronomers, and properly discourse on music as an art confined to the pleasures of imagination." This suggests limits to Jones's "scientific" approach, though he did go on to explain, for the first time in a western language, the principles and terminology of Indian music practice. He gave an illustration of a *vina* and the scale of its fingerboard, which he credited to [F.] "Fowke," whose paper on the instrument had been published in the first issue of *Asiatic Researches.*[51] Jones asked a "German professor of music" to accompany on his violin "a Hindu lutanist, who sung *by rote* [Jones's emphasis] some popular airs on the loves of Krishna and Ra'dha." The professor assured him "that the scales were the same." Jones seems not to have considered the possibility of more accurate pitch measurement. At the end of his monograph he printed an Indian song "in our own characters accompanied with the original notes." In a similar way to Amiot with Chinese music, Jones felt the power of Indian melody. Noting the absence of harmony, in the western sense, in both ancient Greek and Hindu music, he wrote: "Melody . . . alone speaks the language of passion and sentiment."[52]

Customarily coupled with the name of Sir William Jones in the context of Indian music is that of Captain W. Augustus Willard, whose *Treatise on the Music of Hindusthan* was printed in Calcutta in 1834. (In the meantime there had appeared two superbly observed and sumptuously illustrated volumes entitled *Les Hindous* by F. Balthazard Solvyns, printed in Paris in 1810, which had a number of depictions of instruments in players' hands.) Willard was described as being "a skilful performer himself on several instruments"—an early example of a participant observer—and as having "local advantages of observation from his appointment at the native court of the Nawab of Banda." He provided descriptions of some Hindustani musical forms, and a glossary.

Not being a Sanskrit scholar, he made no use of Indian treatises, but, as he tells us, "consulted the most famous performers, both Hindus and Moham-medans ... [also] Hakim Salamat Ali Khan of Barraras, who has written a treatise on music." Willard touched only lightly on the larger aspects discussed by speculative writers, remarking that "the similitude between the music of the classical nations and that of India has never, I believe, been traced, and the following labor will, I presume to hope, be productive of some fruit."

The first person to print westernized adaptations of Indian tunes seems to have been William Hamilton Bird, whose publication (Calcutta, 1789) was entitled: *Oriental Miscellany: being a collection of the most favourite Airs of Hindoostan compiled and adapted for the harpsichord, etc.* It was dedicated to Warren Hastings. Many tunes were indicated as having been taken down from prominent singers, one of whom was a woman. Bird's approach to the tune material, which he made into lessons with variations, was extremely apologetic. He wrote in the Introduction:

> The Compiler of the following airs heartily regrets the great insipidity which must attend the frequent repetition of subject, and their want of variety ... He has strictly adhered to the original compositions, though it has cost him great pains to bring them into any form as to TIME, which the music of Hindostan is extremely deficient in. ... The greatest imperfection, however, in the music in every part of India, is the total want of accompanyments; a third, or fifth, are additions, the Compiler, during a residence of nineteen years in this country, and with the most favourable opportunities, has never heard.

Bird acknowledged that the final Sonata for keyboard with violin or flute (Allegro maestoso; Minuetto; Jigg) was his own, though having "select passages from the airs." He concluded his collection with some short pieces set for guitar.

Bird's forcing of oriental tune material into the straitjacket of western music structure may be compared to a gentler musical impact, also in a situation of conquest and colonization, namely, the Dutch presence in Java. Previous to 1705, when the Dutch East India Company took control of Sunda and West Java, there were from 1656 onward twelve regencies in West Java, ruled by twelve local chiefs as regents *(bupati)* under the hegemony of the Islamic Sultan of the Middle Java kingdom of Mataram. Central Javanese cultural importations into West Java included gamelan, dance and masked plays, sung poetry and *wayang* puppetry. With the Dutch East India Company taking control of Sunda and West Java in 1705, the *bupati* became the colonizer's agents and intermediaries. Ernst Heins has advanced the hypothesis that these intermediaries brought into being, for the Westerners' delectation, a new gamelan, gamelan *degung,* by a combination of two previous genres, *goong renteng* and *goong areng.*[53] In this way they provided for the Dutch an indigenous music suited to their cultural requirements, one that was both feudal and respectable.

In none of the impacts and attitudes discussed up to now was there question of a threat to western culture (unless Doni were to be taken seriously). With Turkey it was for a long time otherwise. In the words of Edward W. Said: "Until the end of the seventeenth century the 'Ottoman' peril lurked alongside Europe to represent for the whole of Christian civilization a constant danger, and in time European civilization incorporated that peril and its lore, its great events, figures, virtues and vices, as something woven into the fabric of life."[54] This paradoxical coexistence of fear and attraction had manifestations not only in the subjects of stage works with music, but also in the structural fabric of the music itself. Besides observation of some Turkish music practices, occasionally at uncomfortably close range,[55] there was some elucidation of the music's nature though not of its theoretical basis. But there was a relatively large amount of utilization, from adaptation of certain elements to total adoption. This last occurred in the case of the military marching music of the Janissary band.

There are descriptions of instruments from the time of Suleyman the Magnificent (1520-66) onward. Michael Praetorius gave some drawings of non-European instruments in the second volume of his *Syntagma Musicum* (1619).[56] Though these pages are indicated in the Index as *Allerley Americanische/Turckische/Mosskowitische/und Indianische Instrumenta,* there is no Turkish instrument, and many of the author's labels do not correspond to the instruments' identities. In the Introduction to the volume Praetorius wrote a veritable tirade against the "tyrannical rule" and "gross inhuman barbarism" of Mahomet, and described Islamic musical instruments in the scurrilous terms of "a devil's bell and a rubbish pail, together with a squeaking shawm, which are still in high esteem among the Turks, and are used at wedding parties and other festivities." He gave an abusive description of a procession with mounted drummers and shawm players, when "children of the Turkish Emperor or of other high persons are circumcised."

Salomon Schweigger of Nürnberg, a contemporary of Praetorius, gave some reasoned cultural comparison in his account of a visit to Turkey. He remarked, surely in humor, that the outdoor music with which he was greeted by a high official was "very charming, lovely music, as if a cooper were hooping a barrel or vat."[57] In a section that contains some factual information on Turkish music, he confessed to finding no sense or skill in it, while noting that the Turks admired music that filled a great open space with fierce and warlike sound. He introduced a short music notation thus:

> The Turks also have various lyrics and songs about their heroes, wars and conquests, which have been stylishly and artistically put into verse. . . . I have in mind the particular melody of a strident sound in an open space, in this manner and harmony:

And they put this forth without any change in the tune, only that they play more vigorously when it comes to a triple rhythm or to imitations [orig: *Fugen*], but they all, whether on wind or brass instrument, play the same melody.

In the same section Schweigger gave a short description of Turkish dancing.[58]

There had developed by the early eighteenth century a demand for more detailed and professional information about non-western as well as about European dancing genres. This appears from such dance manuals as *L'Art de bien danser/Die Kunst wohl zu Tantzen* by Samuel Rudolph Behr, "Maître de danse," published in German in Leipzig in 1713. This has descriptions of Chinese dancing, of the dances of Turkish monks in their mosques with "a certain instrument, after the fashion of cymbals, whose sound rings out very harshly," of Indian dancing to an instrument "that sounds like a bagpipe," and of dancing on the Malabar coast.[59] All these were drawn from the accounts of various travellers. The dancing master Gregorio Lambranzi's *Neue und curieuse theatricalische Tantz-Schul,* printed at Nürnberg in 1716, has an illustration and tune (not of Turkish character) for a dance by four Turks, and similar material for a dance by two Moors showing a Turkish dwarf playing with sticks on both heads of a drum.[60]

A complete chapter on Turkish music appeared in the *Histoire générale, critique et philologique de la musique* by Charles-Henri de Blainville, published in Paris in 1767. Blainville's compositional experiment with a *"mode mixte ou mode hellénique"* was praised by Rousseau. While asserting that "the Turks have no rational system of music," Blainville described most of its practical aspects, with some instrument drawings and notations. He related his experience of listening repeatedly to the singing of his Turkish informant and then trying to imitate it, with poor results, so that he came to the enlightened conclusion that, while still finding Turkish language, customs and dress ridiculous: "superiority aside, one cannot deny that each thing can be good in its kind, and is truly good only to the extent that it is in its own situation." Blainville gave the notation of a song in which he tried to indicate the small intervals used by the Turkish singer, noting that they resembled "the quarter tone that the ancient Greeks used." He also gave notations of a *Marche des Janissaires* and a *Danse de Chypre.*[61]

An account of the circumstances in which actual Turkish military marching music was introduced into the West was given in Christian Friedrich Daniel Schubart's *Ideen zu einer Ästhetik der Tonkunst,* a work dating from 1784-85 that was published in Vienna in 1806:

As is known, drums are played today among well organized Janissaries, as also are kettledrums, played from notation.

The introduction thirty years ago of Turkish music into various regiments in Germany has brought about the study of the musical instruments of the Turks. The character of this music is so warlike that it makes the breasts even of cowards to swell. Whoever has had the good fortune to hear the music made by the Janissaries themselves, whose bands are commonly eighty to one hundred persons strong, must smile pityingly at the imitations with which we generally distort it.

Once when a Turkish concert was given in Berlin in honor of the Turkish ambassador Achmet Essendi, he shook his head indignantly and said: "It is not Turkish!" Ever since then the King of Prussia has taken two Turks into his service, and has introduced the true Turkish music into some of his regiments. In Vienna also the Emperor keeps an excellent band of Turkish musicians, which the great Gluck has already used in operas.

The instruments of this music consist of: shawms, which the Turks usually make out of tin, in order to sharpen the tone; curved horns, whose timbre closely resembles that of our bass horns [*Basshörner*][62]; a large and small triangle; the so-called tambourine, with great effect made by the shaking of the jingles, which with the Turks are made of silver; also, two cymbals of the finest bronze or of bell metal, which at each beat are struck together; and finally two drums, the smaller of which is always rolled and trilled, while the larger is always damped and stroked underneath with a switch.

The Germans have strengthened this music with bassoons, trying to get a bigger effect. The sound of trumpets [*Trompetenstöne*] can very well also be added. In short, Turkish music is the first among all war musics, but also the most expensive if it is as perfect as its nature and its heroic scale demand. Since Turkish music is not played from notation (though we Germans are the only ones who have tried to put it into those symbols) nothing more can be said about its theory ... It uses only two-four time, though we have also made very successful experiments with other measures. In this connection, no other genre of music requires such a steady, persistent and powerfully beaten pulse. Every first beat of the bar is emphasised anew by a vigorous beat, so strongly that it is almost impossible to get out of time. The keys preferred by the Turks seem to be F major and B flat major, since in those keys the ranges of all their instruments coincide most exactly. However, we Germans have experimented successfully with D major and C major, in which keys the great weightiness of Turkish music is clearly brought out.[63]

In a comprehensive article on the historical background and operatic antecedents of Mozart's *Entführung aus dem Serail,* Walter Preibisch dealt with subjects of Turkish lore in western musical theatre. Preibisch surveyed the story material used in plays from Prosper Bonarelli's *Soliman* of 1619 to Goldoni, *Türkenopern* in Italian opera seria from Marc Antonio Ziani in 1689 to Johann Adolf Hasse's *Soliman* of 1753, and settings of *Entführung* by four composers, including Mozart. Preibisch considered Hasse's *Soliman* the prototype of all later *Türkenopern* by reason of its use of dramatic characterization in the place of the purely sensuous charm of the exotic.

(Nevertheless, the spectacle aspect was attended to; according to a manuscript score in the British Library, the opera was produced "with 800 persons, camels, elephants, etc."[64]) Preibisch pursued his study with reference to opera buffa, and to operatic events in France, with Gluck's *La Rencontre Imprévue, ou Les Pélerins de Mecque* as centerpiece, and in England and Germany. Judging from his examples of the musical stuff involved, one could deduce that composers adapted actual Janissary sound in such pieces as marches and *sinfonie turchese,* and developed a set of conventions for "Turkish music." These helped to convey to listeners at first the "wild, fanatical orientals" in all their "ferocity and cunning."[65] Later, under the influence of Rousseau, when "the savage Turk is replaced by the noble one" the music is apt to be associated with grandeur of character. This last observation, from Herman Abert's *Mozart,* was quoted by Bence Szabolcsi in a paper on "Exoticism in Mozart," where he pointed to the striking resemblance of the music of a surviving Hungarian masked dance called Torokos (= *alla turca*), noted down in 1786 and again in 1937, to the Gluck-Haydn-Mozart type of Turkish march music. He thought it not improbable that such tunes could have been a source of indirect transmission of "genuinely Turkish march or dance melodies."[66]

The extensive use of Turkish music in the contexts of military music and the theater is in contrast with the situation of Chinese and Indian musical material. With Janissary music, the process was one of conscious incorporation (a phrase used earlier in this essay) into western usage of both the music sound and its original functions, which were those of contributing to the prestige of a ruler, and inspiring martial ardor in his soldiers. William Lichtenwanger has pointed out that with westernization in Turkey in the 1830s, the "ancient music of the Khans was replaced by bands in the still-developing European style. Paradoxically, it was important elements of that same style which had first appeared in Western Europe, less than a century before, under the name of 'Turkish Music.' "[67]

In the genre of interludes of song or dance in spoken stage works, it seems again that producers did not deliver, nor audiences expect, exotic music with exotic stage characters. The situation is exemplifed in the internationally aware Amsterdam theater. In 1633 there was published in that city the wordbook of a play with incidental songs, entitled *Monsieur Sullemans soete vryagi,* described as a *Boertighe Klucht* (comical farce). The tunes of a sung dialogue of Sulleman and Truyte at their first entry are in galliard style. A seven-part collection of dance music used in Dutch theaters, published in Amsterdam from 1697 to 1715, has a "Menuet voor de Mosselman" (in the usual rhythm but perhaps deliberately naive), a tune "Mahomet in 't Duyte Doosie" (a sort of *bourrée,* perhaps for a comic interlude), a "Menuet voor Mahomet," a tune "D'Groote Maggol" and a "Menuet voor de Turk." All these are in standard style. In another printed tune collection are a "Gigue van de Janitzers," a "Marche der Turken" (which possibly has a Turkish convention opening) and a

"Moorsche Mars." A "Turksche huldiging" with dancing, done after *De Burgelyke Edelman (Le Bourgeois Gentilhomme),* printed in Amsterdam in 1700 and played at the Amsterdam Schouwburg, may have used Lully's music. As late as 1824 there is record of a successful Turkish ballet in the same theater.[68]

Throughout the deployment of Turkishness in music, whether authentic or conventionalized, there was relatively little writing on Arabic music practices in general. The observations of Persian music by Jean Chardin (1711) and Englebert Kaempfer (1712) were notable exceptions.[69] Some elucidation of the Arabic music system and its terminology and instruments was given by La Borde in the chapters "De la Musique des Persans et des Turcs" and "De la Musique des Arabes" in his *Essai.* The information there was credited to "Monsieur Pigeon de S. Paterne, Interprète pour les Langues Orientales." It was supplemented by a chapter, "Des Instrumens Arabes," with some tune notations, attributed to a "Voyage en Arabie" whose author was not named. This in turn had a "Supplément" on the scale of Arabic music, communicated by a Baron de Tott.[70]

Edward W. Said observed that "after William Jones and Anquetil-Duperron [the latter was a translator of Sanskrit literature] and after Napoleon's Egyptian expedition, Europe came to know the Orient more scientifically, to live in it with greater authority and discipline than ever before."[71] One of the fruits of Napoleon's grand plan for Egypt was the first elucidation of the Arabic music system there. Its author, Guillaume-André Villoteau, had been a priest, a cathedral singer and canon, and then leader of the chorus of the Paris Opéra, before becoming one of an academy of *savants* taken to Egypt by General Bonaparte. His commission was to collect facts and materials about the music of the various oriental peoples living on Egyptian soil, particularly Arabs, Copts and Armenians, and also Greek monks. On his return and after a period of library research in Paris, Villoteau wrote four sections on music for the Napoleonic *Description de l'Egypte,* which was published in twenty-three volumes between 1809 and 1828. Of Villoteau's sections, published in 1822-3, the first two deal with music in ancient Egypt, the third with its current state and the fourth with oriental organology. This exposition of Egyptian musical culture was made a part of Napoleon's overall purpose—to render Egypt "completely open, to make it totally accessible to European scrutiny. From being a land of obscurity, Egypt was to become a department of French learning."[72]

By the end of our period, some attempt at a comprehensive western view of oriental musics had become possible. This was essayed by François-Josef Fétis in the "Résumé philosophique de l'Histoire de la Musique" prefixed to the first edition of his *Biographie universelle des musiciens,* published in 1835. For his discussion of oriental musics Fétis relied principally on Amiot, Jones, Sir William Ouseley (three volumes of whose *The Oriental Collections* had appeared in London from 1797 to 1800)[73] and Villoteau. In the five volumes of his unfinished *Histoire générale de la musique* (1869-76) Fétis attempted the grand plan of a history of the music of all peoples. By relating music to ethnology and language, he became a protagonist of ethnomusicological criteria.[74] Shortly after, one writer on "national" musics, Carl Engel of London, felt an end point had come, putting the query: "Isn't the subject exhausted?"[75] However, at that very time a new line of investigation into the music systems of the world was being pursued by Alexander John Ellis, fellow of a Cambridge College, whose main subject was phonetics and who became interested in musical pitch. His devising of a new unit of pitch-interval measurement, the hundredth part of a tempered semitone, and the means to apply it experimentally, began a new era of research in music-systems. In 1895, in a paper entitled "On the musical scales of various nations," Ellis presented some results of his investigations to the Society of Arts in London.[76] He had worked mainly with instruments, but in some instances with players within the tradition concerned, as with Javanese players at the London Exhibition of 1882, and with six Chinese musicians with their instruments at the International Health Exhibition in London in 1884. In the process of his experiments Ellis came to the conclusion that "there is no practical way of arriving at the real pitch of a musical scale, when it cannot be heard as played by a native musician, and even then [this gives] a particular musician's usage, not theory." His final conclusion was the direct reverse of the musical universality that Kircher had proposed on a geographical basis, and Roussier, in reverse, on a historical basis. Ellis's conclusion was: "The Musical Scale is not one, not 'natural,' nor even founded necessarily on the laws of the constitution of musical sound so beautifully worked out by Helmholtz,[77] but very diverse, very artificial, and very capricious."[78] Ellis's work, though fundamental and in a sense essential, was concerned with a single element—pitch—in western and non-western musics. His conclusions about the latter, expressed in the terms of his time, still betray something of earlier Eurocentric attitudes.

Shifts in western perceptions, elucidations and utilizations of eastern (and other non-European) musics in the century or so since Ellis's publications have been as culturally determined as were the attitudes of Ellis and his predecessors. Nevertheless, one of the most significant current shifts is that concepts and methodologies developed in the first instance for the elucidation of non-western musics (for example, the ideas of culturally determined music vocabularies and occasion-oriented usages) are increasingly being applied to the study of much western music also.

Notes

1.   Hector Berlioz, *Les Soirées de l'orchestre* (Paris, 1854), p. 284. This is the present author's translation, as throughout this paper.

2.   Félix Clément and Pierre Larousse, eds., *Dictionnaire lyrique ou Histoire des opéras* (Paris, 1869; rpt. of the 1905 ed., 1969), s.v. "Le Calife de Bagdad."

3.   Edward W. Said, *Orientalism* (London and Henley, 1978).

4.   Marin Mersenne, *Harmonie universelle,* 3 vols. (Paris, 1636-37; rpt. 1963), 3:227-28, "Expliquer quelques instrumens des Indes, et de la Turquie."

5.   Ibid., p. 147.

6.   Athanasius Kircher, *Musurgia universalis,* 2 vols. (Rome, 1650; rpt. in one vol., 1970), 1:568.

7.   Ibid.

8.   *Histori und eigentliche beschreibung... durch Egidium Albertinum auss Italienischen Tractâtl verteutscht* (Munich, 1608), p. 127. The title may be translated thus: "History and true description, firstly, by what means through the special help and disposition of the Almighty, but also through the zeal of the Reverend Fathers of the Society of Jesus, and with trouble, work and danger, they brought the Gospel and teachings of Christ into the great and enormous kingdom of China, and secondly, the way they found out how all the political and secular affairs and occasions stood—all pleasant and useful to read."

9.   Reprinted as *Descrizione degl' instromenti armonici* (Leipzig, 1974).

10. This has not been found; a publication that may relate to the same embassy, entitled *L'ambassade de la compagnie orientale des provinces unies vers l'empereur de la Chine* (Leyden, 1665) does not have the illustration referred to.

11. Extracts from the translation are printed in Frank Ll. Harrison, *Time, Place and Music* (Amsterdam, 1973), pp. 161-66; the five tunes printed by Du Halde are reproduced on pp. 207-8 of that volume.

12. Amiot, *Mémoire* (rpt. 1973), pp. 2-3.

13. Rameau, *Code* (rpt. 1969), pp. 189-237.

14. François-Josef Fétis, *Biographie universelle des musiciens,* 8 vols. (Paris, 1835-44), s.v. "Roussier."

15. Roussier, *Mémoire,* pp. 26-28.

16. La Borde, *Essai* (rpt. 1972), 1:128, 360 note, 366. The writers of the articles on La Borde. D'Alembert and Blainville (see later in this paper) in *The New Grove* do not refer to the observations of those authors on non-European musics.

17. Paul Tannery, Cornelis de Waard and Rene Pantard, eds., *Correspondance du P. Marin Mersenne,* 3 vols. (Paris, 1945), 3:509.

18. Amiot, *Mémoire,* pp. 176-85.

19. Ibid., p. 179.

20. Original German in Harrison, *Time, Place and Music,* p. 184, translated p. 186.

21. *Musikalischer Almanach* (Leipzig, 1784), pp. 233-74.

22. Harrison, *Time, Place and Music*, p. 194.

23. *Gluck-Jahrbuch* 1 (1913):54-81. For the attribution to Grétry see K. Hortschansky, *Parodie und Entlehnung im Schaffen Christoph Willibald Glucks* (Cologne, 1973), p. 268.

24. This and other Chinese festivals had been described in Pierre Bourdelot and Jacques Bonnet, *Histoire de la musique et de ses effets* (Paris, 1715), pp. 175-86; rpt. of the Amsterdam edition of 1725 (1966), pp. 121-27.

25. Castil-Blaze, *De l'Opéra en France*, 2 vols. (Paris, 1820), 1:369.

26. *Karl von Dittersdorfs Lebensbeschreibung* (Leipzig, 1801), pp. 71-72; rpt. (1967), pp. 80-81.

27. See *The New Grove*, s.v. "Murky."

28. See Frank Ll. Harrison, "Universals in Music: Toward a Methodology of Comparative Research," *The World of Music* 19 (1977): 30-36.

29. Albert van der Linden, review of Charles van den Borren, *Geschiedenis van de Muziek in de Nederlanden*, in *Revue Belge de Musicologie* 3 (1949):37.

30. For a facsimile of the letter see Harrison, *Time, Place and Music*, plate E.

31. Rousseau, *Dictionnaire*, s.v. "Musique."

32. La Borde, *Essai*, 1:146-47.

33. Ibid., p. 145.

34. At p. 34 of the tune section.

35. Ibid. On pp. 176-77 La Borde printed ten more Chinese tunes without acknowledgment. The first is Du Halde's no. 2, the ninth is Du Halde's no. 5, the tenth is Du Halde's no. 3; all three are varied more or less (see Harrison, *Time, Place and Music*, pp. 207-8).

36. This section of the earlier offprint has a notated "Air des Malegaches ou Habitants de l'Isle de Madagascar," on plate XVI *bis*.

37. Jones, *Lyric Airs*, music section, p. 29.

38. Harrison, *Time, Place and Music*, p. 169. For extracts from Barrow's book and his notated Chinese tunes, see pp. 192-94 and 209-12 of that work.

39. Jones, *Lyric Airs*, pp. 30-31.

40. Crotch, *Specimens*, I, nos. 316-320. Crotch's no. 318 is not, however, in Du Halde; it is the seventh of La Borde's group of ten.

41. Kambra's form, with pseudo-Chinese text, and his adaptation as a song with bass to a text by Dr. Scott, surgeon in Macartney's embassy, is in Harrison, *Time, Place and Music*, pp. 213-14. Works by Kambra were published in Leipzig and London, where he lived around the turn of the century. For Barrow's form, see Harrison, *Time, Place and Music*, p. 210.

42. Harrison, *Time, Place and Music*, pp. 215-17.

43. Facsimile in Peter Gradenwitz, *Musik zwischen Orient und Okzident* (Wilhelmshaven, 1977), p. 169. The author did not make the connection with Du Halde's Tune II. This song is not in the standard lists of the composer's works.

44. Friedrich W. Jähns, *Carl Maria von Weber in seinem Werken* (Berlin, 1871), pp. 87-89; the orchestral score of *Turandot* is reprinted, ed. Hans-Hubert Schönzeler (Zurich, 1975).

45. La Borde, *Essai,* 1:435-36; *Allgemeine musikalische Zeitung* 7 (Oct. 1804-Sept. 1805), cols. 265-76. These instances are in addition to passages from Adam Olearius on Persia (1669), Simon de la Loubère on Siam (1693) and Englebert Kaempfer on Japan (1727), printed in Harrison, *Time, Place and Music,* pp. 63-72, 86-88, 151-54.

46. Harich-Schneider, *A History of Japanese Music* (London, 1973), pp. 445-86.

47. See above, p. 6.

48. This was reprinted in S.M. Tagore, *Hindu Music from Various Authors* (Calcutta, 1875), in Ethel Rosenthal, *The Story of Indian Music and its Instruments* (London, 1929) and from the latter in *Music of India* (Calcutta, 1962). A German translation by J.F.H. von Dalberg, under the title *Ueber die Musik der Indier,* dedicated to Joseph Haydn, was published in Erfurt in 1802. This has a great deal of additional material, in text, notations and illustrations, on various oriental musics, drawn from Chardin, Amiot, Ouseley (see note 73 below) and others. Thirty music notations were taken from William Hamilton Bird (see p. 21), printed without the left hand of the keyboard score and without Bird's variations.

49. Said, *Orientalism,* pp. 77-79.

50. Jones, *On the Musical Modes* (rpt. 1962), p. 88.

51. This was reprinted in Tagore, *Hindu Music.* Edward Jones acknowledged to him a Persian tune and an "Eastern Air" (*Lyric Airs,* music page 25), noting that Fowke "had learnt them in the East Indies."

52. Jones, *On the Musical Modes,* p. 95.

53. See Ernst L. Heins, "Goong Renteng," Ph.D. diss., University of Amsterdam, 1977, passim.

54. Said, *Orientalism,* p. 59.

55. *Die Musik in Geschichte und Gegenwart,* s.v. "Oper." This article contains an illustration of a scene from Johann Wolfgang Franck's *Der Glückliche Gross-Vezir Cara Mustapha... Nebenst Der grausahmen Belagerung und Bestürmung der Kayserlichen Residentz Stadt Wien,* performed in Hamburg in 1686; it was followed two nights later by a sequel, *Der Unglückliche Gross-Vezier....*

56. Praetorius, *Syntagma* 2, *De Organographia* (Wolfenbüttel, 1619; rpt. 1958), plates XXX and XXXI of the *Theatrum Instrumentorum.*

57. Schweigger, *Ein newe Reyssbeschreibung auss Teutschland nach Constantinopel und Jerusalem* (Nürnberg, 1608; rpt. 1964), p. 39, with an illustration of the greeting party with their instruments.

58. Ibid., pp. 207-10.

59. Behr, *L'Art / Die Kunst* (rpt. 1977), pp. 107-11.

60. Lambranzi, *Tantz-Schul* (rpt. 1975), nos. 38 and 39 in the second set of items.

61. Blainville, *Histoire générale,* pp. 61, 64.

62. According to the article, "Bass-horn," in *The New Grove,* that instrument was invented in the 1790s.

63. L. Schubart, ed., *Christ. Fried. Dan. Schubart's Ideen zu einer Ästhetik der Tonkunst* (Vienna, 1806; rpt. 1969), pp. 330-31.

64. London, British Library, Add. MS 32146.

65. Preibisch, "Quellenstudien zu Mozart's 'Entführung aus dem Serail'," *Sammelbände der Internationalen Musikgesellschaft* 10 (1908-09):430-76.

66. Szabolcsi, "Exoticisms in Mozart," *Music & Letters* 37 (1956):323-32.

67. Lichtenwanger, "The Military Music of the Ottoman Turks," *Bulletin of the American Musicological Society* 11-13 (1948):55-56.

68. Information in *Hollantsche Schouwburg* (Amsterdam, 1697-1715); *Oude en Nieuwe Hollantse Boeren Lietjes en Contredansen* (Amsterdam, ca. 1700-16; rpt. 1972); J.A. Worp, *Geschiedenis van den Amsterdamschen Schouwburg* (Amsterdam, 1920); E. Rebling, *Een Eeuw Danskunst in Nederland* (Amsterdam, 1950), p. 147; all by courtesy of Joan Rimmer.

69. Extracts from both in Harrison, *Time, Place and Music*, pp. 120-50.

70. La Borde, *Essai*, 1:162-98, 379-85, 191, 436-39.

71. Said, *Orientalism*, p. 22.

72. Ibid., p. 83.

73. Ouseley had not been to the East. Indian music items in his miscellany were credited to his brother Gore, a resident there; three Chinese tunes (which are also in Barrow) were acknowledged to Eyles Irwin, Member of the Royal Irish Academy, who had been with Macartney's embassy.

74. See Lauro Ayestarán, "Fétis, un Precursor del Criterio Etnomusicológico en 1869," *Primera Conferencia Interamericana de Etnomusicologia* (Washington, D.C., 1965), pp. 15-37.

75. *The Musical Times* 20 (1879):134.

76. Ellis, "On the Musical Scales of Various Nations," *Journal of the Society of Arts* 33 (1885):485-527, and the Appendix to the same paper, ibid., pp. 1102-11.

77. The reference is to Hermann von Helmholtz, *Die Lehre von den Tonempfindungen als physiologische Grundlage für die Theorie der Musik* (Brunswick, 1863), translated by Ellis as *On the Sensations of Tone as a Physiological Basis for the Theory of Music* (London, 1875).

78. Ellis, "On the Musical Scales," pp. 490-91, 517.

Johann Hermann Schein as Poet and Composer

Basil Smallman

Amongst the works which Schein published, in sacred and secular collections, or as separate prints, during his period as *Thomaskantor* in Leipzig,[1] there are a number which originated as occasional compositions for important family events, such as weddings and funerals. Church pieces of this type include wedding and funeral hymns—some among the latter tragically recording the deaths of the composer's first wife, Sidonia, and various of their children in infancy—which were later absorbed into the *Cantional* (1627)[2] under such section headings as "Bei Braut-Messen" and "Bei Begräbnissen." There are in addition several motet settings of traditional texts, such as "Drei schöne Ding sind" and "Wem ein tugendsam Weib bescheret ist" for weddings, and "Die mit Tränen säen" for funerals, which were published in *Israelsbrünnlein* (1623),[3] a collection appropriately designated in its dedicatory preface: "... bei fürfallenden occasionen musicieret." However, by no means all the occasions requiring music took place in church, or were of a solemn or somber character. Wedding festivities in Leipzig at the period frequently involved much lively domestic music,[4] both for voices and instruments, and for these events Schein was given ready scope for his combined skills as poet and composer, producing numerous German villanellas and madrigals on pastoral and amatory themes, and supplying through them an elegantly oblique expression of the social virtues of love, friendship, loyalty and comradeship.[5] Various pieces of this kind were used as the basis for his two principal secular collections of the period: *Musica boscareccia* (three volumes, 1621, 1626 and 1628),[6] a set of 50 *tricinia* in villanella form for SSB (with optional continuo, and with instruments indicated as possible substitutes for one or two of the voices), and *Diletti pastorali* (1624),[7] a collection of 15 German madrigals for five voices SSATB and continuo.

In his secular works Schein stands out from his contemporaries by the richness and variety of his musical language, and, in particular, by the sensitive interrelationship he succeeds in creating between his texts and their musical settings. Taking as his models the vivid and original villanellas of Jacob

Regnart (the widely renowned *Kurzweilige teutsche Lieder* of 1576, 1577 and 1579), together with the madrigals and canzonets of Hassler, and the German partsongs of Lechner, he brought the *Gesellschaftslied* to new heights of refinement and expressiveness. The influence is clear in his music of the work of the great Italians of the period, particularly Giovanni Gabrieli, Marenzio, Viadana and Monteverdi; but it is equally obvious that through his friendship and professional collaboration with Samuel Scheidt and Heinrich Schütz,[8] he became thoroughly steeped in the current Italo-German styles, and eagerly grasped the opportunities they afforded him for individuality of expression.

As a poet Schein's claims to recognition are less significant but by no means negligible. Drawing upon a verse style and a world of imagery derived from Petrarch[9] and Tasso, he adopts the typical love formulas and poetic artifices of his models while at the same time retaining various turns of phrase, metrical patterns, and even naivetés of prosody and grammar related to folk-song, which reveal the genuinely popular inspiration behind his baroque forms. A musician-poet, a figure somewhat akin to Thomas Campion in England, Schein confines himself almost entirely to the creation of *poesia per musica,* contriving nonetheless to produce through this modest medium some of the most imaginative verse of the period—a period, admittedly, of meager literary achievement in Germany. Particularly influential upon his work was the pastoral element characteristic of one branch of the Italian madrigal, an element derived largely from Tasso's *Aminta* (1573)[10] and Guarini's *Il Pastor Fido* (1585), with their evocation of a make-believe world of shepherds and shepherdesses, and of the mythological deities who control their destinies. Translations of both these works appeared in Germany during the first quarter of the seventeenth century, Tasso's drama in a Latin version at Frankfurt in 1615, and in a German translation by Dietrich von der Werder in 1625; and Guarini's pastoral in a German version by Eilgerus Männlich, published at Mühlhausen in 1619.

Much interesting information can be gleaned from Schein's secular publications about the social and cultural life of the educated bourgeoisie of Leipzig in the early seventeenth century.[11] Although there is nothing to suggest the existence in the town at this time of a formal literary society, comparable to the *Königsberger Kreis* or, in its different way, the nationally renowned *Fruchtbringende Gesellschaft,*[12] it is clear from the title pages and dedicatory prefaces to Schein's works and from other documentary sources[13] that the composer had gathered about him a large and admiring group of literary friends and acquaintances, several of them leading citizens, for whom the exchange of occasional verse to mark significant family and personal events was a normal part of a cultured person's life. The fruits of their labors are evident on the opening pages of many of Schein's volumes, which bear laudatory Latin (and sometimes Italian) poems, in elegant style, by such local authors as Andreas Corvinus (a public orator), Martin Cramer (a co-rector of the *Thomasschule*), Friedrich Deverlin (a senator) and Bartholomaeus Hahn (an actuary).[14] No doubt the cult of pastoralism played a large part in the lives of these Leipzig *literati,* their studies embracing not only the writings of classical authors, such as Theocritus and Virgil, but those also of Spenser, Sidney, de Montreux and d'Urfé[15] (together with the works of Tasso and Guarini, already mentioned), the vogue for which was sweeping Germany at the time. No doubt also they followed Schein's example by adopting various forms of pastoral disguise, concealing their identities behind pastoral pseudonyms or conveying secret messages by the use of acrostics or anagrams. Such rituals, and even pastoral masquerades, began to flourish overtly in Leipzig at a slightly later date, after Schein's death in 1630. The composer's own more modest practice was simply to refer to himself on his title pages as "Coridon," and to his "beloved" (whoever she may have been) as "Filli" ("Filli zart"). In one entertaining instance, on the title page of his *Balletto pastorale* (September 1620),[16] he styles himself "Jonah Heischermann," an anagram of his full name in its original spelling, with single "n's." Also, he not infrequently adopted the appropriate poetic conventions to transform the woods and meadows at Rosenthal, on the outskirts of Leipzig, into a type of Arcadia, an imaginary paradise where he could manipulate his shepherd swains and nymphs, and the concepts they symbolized, like actors—or puppets, even—on his pastoral stage.

Notwithstanding the adulation of his literary colleagues in Leipzig, it is probable that Schein was quite modest about his own talents as a poet. In some Latin verse which he composed in 1629 for the wedding of Benjamin Schütz, the youngest brother of the famous composer,[17] he took pains to decry his own skills, protesting (whether ironically or not it is impossible to say) his inability to emulate the new German style of Martin Opitz[18]—("Non me Teutonicos docuit componere versus/Musa MODO ludens OPITIANA NOVA")—and declaring himself capable of producing only the crudest type of pastoral verse—("Sed Damon rauco sylvestrem stridere cantum/Gutture per Panos Valle-Rosetta[19] dedit"). Nevertheless, as many modern critics have acknowledged, there is evident in his writing an elegance of expression, a tenderness of feeling and, at times, a virtuosity with words which raise the standard of his poetry well above the mediocre *Knüttelvers* found frequently in the work of the earlier German musician-poets.[20] Summing up his achievement, in his *Geschichte des deutschen Liedes,* Gunther Müller writes: "As a poet Schein opened up no new paths ... but he brought together various offshoots with expert skill. His song-poems represent a highpoint of the early baroque period which was not attained even by the Opitz circle."[21]

The aim of the present essay is to examine some of the simple but strikingly effective ways in which Schein seeks to achieve congruence between his verse and his music; and for this purpose various villanellas from *Musica boscareccia* will provide the principal focus of study.[22] Of the 50 short works contained in the collection only seven are positively known to have originated as Leipzig wedding pieces, six of them (Mb. I^9, II^7, II^9, III^5, III^6, and III^{10}) with their original verse and music preserved virtually intact and the seventh (Mb. I^{14}) with almost entirely different music set to the original poem. Several other wedding villanellas with the same scoring have survived, but these, for reasons which may only be conjectured, were not incorporated into the larger collection.[23] Examples include the *Villanellischer Holzgang* (1619), "Mirtillo gut in einem Wald," which may well have been omitted because of its long narrative text in ten stanzas; and the *Aria à 3* (1624), "Ach Äsculapi wohl erfarn," together with the *Cura d'Amore* (1625), "Fürwahr Cupido klein," both composed for the weddings of local physicians, which were probably excluded because their texts are so heavily interlarded with humorous medical allusions of an over-specific nature.[24] If, therefore, as the surviving evidence seems to suggest, it was on the basis of only some six or seven original wedding pieces that the entire *Musica boscareccia* came into being, it seems surprizing that the collection should have grown to such large proportions over such an extended period of time. No doubt the composer was encouraged by the exceptional popularity of what he apologetically called his "schlechte Wercklein."[25] And he may have been attracted to the idea of accomplishing in his work a rounded artistic whole, embracing within his three volumes three diverse aspects of his Arcadian scene—the love of Coridon for Filli, the wiles of Amor (Cupid), and the beauty of Filli, the dearest treasure of the woods. This arrangement artfully echoes the three-stanza arrangement of many of his individual poems, in which different facets of a chosen love theme are similarly surveyed in turn. But it is also likely that he was fascinated with the villanella, with its concise binary form structure and sectional repeats, as a medium for experimentation, particularly with the technical problems of word setting using small units of verse in strophic arrangements.[26]

The *Musica boscareccia* poems are generally simple in construction, consisting typically of three eight-line stanzas with four rhymes to each stanza in a variety of schemes—the main exceptions being poems with additional verses (to a total of six, in rare cases) and ones with a lesser or greater number of lines (between four and ten) to each stanza. Often using short lines, with no more than three or four feet, Schein consistently achieves a striking directness of poetic expression, full of freshness and vitality, and reinforced not a little by his choice of colorful words and phrases—"O lachende Flämmelein!" "O spielende Demantlein!"—repeatedly ornamented with the ringing diminutive "-lein." The poems in the later volumes show an increased elegance of phraseology and depth of emotional content, testifying to the poet's developing skills, and at the same time emphasizing the not inconsiderable variety of his verse styles.[27] At one end of the range there are poems of a modest, *Volkslied* character, such as Mb. II^9, "Viel schöner Blümelein" (originally a wedding poem entitled "Giardinetto d'Amore," dating from May 1623), with its irregular metrical pattern, limited rhyme scheme and calculated air of sentimentality:

> Viel schöner Blümelein
> Jetzund von neuen
> Im kühlen Maien
> Hervor gewachsen sein.
> Aus diesen Blümlein allen
> Tun mir die zwei gefallen:
> Jelangjeliebr, Vergissnichtmein.

And at the other extreme there is to be found verse of a richly colourful, almost Romantic character, such as Mb.III[4], "O Sternenäugelein," which displays an intensity of (apparently) personal emotion altogether unusual for the period.[28] The following lines, from the end of the third stanza, portraying the frustrated lover's despair, seem to strike a quasi-religious note, anticipating the sacred songs (both Catholic and Protestant) of such poets as Friedrich von Spee and Andreas Gryphius, which were to gain wide popularity during the course of the century:[29]

> O Musik, edler Freudenschall!
> O Seufzen, Heulen, Herzensknall!
> O Leben lieb, o bitter Tod,
> Ach wechselt um es ist die Not!
> Wie könnet ihr doch alle sehn
> Ein liebend Herz zu Trümmern gehn?

In setting verse of this character to music Schein leans naturally toward two main interpretative approaches which were to become central to the practice of the entire Baroque period: the expression of an overall mood *(Affekt)* and the detailed depiction in music of individual words and phrases. A principal role is played in the characterisation of *Affekt* by the composer's choice of "key," major "keys" being used generally to signify a joyful mood and minor "keys" a sad one, though the picture is sometimes confused by a degree of tonal ambiguity, due to the residual effects of the church modal system. Also a special function is reserved for the Dorian G minor used in a great many of the settings (including "O Sternenäugelein") which often proves equivocal, giving chameleon-like expression to a shifting spectrum of emotions between joy and sorrow. Of the other "keys" used, D minor (Dorian) is majestic and serious, and A minor (Aeolian) together with D minor (transposed Aeolian) unrelievedly sad, while G major (Mixolydian) has warmth and liveliness, and F major (transposed Ionian) a strong element of graceful humour.

For the illustration of textual detail Schein relies to a large extent on a concept of musical expression (still at that time evolving and still subject to rigorous codification by such theorists as Burmeister, Nucius and

Thelamonius) as the embodiment of an aesthetic doctrine—the "doctrine of figures" *(Figurenlehre)* by means of which a relationship is sought between musical patterns and the figures of speech common in classical rhetoric.[30] Significantly, Schein himself was the author of a treatise on the subject, the so-called *Hermann Scheins manuductio ad Musicam poeticam,* which is unfortunately lost. This system provided the means of creating a symbolic musical language, using in particular the elements of contrast and repetition— in relation to pitch, rhythm, texture, mode, melodic patterns and so on—as a way of underlining emotional expression with varying degrees of rhetorical emphasis.[31] The resultant "language" is capable of being applied, notwithstanding the "rules" of the theorists, with much freedom in practice, a limited number of musical patterns proving adaptable, by virtue of their "semantic" simplicity, to a wide range of verbal meanings. Inevitably less accommodating—because less equivocal—are the devices of direct word painting and descriptive vocal coloratura which Schein employs to great effect in a number of his villanellas: rapid scales to depict the flight of Amor's darts, syncopations to represent fear and bewilderment, highlighted rests *(sospiri)* to mark the lover's sighs and black notation *Augenmusik,* producing a sudden change to triple time, to symbolize Cupid's blindness or the funereal darkness of the rejected lover's despair. At their most extreme these descriptive devices result in passages demanding astonishing virtuosity in performance, such as the following, from the second half of "O Schäferin, o Filli mein" (Mb. II[2]):

Ex. 1

Such graphic forms of pictorialism, derived partly from the madrigal and partly from early forms of monody, are found most commonly in the earlier dated volumes in the collection, and their use may be regarded as a relatively immature stylistic trait. There are, for instance, six examples of black notation *Augenmusik* in the first two volumes and none in the third, and fifteen examples of richly ornamented melismas "painting" particular words and phrases in the first two volumes as compared with only five in the last volume. It is clear that the composer-poet's cultivation, in the pieces gathered together in the 1628 set, of an introspective, near Romantic type of poetry was matched by a more restrained, more subjective kind of musical setting in which the extended and brilliant melisma (the *Riesenkoloratur,* to use Rauhe's picturesque term),[32] exploited so strikingly in Mb.I[1] and Mb.II[2] (see ex. 1 above), was no longer appropriate. Nevertheless, an exceptional case can be seen in the penultimate song of the whole collection, the gently humorous "Einsmals von einem Bienelein" (Mb.III[17]), an account of Amor's bizarre adventure with a beehive, possibly inspired by act 1, scene 2 of Tasso's *Aminta.* Here Schein selects the word "zarten" (gentle, tender), in the context "in seinen zarten Fingerlein," for treatment by means of a long and elaborate melisma which is beautifully shaped and unusual in the fact that all three voices contribute equally to it, using short imitative tags. The poetic aptness and charm of this mature style of illustrative writing produces an effect far removed from the brittle virtuosity of the more vividly ornate passages found in the earlier volumes:

Ex. 2

Quite different in character is Schein's system of building thematic fragments into a coherent and expressive language using altogether subtler, more subdued methods of text interpretation. A telling example is provided by "O Filli, schönste Zier" (Mb.III[14]), the poem of which, although mannered and overflorid in style, inspired one of Schein's finest musical settings. The opening stanza is as follows:

O Filli, schönste Zier,
Was läufst du lang vor mir?
Ach, Korallenmündlein rot,
Willst du mich gern haben tot,
So müsst du sein mein Herzelein,
Sonst ist umsonst das Wollen dein.

The verse structure is a little unusual, consisting of three rhyming couplets, each of which has a greater number of syllables than its immediate predecessor (6.6.7.7.8.8.), producing a marked heightening of the emotional tension. Also powerfully rhetorical is the effect created by consecutive strong accents between the end of line 2 (on "mir") and the beginning of line 3 (on "Ach"), producing a temporary change from iambic to trochaic meter. The division of the music into two main sections with repeats occurs after lines 1 and 2, the first half being amplified by an extended melisma on 'O' and by several repetitions of the second line. Schein's treatment of fine detail—in particular his use of contrast and repetition "figures"—is clearly illustrated in the excerpt, given below. Set in D minor (Dorian) the music moves at once to the dominant chord where, over a sustained pedal, ascending scales portray the nymph's flying footsteps. At the double bar a tellingly placed crotchet rest *(sospiro)* and a diminished fourth leap in soprano 2 highlight the asymmetric accent on "Ach," while an overlapping entry in soprano 1 presses on towards a glowing C major cadence, depicting the "Korallenmündlein rot"; immediately, however, a fall in pitch, a change to minor harmony, and a shift to the "insecurity" of a half-close touchingly underline the lover's bitter reproach: "Willst du mich gern haben tot."

Ex. 3

Equally characteristic is Schein's use of sound painting with words *(Klangmalerei),* a simple example of which may be seen in the following extract from "Concordia zu jeder Zeit" (Mb.III[5]), originally a wedding piece entitled "Commendatio Concordiae" and dated November 1626. The second half of the first stanza, which extols generally the virtues of peace and concord, comprises the following foursquare, rather pedestrian lines:

In allem Stand,
Ja Leut und Land

Sie vielmal hat erhalten,
Die sind verstört
Und ganz verheert,
Wenn sie sich han zerspalten.

Here Schein seizes upon the significant words "verstört" (troubled) and
"verheert" (laid waste) and provides special emphasis for them by contracting
their rhythm against the poetic *ictus* (corresponding to the musical *tactus*)
established by the matching short-line sections, achieving in the process not
only a welcome degree of added metrical freedom, but also an appropriate
expression of agitation:

In al - lem Stand, / Ja   Leut   und   Land

Die sind ver-stört / Und ganz ver-heert, / Wenn sie...

Although the musical setting has a symmetrical phrase structure and regularly
spaced cadences, the variation in the verse-rhythm, seen above, results in a
subtle feeling of dislocation, creating an artificial type of enjambement by
postponing the cadence expected at the end of line 5 until the second word of
line 6. Furthermore, additional emphasis is supplied for "verstört" and
"verheert" by the use of dissonant suspensions in the soprano 2 line; and an
ornamented repetition of the phrase "Wenn sie sich han" delays and thereby
enhances dramatically the final climactic word, "zerspalten" (split):

Ex. 4

A special problem is posed by the additional stanzas of each villanella, which rarely match the basic musical setting with anything like the same precision as the opening verse. Indeed, the very richness of Schein's material and the elaborate pictorialism which he so often cultivates are ingredients which militate against a wholly successful strophic treatment. Rauhe puts forward the view that, as in strophic works of the period generally, Schein's music was fashioned solely to fit the poetic ideas expressed in the first stanza, the remaining verses being arranged so as to observe only the metrical pattern; such occasional "good matches" of verse and music as exist he takes to be simply the result of "accidental conformity" *(zufällige Uebereinstimmungen).*[33] Two factors suggest, however, that Schein's intentions may have extended somewhat beyond these limits: one is the unusual strength of his position as creator of both the poetry and the music, which must surely have encouraged him to attempt an integration of these elements over as broad a range as possible; and the other is the surprisingly large number of individual cases where the various types of musical word painting are in fact aptly matched with poetic detail in the later stanzas. One example occurs in "Einsmals von einem Bienelein" (Mb.III[17]) where the melisma used to color the word "zarten" (see ex. 2) is associated in the later stanzas with the words "Rosenlipplein" ("Auf Filli Rosenlipplein zart") and "küsst" ("Die Schäfrin küsst wusst nichts davon") with an aptness which seems unlikely to have occurred simply by chance. Another is to be found in "O Schäferin, o Filli mein" (Mb.II[2]), where a short passage of rippling semiquavers, used in stanza 1 to illustrate "lachen" ("Frau Venus wird es lachen"), is effectively set to "Parlieren" ("Mit lieblichem Parlieren") and "resonieren" ("Das wird wohl resonieren") in the second and third verses, respectively. At the same time, cases to the contrary are of course equally demonstrable; in the plaintive setting, "In grosser Traurigkeit" (Mb.I[5]), for example, the tiny pictorial touch of a rapid descending scale, used in the first stanza to illustrate "Pfeil" (arrow), is deprived of much of its effect in the ensuing verses where the equivalently placed words are "bald" ("Die Kraft wird bald durchdringen") and "sie" ("Drum lass mich sie empfangen").

Only in certain limited contexts are points of illustration preserved through successive stanzas with any degree of uniformity. One category consists of short, contrasting passages in triple time, which usually occur either in response to text references to dancing, singing, drinking or other forms of rejoicing, or else as the result of black notation eye-music, portraying symbolically such phrases as "Göttlein blind" or "grosser Traurigkeit." In the former instance it is customary for the text sense to be preserved consistently in all stanzas, often by means of an exactly repeated refrain, while in the latter case the invariable practice is to drop all reference to "blackness" in the later verses—possibly in deference to the views of the performing *cognoscenti* who, having smiled knowingly over the conceit in the first stanza, might well have regarded its repetition in later verses as otiose, or even tasteless. Then again, exclamations such as "O" or "Ach" at the start of various opening verses, which frequently attract special musical treatment, are commonly preserved unchanged throughout (or are occasionally replaced by "Drum"); while passages of "giant" coloratura [34] (found only in the earlier volumes) are usually provided either with words containing conveniently singable vowel sounds, such as "Gesang," "Wäldern" and "Rosildo" in Mb.I[1], or with ones chosen for their special relevance to the poetic context, such as the modish Italianate expressions, "Manieren," "passeggionieren" and "askoltieren," set in Mb.II[2] to a 56-note gorgia, almost certainly with satirical intention [35] (see ex. 1).

In cases where the word painting is of a less obvious kind, strophic treatment not infrequently leads to surprising anomalies. Clearly, within the limited framework of any individual poem it would have been perfectly possible for Schein to supply each later stanza with words and phrases precisely equivalent in meaning to those "painted" musically in the opening verse. The fact that he does not do so suggests that he may have regarded such a procedure as excessively mechanical (particularly if sustained, setting after setting, through the whole collection) or as detrimental in some other way to the natural flow of his poetic thought. Nevertheless, the disparity between the precise handling of the various opening stanzas and the relatively wayward treatment (sometimes extending even to aberrations in rhythm, meter or accentuation) [36] accorded to the later verses is often hard to explain. A detailed example of the problems involved can be seen in "Wenn ich durch Ach mein Liebesqual" (Mb.III[9]), based on the following text:

1. Wenn ich durch Ach mein Liebesqual
   Mit Schreien könnt kurieren,
   So wollt ich schreien tausendmal
   Ach, ach stets repetieren.
   Abr so, je mehr ich schreien tu
   Je mehr nimmt meine Marter zu.

2. Wenn Seufzen hatte eine Macht,
   Die Schäfrin zu bewegen,
   So wollt ich seufzen Tag und Nacht,
   Mein Herz zu Ruh nicht legen.
   Abr so, hilft mich kein seufzen nicht,
   Nur feindlicher sie mich ansicht.

3. Könnt ich durch sehnlich Flehn und Bitt
   Bei Filli Hilf erlangen,
   Zu bitten ich aufhörte nit
   Wollt stets von vorn anfangen.
   Abr so, hilft gar kein Bitten, Flehn,
   In ihrer Lieb ich muss vergehn.

In a poem noteworthy for its symmetry and its high degree of motivic integration, each stanza displays a neat balance between the "hopeful" aims expressed in its initial quatrain and the "despair" conveyed by the final couplet, the latter a type of mock refrain, introduced at each appearance by the words "abr so." The uneven split produced by the verse structure is modified in the musical setting by repetitions of the "refrain" lines, with rising sequences to emphasize the prevailing mood of hopelessness, so that the second half in fact slightly exceeds the first in length. The lover's anguished search for release from his torment is symbolized in the music by a wayward, unsettled tonality, with no clear statement of the principal "key" until the cadence at the end of the first section; and an atmosphere of relentless suffering is created by the music's march-like pulse and largely homophonic style.

Particularly ingenious from the structural point of view is the use in each stanza in turn (and in that stanza alone) of a predominant key word—successively "Schreien" ("schreien"), "Seufzen" ("seufzen") and "Bitt" ("bitten," "Bitten"). Musical word painting is used to underline these key words at least once in each stanza, a pattern being established in the opening verse whereby "Schreien" (or "schreien") is "painted" no less than three times, the occurrences in the second and fifth lines being closely interrelated thematically.

Ex. 5

In both the later stanzas, however, the verbal and musical patterns drift slightly out of alignment, the respective key words no longer coinciding consistently with the word painting; the result is the following arrangement of "painted" words, the first and last in each horizontal line being the ones which coincide with the thematically related patterns:

Stanzas:			
1.	Schreien	schreien	schreien
2.	Schäfrin	seufzen	Seufzen
3.	Filli	ich	Bitten

The crucial question is whether this has happened deliberately or by chance. Little difficulty is presented by the first and second stanzas, since obvious unity is imparted by the use of words beginning with "Sch" and "Seu," and there is in any case a clear connection not only between "crying" and "sighing" but also between both of these activities and the shepherdess (Schäfrin) who is the cause of all the suffering. In the third verse the arrangement is more problematic. It is logical enough for the thematically interrelated patterns to coincide with "Filli" and "Bitten," which themselves follow on naturally from "Schäfrin" and "Seufzen" in the preceding stanza. But it is not easy to see why "ich" should have been chosen as a subsidiary keyword to carry the central section of word painting, particularly since a simple rewording of the third line, such as "So würd' ich bitten, rasten nit," would have preserved the pattern established in the earlier verses—"So wollt ich schreien (or seufzen)." By allowing the word painting to coincide with "bitten," the rewording would have maintained the logical sequence of ornamented keywords: "schreien," "seufzen" and "bitten." As in a number of similar cases, the composer here seems closely to approach an ideal solution for his later stanzas, only to prejudice the result by an apparent disregard for some relatively small detail. Significantly, the discrepancy occurs only in the third verse, and thus conforms to a common pattern whereby the later verses reveal in turn a gradually decreasing relationship to the basic musical setting.[37]

Such minor inconsistencies, together with weightier stylistic anomalies found elsewhere in Schein's works, are attributable with hindsight largely to the composer's historical position in a period of transition between two major style eras. Not infrequently conflict arises from the attempt to embrace novel modes of expression within traditional formal structures, devised originally for rather different artistic purposes. Just as in his madrigals, for example, Schein aims at times to set extravagantly "expressionist" ideas, both poetic and musical, in conventional or relatively restricted frameworks,[38] so in his villanellas he apparently endeavors (though not always successfully) to achieve a compromise between his detailed musico-poetic language and the neutral, largely non-illustrative type of strophic treatment in common use at his period.

As a result of stylistic advances in German poetry and music, and the spread of new genres, such as the Alexandrine verse of Opitz, and the solo songs[39] of Heinrich Albert and Kaspar Kittel, several facets of Schein's work became somewhat outmoded after his death in 1630. Nevertheless, his monumental villanella collection continued to appear in new editions, apparently providing later generations of Lied composers with an enduring model for the apt interrelationship of verse and music. In his *Grundlage einer Ehren-Pforte,* published over 100 years later, Johann Mattheson still felt justified in recalling the admiration which Schein's work had evoked. "Proof and evidence," he wrote, "of the esteem which the musical world felt for (Schein's) work are provided by the publication ... at Erfurt, in 1651, of one of his posthumous compositions, known, according to the nature of its text-underlay, sometimes as *La Musica boscareccia sacra,* sometimes as *cantilenas sylvestres* or *Waldlieder,* and sometimes as *Odas amorum.*"[40] Significantly, perhaps, Mattheson gives pride of place to the version he describes as "sacra,"a strange compilation in which sacred texts (published anonymously, but now identified as the work of one Eckart Leichner, a medical practitioner) were allied to Schein's music, probably with the intention not so much of suppressing the original mildly erotic verse as of offering in conjunction with it poetry more in line with contemporary taste. The addition of religious texts to Schein's amorous little pieces, grotesque though it may seem at first sight, is not perhaps entirely surprising when one considers, on the one hand, the high artistic caliber of the music and, on the other, the intense and manifold religious preoccupations of the age.[41] What is indeed remarkable is the precision with which the new verse is fashioned to match expressive details in the music—ample evidence it would seem not only of the integrity of the new author, but also of the decisive influence which Schein's impressive demonstration of the *musica poetica* concept was already beginning to exercise in Germany by the middle of the century.

Notes

I gratefully acknowledge the help and advice given by my friend and colleague, Mr. W.H. Fox, in connection with the various literary matters involved in this essay.

1.   From August 1616 until his death in November 1630.

2.   *Neue Ausgabe Sämtlicher Werke,* 2, ed. Adam Adrio.

3.   Idem, 1, ed. Adam Adrio.

4.   See R. Wustmann, *Musikgeschichte Leipzigs* (Leipzig and Berlin, 1908), pp. 83-85.

5.   For a detailed study of the background to Schein's secular works, see A. Prüfer, *J.H. Schein und das weltliche deutsche Lied des 17. Jahrhunderts* (Leipzig, 1908).

6.   *Sämtliche Werke,* 2, ed. A. Prüfer.

7.   *Neue Ausgabe Sämtlicher Werke,* 8, ed. Adam Adrio.

8.   See Adam Adrio's article on Schein in *Die Musik in Geschichte und Gegenwart* 11, col. 1644.

9.   The Petrarchan features in Schein's poetry are strongly Renaissance-oriented. During his lifetime they were gradually superseded as Baroque elements began to play an increasing role in his verse style.

10. It was probably from the subtitle of Tasso's *Aminta*—"favola boscareccia"—that Schein derived the Italian name for his large villanella collection. His alternative title, *Waldliederlein,* suggests a possible relationship with the commonly used literary term, *Poetische Wälder,* usually indicating a somewhat haphazard collection of poems, indeterminate in number and widely varied in mood, form and purpose.

11. See David Paisey, "Some Occasional Aspects of Johann Hermann Schein," *British Library Journal* 1 (1975):171-80.

12. The *Königsberger Kreis* was founded toward the end of the sixteenth century; its most gifted poet was Simon Dach (1605-59). The *Fruchtbringende Gesellschaft* (modelled on the *Accademia della Crusca* of Florence) was founded in 1617, under the presidency of Duke Ludwig of Anhalt-Cöthen.

13. E.g., four volumes of occasional verse in the British Library, pressmarks c. 107 e. 19-22. See Paisey, "Some Occasional Aspects," p. 171.

14. Poems by these authors are to be found in the prefaces to *Israelsbrünnlein, Musica boscareccia* and *Diletti pastorali.*

15. In particular, Spenser's *The Shepherds' Calendar* (1579) and *The Faery Queen* (1596), Sidney's *Arcadia* (1590), de Montreux's *Les Bergeries de Juliette* (1585-93), and d'Urfé's *Astrée* (1607-27).

16. *Sämtliche Werke,* 2, ed. A. Prüfer, p. 26.

17. See Paisey, "Some Occasional Aspects," pp. 176-77.

18. Martin Opitz's *Das Buch von der deutschen Poeterey,* published in 1624, was to influence the development of German poetry for the next 150 years.

19. A typical reference to the Rosenthal countryside near Leipzig.

20. Important critical appraisals of Schein's poetry are contained in Walter Brauer, "Jacob Regnart, Johann Hermann Schein und die Anfänge der deutschen Barocklyrik," *Deutsche Vierteljahrsschrift für Literaturwissenschaft und Geistesgeschichte,* 17. Jg., 1 Referatenheft, 1939, pp. 371-404; A.G. de Capua, *German Baroque Poetry* (Albany, 1973), pp. 21-24; H. Kretzschmar, *Geschichte des neuen deutschen Liedes,* 1 (1911), 10-13; Gunther Müller, *Geschichte des deutschen Liedes vom Zeitalter des Barock bis zur Gegenwart* (Munich, 1925), pp. 22 ff.; R. Hinton Thomas, *Poetry and Song in the German Baroque* (Oxford, 1963), pp. 21-33.

21. Müller, *Geschichte des deutschen Liedes,* 1, 24.

22. In all references to pieces contained in *Musica boscareccia,* the title will be abbreviated to Mb., followed by the volume and item numbers, e.g., Mb.I[14].

23. The additional wedding pieces are to be found amongst the "Weltliche Gelegenheits-Kompositionen" in J.H. Schein, *Sämtliche Werke,* 2 ed. A. Prüfer, 126-59.

24. E.g., in the *Aria à 3* "Wenn's nur ein krankes Herzelein / Mit seinem Mund anhaucht, / Von Stund an neue Kraft behend / Empfindt davon der Patient, / Als wär ihm nichts gewesen."

25. In the dedicatory preface to *Musica boscareccia,* 2.

26. Strophic settings are not uncommon amongst the works of Schein's predecessors Lechner, Hassler, Demantius and others; but often they adopt a style of composition which is insufficiently complex to produce significant difficulties with the later stanzas.

27. The only certain basis for assumptions about chronology is the terminal publication dates of the three volumes. Nevertheless, the "natural" expectation that the later volumes will contain more mature individual items, both poetry and music, appears to be well supported by internal stylistic evidence—admittedly a circular argument.

28. See Brauer, "Jacob Regnart, Johann Hermann Schein," pp. 390-91.

29. See de Capua, *German Baroque Poetry,* pp. 88-106.

30. The principal German theorists involved in promoting the concept during Schein's lifetime were: Seth Calvisius (*Melopoeia . . . ,* Erfurt, 1592), Joachim Burmeister (*Musica poetica,*

Rostock, 1606), Joachim Thelamonius (*Tractatus de compositions sive musica poetica,* 1610), and Johannes Nucius (*Musicae poeticae...praeceptiones,* Neusse, 1613). Some discussion of the general background to the subject, particularly in relation to Burmeister's work, is to be found in Maria Rika Maniates, *Mannerism in Italian Music and Culture, 1530-1630* (Chapel Hill, 1979), pp. 209-12.

31.   For a detailed study of the subject see Hermann Rauhe, *Dichtung und Musik im weltlichen Vokalwerk Johann Hermann Scheins* (Hamburg, 1959); for discussion of the important role which rhetorical "figures" play also in the later works of Leonhard Lechner, see *Leonhard Lechner Werke,* 13, ed. Walther Lipphardt, xi-xvi.

32.   Rauhe, *Dichtung und Musik,* p. 72.

33.   Rauhe, *Dichtung und Musik,* p. 74.

34.   Strophic arias with equally elaborate forms of coloratura treatment are to be found in Caccini's *Le Nuove Musiche* (1602); a typical example is the *Aria seconda* "Ardi cor mio," where the words "Ardi," "Canta," "Luci," "Laccio," "Felice," and "Almo" are each set, twice in successive stanzas, to melismas of 47 notes and 36 notes respectively. See G. Caccini, *Le Nuove Musiche,* ed. H. Wiley Hitchcock (Madison, 1970), pp. 120-22.

35.   The musical satire here is clearly linked with the literary satire inherent in the French style "-ieren" endings, the pretentiousness of the alleged user being gently mocked.

36.   E.g., in the last stanza of "Der Hirte Coridon" (Mb.I[14]), where the final four lines have an aberrant syllable count of 6.7.7.6. instead of 7.6.6.7, and can only be made to fit the music by means of contractions and expansions of words, e.g., "setzet" to "setzt," or "sein" to "seinen." The original poem, entitled "Residenza d'Amore," was set as a wedding piece (November 1618) for six voices and continuo, and was through-composed.

37.   A typical example is provided by "O Berg und Tal" (Mb.II[13]), where a rapid ascending scale of F major, used to illustrate "Pfeil" (arrow) in stanza 1 is linked in subsequent verses with "Wind" (wind), "Grausamkeit" (cruelty), and "mitleidentlich" (sympathetically), so that "activity" description gradually and inappropriately gives way to "emotion" description.

38.   The madrigal "Aurora schön mit ihrem Haar" (*Diletti pastorali,* no. 13), with its clear stylistic debts to Monteverdi and Giovanni Gabrieli, provides a good example. It is noteworthy, however, that in this setting the inbuilt conflict between content and form seems to contribute significantly to the intensity of the emotional expression.

39.   Schein's only surviving secular solo song is "Jocus nuptialis," a wedding piece dating from October 1622 for tenor voice and theorbo printed in *Sämtliche Werke,* 2, ed. A Prüfer, 131. Among the more notable ensemble songs of the next generation are those of Thomas Selle of Hamburg, who was possibly a pupil of Schein, such as *Deliciarum juvenilium decas harmonica-bivocalis,* à 2 (1634), and *Amorum musicalium...decas I,* à 3 (1635).

40.   Johann Mattheson, *Grundlage einer Ehren-Pforte* (Hamburg, 1740), p. 316.

41.   Leichner's sacred texts are incorporated throughout in Prüfer's modern edition, *vide supra.* It is worth noting that the *Poetische Wälder* concept (mentioned in note 10 above) would readily allow for the inclusion also of sacred texts.

John Blow: An English Harpsichord Composer

Watkins Shaw

The dominant figure in London music during the last 30 years of the seventeenth century was John Blow (1649-1708). To speak thus is not perversely to ignore the achievements of Henry Purcell, but to make some attempt partly to view the period as a whole, partly to see it as it might have appeared to contemporaries. For though the brilliance of the younger musician was acknowledged, Blow's own reputation also stood high, the two of them being bracketed in one encomium as a "Mighty Pair! Of Jubal's sacred art / The greatest glory"; and when Purcell died it was announced in the press that his post of organist of Westminster Abbey was disposed of to "that other great master, Dr Blow." The number of important positions which Blow combined—as composer and musician-in-ordinary at Court, as organist of Westminster Abbey both before and after Purcell, as master of the choristers of St. Paul's Cathedral at an important juncture, as one of the organists and, above all, for 34 years master of the Children of the Chapel Royal—all betoken the preeminence of his professional position. If we add his influence over very many pupils of some successive generations, embracing not a few celebrated figures, as well as the scope of his output as a composer from about 1670 to 1705, it may be thought that the epithet "dominant" is not without justification; and it may follow that both the strengths and the weaknesses of English music of those days will be better understood by an examination of his works.

In large degree the works of both Blow and Purcell lie parallel, especially the secular odes, church music, and solo vocal music. In three other departments the parallel, though discernible, is much less marked. After his fascinating little opera *Venus and Adonis,* Blow displayed no further interest in stage music, and he seems to have written but one trio sonata. On the other hand, though Purcell wrote a certain amount of well-turned harpsichord music and a trifling quantity of unimportant organ music, it was left to Blow to address himself assiduously to composition for the keyboard. From one point of view it is probable that aspects on which they laid different emphasis will most clearly reveal their separate individualities. And certainly in his keyboard music Blow's achievements rather than weaknesses (which there are) may be seen more fully than in some other branches of his compositions.

Blow's works specifically for harpsichord (or spinet) embrace pieces ranging from easy trifles of only a few bars to relatively extended works, many in dance forms but others in the abstract character of preludes, grounds and chacones. ("Chacone" was a distinctive anglicized use of the period. Throughout this paper, in dealing with acclimatized forms, I shall correspondingly employ "Almand," "Corant," "Gavott" and "Jigg.") In "The Harpsichord Music of John Blow: A First Catalogue" (contributed to *Music and Bibliography,* ed. Oliver Neighbour, London and New York, 1980) I identified 70 pieces with their sources. Since then Peter Holman has drawn attention to MS. 15.139Z in the Conservatoire royal de Musique, Brussels, which adds five more. This establishes Blow as being, by virtue of bulk of output, if nothing more, the leading English composer of his day in this genre. He appears to have been the central pillar of a little school. After Matthew Locke, and apart from nonentities, the leading composers of keyboard music— John Barrett, Ralph Courteville, William Croft, Jeremiah Clarke, Francis Pigott, Henry Purcell—were all pupils of his, the only significant figure outside that circle being Robert King, who does not seem to have served under him though he became a colleague at Court.

Twenty-five pieces were published in his lifetime and may be studied in two reliable modern editions, *Musick's Hand-maid: II,* edited by Thurston Dart, and *John Blow: Six Suites,* edited by Howard Ferguson (both London, Stainer & Bell, 1958 and 1965 respectively). With one exception, the so-called "Morlake's Ground," these are all dance movements or the like. The remaining 50, which include all the other grounds and non-dance movements, must be recovered from manuscript sources, some of them surviving in as many as five extant transcripts, though none of them in Blow's hand.

Attributions in manuscript copies are casual. Many are anonymous, leaving the composer to be identified, if possible, by reference to some other source. Fortunately, after sifting, there seem to be few treacherous instances of misattribution in Blow's harpsichord music, certainly nothing so misleading as the inclusion among his organ music in GB-Lbm (bl), Add. MS 31468, fol. 16, of a piece by Frescobaldi. There is however the interesting instance of an Almand in D minor printed in G.B. Draghi's *Six Select Suites of Lessons for the Harpsichord* (c. 1707), which is ascribed to Blow in both GB-Lbm(bl), Egerton MS 2959, fol. 10, and B-Bc, MS 15.139Z, both probably from the first decade of the eighteenth century. (Robert Woolley has kindly drawn my attention to Draghi's publication.) But, still on the subject of attribution, it is unfortunate though perhaps opportune to record that Oesterle and Aldrich's anthology, *Early Keyboard Music* (Schirmer, 1904), includes four pieces ascribed to Blow for which at no time have there been any grounds whatsoever to attribute them to him: Almand I in A (printed oddly as a tripartite piece, the first of its elements being by Robert King), Prelude, Courante, and Fugue in C (all anonymous in GB-Lbm(bl), Add. MS 41205). These same misattributions are found in an earlier London edition by Ernst Pauer.

This brings us to the question of a definitive text of this oeuvre, about which, though it is not our prime concern here, at least something must be said in the absence of an accepted standard edition for reference at present.

Two-thirds of these pieces have come down to us in more than one source, whether printed or manuscript, and most of those having one source only are among the least significant—an interesting if accidental sifting. Some have as many as five, six, or seven sources. After collation these do present some few acute difficulties which seem incapable of convincing resolution. In addition a very few differences suggest that the text from which the transcribers worked (maybe Blow's original) was not clear, perhaps because what was intended to be the final version was arrived at after heavy correction. One instance even suggests that Blow (or someone else after him) had attempted a slightly more elaborate working-out, but abandoned it without the transcriber's understanding what had happened. But, with these allowances, it is comparatively rare to find crucial disagreement on what I will call essentials: the true bass; the fundamental harmony whether explicit or implied; the primary melodic outline, or the keyboard figures. This being so, our present survey can be made without the existence of a fully critical text. On the other hand, the really extensive differences between sources (other than ornamentation which of course varies enormously) concern what I will call glosses: enrichment of the sonority of the bass; elaboration of melodic outline; rhythmic refinements; more explicit harmony in the mean part of the texture. Accepting that a textual scholar will be on guard against little features which might wander from contemporary style in a somewhat later transcript, large quantities of the remaining variants can be accepted as within the legitimate discretion of the performer. But it follows that, even if an editor could publish a comparative text (feasible with two sources even though expensive, but manifestly impracticable with more), neither one nor another can have final authority. As for a collation of such variants, sometimes running through bar after bar, its expression in tabular form would be of such complexity as to defeat any useful purpose whatever. And though the survival of but a single source may relieve an editor of some labor, it cannot relieve the uncomfortable certainty that should another have existed it would assuredly have displayed these kinds of differences.

Ideally, what is required is, first of all, to postulate, behind the sources which we have, a kind of basic text over which one may, as a hypothesis, suppose them to have worked; and next, from an analytical study of these variants, to build up a vocabulary of discretion for performers to study. In that way, when confronted by such a basic text, they may apply a sense of style without an editor's crystallization of any one feature. The accomplishment of that combined task is probably a chimera, but to go some way towards accomplishing the second part would be a very desirable undertaking.

Understanding of this body of Blow's music would be enhanced by some inkling of its chronology. But external evidence is all but totally lacking. The few (and not particularly telling) pieces in *Musick's Hand-maid: II* must, obviously, have been written by 1689. Blow's six published suites may have been composed at any time before 1698 (nos. 1-4) or 1700 (nos. 5 and 6), and that tells us really nothing. A decline in his output generally suggests that he wrote next to no keyboard music after 1700, and those six suites probably represent an assortment of music from earlier years, now suitably grouped and published in response to the demand for that kind of thing which seems to have sprung up just before the turn of the century. Of the large-scale pieces among those remaining in manuscript, the only scrap of information available is that the Chacone in G minor is dated 3 June 1687 in B-Bc, MS 15.139Z. If that is not the actual date of composition, at least it gives a latest possible date. This unusual piece is quite mature in manner and seems to indicate that there is no stylistic reason why any of his other pieces could not have been written (even if they were not) by that date. As for internal indications of chronology in point of style, the external evidence provides too few pointers to act as controls. But if, for instance, there was (as may be supposed) a movement over the years towards more symmetry, regularity, and refinement, this supports our suggestion that the suites published in 1698-1700 represent a pool of material collected over a period of some years.

When one thinks of the great number of Chapel Royal choirboys for whose teaching Blow carried responsibility for so many years, it is not surprising that a few of his harpsichord pieces should have every appearance of instructional material for beginners: five-finger work, easy extension of the hand, simple scale passages. But one supposes that the wider circle of domestic players would chiefly be interested in his dance movements, the sort of thing which secured publication in suite form.

As with Purcell, the roughly standardized form of Blow's suites (to which there were exceptions) was Almand, Corant, and Saraband, sometimes followed by a lighter movement, maybe Air, Gavott, Minuet, or Jigg. These last, when they occur, are only miniatures, and their more polished manifestations, for example the Gavott from Suite No. 4 or the Minuet from Suite No. 5, have the immediate appeal of a bonbon. Something of the same is evident in the more refined Corants (Suite No. 4) or Sarabands (Suite No. 3). The Jigg of Suite No. 1 smacks a little of a country dance with a certain not unattractive lumbering gait. But in other examples of such movements Blow's invention seems to lack spontaneity and clear direction. What should be noted, however, is that the more finished instances, with their agreeable melody, regularity of rhythm, and balanced phrases, might perfectly well have been written by some other hand, Courteville's for instance.

As for Almands, the idea of a common rhythmic figure running through all movements so entitled sat lightly on Blow, Purcell, and their fellows, even though frequently enough (but far from invariably) sixteenth note patterns were in evidence after a beginning in the form of an upbeat eighth (or sixteenth) note followed by a quarter note tied to the first of a group of four sixteenth notes. But in his Suite No. 2, where a very slightly quicker tempo is implied, there are no groups of sixteenth notes, but instead a pleasing sprightliness conveying a clear-cut melodic outline. Its readily perceived phrase structure is in marked contrast to the Almand of Suite No. 5, which would baffle the ear listening for any such thing. One must accept this rather as a passage of continuously unfolding, perhaps somewhat wayward invention. In Suite No. 6 Blow renounces the upbeat beginning and delivers a delicately lyrical cantilena-like phrase opening thus:

Ex. 1

(Almand, Suite 6. Ornaments omitted)

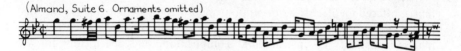

Especially interesting is the first movement of Suite No. 2, entitled simply "Ground," but which by its rhythmic patterns combined with its position in the suite must be regarded as "Almand (on a Ground)." The theme is in two halves, *(a)* cadencing on the dominant, *(b)* cadencing on the tonic. Instead of setting out his variations on the whole of this each time, Blow disposes the movement as follows:

Initial statement of *(a)*—1st variation on *(a)*;
Initial statement of *(b)*—1st variation on *(b)*;
2nd and 3rd variations on *(a)*;
2nd and 3rd variations on *(b)*.

This slightly loosens the limbs of a fairly tight framework while maintaining unity. The movement has a considerably higher degree of perspicuity and regularity than much of Blow's other music of this kind. Yet another approach is revealed in an unpublished movement in G which was nevertheless popular, to judge by the number of surviving transcripts. Under cover of the "Almand" title Blow introduces the same rhythmic figure (the "Scotch snap") which he had used in act 1 of *Venus and Adonis* for the Hunters' Music, whence this piece got its nickname "The Hunting Almand." Each half of it works at this figure symmetrically in an exceedingly un-Almand-like style, despite the perfunctory gesture of the upbeat and tied note at the outset. (This piece is no. 30 in my published catalogue, reference as above, which quotes incipits and cites sources. From this point, in dealing with items unpublished in Blow's lifetime, I shall cite these numbers for purpose of identification.)

Consideration of these varied Almands suggests that Blow's approach, fully as much as Purcell's if not more so, was fundamentally that of an abstract composer. Not for him to write varied exemplars in the pattern of any regular convention. Rather he would put down the title "Almand" and a common time signature, and then proceed to compose at will, but within the accepted span of a dance movement. If that point of view does indeed represent his mind, it is perhaps curious that not one of his suites, published or in manuscript, has a prelude in which he would have been free of all restraint, and that there are only four independent preludes by him. One of these, however, is a particularly impressive bit of work. In its compact form, the Prelude in G (70) evinces in every bar of its toccata-like content the inventive powers of the composer not less than his delight in the resources of the instrument. Though of no great length, it is one of the most outstanding English pieces of its time.

It seems to have been considered that harpsichord music, unlike organ music, offered no place to counterpoint, and Purcell's preludes to his suites in C major and G minor are exceptional in this respect. And so, as one having a manifest instinct for instrumental composition, and specifically for the harpsichord, Blow sought a larger canvas, having regard to the limited constructional conventions familiar to him, in the ground bass. Purcell, consummate master though he was of the art of composition on a ground, wrote few original examples for the harpsichord, and these, though expertly contrived, are slender in character and fairly brief, as if he deemed strong meat unsuitable in this medium. It was otherwise with Blow, who wrote some notably extensive specimens, full of interest and of no small technical difficulty.

The subjects of his eight examples are as follows, cited in a generalized form, without inessentials of sonority or figuration which do not affect the true bass:

Ex. 2

Ex. 2 (continued)

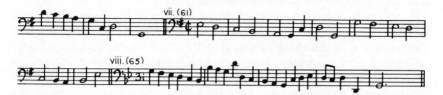

As customary in England at that date when composing for the harpsichord, the theme was not announced solo but given out as the bass of a fully realized texture.

The first of these, the Ground in C (58), does not depart from the obvious harmonic implications of its unfruitful subject, and some of its 16 statements carry only primitive melodic decorations. Elsewhere there are easy instances of a principle put to a higher power in some other of Blow's works, breaking up the bass theme itself and harking back to the older "division on a ground" (cf. ex. 3, below). Such interest as the piece has lies in a question of keyboard performing technique. In one passage of mainly conjunct sixteenth note movement for the right hand, the scribe of the solitary contemporary manuscript writes one note a third below the first sixteenth note and writes beside it "3ds" to indicate that the whole passage should be played thus, a considerable technical requirement. The passage would be perfectly effective and sensible without the thirds. Was that how it was in the copy from which the scribe was working, and did he, having been struck by the idea of thirds, make a jotting to that effect on his own account? Or did the copy before him contain the thirds while he himself saved trouble by not writing them in extenso? Later, a similar passage is marked "6ths" in the same way, so that it could hardly be played at any reasonable tempo unless the left hand, by releasing the dotted half note of the bass, came to the aid of the upper parts. A considerably later transcript of the work (late enough to contain music by Handel) accepts these thirds and sixths. This lends them a certain support, but on the other hand they might represent the view held more than 50 years after Blow's death. But whether they emanate from Blow or not (and it cannot certainly be said they do not) the fact that a source for his work dating from the earliest years of the eighteenth century envisages them is interesting testimony to contemporary keyboard technique. Although the actual musical substance of this curious piece is only conventional, if we accept it in this form then it makes a fairly demanding étude. Yet the title of "The Hay's" suggests some lurking popular allusion. Its meaning remains unexplained; but there was a country dance called "The Haymaker's Jig," and in *Kenilworth,* chapter 4, Sir Walter Scott makes Wayland Smith say "I'll dance the hays yet with any merry lass in Warwickshire."

Another ground in C (60) need not detain us. Vapid in content, it suffers from the further defect that the themes, and hence the whole piece as it appears to stand, concludes in the dominant. But it comes to us from one source only; and if indeed it is by Blow (it would be no loss to his oeuvre if not) one wonders whether it was designed to be followed by a second section consisting of variations on a second limb of the ground bringing it back to the tonic.

The only ground published in his lifetime acquired the sobriquet "Morlack's" or "Morelake" Ground. Easily poised amidst unflorid melodic decoration, easy divisions for the left hand, and chordal sonorities, it breathes the air of what would be agreeable in the parlor without making great technical demands. It is noticeable that three out of four manuscript sources of this piece (as distinct from its publication in *Musick's Hand-maid: II*) include one additional variation, so contrived as to carry the mind forward from the mild climax of the published version to a slightly intense change of mood, by time and tempo, to a tiny coda in slow common time bearing no relation to the theme, and which, by a slight chromatic turn to G minor, imparts an altogether different character to the ending. Such a mood, with chromaticism, is to be found at the end of some other of Blow's works.

Four other grounds by Blow are much more worth attention, each conveying an impression of some overall mood. In the Ground in C (59) that is one of sonority and a spaciousness which is maintained in the more bravura passages. It opens thus:

Ex. 3

At each repetition of the theme the simple device of treating the first half of bar 1 as the end of a statement and the second half as beginning the next helps the continuity of what, in sum, is an English work of unusual dignity in this form at this date. Two statements in 12/8 time give relief before reverting to common time for a clinching recall of the opening gesture by way of conclusion.

The first of two Grounds in G (63) concentrates on building up brilliance. A gentle opening of melodious charm and delicacy gives way gradually to increasingly arresting passage work of greater and greater sweep, which at one point is almost violinistic:

Ex. 4

After the climax, the final variation allows the tension to relax in *style brisé* together with a touch of chromaticism which hints at ritardando:

Ex. 5

     If in the two works just discussed Blow has harnessed his treatment of the form to sonority in the one and brilliance in the other, it is lyricism that characterizes a third, also in G major (64). This is secured by maintaining the surface of the harmony close to melody and preventing a bravura element from becoming dominant. A smooth flow of thought is assisted in its later part by treating the last note of the theme as the initial note of its next statement. In one variation the composer treats his bass as capable of some rhythmic elasticity, the texture meanwhile hinting at counterpoint:

Ex. 6

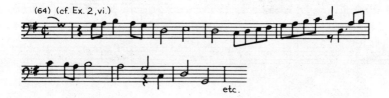

The particular expressive manner of this piece, somewhat gentle and slightly poetic, is rare, not just among his own music but also in that of Blow's English contemporaries and makes it quite distinctive.

Blow's most extended (perhaps slightly overextended) composition in this form is the Ground in E minor (61). Beginning quietly but promisingly enough with the initial statement of the theme harmonically clothed, it then proceeds in recognized manner to accumulate activity by melodic and rhythmic decoration for the right hand, the ground itself remaining in its plain form. By the end of the thirteenth statement, however, the ear has had enough. In spite of the length of the ground and the benefit of its internal shift of mode, the lack of harmonic variety and the monotonous harmonic rhythm show through the decorative procedure, while more than one variation displays a family likeness to another, and there is uncritical overuse of the rhythmic figure ♩. ♪ ♩. ♪ ♩. ♪ .

But from this point (bar 105) a new vitality seizes the music, and it now moves forward with almost magisterial effect to a striking climax, from which it quickly subsides to a conclusion. Harmonic variety is still not much in evidence. The source of the fresh vitality of invention is in the use of transformations of the ground bass itself, for example:

Ex. 7

While not creating much new harmonic resource these do relieve the ear by altering its rate of change. More importantly they generate rhythmic vigor which passes over to the upper parts until both hands grasp it together and, in an exciting moment, share the exuberant climax.

Ex. 8

Ex. 8 (continued)

Collation of the sources for this work reveals that one of them concludes at the end of the thirteenth statement. Is it then possible that, as first composed, it did indeed finish there, and that some time later the composer took up his pen to add the more powerful succeeding variations? If so, perhaps he might have done well to prune the earlier ones which slightly mar an otherwise outstanding piece.

The triple time Ground in G minor (65) raises a problem, for it exists also (in a rather longer form—144 bars as against 112) as a one-movement trio sonata (GB-Lbm(bl), Add. MS. 33236). Which came first? Even though Blow showed little interest in that medium, the idea of such a trio movement is well exemplifed in no. 6 of Purcell's second set of sonatas. The keyboard version of Blow's piece is largely two-dimensional, consisting mainly of a single line in the right hand (corresponding to violin 1, or to violin 2 when more prominent), the left hand mainly concerned with the ground bass only though touching in a little harmony here and there. When unrelieved, such a texture is uncharacteristic of its composer's keyboard writing. If the trio version was worked up from the keyboard form, then the second violin part would be something of a *parti de remplissage*. Though not very distinguished, it does not seem to me to be quite that, and there are some moments corresponding to it in the keyboard version where a violinist's bowing arm comes to mind. This right-hand passage is note-for-note with violin 2 of the trio:

Ex. 9

Finally, the bass theme itself has a cantabile quality more idiomatic of a string bass than reminiscent of Blow's keyboard style. The extra variations found in the trio are such that a single right-hand line on the harpsichord could not do justice to the intertwining of the two violin parts, while at the same time neither could those be jointly transferred to the keyboard. On balance my speculation is that in origin this is a trio sonata movement, although the number of surviving transcripts of the keyboard form (including one at least post-1750) attests to its acceptance in that state.

There is little room for doubt that Blow found ground bass form congenial enough to provide for comparatively extended work, perhaps stimulating his invention by challenging it. But there were limitations. It divided a work into prescribed regular lengths, it precluded key contrasts unless the theme was shifted in pitch, and when nothing more could be extracted in the way of variety there was an end. In a couple of different works which he called by the term "chacone" he escaped from these conditions. Free from the ostinato principle, they have nothing in common with the standard chaconne form other than triple time and the fact that they are constructed by an aggregation of sections. Restricted only by the meter and the composer's capacity to go on inventing material of sufficient interest, they are really fantasias, and may loosely be thought of as the late seventeenth-century counterpart of the older English "Fancy."

The main problem was to avoid inconsequence. The shorter example, the Chacone in G minor (57) is successful perhaps because within itself there is a miniature ground bass section and some consolidating repetition. But as to the impression of its musical content and effect it is worth recording that after a performance by Ruth Dyson broadcast by the BBC some four years ago, an impartial critic, reviewing all the music of the week, mentioned this as having particularly impressed him.

The Chacone in F (56) is, by English standards of its time, a truly big work, with a span of 188 bars. Construction by sections is not much disguised, but their varied extent obviates predictability and some have a tiny element of internal development. Growing longer towards the climax, some are unassuming, some brilliant, some sonorous, some even lightly suggestive of counterpoint, presenting overall plenty of variety of keyboard resource and sound. All these devices are the more called for because within the convention in which he worked it did not occur to Blow to move firmly to a new key. Nevertheless, within a section he was freer than in ground bass form to touch on related tonalities—generally to the flat side, major or minor; the dominant is not emphasized—and could resort to more languorously changing harmonies as in this skeleton quotation:

Ex. 10

A change to the lilt of compound time comes at a well judged moment to afford relaxation from all that had gone before and heightens by contrast the splendidly resounding finale when simple time is reestablished. Mere quotation of one section from this fascinating work can give but little idea of it, but one cannot forbear to show how, at the end, having stated his mass of harmony in full, reiterated chords, the composer displays his desire for the grandest tone he can get by restating it thus:

Ex. 11

Like the Ground in G minor (65), the Chacone in F exists in two forms. There is a version for four-part string ensemble (GB-Ob, MSS Mus.Sch. e. 443-5 and f. 570) but in G major. If on the one hand the keyboard version was original, then some advantage can be seen in a transposition to G for strings; but there seems no persuasive reason, if transcribing from the string version, to transpose to F for keyboard. On the other hand the nature of the figure on which a compound time section is based is so like some used at that period in the imitative sections of overtures for instrumental ensemble that it inclines one to accept the string version as the original. Even so, were the existence of the alternative not known, one would not suspect that either was a transcription. Furthermore, certain characteristic sections in each have no counterpart in the other, and, whichever came first, there are some patches of rewriting. Both are perfectly effective and, if the string version did indeed come first, one may justifiably regard the keyboard version as existing in its own right, rather than as an arrangement of it. Be that as it may, the work is on the grand scale and occupies a unique position for its time and surroundings.

Why did Blow write these larger specimens of non-dance movements? They would hardly appeal to most users of such things as *Musick's Hand-maid* or *The Harpsicord Master* and could not expect publication. In an age of *Gebrauchsmusik* they were not called for by his professional work. The best of his pupils—Purcell himself, perchance—may well have played them privately, and it is faintly possible, perhaps, that they had an airing at one of the public "consorts" of music which became fairly common in the 1690s at such places as York Buildings in Villiers Street, near Charing Cross. But most likely, as with Purcell and his String Fantasias, they represent the composer's personal response to his urge to create in a medium so evidently congenial to him. And though he was, as we have remarked, at the center of a group of composers for the harpsichord, not a few of his works remain unparalleled in the output of his contemporaries and followers. They constitute a significant element in his claim to a small yet distinctive place in the gallery of English music of his time.

The Musical Sources for Handel's *Teseo* and *Amadigi*

Winton Dean

The manuscript sources for Handel's operas are an uncharted wilderness, an astonishing state of affairs in view of his stature as a musical dramatist and the accessibility of much of the material. It is common knowledge that the vast majority of his autographs and many copies are in the British Library, nearly all his performing scores in the Staats- und Universitätsbibliothek, Hamburg, more copies and many autograph fragments in the Fitzwilliam Museum, Cambridge, and contemporary scores and parts for almost all the major works (the Newman Flower Collection, acquired in 1965) in the Henry Watson Music Library, Manchester. Many other manuscripts, some of prime importance, survive in public and private collections in several countries. There has been no systematic attempt to examine, collate and digest this mass of material, and until very recently even individual operas have attracted no attention from scholars.[1]

Two explanations may be advanced for this: the traditional view, shaken in recent years but not quite exploded, that eighteenth-century *opera seria* of whatever provenance is irredeemably archaic and has little to offer to the modern theater, and the apparent finality of Chrysander's monumental edition, now a century old. Chrysander did not have access to all the material now known, and his treatment of what he did have was not impeccable. His edition (HG), despite all its virtues, is inevitably out of date—for some operas much more than for others. Arnold in his collected edition (1787-97), a heroic effort for its time, included only four of the 39 surviving operas. The new Hallische Händel-Ausgabe (HHA) has so far published three.

There have been two helpful incursions into one sector of the field. As a by-product of his study of *Messiah* (1957) Jens Peter Larsen examined nearly all the Handel manuscripts in public collections with a view to identifying the copyists and dating the copies. The now familiar sigla he gave them, S1-S13, RM1-RM9, etc., laid a sound foundation on which later Handelians have gratefully built; but he was refused access to the Newman Flower Collection (then in private hands) and was unaware of the very important collections of Gerald Coke and the Earl of Malmesbury, which contain some of the earliest datable manuscripts. In 1972 Hans Dieter Clausen published his important study of the Hamburg performing scores, in which he identified a further group of copyists (H1-H12) and, working with the printed librettos, threw light on the progress of the text in Handel's revivals. His conclusions are occasionally vitiated by unfamiliarity with the non-Hamburg sources (he was of course aware of the British Library and Fitzwilliam collections) and reliance on faulty statements in Deutsch's *Documentary Biography*.

While the text of every Handel opera presents problems to the scholar, these are particularly acute in the first five he composed for London, *Rinaldo, Il Pastor Fido, Teseo, Silla* and *Amadigi,* none of which survives in complete autograph. *Il Pastor Fido* and *Silla* (Handel's only opera not written for the public theater, and never revived since its first production in June 1713) are relatively minor works, but the other three, on magic subjects taken from Renaissance epics or classical myth, are not only ambitious and spectacular but contain some of his boldest and most imaginative music. The autograph of *Rinaldo,* like that of *Il Pastor Fido,* fell apart at an early date and is divided between the Royal Music and Fitzwilliam collections; even when the fragments are combined many gaps remain. Of the *Teseo* autograph only a few pages survive; of *Amadigi* none at all. Whereas *Rinaldo* was such a popular success that substantial sections of the music were promptly published by John Walsh, in score and parts, *Teseo* and *Amadigi* were comparative failures. A handful of arias appeared in print, in short score with added English texts of an insipid and irrelevant complexion; but the operas made so slight an impact on the memory of London's principal music publisher that some years later he took them for a single work and, as noted below, garbled the titles and the contents.

The scarcity of autograph and contemporary printed material for these two operas confers high importance on the manuscript copies, especially if they can be dated. As it happens they are exceptionally numerous—there are more copies of *Amadigi* than of any other Handel opera, though not all are complete—perhaps because Handel's patrons and admirers, who could buy Walsh's publications for *Rinaldo,* needed the service of copyists if they wanted *Teseo* and *Amadigi.* Here we encounter another problem, and a very interesting one. Larsen has demonstrated that from the foundation of the Royal Academy in 1719 Handel's principal copyist was the elder Smith, who with the aid of various assistants had to satisfy the demands of patrons and— more important—to prepare performing scores for Handel's use in the theater. The date of Smith's arrival in England is uncertain, but was probably about 1717 (the earliest known manuscript copied by him is dated 1718),[2] some time after the production of *Amadigi,* the latest of the first group of London operas, in May 1715. How did Handel organize the preparation of his performing scores during this period, and who copied them?

Not all the evidence can be presented here,[3] but something needs to be said to clarify the tables given below. Larsen and Clausen identified as "early Smith"[4] the work of a copyist who was active as early as 1712, when Smith was certainly not in England. This copyist was D. Linike, a viola player in the Haymarket orchestra (his name is variously spelled Linikey, Liniken, Lunican, Lunecan, Lunicon, etc.) He was Handel's principal copyist, certainly from 1712 and perhaps from his arrival in London late in 1710,[5] and like Smith later he worked with a number of colleagues whose hands sometimes appear in the same manuscripts. After 1718 he collaborated on occasion with Smith himself; indeed there is evidence that the latter, a tradesman in Ansbach, who is not known to have been a copyist or even a musician before Handel brought him to England in a secretarial capacity, served a kind of apprenticeship under Linike.

The earliest surviving copies of *Rinaldo* (RM 19 d 5), *Il Pastor Fido* (RM 19 e 4), *Teseo* and *Amadigi,* the last two in Gerald Coke's collection, are all in Linike's hand, and those of *Il Pastor Fido* and *Teseo* can be shown to antedate the first performance of the operas. RM 19 e 4 is the earliest copy of any of Handel's London operas to which a definite date can be assigned (October 1712). Handel used RM 19 d 5 and RM 19 e 4 in the preparation of later revivals of *Rinaldo* (1731) and *Il Pastor Fido* (1734). That only proves that the scores remained in his possession; but it is more than likely that this group includes his earliest surviving London performance scores. (RM 19 d 5 cannot be the 1711 performing score of *Rinaldo,* both on account of its contents and because Linike's hand, which developed over the years, shows intermediate clefs and rests datable to about 1715.) Those of the two operas produced in Italy, *Vincer se stesso è la maggior vittoria* (*Rodrigo,* Florence 1707) and *Agrippina* (Venice, 1709/10), are lost—they may have remained the property of the theaters—but there is ample evidence that they existed. The performing score of *La Resurrezione* survives, and possibly that of *Il Trionfo del Tempo.*

The librettos of *Teseo* and *Amadigi* were adapted, probably by Nicola Haym, from French *tragédies-lyriques:* the former from *Thésée* by Quinault and Lully (1675), the latter from *Amadis de Grèce* by Houdar de la Motte and Destouches (1699). This accounts for peculiarities in their design, notably the loose employment of the exit aria, *Teseo*'s five acts and the relics of ballet in *Amadigi.* Handel performed *Teseo* in a single season (1713), *Amadigi* in three (1715, 1716 and 1717). He revived neither later, though a little of the music reappeared, generally altered, in other works. As with most of his operas, some pieces are found in more than one setting, or modified and transposed, or replaced by others. Such variants were composed for revivals, for later performances in the original season, or were rejected before performance, though they might still appear in copies, especially those made for patrons and friends like Charles Jennens. At least four such pieces are known for *Teseo* and five for *Amadigi;* but the almost complete disappearance of the autographs and the scarcity of printed librettos (none are known for the two *Amadigi* revivals) make it difficult to identify the occasion for which they were written. Doubtless the *Teseo* additions included the "several New Songs" advertised for the thirteenth and last performance on 16 May 1713, when Handel took a benefit.

B, C, D and E (and of course A) are important sources for the text; G, though it needs to be treated with caution, throws light on the orchestration; B, E, I, RM 19 c 9 and a Walsh print of 1724 contain music not in HG. (See Table 1.) B in particular is a fascinating document; to appreciate its significance we need to glance at the libretto printed for the first production.

The cast includes one character, Medea's confidante Fedra, who appears in two scenes (II, i and ii) but has not a word to sing. Nine passages of recitative in five scenes (I, v; III, iii; IV, vii; V, iii and iv), some 85 lines in all, are marked with *virgole* as omitted in the performance. The original state of B contains music for Fedra in II, i and V, ii (seven and twelve bars of recitative respectively) and settings of more than half the lines in *virgole*. It seems likely that, with the exception of seven lines in IV, vii, Handel set all of them; one or more pages have been replaced in I, v, and one torn out in III, vii. Since he did not finish the opera till 19 December 1712 and it was first performed on 10 January 1713, and since Fedra's lines were removed and the *virgole* added before the libretto was printed (it must have been available as usual on the first night, or the press announcements would have contained an apology), Linike could only have copied B—or at least finished it— in the latter part of December. This suggests a very close working arrangement with Handel, of the type later enjoyed by Smith.

Fedra's two scenes and all the *virgole* passages—including the only one in the surviving fragment of A, printed by Chrysander in brackets on HG 99[6]— were cancelled, folded over or torn out in B, and linking bars supplied where required. The manuscript contains an otherwise unknown version of Arcane's aria "Più non cerca libertà" (HG 55) as a binary arietta without *da capo,* followed by the direction *Arcane parte. Segue il Rittornella* [*sic*]. This ritornello follows on the next page; it is a slightly extended variant of the melody on four staves, including a viola part that does not appear elsewhere in the aria, the recorders sometimes in unison with the violins and sometimes an octave above. Handel then changed his mind, and the whole page was cancelled and replaced by the simpler ritornello, B section and *da capo* as printed. Four unpublished bars are cancelled after bar 3 of "Ah! cruda gelosia" (HG 18) and another in the ritornello after the B section. The B section of "Tengo in pugno" (HG 97) is crossed out, though it appears in all other copies.

Another striking feature of B is the exceptionally full specification of scoring and dynamics, itself a sign of early date. It contains hundreds of detailed markings, including slurs and trills, that do not appear in Chrysander's score; and since Linike was working at Handel's elbow they are unquestionably authentic. Almost every number, whether or not it includes the oboes, is rich in *soli-tutti* alternations and expressive dynamic contrasts. Three outstandingly beautiful pieces may be cited as examples. "Dolce riposo" (HG 30) begins *forte e staccato* with many more violin trills in the first bar and a half, then changes to *pian sempre* with the quavers regularly slurred in pairs and *senza cembalo* at the pianissimo in bar 6. The exquisite love song "Vieni, torna" (HG 56), which had not yet acquired a tempo mark, has additional bassoon trills, appoggiaturas and graded dynamics, notably in bars 9-11, where the repeated figure in thirds is first *forte,* then *piano,* then *pianissimo.* "Deh! v'aprite" (HG 74) is Adagio with all the violins muted; further interesting points about this aria are discussed below. Seven pieces have tempo marks not in HG, and there are many differences in scoring, especially in the treatment of the oboes. The first Allegro of the overture has three violin parts, the oboes taking the top line in unison (HG 2).

It may be thought unfortunate that these particulars were not available to Chrysander. But they were available: B was the copy used by Arnold for his edition, as his signature on the inner cover with the date 24 April 1787 confirms. Although Arnold made careless mistakes, he reproduced the vast majority of B's unique readings correctly. So deep-rooted was Chrysander's contempt for English editors and all their works, and for Arnold in particular, that he rejected them without ceremony. He did the same in his edition of *Agrippina,* lambasting Arnold's score as "so defaced by omissions, extensions and mistakes as to be barely recognisable"; yet it can be proved that Arnold's text was derived from Handel's lost performing copy and therefore much closer than Chrysander's to the Venice production. In both these operas Chrysander repeatedly altered Arnold where he is right and followed him where he is wrong. In bar 12 of "Deh! v'aprite" Arnold, copying a mistake by Linike, printed the second violins' phrase one beat too late, spoiling Handel's double echo of the voice, and in bar 13 gave the fourth note of the voice as c″ instead of b′; Chrysander did the same, though his main source (C) is correct in both places.[7] In bars 47-8 of "E pur bello" (HG 12) Chrysander was confronted with alternative readings for the first and second violins—that of Arnold (and B) (i) and that of C (followed by later manuscripts [ii]); liking neither of these, he produced an emendation of his own (iii), and apparently pencilled it into C. D, G and J added yet another variant (iv), a conflation of those in B and C (see page 70).

C, Chrysander's principal source (he also used the RM 20 c 12 segment of A, but not the printed libretto, hence the omission of many important stage

Table 1. Sources for *Teseo*

Location	Date	Copyist and Contents (full score except where stated)
A. RM 20 c 12 (16 leaves) RM 20 f 11, fol. 8[1]	Dec. 1712	Autograph: fragments covering IV, i and ii (HG 69-73), 8 bars of recitative in IV, vi (HG 80), and the close of the opera from the middle of Teseo's accompanied recitative in V, iv (HG 98-112), with the exception of Agilea's aria "Si, t'amo"; dated at the end 19 Dec. 1712. There are 4 sketches for *Teseo*, one of them not used, on a blank page in the *Rodrigo* autograph (RM 20 c 5, fol. 48 verso).
B. Coke I	Dec. 1712	Linike (active 1712-21), modified by Handel 1713.
C. RM 19 e 6	? 1713	RM1 (active ?1713-25), modified by Handel ?1713, 1734, 1739.[2]
D. Munich private collection	ca. 1714	Linike (p. 1) and RM1 (text ?Linike); addition by S2 (active ca. 1723-46) and note by Jenners.
E. Malmesbury	June 1717	Linike ("Transcribed by Mr. Linike June 1717" in hand of Elizabeth Legh); contemporary insertion by RM1, modification probably by Handel.
F. RM 19 g 4	early	RM2 and another; no recitatives.
G. Manchester MS 130 Hd 4 v. 258-64	? 1720s	S2; complete instrumental parts, extracted from D, omitting overture and recitatives.
H. Coke II	early	Overture in very early hand, remainder much later (not unlike S9, ca. 1760).
I. Coke III	early	2 unknown hands in collaboration, later supplemented by a third; 13 items from *Teseo*, others from *Amadigi* (q.v. Source **K**), *Il Pastor Fido* and *Silla*.

(Table 1 continued)

J. Coke IV	? 1730s	Eccentric English copyist who sometimes reflects early sources; omits recitatives and some other movements.
K. Shaftesbury	ca. 1736	S4
L. Lennard (Fitzwilliam Mus.)	late	Smith.
M. Granville (BL Egerton 2916)	late	S5 (active ca. 1740-60).
N. RM 19 d 8	late	S13 (active after 1750).
O. Fitzwilliam Mus MS 74	? 1767	Same copyist as Fitzwilliam scores of *Amadigi* and *Muzio Scevola*. "R. Fitzwilliam 1767."

Detached vocal movements: Tenbury 884 (Smith, ca. 1719), RM 19 c 9 (S2), Shaftesbury (S4, ca. 1736), BL Add MS 29386, RCM 1125, Coke (5 arias with a little contemporary ornament).

Harpsichord arrangements of overture by Handel: Malmesbury (2 copies, RM1), ca. 1717. Smith, ca. 1728. Coke Wesley MS (H1, ca. 1721): revised version RM 18 c 1 (S2, ca. 1728) and Walsh print, ca. 1728.

Printed excerpts: 9 arias, short score with English versions, in fugitive publications ca. 1715-25; overture in parts ca. 1725; aria and duet as altered for revival of *Il Pastor Fido* 1734.

Full scores: Arnold (1788), Chrysander (1874).

1. Not identified in Barclay Squire's *Catalogue of the Royal Music Library.*
2. Transpositions of "Deh! v'aprite" for use in *Il Pastor Fido* (1734) and *Jupiter in Argos* (1739).

(Example mentioned on page 67)

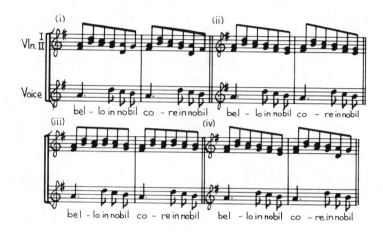

directions), has a number of corrections and amendments written by Handel; this is the copy mentioned in the HG Preface. Handel altered the bass in bars 3 and 4 of the overture's second Largo, added the tempo *Andante ma non troppo allegro* on "Vieni, torna," improved the underlay in bars 58-9 of "Sibillando" (HG 67; the words "che mi scherni" should be repeated three times, but Chrysander ignored this), corrected the genders in the A section of "Cara, ti dono" (HG 84) and the clefs in the Minerva recitative, where RM1, understandably confused by A, had written the notes and words of the bass version with a soprano clef,[8] and removed some minor errors. C contains a few more tempo marks not in B (written by RM1, again ignored by Chrysander), but far fewer indications of dynamics and scoring.

It seems likely that Handel made these changes before or during the 1713 run, and that he used C or B or both for performance in the theater. B has an interesting autograph modification, mentioned below; and the cancellation of the B section of "Tengo in pugno" is most easily explained as a cut made at one of the later performances. Neither copy resembles the standardized Smith performing scores of later years; but we know nothing of Handel's London practice in this respect before 1720 except what can be deduced from Linike and RM1 copies.

D, if it does not antedate C, is based on an earlier source, for it contains none of Handel's changes except corrections of a few wrong notes. Some of its instrumental details are unique. Every movement has a tempo mark except the duet "Addio" (HG 19), which lacks one in every source. E, likewise unknown to Chrysander and not hitherto described in print, has a correction apparently written by Handel (Elizabeth Legh was a close friend). It was not copied directly from B or C, though it includes most of the former's instrumental and dynamic detail, but is closely related to D. In both D and E the copyist has corrected the mistake in bar 12 of "Deh! v'aprite" and in a number of places added the words *segue subito* or *subito* to emphasise dramatic continuity (a feature generally ignored in modern productions of the operas, though it is stressed in various early copies).[9] The most interesting feature of E is its inclusion of two unique alternative versions, both inserted at a very early stage before the binding of the volume with Elizabeth Legh's arms on the cover. The first, written by RM1, is a setting of "Deh! v'aprite" for alto voice in C major with a single unspecified treble line and bass. The material is that of the G major version, but the A section is six bars longer. At the point where these bars are added Handel marked the first Linike copy (B) with the idiosyncratic symbols for insertion found frequently in his autographs. Both sections of the aria have delicate vocal ornaments in the hand of RM1; they may well derive from Handel. The second insertion, written by Linike, is a reworking of the duet "Cara, ti dono" for two altos in F major accompanied by two violins and bass. The first part is essentially unchanged, apart from simplification of the string parts to eliminate the viola and improvements to the coloratura; but the B section is quite different and much shorter, 12 bars instead of 32. It differs also from the version used later in *Il Pastor Fido*. It is likely that these pieces were composed for an alto Agilea at one of the 1713 performances, her other arias perhaps being transposed or cut. A copy in RM 19 c 9 of "Deh serbate" (HG 14) transposed down a tone to A minor may reflect the same occasion.

K gives an early text apparently based on C, incorporating some but not all of Handel's changes. The remaining copies contain no major variants. However two forgotten arias connected with *Teseo* are found in none of the scores. Walsh prints are the only source for "Nò, non piangete," a different aria from that beginning with the same words in *Floridante*. It appeared, always associated with "Deh serbate," first in *The Monthly Mask of Vocal Musick* for August 1724, then in volume 2 of *Apollo's Feast* (November 1726), then in an eccentric compilation entitled *The Favourite songs in ye Opera call'd Thessus* [*sic*] *& Amadis* (1732), of which a unique copy was recently discovered in the Schoelcher Collection in Paris.[10] Its 17 items, reprinted from old plates, include six arias from *Teseo,* two from *Amadigi,* one each from *Il Pastor Fido* and *Silla,* one added to *Giulio Cesare* in 1730, one apparently contributed by Handel to a revival of Scarlatti's *Pirro e Demetrio* (see below, p. 76), and five by other composers. The second additional aria, "La crudele lontananza," a beautiful F minor piece, is found in I, RM 19 c 9, Tenbury 884 (source L for *Amadigi*), and one of the supplements to the Malmesbury score of *Rinaldo*. It may have been sung in a revival of that opera.

The instrumental parts (G) were copied for Jennens, though it is not clear why he wanted them. Their chief significance lies in their demonstration of how a copyist from Handel's immediate circle extracted parts from scores (those he used can sometimes be identified). It is clear that S2 had to exercise his judgment as to when and what the oboes were to play. Sometimes his decisions can be refuted by the autograph or performing score, but his practice was consistent. When oboes are included, they play with the violins, usually in intermediate as well as main ritornellos, but are silent when the voice enters. There are a few exceptions, chiefly where solos or obbligatos are indicated. In arias (but generally not ensembles) with two treble instrumental lines, wherever S2 found the word *Tutti* against the top part he made both oboes double the first violins. This is undoubtedly correct, and confirmed by Handel's preference elsewhere for strong treble and bass lines and lighter inner parts. Chrysander's almost invariable custom in such movements of making the second oboe double the second violin, for example in much of "M'adora l'idol mio" (HG 45) and "Benchè tuoni" (HG 72)—and in the opening Largo of the overture (though this is not in the parts)—frustrates Handel's intention. The most reliable sources, including B,D, E and G, have the top lines of "O stringerò" (HG 48) alternating between *Tutti* and *Violini*.

The loss of the *Amadigi* autograph has deprived us of Handel's date for completion. He probably composed the opera in April/May 1715 for the return of the great castrato Nicolini after an absence of three years. It was first performed on 25 May—later in the season than any other Handel opera—and repeated five times. Anastasia Robinson, who played the heroine Oriana, was taken ill after the first night and replaced by an unknown substitute. She was back however for both revivals, on 16 February 1716 (six performances) and a year later on 16 February 1717 (five performances), when *The Daily Courant* announced that "Mrs. Robinson will perform all the Songs which was [sic] Originally Compos'd for this Opera." This suggests either that she omitted some of them in 1716 or (more probably) that her substitute had sung different music in 1715. In each of the revival seasons Mrs. Robinson had a benefit, on 3 March 1716 and 21 March 1717. For the latter *The Daily Courant* advertised "the Addition of a New Scene, the Musick compos'd by Mr. Handel, and perform'd by Signor Cavaliero Nicolino Grimaldi [Nicolini] and Mrs. Robinson." There were also two benefits for the orchestra, on 20 June 1716 and 30 May 1717 (as well as one for Nicolini on 11 April 1717). On the first occasion Handel added "Two New Symphonies." One of these was the first movement of the concerto grosso in F (Op. 3 No. 4), sometimes known as "the Orchestra Concerto"; the other may have been the second Allegro in the overture to *Teseo,* copied on the same page as an *Amadigi* aria in I. They were probably identical with the "Two Pieces of Musick between the Acts" played at the orchestra's 1717 benefit. Apart from the enforced retirement of Anastasia Robinson in 1715, the single cast change was the substitution of the alto castrato Antonio Bernacchi for the contralto Diana Vico as Dardano in 1717.

The only autograph items pertaining to *Amadigi* (apart from insertions in two copies), an altered and ornamented version of the aria "O caro mio tesor" (HG 34) with figured bass accompaniment and a shortened keyboard arrangement of the overture with embellishments, though of the highest interest, are not strictly sources for the score.[11] The former, perhaps prepared for a singer at some concert, is so modified—even recomposed—as to be unusable with the upper instrumental parts; it cannot have been intended for Anastasia Robinson in 1715.[12] The latter may have been made for teaching purposes; the paper suggests a date about 1724-26. But the exceptionally large number of early copies—at least 10 dating from before 1720 and three more reflecting the text at the same period—do enable us to throw fresh light on the early history of the opera. Three of them—B, E and L—and a volume in the Coke collection contain music not in HG. (See Table 2.)

Both the published full scores are based on F. Chrysander used it exclusively in the belief that it was Handel's performing score; so it may have been, but not for the 1715 season. Knapp, though aware of most of the copies listed in Table 2,[13] took little note of them where they differ from F, apart from printing four unpublished arias in an appendix. While Handel's changes in F are of course authoritative, the fact that, minor variants and obvious mistakes apart, all early copies follow its unmodified text and some are much fuller in detail and freer from error indicates that F is by no means the earliest copy and does not give the opera as first performed. Although only B is precisely dated, it is possible by tracing the activity of the copyists, the development of their handwriting and the gradual deterioration of the text to place the copies in approximate chronological order. Certainly A, B and C, and probably several others, antedate the original state of F, which already incorporates one change that appears in no other copy before L, a simplification of the violin part in bars 14 and 15 of "Ch'io lasci mai d'amare" (HG 69). By the time Linike copied F many details of scoring and dynamics and some stage directions had dropped out, and numerous minor errors crept in. Besides the substantive changes listed below Handel corrected a number of wrong notes—as did later hands, including Chrysander's—but understandably did not bother with the rest.

For the closest approximation to the lost autograph we must look to the nearly related A, B, and C, in particular the first two. Only a little of the new information they supply can be given here. The overture has many extra *solo-tutti* contrasts, especially for the cello; the viola part in the A section of "Ah spietato" (HG 17) is for bassoons as well—hence the tenor clef; the bass of "O caro mio tesor" is *senza cembalo* when the voice enters; the violins double the oboes in bars 55-6 of the duet "Crudel, tu non farai" (HG 55); there are several oboe solos in "Se tu brami" (HG 63) and "Dolce vita" (HG 76); the final ritornello of "Io già sento" (HG 89) is *pianissimo* (*piano* in some copies); in "Sento la gioja" (HG 92) the voice has a long trill beginning at bar 54. As in the

Table 2. Sources for *Amadigi*

Location	Date	Copyist and Contents (full score except where stated)
A. Coke I	probably 1715	Linike.
B. Malmesbury	1716	Newman ("Elizabeth Legh: 1716"), additions by Handel.
C. Manchester MS 130 Hd 4 v.46	ca. 1716	RM1, text Linike?
D. Washington, L of C M 1500 HI3 A44 (Littleton)	ca. 1716-17	RM1, text Linike?
E. Washington, L of C (Landon)	ca. 1716 (ca. 1719)	Linike (Smith); incomplete aria collection, two fascicles; contains arias from other London operas of ca. 1713-16 and one addition in a later hand.
F. Hamburg MA/1003	ca. 1716-17	Linike, amendments and corrections by Handel.
G. BL Add MS 47848	ca. 1717-18	RM4 (active 1717-21).
H. RM 19 g 2	early	RM2; omits recitatives and sinfonia in III, vi.
I. RCM 902	early	Unknown; 12 arias only.
J. Coke II	after 1717	RM1 (overture) and another; reflects very early source.
K. Coke III	early	2 unknown hands in collaboration, later supplemented by a third; 14 items from *Amadigi*, others from earlier Handel operas (cf. *Teseo* Source I).
L. Bodleian (Tenbury 884)	probably 1719	Smith; omits recitatives and some other pieces, but includes arias, many unpublished, from various early operas.

(Table 2 continued)

M. Manchester MS 130 Hd 4 v.303-9 and 265	? 1720s	S2; instrumental parts (omitting overture, Act III sinfonia and Ballo), reflecting early text before Handel's alterations to F.
N. Shaftesbury	ca. 1736	S4
O. Lennard (Fitzwilliam Museum)	after 1740	S5; derived from F.
P. Granville (BL Egerton 2917)	after 1740	S5; derived from F.
Q. RM 19 c 5	after 1750	S13; derived from F.
R. Fitzwilliam Mus MS 75	? 1767	Same copyist as Fitzwilliam scores of *Teseo* and *Muzio Scevola;* copied from O. "R. Fitzwilliam 1767."

Detached vocal movements: Add MS 31571 (Smith, ca. 1719), RM 18 c 1 (S2), Shaftesbury (S4, ca. 1736, 3 arias), RM 19 d 12 (H9 and ? RM2), Durham Cathedral Lib. Bamburgh MS 70 (Edward Finch, Prebendary of York, 1664-1738), 2 volumes in Coke Collection (4 arias with a little contemporary ornament, "Minacciami" in same hand as *Teseo* Source J).

Harpsichord arrangements of overture and other instrumental movements: Malmesbury (2 copies, RM1 and Linike, ca. 1717, Smith, ca. 1728), Coke Wesley MS (Smith, ca. 1721, autograph additions), New York PL Drexel MS 5856 (Smith ca. 1721), Coke Rivers MS (Smith junior, ca. 1727), RM 18 c 1 (S2, ca. 1728), RM 19 a 4 (S2). Add MS 31777 (Gulielmus Bogdani). Some include first movement of Op. 3 No. 4, or even the whole concerto. Coke Rivers and RM 18 c 1 have Handel's shortened arrangement of the overture.

Printed excerpts: 4 arias, short score with English versions in fugitive publications ca. 1718-25; overture in parts ca. 1725; overture for harpsichord (clumsy arrangement 1726; "Second Overture" (1st movement of Op. 3 No. 4) in keyboard arrangement 1728; duet "Cangia al fine" in Favourite Songs from pasticcio *Solimano* 1758.

Full scores: Chrysander (1874, 2 issues), HHA, ed. J. Merrill Knapp (1971).

first Linike copy of *Teseo* nearly every aria has unpublished dynamics, trills or other directions. Important details of scoring, especially for the oboes, are discussed below in connection with M, which also gives the pre-F text.

A number of stage directions, not in the printed libretto, can only derive from the autograph. The full heading of the first scene was evidently *Giardino di Melissa, di dove in lontano si vede la torre di Oriana. Notte.* This appears only in J, which has several stage directions found nowhere else. A and B omit the words "la torre di Oriana," making nonsense. In A, B and C the heading of I, vii ends with the sentence *Oriana discende dal Trono.* Only A, B, C and D have *riguarda nella fontana* after "Sussurrate" (HG 42). Such matters are not purely academic. The omission in F (and most other copies) of [Melissa] *vuol partire mà Oriana la ritiene* immediately before "Ch'io lasci mai d'amare" may well account for Chrysander giving this aria to the wrong singer; it is of course Oriana's.[14]

B, like many Malmesbury copies, is of exceptional interest. Though not quite so free from error as A, it contains three arias not in HG and two additions almost certainly written by Handel but not mentioned in HHA. The three arias, early insertions in Newman's hand, are the second setting of "Io godo, scherzo e rido," "Affannami" tormentami" and "Torni la gioja in sen" (HHA 167-81). Only the second appears in its correct scene, after "Ch'io lasci mai d'amare," which replaced it probably after the first performance in 1715. The libretto has "Affannimi" here, but the music survives only in B. "S'estinto è l'idol mio" (HG 46) adds one to the choice group of arias with ornaments written by Handel, presumably for Elizabeth Legh herself. They are mostly simple but include a short cadenza at the *fermata* (bar 60). The second addition is surprising: Handel added an independent bass to all the passages in "Ch'io lasci mai d'amare" where the voice is accompanied or doubled by upper strings—that is, to the whole aria apart from ritornellos. This copy alone has no tenor voice in the *coro*—probably its original form: the part in all other sources, doubling the soprano at the octave, has a makeshift look. A later hand has written the names Oriana, Amadigi and Orgando against the other parts; there is however no evidence that Orgando was ever sung by a bass.

E is another fascinating manuscript. Its core consists of 24 leaves written by Linike about 1716, containing an aria for one Demetrio (for a revival of A. Scarlatti's *Pirro e Demetrio*?), eight from the pasticcio *Ernelinda* (26 February 1713, revived in the two following seasons),[15] one from the pasticcio *Lucio Vero* (26 March 1715; the aria is in the libretto), and fourteen from *Amadigi* in haphazard order. To this were later prefixed 14 leaves in Smith's early hand (ca. 1719) containing the sinfonia before I, vii, the duet "Cangia al fine" and four arias. Later still a third hand added an aria from *Dario*, probably Ariosti's opera of 1725. The Linike fascicle includes two settings of "Pugnerò" (HG 8), the second in E major, 4/4, otherwise unknown, and two of "Gioje, venite in sen," the second identical with the C major "Torni la gioja in sen" (HHA appendix, 176); Linike wrote in both texts at the same time. The Demetrio aria, "Nò, non cosi severe," is certainly by Handel[16]—it appears also in L—and one or two of the Ernelinda arias could be his on stylistic grounds. They do not appear to be known elsewhere. The Smith fascicle was doubtless copied as a supplement to the Linike; there is no duplication.

Of the other copies with the pre-F text, D and G show a decline in instrumental and dynamic detail and an increase in mistakes. H and I, both incomplete, are related to each other and to J. All three generally name the original singers, and the last two are full of errors in the Italian as well as the music. I never mentions Anastasia Robinson; the only one of her arias present, "Ti pentirai crudel" (HG 52), is ascribed to Elisabetta Pilotti-Schiavonetti (Melissa), as it is also in H. This is the only one of Oriana's arias that would make sense in Melissa's mouth, and these manuscripts could reflect its temporary transfer to her when Robinson was out of the cast in 1715. J (the overture apart) cannot be earlier than 1717, for it ascribes one of Dardano's arias to Diana Vico and another to Bernacchi.

F as first copied resembles D and G in its errors and omissions, and would have little importance but for Handel's modifications, which affect eight movements. He rearranged the underlay in bars 72-97 of "Vado, corro" (HG 21; previously the first line of text was repeated several times instead of the second); put down the first two bars of the following recitative from G♯ minor to G minor; revised the B section cadence of "Agitato il cor" (HG 23; the text as copied was corrupt, and is variously emended in different manuscripts); changed the tempo of "Gioje, venite in sen" from *Largo* to *Larghetto;* cancelled two bars of "O rendetemi" (HG 40) after bar 22; altered the two top instrumental parts in bar 28 of "Sussurrate"; changed the tempo of the duet "Cangia al fine" from *Vivace* to *Larghetto;* and added the word "và" in bar 18 of "Io già sento" (the early copies have a rest here; Melissa died in the middle of a sentence). The tempo change in "Cangia al fine" confirms the evidence of "Il vostro maggio" in *Rinaldo* that for Handel *Vivace* was an indication of mood rather than speed. A quick tempo in either context would be nonsensical.

L is the earliest copy to incorporate any of Handel's changes in F—but oddly not all of them. Entitled "Opera of Amadis & Other Songs by Mr Handel," it is an anthology evidently assembled from a number of sources. It contains no recitatives or purely instrumental movements except the final Ballo; omits five vocal movements and gives the rest in the wrong order; and includes before the *coro* and Ballo a miscellaneous collection of 20 arias from the early operas, many composed for revivals and 13 still unpublished. Among them are three additions to *Amadigi,* the second setting of "Io godo, scherzo e rido," "Torni la gioja in sen" (C major) and "Minacciami, non hò timor" (HHA appendix, 182). L has the amended violin parts in "Ch'io lasci mai d'amare" as in F, follows Handel's revisions in "Vado, corro" and "O rendetemi" but not in "Gioje, venite in sen" or "Sussurrate," and produces a unique variant for the B section cadence of "Agitato il cor." The other three affected movements are not in this manuscript.

N mostly reflects F, but surprisingly includes the two extra bars in "O rendetemi." The four late copies, all based on F, are of no consequence. M, extracted from an unidentified score similar to G, is important for the definition of the oboe parts. Evidently S2's source was sparing of instrumentation on the top line, for in five arias where nearly all manuscripts specify unison violins[17]—"Non sà temere," "Agitato il cor," "Io godo, scherzo e rido," "Ti pentirai crudel" and "Ch'io lasci mai d'amare"—he supplies oboe parts in the ritornellos. HG omits them, probably rightly; HHA adopts them in the first four arias but not in the fifth. A more important point concerns those movements with two treble parts where all sources, early and late, that give any information at all have *Tutti* on the top line: the B section of "Ah spietato," the sinfonia before I, vii, "E si dolce," "O caro mio tesor," "S'estinto è l'idol mio," "Dolce vita" and the *coro*. Except as usual in the *coro*, both oboe parts in M double the first violins. The two printed scores go astray here—and elsewhere. HG, though it includes most of the oboe solos in "Dolce vita," omits the obvious one at bar 38 which is in all early sources except F. HHA omits all oboe solos in this aria, "Se tu brami," "Affannami, tormentami" (B section) and "Torni la gioja in sen"; the last aria is scored for unison violins, unison oboes (reduced to a solo when accompanying or doubling the voice), viola and bass.

Arias are sometimes found in transposed keys. "S'estinto è l'idol mio" is in G minor in the Durham manuscript and one of the Coke aria collections, "Non sà temere" in D in another (K); a third has "Minacciami, non hò timor" in the miniature hand of Source J of *Teseo*. This aria also appears in one of the appendices to the Malmesbury copy of *Rinaldo* and may have been sung in a revival of that opera. Two arias were printed in alien keys, "E si dolce" in C major and "Ch'io lasci mai d'amare" in F major; these are the two *Amadigi* arias included by Walsh, using the old plates, in his 1732 *Thessus & Amadis* collection.

HHA offers no suggestion for the date or context of the four arias in the Appendix. "Affannami, tormentami," if it was sung at all, was probably replaced by "Ch'io lasci mai d'amare" when Anastasia Robinson retired after the first night. The latter was a hit with the public,[18] and no doubt for that reason was retained when Anastasia returned. It seems likely that "Torni la gioja in sen," on the evidence of E an alternative setting of "Gioje, venite in sen," was also written for her substitute (probably Caterina Galerati). It is less easy to account for the second, far inferior, setting of "Io godo, scherzo e rido," since so far as is known Pilotti-Schiavonetti sang Melissa at every performance. It could be a first attempt resurrected from the autograph, and the same might be true of the E major "Pugnerò." The possibility that Handel reset this aria for the new singer Bernacchi in 1717 seems ruled out by Linike's early hand in G. Another motive might be Handel's wish to remove the resemblance between the printed version and Dardano's other act 1 aria, "Agitato il cor": both are fast pieces in the same key and meter (G minor, 3/8) and employ similar rhythmic figures in the orchestra.[19] All four arias so far mentioned belong perhaps to 1715; three of them cannot be much later, since they appear in B, dated 1716. On the other hand "Minacciami, non hò timor," described as "Aditional to Amadis" in the Coke copy but absent from B, could have formed part of the new scene added on 21 March 1717. The low alto tessitura and the text suggest that it was addressed by Amadigi to Oriana during a quarrel, an episode not in the printed libretto. The fact that the voice part begins with the same phrase as "Affannami, tormentami"—inspired no doubt by the similarity of the words—suggests that it was composed after the latter had been abandoned.

Notes

1. The sources for the librettos are not considered here. See D.R.B. Kimbell, "The Libretto of Handel's *Teseo*," *Music & Letters* 44 (1963):371, and "The 'Amadis' Operas of Destouches and Handel," *Music & Letters* 49 (1968):329.

2. This could be Old Style, i.e., up to 25 March 1719.

3. See my article "Handel's Early London Copyists," in *Bach, Handel and Scarlatti, Tercentenary Essays*, ed. P. Williams (Cambridge, 1985, forthcoming).

4. For example, in RM 19 d 5, RM 19 e 4, Hamburg MA/1003 and MB/1570 (part).

5. At least 19 surviving Handel manuscripts in 10 different collections were written in whole or part by Linike.

6. The music is not cancelled in A.

7. In source C Handel pencilled a semiquaver c″ before the b′ to accommodate an extra syllable when adapting the music to a new text ("Caro amor") in *Il Pastor Fido* (1734). The c″ never replaced the b′ but appears as an appoggiatura to it in K.

8. Chrysander created unnecessary confusion over this piece. Handel composed it for soprano, perhaps intending to double the roles of Minerva and Fedra, but altered it for a bass priest (forgetting to change the stage direction) before Linike copied B. The soprano version exists only in A with the bass setting superimposed. The latter should be in the text, the former in the appendix.

9. Including *Amadigi* sources A, C, F, G and J.

10. Bernd Baselt, "Thematisch-systematisches Verzeichnis: Bühnenwerke," in *Händel-Handbuch* 1 (1978):137, note.

11. Both are in the Fitzwilliam Museum: Mus MS 256, 41-3, and Mus MS 260, 7-9.

12. See Winton Dean, "Vocal Embellishment in a Handel Aria," in *Studies in Eighteenth-Century Music*, ed. H.C. Robbins Landon and R.E. Chapman (London, 1970), p. 151. The manuscript is reproduced in HHA, xiv-xvi.

13. The dating and identification of the copyists in the HHA Preface need correction in many particulars in the light of later research.

14. The direction is in the libretto, which Chrysander did not have when he first published the score. He later discovered it and supplied its stage directions in a second issue with the same title page, but did not restore the aria to Oriana. Unfortunately the Gregg Press facsimile (1965) used a copy of the first issue.

15. Two of the eight arias are in the 1713 libretto; later librettos are not available, but new arias were included on 3 April 1714, 24 May 1714 and 4 December 1714.

16. During Handel's time in London Scarlatti's opera was revived with new arias in May 1711 and March and May 1716. The aria is not in the 1716 libretto.

17. The few exceptions may however be significant: "Io godo" has *Tutti* in A and D, "Ch'io lasci mai d'amare" *Unisoni* in B. H has a casual *Unisoni* almost everywhere, but was not S2's source.

18. It survives with two sets of English words, one ("Love grows fiercer by denials") in the Walsh prints, the other ("Be kind, bewitching creature") in manuscript in RM 18 b 16.

19. Amadigi's arias in I, iii and v, "Non sà temere" and "Vado, corro," are also disturbingly alike (*Allegro*, 3/8, B flat with a single upper part indulging in rapid semiquavers). Such close parallels are unusual in Handel, but in the absence of the autograph no explanation can be offered.

Khandoshkin's Earliest Printed Work Rediscovered

Boris Schwarz

At the 1977 Berkeley Congress of the International Musicological Society, one of the "round tables" was devoted to *Eastern European Folk and Art Music.* My contribution was entitled "Russian Violin Music: A Link between Folk and Art Music." The chief representative of this trend, as I pointed out, was Ivan Khandoshkin (1740-1804), who was the first Russian to compose and perform violin variations using Russian folk themes.[1]

While assembling a chronological catalogue of Khandoshkin's violin variations, I pondered one question: why was Khandoshkin's first printed music of 1781, the *Chansons russes variées,* published not in St. Petersburg where he was established, but in Amsterdam where he was totally unknown. Khandoshkin had never traveled abroad but his style revealed a solid knowledge of Tartini's violin technique. This fact did not escape the sharp eye of the astute publisher Jean Julien Hummel, an enterprising businessman. He could hardly expect large sales of Khandoshkin's music in Western Europe, but no sooner had he issued the *Chansons russes variées* as well as Khandoshkin's *Six Sonates pour 2 violons* than he shipped a number of copies to Russia to be sold in St. Petersburg and Moscow. Announcements in the newspapers of both capital cities appeared in December 1781, offering Khandoshkin's music at the same price (2 rubles for the chansons, 3 rubles for the sonatas) though only the Moscow notice stated specifically that the material was printed in Amsterdam—certainly a noteworthy fact.[2] Copies were still offered for sale in 1789, but eventually the Amsterdam edition disappeared from circulation, both in Russia and Western Europe. Soviet musicologists, working on Khandoshkin since the 1940s—Volman, Fesechko, Yampolsky,[3] Keldysh[4]— state unanimously that Khandoshkin's Amsterdam editions of 1781 are "not to be found." They avoid the finality of the word "lost." Perhaps they are right in being so cautious; as late as 1971, Fesechko discovered, among new acquisitions in the Pushkin Museum in Moscow, Khandoshkin's opus 4 which the Geneva Library had owned for a long time.

One must assume that a thorough search of Soviet archives was made to find the missing Khandoshkin Amsterdam edition. Whether the search was equally thorough investigating European libraries is questionable, complicated by 11 different spellings of Khandoshkin's last name. RISM's catalog of works by "Handochkine" is woefully inadequate and lists only two libraries, Geneva and Naples, disregarding Russian and United States libraries.[5]

As I was leafing through the small number of Khandoshkin file cards at the Library of Congress in Washington, my eye was caught by the following card:

Chançons/Russes/Avec des Variations pour UN VIOLON/et l'Accompagnement D'UN BASSE/ dediées/A Monsieur Nikita Akinfiewitsch/de Demidoff,/ Conseiller d'Etat de S.M.I. de toutes les Russes &c &c/ composées/Par/Iwan Handochkin/ ... Russien/ Musicien de la Chapelle de/ l'Impératrice de Russie.

Imprimé à Amsterdam chez Jean Julien Hummel   [1781?]
   au Grand Magazin de Musique.

There could be no doubt that this was the "lost" edition, residing peacefully in faraway America instead of St. Petersburg. No one in Washington was aware of the rarity of the item, as far as I could gather. I brought it to the attention of Donald L. Leavitt, Chief of the Music Division of the Library of Congress. There is no record in the files of the Library as to when and from whom the copy of Khandoshkin's music was acquired. A rubber stamp with the name "Yudin" might indicate a former owner but reveals nothing in addition.

Description of 1781 Hummel Edition

Ten numbered pages contained two untitled Russian folksongs with variations for violin and bass.

Pages 1 and 2 contain the *Basso* part for song no. 1 and 40 variations.

Pages 4 to 8 contain the violin part of an Andante in D minor followed by 40 variations. The Andante can be identified as the song *Kalinushka* which was published, together with its 40 variations, in a separate supplement to *Sovetskaia Muzyka* (June, 1951).[6] It was edited by G. Fesechko, who had discovered the *Kalinushka* variations in a manuscript volume in the Lenin Library in Moscow (the manuscript was not in the composer's hand). In comparing Fesechko's edition with the 1781 original print, I found no major discrepancies, though there are differences in dynamics, bowings, and other details. Here are a few examples.

Theme, voice leading.
  A = Original
  B = Fesechko ed.

Variation 11, penultimate measure
  A = Original
  B = Fesechko ed.

Variation 16.
  A = original
  B = Fesechko ed.

Variation 19.
  A = original changes pattern
       from m. 3 to end
  B = Fesechko ed. adjusts
     pattern (at ⊗)

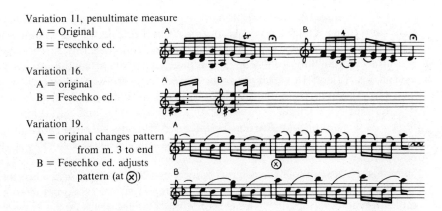

Variation 35 has in the original the indication "sur une corde." In this case it means that the broken thirds *not* be played on two neighboring strings, but on one string—a certain finesse of fingering.

Khandoshkin's original edition is also careful of dynamics, much more so than the Fesechko reprint indicates. Thus we have variation 31 in *pp,* No. 32 in *mez* (mezzo), No. 33 in *p,* No. 34 in *f.* Variation 11 has a variety of dynamic shadings in the original, from *pp* to *p, cresc,* and *f.* It shows that Khandoshkin was sensitive to interpretative refinements.

The most important discovery, however, is the *Basso* part for the *Kalinushka* variations—not merely an ostinato part to be used for theme and variations alike, but a separately engraved and carefully worked out bass part for each individual variation.

Fesechko published his edition of *Kalinushka* plus 40 Variations based on the assumption that it was for *un*accompanied violin; his source, an old manuscript volume in the Lenin Library, had no bass part. Only now, with the rediscovery of the 1781 original Hummel edition, have we become aware of Khandoshkin's through-composed bass part. Since it was engraved on a separate sheet, it became detached and lost so that later copyists assumed the violin part to be complete in itself and to be played "solo."

At this point it must be mentioned that *Kalinushka* is also known in a shorter version with only 18 variations (republished by Yampolsky[7] based on an old manuscript in the Moscow Conservatory Library); here the same ostinato bass serves the theme and all 18 variations. Fesechko assumes that the shorter version was extracted by a dilettante scribe from the complete 40 variations.

In contrast, one can think of Tartini's *L'arte del arco,* the famous variations on Corelli's Gavotte which Khandoshkin used as model. Tartini expanded the number of his variations from 17 (in 1747) to 38 (in 1758) and ultimately to 50. It is most likely that Khandoshkin saw the second edition of 1758.

Pages 9 and 10 of the Hummel 1781 edition contain an Andante con variazioni for violin in C minor (con sordino) followed by 13 variations. The Andante is printed on two staves, the upper in violin clef, the lower in bass clef for the accompanying violoncello. The same bass part serves all the variations, except nos. 12 and 13 which are to be played "sans accompagnement."

The Andante theme is untitled but can be easily identified as the folksong "To teriaiu, chto liubliu" (I lose what I love). Theme and variations are reprinted in Yampolsky's *Russkoe skripichnoe iskusstvo* [Russian violin art],[8] copied from the manuscript volume in the Moscow Conservatory Library. A comparison shows that there are no significant differences between Yampolsky's reprint and the original edition of 1781—except for the last two variations, which are to be played "solo" in the Hummel version, and some indication of fingerings, like "sur une corde" (meaning "on the G string"), better bowings, and more careful dynamics.

Var. 8:

The Hummel 1781 edition appears to have been more or less duplicated by Khandoshkin's opus 4, *Deux Chansons Russes variées pour violon accompagné d'un violoncelle... Chez F.A. Dittmar, St. Petersbourg* (no date). Dittmar owned the publishing firm between 1800 and 1810; thus the publication belongs to that decade. Whether opus 4 was published before or after Khandoshkin's death in 1804 is a matter of dispute among Soviet musicologists, Yampolsky favoring an earlier publication, Fesechko a posthumous one. More important than the precise publication date of opus 4 by Dittmar is its *close similarity* to the Hummel 1781 edition—the same chansons, the same order and arrangements. This was never pointed out because no one—until now—had seen the Hummel 1781 edition; Fesechko ventures a guess that is off the mark. Now that we have a positive identification of Hummel 1781, the similarity with Dittmar opus 4 can be tentatively explained as follows: Dittmar, having acquired a publishing business from Gerstenberg in St. Petersburg in 1800, was in search of music to publish. Khandoshkin's opus 2 (*Chansons russes variées pour deux violons,*1796) was in Gerstenberg's catalogue, and Dittmar continued to publish two additional opus numbers by Khandoshkin: opus 3, *Trois Sonates pour le Violon seul,* and opus 4, *Deux Chansons russes variées pour violon accompagné d'un violoncelle.* Let us assume that Dittmar brought the manuscript of opus 3 from the composer in the early 1800s and published it by 1804. As for opus 4, its similarity with the old 1781 Hummel editions seems more than accidental: Dittmar may have found it convenient to reprint (with minor changes) the old out-of-print edition, giving it a new opus number and profiting by the increased fame of the composer. (Among the "minor changes" are the absence of a bass part for the 40 variations of *Kalinushka*, whose title was changed to "Vyidu ya na rechenku" [Out I'll go to the brooklet]). A posthumous publication date for opus 4 (after 1804) is probable.

The present discovery of the original 1781 Hummel edition of Khandoshkin's *Chansons russes variées* is important inasmuch as it confirms the authenticity of the extant old manuscript copies which are not in the composer's hand. The care with which the violin part has been edited indicates the high standard of Khandoshkin's musicianship as well as his technique. He could fully compete with visiting virtuosi like Lolli and Pugnani, while his folkish repertoire endeared him to his countrymen. He collected his own folk material, not relying on other collectors.

The rediscovered bass part for the 40 *Kalinushka* variations is a most agreeable addition since the variations acquire more musical quality and sound less like exercise pieces. True, the bass part shows limited variety, yet there are occasional flashes of commendable imagination, as shown in the following example from the 1781 Hummel edition:

Var. 29

It is hoped that Khandoshkin's two *Chansons russes avec des Variations pour un Violon, et l'accompagnement d'un Basse* in Hummel's Amsterdam edition of 1781 can be published as an *Urtext* in the near future. In the absence of any autograph score by this composer, an authentic first edition becomes a source of prime importance, especially one so carefully edited. Over and above his significance for Russian instrumental music, Ivan Khandoshkin must be recognized as having reached a level of violinistic accomplishment comparable to his Western confreres with whom he was able to compete whenever they visited St. Petersburg.[9]

Notes

1.   International Musicological Society, *Report of the Twelfth Congress Berkeley 1977*, eds. D. Heartz & B. Wade (Kassel, 1981), pp. 35-39.

2.   Boris Volman, *Russkie pechatnye noty XVIII veka* [Russian printed music of the XVIII century] (Leningrad, 1957), p. 73; Grigory Fesechko, *Ivan Eustaf'evich Khandoshkin* (Leningrad, 1972), pp. 40-41.

3.   Israel Yampolsky, *Russkoe skripichnoe iskusstvo* [Russian violin art] (Moscow, 1951), pp. 76-121; 401-75.

4.   Yuri Keldysh, *Russkaia muzyka XVIII veka*   [Russian music of the XVIII century] (Moscow, 1965), pp. 404-14.

5.   RISM = *Répertoire International des Sources Musicales*, vol. 4, p. 112.

6.   G. Fesechko, ed., in *Sovetskaia muzyka* (June, 1951), Musical Supplement.

7.   Yampolsky, op. cit., pp. 401-07. Here the song has the title "Pri dolinushke."

8.   Yampolksy, pp. 440-45.

9.   Keldysh, pp. 128, 130.

Orchestra and Chorus at the Comédie-Italienne (Opéra-Comique), 1755-99

David Charlton

In the wider sense, this essay contributes to efforts made since the Classical period itself to harness and examine that fascinating musical creature, the orchestra. No apology need, I trust, be offered for presenting a number of fundamental statistics. As Neal Zaslaw recently showed, the available evidence for any comparative study of European ensembles is difficult to interpret and uneven in balance: "one must study an orchestra over a period of time in order to see what it had as its normal working strength."[1] French and English orchestras have been less studied than have German ones: the present article has only one close ancestor and that deals with the Concert Spirituel and Paris Opéra.[2] In the narrower sense, the following essay contributes to our knowledge of a crucial yet largely unstudied topic: eighteenth-century opéra comique. This was a theatrical genre in which France enjoyed musical supremacy, a repertory that prepared the way for the "revolution" wrought by Gluck in Paris, and one on the point of attracting the creative interest of the most avant-garde musicians in Europe.[3]

A brief word may place the Comédie-Italienne in context. It was traditionally a mixed troupe: Italian actors and French actors or actor-singers. Until 1765 it might present Italian-language comedy, mixed Italian-French comedy, semi-improvised harlequinades, French plays, ballet, vaudeville or opéra comique. The French play repertory was withdrawn in 1769 but returned in 1779, at which juncture most of the Italian actors finally disappeared for good. (Actors skilled in the old improvising technique had been getting harder to find since the mid-century.) By 1778 "modern" opéra comique without vaudevilles was thoroughly established, but the Paris Opéra feared competition and ensured the retention of spoken plays and simple vaudevilles on two evenings a week.[4] Some of the Comédie-Italienne's musical repertory was Italian, as for example Pergolesi's *La servante maîtresse,* but it is worth noting that very few actual *opere buffe* were performed, and that these were invariably given in French.

Until 1783 the company chiefly performed at the Hôtel de Bourgogne; it was in rivalry with the Opéra-Comique, which acted at the Foires Saint-Laurent and Saint-Germain until 1762.[5] In 1762 the rival troupes merged and the Comédie-Italienne thereafter possessed and enhanced the whole repertory of opéra comique. Not until 1789 when the Théâtre de Monsieur (later Théâtre Feydeau) was founded did the Comédie-Italienne again have a serious rival. After a decade of competition these companies merged in 1801. The title of the Italian company could have changed to Opéra-Comique with the issuing of royal letters patent on 31 March 1780.[6] But public habit prolonged the appellations Théâtre Italien and Comédie-Italienne until 1793 when, on 5 February, public request to change the name to Théâtre de l'Opéra Comique National was immediately acceded to by the company, though not legally ratified until 17 March.[7]

The Hôtel de Bourgogne, "the first regular theater ever established in France,"[8] was converted for the purpose in the mid-sixteenth century after the death of the last duke of Bourgogne. Of course, the theater suffered more than one set of alterations in the course of time; but nothing could change its dominant narrow proportions, determined by the original design as a tennis court.[9] Its capacity was around 1,500 by the later part of the eighteenth century. In summer 1760 quite extensive remodelling was carried out but the description of this by Gueullette shows nothing affecting the orchestra.[10] Eventually a completely new structure was raised for the Comédie-Italienne, which first performed in it in April 1783. The design, by J.F. Heurtier, was perforce influenced by the great progress then being made in French theater design, but acoustically his auditorium looks to have been a little dry, since it featured projecting rows of open-plan boxes exposing the fabric of the audience's clothes.[11] Naturally, much more room was made available for the orchestra: the width of the pit at the Hôtel de Bourgogne was about twenty feet, while the width of the new proscenium was thirty-six *pieds,* about thirty-nine English feet.[12] The audience capacity, after some remodelling in 1784 by C. de Wailly, was around 2,000.

Only two sources provided the material for the present study: *(a)* the contemporary account and record books of the Comédie-Italienne, called Registres, and *(b)* the annual printed guides to Parisian theaters and music, *Les Spectacles de Paris.* Over 300 volumes of Registres cover the period 1717 to 1832. The Registres were the inspiration and source for Arthur Pougin's *L'Opéra-Comique pendant la Révolution* (Paris, 1891); they were later subject to preliminary investigation for the pre-1789 period by Georges Cucuel, who published a valuable if brief article on them in 1913. This touches on instrumental matters but is chiefly an analysis of trends in the reception given to various works.[13] The Registres were then rediscovered a generation later by Léon Chancerel and used in the editing of the Gueullette manuscript mentioned in note 10. (Neither Cucuel nor Chancerel mentioned the work done by their predecessors.) The main postwar study of them was Brenner's chronological transcription of the stage repertory up to 1793 by title, with a substantial introduction and description of sources.[14] For our purposes Registres (henceforth R.) 37-83 and 115-24 provide details of musicians' employment not only month-by-month but on single occasions; purchase, hire and repair of instruments; functions of musicians in the theater; organization and discipline, and so on. Each volume of the first type, R. 37 to R. 83, measuring about 46 cm. tall by 30 cm., runs from after the Easter recess one year to the beginning of the equivalent break in the next. This pattern was changed only in the late 1790s.[15] They contain daily entries whenever there was a performance with titles, receipts and (until 1773) names of players. At the end of each month's entries many pages of accounts are made up; against income from hire of boxes and the gate are the listed outgoings, set out in sectionalized fashion. The sections containing our information are either the monthly salary lists, *mandements,* or else authorized payments to individuals, *frais courants,* current expenses. These can have a subheading for *Instrumens extraordinaires,* hire of extra players. Finally there is the annual list of *gratifications,* gratuities. Certain Registres commence with a complete list of the permanent employees corrected after Easter, which can give extra information or provide a check on other evidence.

The above Registres do not, however, lay before one all the desired facts upon a plate. The orchestral lists do not append the instruments played, and the actor-singer lists do not specify, until 1795, which of the personnel sang in the chorus. The high degree of exactitude that is possible in our task requires the use of *Les Spectacles de Paris,* which itself contains a high degree of unreliability. It lists names and corresponding instrument(s) or voice, addresses of personnel, provides snippets of biographical information, and much besides. As its editors made clear, it went to press in July (later August) of the year preceding the one named on the title-page. This increased the degree to which it could give out-of-date information.[16]

The third basic type of source used is contained within R. 115 to R. 124, which form part of a series of 21 Registres predominantly consisting of committee minutes, July 1781 to 1828. The first nine were described in Brenner's study (pp. 40-42), the tenth (R. 124) being just outside his terms of reference and reaching May 1799. Certain volumes contain minutes actually taken during meetings and signed by those present (R. 115, 117, 118 etc.) while others duplicate these minutes in a more orderly way, merely noting signatories (R. 116, 119 etc.). The great advantage of the former set is its inclusion of original letters and submissions discussed in committee. Registre 123 is exceptional, being neatly copied contractual agreements with artists and others, and with some legal declarations of fundamental importance. Unfortunately there are gaps in the coverage. After the close of R. 122 in March 1791 we lack minutes and ordinary reports for six and a half years, and R. 124

closes in 1799, which is significantly short of the closure of the Opéra-Comique company in 1801.

The genesis of these committee volumes, described in R. 116, were the Orders in Council of 20 June 1781, designed to set to rights the too haphazard system of deciding precisely what was to be staged. Henceforth a committee of seven members would meet and make initial decisions about scripts submitted. (Those that passed the hurdle were read to the general assembly of members and voted upon.) However, these Registres reveal a whole range of executive decisions taken both by the committee and by the assembly.[17]

Let us begin our acquaintance with the musicians of the Comédie-Italienne by applying the historical magnifying glass provided by R. 115 to R. 124. We can see, for example, how they joined the company, were disciplined or even dismissed, and how cared for after long service; it was a close-knit community as well as a theater company.

By 1781 an official prodecure had been laid down for admitting orchestral players, but the minutes of 25 November referring to this is couched in revealing negatives: "not to admit to the orchestra except by audition" and "only to prefer those who are adjudged the most capable." Obviously the backdoor procedure had long reigned, and was indeed tried again (minutes of 28 November 1783). At least three other methods of entry can be detected: when the leader's nomination of a known player was accepted by the assembly (3 September 1783, 21 January 1784); when the assembly offered a post to a particularly good outside player (21 January 1784, 4 November 1790); or when a nomination by the composer Grétry, the company's permanent "artistic adviser" as we would say, was accepted (25 March 1784). Various methods were adopted in recruiting chorus singers, the chorus—once such a concept had come into being—not initially having an exclusive or rigid constitution. A singer could propose him- or herself, be agreed in assembly to be put on probation, and eventually accepted (25 February 1784). Or it could be decided to employ two copyists, these being needed at the time, who would also sing in the chorus (25 July 1790). Two ladies of the ballet were permitted also to sing in the chorus (18 April 1787).

Disciplinary provisions or proceedings form a consistent thread throughout the Registres that sometimes enables us to get as close as can ever be hoped for to the quality of music making itself. As far as the orchestra was concerned, what the company would dearly have liked was a band who would all arrive at 5:30 P.M. exactly, go down to the pit when the bell rang and tune up, never leave the pit before the end of an act, never use a substitute, and attend all rehearsals punctually (internal constitution of Ventôse An 5, February-March 1797). But of course, absenteeism and lateness were common enough for a system of fines to be used: even the musical director La Houssaye could be fined for missing the overture (11 July and 31 August 1782). At the time of the move to the new building there was a need to "reestablish the good order and subordination necessary to attain *ensemble,* on which depends the perfect performance of the orchestra" (1 April 1783). La Houssaye was then given "full power" to oversee players, but a more effective method was brought in when the names of latecomers were noted by officials and read out in assembly (6 January 1784). After this things seem to have stabilized into a pattern of casual indiscipline probably connected with the difficulties of La Houssaye's final years in office (see below). The committee meeting of 18 April 1790 encouraged his successor to be firm in spotting evidence of "the negligence and abuses introduced in recent years."

For the loyal player, though, the company acted in its best traditions of charitableness. On 22 March 1786 it voted a retirement pension to a violinist whose stipulated 20 years of service had not—as the rules laid down—been uninterrupted, but in two blocks. He received half what his annual salary had been.

Discipline problems in the chorus were considerably greater, at least from time to time, and as will be seen later came to a head in March 1788 with the wholesale reauditioning of members. "Extreme" dereliction of duty, not to mention their "indecent" comportment on stage, was noted of certain ladies of the chorus in February 1784. Higher fines were brought in, followed by a circular letter in March and an offer of help by M. Raymond in June. Yet the same problems were being tackled in May 1785 when nine ladies' names were read out in assembly as a warning. Until the appointment of a new trainer in 1788 there were consistent complaints of inadequate rehearsal and performance standards.

We must turn to the question of the character of orchestral performance practice at the Comédie-Italienne first by looking at the four musical directors who were employed during the 40 years under discussion. In the first period considered below, A.B. Blaise was both *maître de musique* and bassoonist, as well as an active composer and arranger. As *maître* he might well have played the keyboard. Zaslaw, without coming to any firm conclusion, reminds us that on one hand the *maestro* might perform a continuo role, while on the other certain moves were being made generally from the 1760s to remove the harpsichord from ensembles. At the Comédie-Italienne no listed orchestra player was charged with playing the harpsichord at any time (or later the piano: from 1791 payments were made to the tuner of the "piano forté").[18] Information to be published by M.E.C. Bartlet shows that a continuo player was paid within the category of general employees.[19] Of the performance of popular vaudevilles we still know little; but there is evidence for a reduced size of orchestra on the two days when such entertainments were given, with a total of six violins (13 January 1782). The other instruments used were mentioned on 19 April 1788, when fines were imposed after particularly slovenly renditions in the vaudeville divertissement, *La fête du château,* first performed in 1766:

> The assembly agreed to fine indiscriminately all persons charged with accompanying in yesterday's performance, the violins only, the cellos *(basses)* and wind instruments not to be missed from the said fine of six *livres.*

But all these need not have played all through; again, however, the continuo finds no specific mention.

Blaise's successors were eminent string players. Le Bel, chief from 1761 to 1781, had been a violinist with the orchestra under Blaise, and before that at the Opéra-Comique: he was often referred to as "premier violon." Pierre La Houssaye, chief from 1781 to Easter 1790, was a renowned violinist-director, a student of Tartini and on appointment already in charge of the Concert Spirituel. He was succeeded by M.F. Blasius who, although a composer practiced in various genres, had certainly appeared as soloist in his own violin concerto at the Concert Spirituel in 1784.[20] That he carried a violin is suggested by the experimental employment of a *batteur de mesure* in his orchestra for some five months during 1794.[21]

Grétry provides a vignette of Le Bel in 1768:

> I went down to the orchestra pit. My intention was to commend myself to the first violin *(Lebel).* I discovered him poised to strike the first down-bow; his eyes were ablaze, his features altered almost beyond recognition: I retreated without a word...[22]

But the *Correspondance littéraire* in 1772 made a devastating comparison between Le Bel's ensemble and that of the Mannheim opera, whence the writer had recently returned.

> As for the astonishing, sublime performance standard of the Mannheim orchestra, possibly unique today in Europe, I do not know how long it will take me to forget it and adjust my ears to the discordance of those scrapers of the accompaniment at the Comédie-Italienne, without nuances, without soul and without sensibility.[23]

Much later, when Michael Kelly first went to Paris early in 1787, he could write with utmost approval in the light of his own professional musical experiences elsewhere in Europe:

> My object in Paris, was to see all the theatres, and I therefore visited one or other of them every evening... but my favourite theatre of all was, the Théâtre Italien, in the Rue Favart, where French comic operas were performed; the orchestra was very good, and the actors and singers equally so....[24]

For La Houssaye's period of office we are fortunate to have in R. 119 extraordinary details of an eighteenth-century music director in action. He was obviously not on the best terms with the executive committee towards the end of the 1780s and after the performance on 3 March 1788 the committee discussed him. First they agreed to tell him to make progress with preparing the 700 *livres'* worth of music he had got them to buy (presumably for incidental and ballet performance); then they urged him to exert his authority over slack players; finally they entered his artistic preserve:

> It was agreed to propose to M. La Houssaye to lead [*conduire*] the orchestra from full score and to beat time as need be with his bow and to follow the actors in their singing and also to take care to maintain poise [*aplomb*] in the chorus, which up to this time has not been performing as it ought.

Do we have here some of the birth pangs of modern conducting practice? After all, it is hardly practicable to play violin from full score, owing to page turns, let alone conduct as well. Assuming that the committee realized this, we conclude that basically they intended him to cease playing and to become a "modern" conductor. Or was it merely an attempt to get La Houssaye over a period of indifferent leadership by suggesting some unexceptionable, well-tried methods?

We have near proof here that a first violin part or short score was used by the director prior to March 1788 but there is unfortunately nothing to show that he complied in the use of a full score after then. Complex textures, offstage ensembles, new instrumental techniques, all were fast becoming part and parcel of opéra comique; yet the orchestral musicians appear to have remained in an artistically subordinate role within the company. Its demarcation line of artistic responsibility was wrongly drawn. As if to test this La Houssaye, either through accident or design, had a trial of strength with two singers a few weeks later, which he lost.

> It was agreed to fine M. La Houssaye two *louis* for having been unwilling to follow M. Rosière and Mad[emoisell]e La Caille in the speed that they had taken in the duet "On ne peut élever l'enfance" in [J.P.E. Martini's opéra comique] *L'Amoureux de 15 ans* and for having publicly shown ill temper (R. 119, 19 April 1788).

This fine was never imposed because La Houssaye, having had sick leave for a sprained hand, presented detailed objections to the committee on 27 August. (These do not survive, at least in the Registres.) By 16 October 1789 he had given his notice to leave, since that day the committee decided to approach Blasius. It would seem that the committee wanted La Houssaye to change his methods in the attempt to improve standards, but also that they themselves could or would not delegate the effective disciplinary authority he needed to implement that attempt. La Houssaye was certainly not on the committee, and a player could perhaps easily argue his way out of a disciplinary hearing. Brenner noted how the most flagrant misbehavior by members of the ballet went ultimately unpunished; and no less a figure than Grétry put his weight behind La Houssaye in a near-contemporary document.

> I frequently hear the musicians of the Comédie-Italienne adding a few notes here and there to my [orchestral] accompaniments... The performing musician who oversteps the limits of his duty not simply tutors the composer, but with respect to his colleagues projects a tone of pretension which in the course of time singularly harms their reputation. If one day the Comédie gives less limited power to the skillful artist *(M. de La Houssaye)* who conducts the orchestra, I have no doubt that he will check this corrupt practice (Grétry, *Mémoires* 1:37-38).

La Houssaye's next post was the orchestral directorship of the rival Théâtre de Monsieur, where he rapidly created a reputation for excellence and precise playing.

The "regular" ensemble instruments were by no means the only ones heard at the Comédie-Italienne. The Registres reveal an unexpected number of references to instruments such as the harp, viola d'amore and so on, and to groups of military instruments, all of which are discussed in the appropriate section below. Occasional reference of this kind is sometimes made to operas now lost, about which therefore we can glean small pieces of information. For ease of presentation the remainder of this study is divided into five roughly equal chronological periods. These have been created for the convenience of the reader rather than to imply discontinuity in the life of the Comédie-Italienne. In the commentaries below any mention of a year or pair of years is liable to signify Easter onward or Easter in one to Easter the next; this is the way the company organized itself. Plain figures in the tables referring to instrumentalists signify known salaried posts, while those within square brackets signify conjectured salaried posts and those within parentheses signify a part-time post or doubling with another instrument. The mention of a specially-hired instrument refers normally to the first occasion of its appearance, but this does not imply only one such appearance. If the piece was a success, the extra player(s) continued to be hired.

Table 1.   Period 1: 1755-62

	vl 1	vl 2	vla	vlc	cb	fl ob	cl	fag	cor	tr	tb	timp
Easter 1756- Easter 1760	3	3	[1]	3	—	2	—	2	2	—	—	(1)
Easter 1760- Easter 1762	4	4	2	3	1	2	—	2	2	—	—	(1)

Registre 37 for 1755-56 provides insufficient evidence for us to be certain of figures: physical deterioration of the "Etat des pensionnaires" (the opening annual list of employees) and absence of mention of their tasks even makes guessing too hazardous. During that year horns and timpani were paid by the month as required. Indeed, the Comédie-Italienne, to the end of the century, almost never paid an individual exclusively as a timpanist: the job was doubled with a violinist or violist. In 1758 (R. 39, February, March) the timpanist was Soret, either the violinist himself or possibly even his father: Les Spectacles... 1757 calls the violinist "Soret fils." The horns became salaried rather than paid ad hoc in 1756, remaining on the payroll thereafter except in 1758-59 and maybe 1759-60, for which R. 41 lacks the "Etat des pensionnaires." Although no violist was identified until Les Spectacles... 1759 and R. 43, I feel that Vesou, violist in this publication and salaried player since R. 38 if not before, must have played viola. The year 1759-60 may have seen an increase to seven violins, as suggested in *Les Spectacles... 1760;* indeed, the new double bass player, though not listed in the latter, may in fact have played before Easter 1760: we cannot know.

Specially hired instruments mentioned in Registres included a serpent in the ballet *Les Noces chinois* (May 1756), an entertainment also requiring 14 soldiers. The use of soldiers, later with instruments, or other citizens as extras was a continuing feature of stage life at the theater. A trumpet was heard in the spectacular comedy *Le Prince de Salerne* in 1756 (the play itself dating from 1746), a musette in *Timon le misanthrope* (1758, originally given 1722), a hurdy-gurdy in *La Soirée des boulevards* (première November 1758) and a harp in the perennial *Soliman II* which was played by the author's wife, Mme. Favart (1761). We learn about participation of the mandolin from Gueullette, however. Writing of *Le Charlatan* (November 1756), a parody of *Tracolo* then being given by the bouffons at the Opéra, he noted, "The music was arranged by Mr. Sadi, who plays the mandolin in the orchestra."[25]

In 1760-61 Blaise *(maître)* and Le Bel (first violin) drew equal salaries, Blaise having taken a cut. From Easter 1761 Le Bel took the highest remuneration; at the same time the composer Duni took up a salaried position, described in *Les Spectacles... 1762* as "Directeur de la Musique." He had come from Italy in 1757 and settled in Paris, writing opéras comiques for the rival Opéra-Comique troupe. During Period 1, in fact, the Opéra-Comique took a most significant artistic lead through the first performances of several opéras comiques not only by Duni, but also Philidor and Monsigny.[26] These attracted large numbers of spectators. An idea of this rival ensemble may be provided from *Les Spectacles de Paris.* Already from 1755 there were six violins, a viola, two or three cellos and at least one double bass, plus the usual six wind players. In 1758-59 the total of violins seems to have increased to eight, one of whom was the new leader J.C. Trial, later co-director of the Opéra. These facts apparently spurred the Comédie-Italienne to take similar steps. The fusion of the two companies took effect from 3 February 1762, but the size of the Comédie-Italienne orchestra remained stable until after the Easter break.

There was no chorus as such at the latter theater for many years, and opéra comique confined itself to small-scale canvases with a handful of actor-singers participating. Yet the desire to see larger numbers of actors was natural and one which was for the moment satisfied not only by the use of extra personnel such as the soldiers earlier mentioned, but particularly by the ballet dancers. While for most of period 1 there were around 18 actors, including the Italian players impersonating Harlequin, Pantaloon and Columbine, the number of dancers was around 25.

Period 2: 1762-71

During 1769-70 the addition of Ebling "hautbois" to the regular flute-oboe team of Rostenne and Capelle remains unexplained: as R. 52 is only a daybook we cannot ascertain whether this arrangement continued into 1771. The phenomenon may be connected—it is pure guesswork—with two early works of Grétry, almost the first published operas comiques to specify the clarinet, namely *Le Huron* (1768) and *Les Deux Avares* (1770), albeit only in a single movement each. The normal procedure in later cases was for extra hired clarinetists to be used, but the Registres never show any such payments for the above operas, though they held the stage for some years. In short, we have no positive evidence that Grétry's demands were met by doubling within the orchestra, which is why clarinets are not indicated in the table for period 2. However, two anonymous clarinetists were paid for in March 1767 (R. 48, *Mandement* 3) for their participation in a revival of *Gilles garçon peintre*, a "parade" created in 1758 at the Foire Saint-Germain with music by La Borde. The instruments were by no means new in Paris and had been used occasionally at the Opéra since 1749. Cucuel, who quotes some of their music from the overture of *Gilles*, says that the clarinets "seem to have won the freedom of the city at the Foire" in this work.[27]

Table 2.   Period 2: 1762-71

	vl 1	vl 2	vla	vlc	cb	fl ob	cl	fag	cor	tr	tb	timp
Easter 1762- Easter 1763	5	5	2	3	1	2	—	2	2	—	—	(1)
Easter 1763- Easter 1768	5	4	2	3	2	2	—	2	2	—	—	(1)
Easter 1768- Easter 1769	5	5	2	3	2	2	—	2	2	—	—	(1)
Easter 1769 Easter 1770 (1771)	5	5	2	3	2	3	—	2	2	—	—	(1)

From *Les Spectacles... 1763*, R. 50 and elsewhere we learn that Le Bel's assistant violinist Lebreton (also called Mahoni) acted as *répétiteur*.[28] The viola player Moreau joined the company after Easter 1762, and although he was to be credited as doubling on timpani in *Les Spectacles... 1765*, he may well have played both instruments before, at least after the 1762-63 season during which an extra musician, Canu, was being paid as *ad hoc* timpanist. The tambourin was heard in various pieces during period 2 including Duni's *La Fée Urgèle* (May, June 1766); none is notated in the appropriate dance on page 130 of the printed full score. The mandolin was paid for unspecified "various pieces" (July 1765) over 20 nights.

If the orchestra experienced relative stability, the genre of opéra comique during period 2 was undergoing profound internal changes. Tentative beginnings were made in choral music, principally by Philidor, which led towards Monsigny's *Le Déserteur* (1769) wherein the four-part chorus played a climactic part in both the musical and the dramatic structure. At first, the occasional movements labelled "chorus" might lead us to imagine something of a crowd, but this would be false. For example, the rather Handelian "Chantons la bienvenüe" in Philidor's *Sancho Pança* (1762) bears in the libretto the rubric, "choeur, qui entoure et salue Sancho" (chorus which surrounds and greets Sancho); the score reveals four staves each with two named singing parts per stave. There were few if any available singers in excess of these eight. When, for example, *Sancho* was acted on 17 February 1763, on the same night as a new divertissement, a total of five women and seven men were paid. Philidor's *Le Sorcier* (1764) contains a "Choro" whose music this time has a little contrapuntal development, but the opera was acted on 21 January 1764 (for example) by three women and four men only. The four-act *La Fée Urgèle* (1765) features the entourage of Queen Berthe, knights, dames, courtiers etc. with choruses modest in length but in up to four parts in texture in acts 1, 3 and 4. The daily records of the Registres show that this work was acted by about five singing women and six singing men in all. On 19 June 1769 it was produced with only four women and five men. *Le Déserteur* was repeatedly acted at the time by some four singing women and seven men. Thus in his turn Grétry was writing in hope rather than certainty when for *Les Deux Avares* (1770) he requested a miniature chorus of three named male parts and "seven other Janissaries." In the revival of January 1772 only seven or eight men sang, and only five performed on the fifteenth of that month.[29]

Table 3.   Period 3: 1771-83

	vl 1	vl 2	vla	vlc	cb	fl ob	cl	fag	cor	tr	tb	timp
Easter 1771- Easter 1773	5	5	2	3	2	2	—	2	2	—	—	(1)
Easter 1773- Easter 1777	6	5	2	3	2	2	—	2	2	—	—	(1)
Easter 1777- Easter 1783	6	6	2	3	2	2	—	2	2	—	—	(1)

No special administrative division occurred here; the years of period 3, however, were ones of orchestral innovation for opéra comique in general. The composer Grétry almost presided over the repertory not only on account of his prolific output but also because the Comédie-Italienne, in September 1771, decided to give him a salary, larger than Duni's, "in order to recognize his daily services" and that he should "watch over everything concerning this type of music, the singing and the orchestra."[30]

A sidelight on performance practice is the monthly appearance of payment for two violins and cello for rehearsal duties, from May 1774. Even by 1790 when N.E. Framery anonymously published *De l'organisation des spectacles de Paris,* a keyboard player was not being used in the rehearsals (p. 132).

Grétry's celebrated *Zémire et Azor* was first performed at the theater in December 1771: it requires clarinets in the offstage wind sextet in act 3 (the "magic picture" scene) and offstage horns and flutes in act 4, for the evocation of Azor's wild garden. Two veteran clarinetists (Gaspard [Procksch] and Flieger) and a horn player (Mozer) were duly hired, and similar hirings were made whenever the work was performed (R. 53, December, *Mandements* 20, 22, and "Suitte des frais courants").[31] An extra *Zémire et Azor* flute began to be hired from March 1774. In the same composer's *Le Magnifique,* overture only, trumpets were required, perhaps for the first time in a published opéra comique score (March 1773). Extra players were used from the start and paid for in May that year (*Mandement* 4). All these extra demands were dwarfed in November 1774 when Martini's *Henry IV* was staged. This portrayed nothing less than the battle of Ivry in its second entr'acte, albeit offstage, with the help of military music performing standard musical signals. In act 3 military music and orchestra played together for the victors' parade and defile. Martini's score suggests the use of fifes, clarinets, oboes, horns and bassoons. Two extra trumpeters, a timpanist and twenty military players (with a further thirteen on the very first night) were employed, placed in the musical charge of the regular orchestra's bassoonist. This began a trend. Similar forces were subsequently heard in Bianchi's *La Réduction de Paris* (September 1775), *Les Mariages samnites* (by Grétry, June 1776), *Matroco* (also by Grétry, February 1778; no longer extant), *Zulima* (by Dezède, May 1778) and others.

L.B. Desormery had used clarinets in *La Fête du village* in June 1775, judging from the extra payments made. Clarinets were then called for in the December 1776 revival of Rodolphe's 1767 *L'Aveugle de Palmyre:* the printed score of this work indicates only string accompaniments. In March 1778 the anonymous ballet score *De l'Art et de la nature* also required two clarinet players, with three trumpeters and timpanist, not to mention 21 musicians from the "dépot des Gardes." One of the trumpeters was Guthmann, a player of versatility who joined the Comédie-Italienne violins in September 1785 and by the following Easter received his gratuity in respect of playing violin, viola and horn. To these he added the trumpet a year later. (In a manuscript book it was noted, evidently from an interview in 1789, that he also played trombone and harp.[32]) His case, if a little exceptional, is a reminder that we can never be dogmatic about orchestral practice simply from the statistics. Borrel (see note 2) found that the Opéra orchestra in 1781 could summon supplementary horns, trumpets, trombones and timpani from the other sections.

It is unclear who played timpani regularly at the Comédie-Italienne at this time. Three different players were paid as "extra" timpanists in 1778-79 but after January 1779 no further such payments appear for some years. The violinist Lescot received gratuities in respect of timpani playing at Easter 1782 and continued to do so until 1789, but he had been a violinist since 1768 and could have doubled on percussion after the violist-timpanist Moreau departed in 1773. Continuing formations of extra instruments included two flutes with two horns in Dezède's *Cécile* (February 1780) and five players in Benda's melodrama *Ariane abandonnée* (July 1781): the evidence of the autograph of *Ariane* used in Paris suggests that they performed fanfares scored for four trumpets.[33]

During 1773 daily records ceased to be made of exactly which actors had worked on a given evening; it becomes more conjectural to gauge the exact size of the available chorus in period 3. Irritatingly, these are years when interesting demands were made on these singers. Information from R. 74 (noted below) shows that the chorus was drawn from one particular group of actor-singers: those paid monthly and known as *appointés,* salaried staff, as opposed to those with a permanent share in the company. By 1776-77 there were some nine male and six female *appointés* (the numbers were naturally fluid). This total was reduced to some 12 in 1779-80 when the Italian players withdrew, rising slightly thereafter. A "chorus" in period 3 can have meant no more than two or maybe three voices per part. However, there was no mistaking the musical ambitions which composers now had for the chorus. Explicit acknowledgement of this was made when an agreement concluded with the Opéra on 16 October 1779 imposed restrictions on the dramatic context and function of the Comédie-Italienne's choral music.[34] The Opéra protected itself from competition by prohibiting any "ornate chorus" or the use of extra singers for any chorus that did not arise dramatically from the "natural" coming together of actors on stage in response to the demands of the plot. It specified, in fact, the choral "rendition of a tumultuous acclamation [rather] than a chorus properly speaking." Works that were already in the Comédie-Italienne repertory were allowed to remain as they were, however.

Period 4: 1783-93

We are fortunate that the information in R. 115 *et seq.* covers the events of 1783, principally the opening of the new season on 28 April in the newly completed theater, rue Favart. Prompted by the knowledge that more space would be available the committee took several decisions on 1 April:

> The Committee, deliberating on the means of improving the orchestra and of augmenting it insofar as is needed for the new theater, has agreed as follows:
> 1. To augment the violin section by four players of whom two shall be regular orchestral members, and two supernumeraries, all four to be selected by audition.
> 2. To take on one more cello, this position to be given to M. Dourde, a longstanding supernumerary, and also a fifth player as supernumerary to form five cellos in the orchestra of the new theater.

In fact on 19 April the *comité des simphonistes* (orchestral committee) selected five violinists and three cellists, on La Houssaye's advice. One violin was to replace Rollot, who retired on Easter 1783, resulting in the 16 as desired, and as were listed in May. But one Battu thereupon disappeared, leaving 15 salaried players from June. As for cellos, the more generous final plan provided five regular and one supernumerary players.

The duties of supernumeraries were to double for indisposed players and—at least as violins were concerned—to play as a "foundation service on Tuesdays and Fridays independently of the six violins obligatory on those days" (the spoken play and vaudeville nights). This was spelled out on 13 January 1782, at which time it was decided to employ two such violinists: presumably they would be paid, as was Dourde, through gratuities. In the figures below therefore, the string figures may be misleading in the sense that at the start at least, only 14 violins and five cellos need regularly have played in the main orchestra.

Table 4.   Period 4: 1783-93

	vl 1	vl 2	vla	vlc	cb	fl ob		cl	fag	cor	tr	tb	timp
Easter 1783-Easter 1784	8	7	2	6	2	2		—	2	2	—	—	(1)
Easter 1784-Sep. 1785	8	7	2	6	2	3		—	2	2	—	—	(1)[1]
Easter 1785-Easter 1786	8	8	2	6	2	3		—	2	2	—	—	(1)
Easter 1786-Easter 1790	9	9	2	6	2	3		—	2	2	—	—	(1)
Easter 1790-Easter 1791	8	8	3	5	3	3		2	2	4		—	(1)
Easter 1791-May 1793	8	8	2	5	3	1	2	2	3	4	1	1	1 (July 1791)

1.   My figures for 1784 come not from the Registres, the relevant one being missing, but *Les Spectacles de Paris*...1785. It should also be noted that only 7 second violins were listed October 1791-Easter 1792.

Likewise, later in period 4, not all the violins need be assumed to have been heard on every evening.

The years preceding 1790 saw the repeated hiring of two trumpets for works like Grétry's *Aucassin et Nicolette* (1779), Dalayrac's *Sargines* (1788) and his *Raoul sire de Crequi* (1789), so their eventual incorporation was a natural consequence of a continuing development of taste. The hiring of clarinets in the 1780s became far less prominent, however, suggesting doubling within the orchestra: but it is a fact that few opéras comiques before 1790 needed clarinets at all. Once they were permanently available there was an upward leap in their employment.[35] The penchant for military musical styles before the Revolution can be detected merely from the continued hiring of extra military musicians in a play like *L'Incendie du Havre* for example (February 1786), or "deux trompettes du depôt" in a parody of Salieri's *Tarare* in 1787. What is revealing in the assembly minutes of 28 March 1790 (R. 122) is that making the trumpets salaried was a business decision. It had cost 2,630 *livres* to hire all extra instruments in the preceding twelve months, and it was consequently decided to move Guthmann from violins to trumpet and horn and simply hire one new permanent player (Frédéric [Duvernoy]) to second Guthmann; the new salary was only 800 *livres* p.a. It was also ordained that on one day a week Guthmann and Frédéric would relieve the regular hornists Tourtourelle and Schwend. Regrettably, no mention of the decision to take on clarinetists is found.

The new violist in 1790 was also a timpanist, Ambezard. He left after a year to join the Opéra, but it is doubtful whether his successor Hardouin (July 1791) actually played viola from the beginning: this is because R. 78 (October 1793, *Mandement* 19) states that he only then began to receive payment in respect of the viola, and because extra viola music had to be copied at the time, being paid for in January 1794 (Nivôse An 2, *Mandement* 13). Back-desk violinists might have played viola in the late 1780s, for the preferred ratio of violas to violins at the Opéra and Concert Spirituel in the Classical period was one to five or six; our figures stand at one to eight or nine.[36] On the other hand, neglect of the viola section is, on paper, well documented in other orchestras of Europe.[37] The strong cello section of the Comédie-Italienne compares closely with Parisian practice elsewhere.

The addition of a trombone in 1791 was entirely characteristic of this period in Paris. The Théâtre Feydeau orchestra seems already to have included the trombonist Mariotti, "astonishing in his precision on this instrument, whose fine effect was unknown in France."[38] Unfortunately the relevant committee minute of 21 December 1790 (R. 122) reveals nothing of the motives of the Comédie-Italienne in determining to appoint a trombonist: only that they wanted "one of the best musicians of this kind" to be procured from Italy or Germany. In Cherubini's *Lodoïska* (Théâtre Feydeau, July 1791) Mariotti was asked to play reinforcing bass lines, sometimes just with the wind choir, and this style was adopted in the first Comédie-Italienne works printed with trombone parts: Kreutzer's *Lodoïska* and Dalayrac's *Philippe et Georgette* (first given in August and December 1791). Less is known about the role of the third bassoon, since no opéra comique is known to have required three real parts for that instrument. The overall growth of attention to the wind sections was, as Zaslaw showed, endemic to the orchestra everywhere in the period, but the use of a single trombone in an ensemble seems to have been very rare before 1796 outside Paris.

Definite moves were made in period 4 to regularize the constitution and musical efficacy of the chorus. Prior to 1783, for example, the smallness of the choral body was inseparable from a sort of arbitrariness as to who constituted it. We have a letter, presumably autograph, from Mlle. La Caille, attached in

R. 115 to the relevant committee deliberations for 16 July 1782. La Caille had joined the company in 1780 and sang many leading opéra comique roles. Her letter complains of harassment by Mlle. Le Roy and others.

> ... If sometimes my *mances* [performance gratuities] surpass hers, it is because it pleases me to appear in the choruses, and because I have played roles which are outside [the terms of] my employment.

However, the size of the pool of salaried actor-singers grew as though inevitably: 18 in 1783-84, 24 at Easter 1787, 26 by Easter 1791. The lists of these *appointés* (one for women, one for men) in *Les Spectacles de Paris* are subdivided by a line starting with the issue for 1787 (compiled 1786). This seems to indicate a choral subgroup, which consisted of 10 names in that year rising over the next three years to 14, then 16 in *Les Spectacles . . . 1791,* the male singers now headed by the "Chef des Choeurs," Testard. Over the following two years the numbers rose to 19, then 20.

In the meeting of 1 April 1783 the executive committee made an attempt to grapple with the problems of the chorus and deputed the singers Narbonne and Dorsonville to oversee it, but also to use one M. Murgeon to rehearse the chorus prior to general rehearsals. The arrangement did not last and if the following initiative had not occurred, the solution might have been much longer in appearing:

> Assembly minutes, 9 July 1783
> Letter read from M. La Caille who proposes his services to the Comédie for choral ensembles, which he aims to perfect by demonstrating the parts to the choristers separately, and having them rehearse together . . .

The proposal was voted in favor. From the end of the 1783-84 season La Caille received a gratuity for his work annually, and from April 1787 was paid monthly for "L'étude des choeurs." But by 25 May 1785 not only was the chorus being rehearsed "negligently" but the music was being performed with "lack of exactitude." Consequently a new inspector, the actor M. Valroi, was given power to order "as many rehearsals as he believes necessary" and La Caille ordered to abide by all Valroi's decisions. Finally La Caille's competence was called into question when action was taken at the highest level: it was announced on 24 March 1788 in committee that the Gentlemen of the Chamber,

> intending to establish good order in the chorus section, overly neglected until now, have chosen M. Testard to be its conductor [*conducteur*] and in consequence direct all members of the Comédie-Italienne chorus to the Ecole Gratuite [the recently-founded singing-school headed by Gossec] at the Menus Plaisirs, rue Poissonnière, on Wednesday 28 March next, where the professors *(maîtres)* of the School will be found with M. Testard and the Committee of the Comédie-Italienne.

In the presence of Des Entelles of the Chamber and the Duc de Frousac all chorus members were re-auditioned: no minutes report the need for a subsequent influx of new singers, however. La Caille was discharged and given a year's salary as gratuity. This Draconian episode did not put a stop to further indiscipline but Testard held on to his position to the end of the century and presumably kept matters under reasonable control.

Table 5.   Period 5: 1793-99

	vl 1	vl 2	vla	vlc	cb	fl	ob	cl	fag	cor tr	tb	timp
June 1793- Aug. 1793	8	7	2	5	3	1	2	2	3	4	1	1
Sep. 1793- July 1794	9	8	3	5	3	1	2	2	3	4	1	(1)
July 1794- March 1795	9	8	3	6	3	1	2	2	3	4	1	(1)
March 1795- Feb. 1796	10	9	4	7[1]	3	2	2	2	2	5	(1)	(1)
Feb. 1796- April 1796	10	10	5/6[2]	7/8	3	2/3	2	2	3	5	(1)	(1)
April 1796- Nov. 1796	10	10	6	9	3/4[3]	3	2	2	3	5	1	(1)
Nov. 1796- March 1797	10	9	6	9	4	3	3	2	3	5	1	(1)
March 1797- June 1797	9	9	5	8	3	3	3	2	3	4 2	1	(1)
Oct. 1797- Jan. 1799	9/8[4]	8	6	8	3	3	3	2	4	4 2	1(2)	(1)
Jan. 1799- 22 Oct. 1799	8	7	5	7	3	3	2	2(3)	3	4 2	2(1)	(1)

1.   The cellos stood in fact at only six players from Fructidor An 4 to Nivôse An 5 (August 1795 to January 1796).
2.   Second alternative figures in this line with effect from Germinal An 4 (21 March).
3.   Second figure with effect from Thermidor An 4 (19 July).
4.   Reduction to eight in Prairial An 6 (20 May 1798).

The changes of pattern in dating coincide with the adoption of the Republican calendar, though all dates above have been converted to the Gregorian equivalent. (Use of the new system commenced on 1 Vendémiaire An 2, i.e., 22 September 1793. The bookkeepers of the Registres transferred to the new dates by running December 1793 on until the end of Nivôse An 2, i.e. 19 January 1794.) The theater closed in summer 1797 for refurbishment, but otherwise kept up its traditional pattern of performances all the year round; after 1792 the Easter recess no longer took place. Many rapid changes are apparent in the orchestra, but the numerical apex of its constitution was reached steadily, that is with 55 players in 1796-97. The regular salary lists have continually to be counterbalanced in the Registres by reference to the occasional payment lists in order that one may arrive at the true state of affairs.

We noted above that brass players doubled between horn and trumpet. Several works from the mid-1790s maximized available resources by requiring four horns without trumpets.[39] For a period in 1795-96 the trombone was doubled by a violinist, Kerstan (= Kerstein). Six violas and eight cellos were first engaged during March 1796 (Germinal An 4), together with the three flutes. The fourth double bass first joined in July 1796 (Thermidor An 4). Some ambiguity remains concerning the duties of Perret, the regular trombonist from 1796, who is listed in 1799 with the clarinets from Pluviôse An 7 onwards (R. 83) while Kerstein is listed as the trombonist. The *Almanach des spectacles de Paris... An VIII* (? 1799) listed both musicians as trombonists, and indeed two are required in Boieldieu's *Zoraïme et Zulnar* (May 1798).

During period 5 the theater purchased a harp, in June 1797, having previously been obliged to hire one at intervals. It also bought what may have been a bass trombone, since Perret was reimbursed in May 1798 for a "grande trombone" (Floréal An 6, *Mandement* 63). A viola d'amore was also acquired, for what purpose is not known, in October 1798 (Vendémiaire An 7, *Mandement* 36).

The proportions of orchestral strings demonstrate a decisive swing to the ratio two (violins) to one (cello), the pre-revolutionary norm in Paris being three to one. However, this involved little actual change in the numbers of violins. In fact in 1799 the same number of violins if not fewer than existed before the Revolution had to balance 150% more lower strings and up to 200% more wind players. Essentially the orchestra had become "modern" in its resources by 1790; but within a few years with the addition of trombone and multiple woodwind it had become idiosyncratic, matched in the 1790s perhaps only by the Koblenz court ensemble with its 13 violins, 12 woodwind and eight brass.[40]

The first specific chorus lists in the Registres occur in the introduction to R. 80 (1795-96) when the salaried actors were classed as either "Rôles" (twelve women, eight men) or "Choeurs" (17 men, 18 women). This represented a large increase in the probable size of the chorus for the year before when the total *appointés* numbered only 31, some 25 of whom could have sung in the chorus. This is a deduction based on the names of those who were soloists in R. 80. In turn, this represented an increase over 1793-94 when there were only about 25 *appointés*. Registres 81 and 82 gave only composite actor-chorus lists between spring 1796 and autumn 1798 (around 49 and 41 people respectively). In February 1799 (Pluviôse An 7), however, R. 83 made a separate entry naming 15 female and 17 male chorus members. These numbers remained valid for the whole year.

The lack of full committee minutes for much of the 1790s deprives us of the reasoning behind the statistics, although many other stories of interest are found in those which survive. We nevertheless know that the need to attract customers became pressing, so that larger and larger numbers of performers were probably hired in accordance with the laws of supply and demand. (The refurbishment of the theater in summer 1797 was a desperate bid to revive public interest, an operation for which the company persuaded its employees to take half wages for three months with no guarantee that they would ever be repaid.) The printed scores of works given during the decade reveal a corresponding increase in the number of wind instruments employed, until at last in 1797-98 Grétry's *Lisbeth* and Dalayrac's *Gulnare* required nine woodwind parts simultaneously with a piccolo in addition to two flutes. If all four bassoonists were used, 11 players would have sounded at once. Boieldieu's *Beniowsky* demanded eight woodwind and eight brass parts simultaneously, and Méhul's *Bion* overture, also 1800, was the first work at the theater to require at least nine woodwind and either eight or nine brass parts at one time (depending on whether one or two trombones played).

Thus from a simple group of musicians in the 1750s accompanying doubtless in fundamentally *style galant* manner, the Comédie-Italienne orchestra was inflated to match the expectations of a public who in turn were served with a drastic development in style by Parisian composers. The chorus grew from nothing to over thirty members. The deliberate cultivation of an indigenous repertory and the cultural continuity that obtained, even in the midst of social upheaval, were not achieved by any myopic or sentimental view of what musical forces were required to express and embody this interesting branch of French operatic art. On the contrary, the Comédie-Italienne had reason to be proud of the better works written for it, opéras comiques that were taken up in cities and towns all over the civilized world, and whose scores were often, even later, seen as touchstones of taste and quality. It had even more reason to chafe under the financial and artistic restrictions imposed on it until 1791 by the Paris Opéra. Without these, some most exceptional pieces would have been created. Notwithstanding this, the Registres show that the orchestra and chorus mirrored the experiment and expansion evinced in the theater's dramatic output. The musicians were not an ensemble dedicated to the polished perfection of a rich patron's favored repertory. The orchestra was neither "great" nor negligible, but multipurpose and overworked. It suffered exactly the same pressures of tension and complacency as any of today's groups at once salaried and pensioned, but forced to perform publicly five, if not six or seven nights per week: except for the most important religious festivals (e.g., 24 and 25 December) and during Lent, the Comédie-Italienne entertained Paris daily.

Notes

I should like to thank the School of Fine Art and Music, University of East Anglia, for the provision of research grants towards this study. Dr. M. Elizabeth C. Bartlet kindly drew my attention to the existence of the Registres some years ago, which she had then recently finished classifying. I thank her also for her scrutiny of a draft of the present paper.

1. Neal Zaslaw, "Toward the Revival of the Classical Orchestra," *Proceedings of the Royal Musical Association* 103 (1976-77):170, 180.

2. Eugène Borrel, "L'orchestre du Concert Spirituel et celui de l'Opéra de Paris, de 1751 à 1800, d'après 'Les Spectacles de Paris'," in *Mélanges d'histoire et d'esthétique musicales offerts à Paul-Marie Masson* (Paris, 1955), 2:9-15.

3. The wider importance of opéra comique has long been recognized in German scholarship, e.g., Heinz Wichmann, *Grétry und das musikalische Theater in Frankreich* (Halle, 1929).

4. Emile Campardon, *Les Comédiens du Roi de La Troupe Italienne pendant les deux derniers siècles* (Paris, 1880), 2:350-58; Pierre Louis Duchartre, *The Italian Comedy*, tr. R.T. Weaver (London, 1929; rpt. New York, 1966), pp. 114-16, etc.; Pierre Peyronnet, "Un thème privilégié des Comédiens-Italiens à Paris: la jalousie," in *Studies on Voltaire and the Eighteenth Century*, 192 (Oxford, 1980):1463-68.

5. See "Paris" §IV,3, and "Théâtre de la Foire," in *The New Grove Dictionary of Music and Musicians*.

6. Information kindly communicated by Nicole Wild.

7. Clarence D. Brenner, *The Théâtre Italien, its Repertory 1716-1793*, University of California Publications in Modern Philology 63 (1961):35.

8. Duchartre, *The Italian Comedy*, p. 307.

9. An engraving and plan of the theater will be found at the end of volume 2 of *Le Théâtre de l'Hôtel de Bourgogne* by S. Wilma Deierkauf-Holsboer (Paris, 1970).

10. Thomas-Simon Gueullette, *Notes et souvenirs sur le Théâtre-Italien au XVIIIe siècle*, ed. J.E. Gueullette (Paris, 1938; rpt. Geneva, 1976), pp. 174-75.

11. Engravings as plate 3 of Alexis Donnet et al., *Architectonographie des Théâtres* (Paris, [1820]).

12. Antoine D'Origny, *Annales du Théâtre Italien* (Paris, 1788; rpt. Geneva, 1970), 3:73.

13. Georges Cucuel, "Notes sur la Comédie Italienne de 1717 à 1789," *Quarterly Magazine of the International Musical Society (Internationale Musikgesellschaft)* 15 (Oct.-Dec. 1913):154-66. The author's early death deprived us of what surely would have been definitive work in this area.

14. See note 7. The Registres are in the Bibliothèque de l'Opéra, Paris.

15. Some Registres, smaller in size, are simply daybooks, containing the takings at the door with titles of works acted: R. 52, R. 65, R. 75, R. 84, R. 85. The Registres for 1784-85 and 1800-01 are missing altogether. Some detailed information from Registres of the Revolution, Consular and Empire periods is in M. Elizabeth C. Bartlet, "Méhul and Opera during the French Revolution, Consulate and Empire: a source, archival and stylistic study," Ph.D. diss., University of Chicago, 1982.

16. *Les Spectacles de Paris... 1785*, p. [iv]: AVIS DU LIBRAIRE. Even *Les Spectacles... 1794*, the last of the initial run, said its deadline was the August preceding. In fact no issues then appeared before An 8 (1799-1800) when the title became *Almanach des Spectacles de Paris*.

17. The seven committee members were nominated directly by the Duc de Richelieu. An earlier committee of five members operated from 1774: Brenner, *The Théâtre Italien*, p. 13. However, Brenner (p. 28) seems not to have taken account of the 1781 script selection system.

18. Registre 76, June, *Mandement* 13 etc. But the theater used a piano in 1779 for a work by Duni: "Payé au Sr. Dubois pour accord. pret et port de clavecin et Piano forté pour l'Ecole de la jeunesse suivant l'arrêté du 3 dud. [i.e., November]... 19 l[ivres]-16 [sols]" (Registre 63, November, *Mandement* 6).

19. See the edition of Grétry's *La Rosière de Salency* in the forthcoming series *French Opera in the Seventeenth and Eighteenth Centuries*, ed. Barry S. Brook (New York).

20. Constant Pierre, *Histoire du Concert Spirituel 1725-1790* (Paris, 1975), p. 325 (concert no. 1118).

21. . Registre 79, Floréal *Mandement* 25; Prairial *Mandement* 17; Messidor *Mandement* 12; Thermidor *Mandement* 9. The conductor was "Berton," perhaps Henri-Montan Berton; the period covered was March to August.

22. André E.M. Grétry, *Mémoires ou Essais sur la Musique* (Paris, Pluvôise An V; rpt. New York, 1971), 1:161.

23. *Correspondance littérarire, philosophique et critique par Grimm, Diderot, Raynal, Meister, Etc.*, ed. Maurice Tourneux (Paris, 1877-92), 9:439.

24. Michael Kelly, *Reminiscences*, ed. Roger Fiske (London, 1975), pp. 146-47. This visit of Kelly's ended in mid-March 1787.

25. T.S. Gueullette, *Notes et souvenirs*, p. 167.

26. For example, *Les Aveux indiscrets* and *Blaise le savetier* (1759), *Le Maître en droit* and *Le Soldat magicien* (1760) and *On ne s'avise jamais de tout* (1761).

27. Cucuel, "Notes sur la Comédie Italienne," p. 165, and the chapter "Les Clarinettes" in his *Etudes sur un orchestre au XVIIIe siècle* (Paris, 1913), pp. 11-23: "After the death of La Pouplinière [1762] the role of the clarinet became more important, as if the best instrumentalists had suddenly been liberated" (p. 21).

28. Dr. Bartlet thinks this may have been in respect of the ballets, as is the case with single *répétiteurs* in the next two decades.

29. The Registres never specify who acted in which play or opéra comique on a given evening. We know the identity of the Italian players; apart from anything else the retirement of seven of their number in 1770 owing to the decline in popularity of their art was well publicized. Yet the Italians seem sometimes to have acted in opéra comique, for example on 13 February 1766 (R. 47) when De Hesse, Champville and Balletti acted in *Le Maître en droit* and *La Fée Urgèle*.

30. Michel Brenet, *Grétry, sa vie et ses oeuvres* (Paris, 1884), p. 80.

31. Both clarinetists had been active in Paris since 1753. See G. Cucuel, *La Pouplinière et la musique de chambre au XVIIIe siècle* (Paris, 1913; rpt. New York, 1971), pp. 331, 339, 348.

32. Paris, Bibliothèque de l'Opéra, Res. 1025 (2), entry for 30 March 1789.

33.   Registre 66: the names of four of the five were associated with brass instruments: Neufer, Ernest, Braun, Heina, Wunderlich. Information on Benda's score was provided by the late John D. Drake.

34.   Campardon, *Les Comédiens du Roi,* 2:352-53.

35.   D.P. Charlton, "Orchestration and Orchestral Practice in Paris, 1789-1810," Ph.D. diss., Cambridge University, 1973, pp. 114-20.

36.   Borrel, "L'orchestre du Concert Spirituel..."

37.   Zaslaw, "Toward the Revival of the Classical Orchestra," p. 180 and note 47.

38.   *Almanach général de tous les spectacles* (Paris, 1791), p. 54.

39.   Méhul, *Stratonice* (1792) and *Mélidore et Phrosine* (1794) are the first.

40.   Zaslaw, "Toward the Revival of the Classical Orchestra," p. 172.

Tändelnde Lazzi: On Beethoven's Trio in D Major, Opus 70, No. 1

Joseph Kerman

Beethoven's Piano Trio in D major, composed in 1808, published as the first half of opus 70 in 1809, and soon thereafter provided with the sobriquets *"Fledermaustrio"* and *"Geister,"* has been poorly treated in the Beethoven literature. Bibliographical control in such matters is a chimera, of course, but a conscientious scan has not turned up more than one or two articles or sections of books in which the music is discussed in any sustained way. The one important recent article devoted to the Trio does not treat the music extensively, for in "Stages in the Composition of Beethoven's Piano Trio Op. 70, No. 1" Alan Tyson had his hands full dealing with the sketches and the newly-emerged autograph.[1] His study was a breakthrough—a crest breaking on the new wave of Beethoven scholarship, one might say—in that here for the first time a long draft in a sketchbook was identified confidently as the precise source from which Beethoven derived the autograph; and I admire it. But I have had occasion to remark before on the absurd situation in which the Beethoven bibliography grows by several hundred items every year, year in year out, while major works remain undiscussed in any kind of analytical detail.

One discussion of the "Ghost" Trio is, however, famous and distinguished. This is E.T.A. Hoffmann's review of the original edition of opus 70, published in the *Allgemeine Musikalische Zeitung* of 1813. Parts of this review and parts of Hoffmann's even more famous 1810 review of the Fifth Symphony went to make up the article "Beethoven's Instrumental Music" which appeared in the *Fantasiestücke in Callots Manier* of 1814 and was widely influential. But in recasting his work in a musical journal for a literary collection, Hoffmann not surprisingly left out the bulk of his technical analysis in both articles (and much of what he left has sometimes been excised by later editors). Carl Dahlhaus has recently stressed in several of his writings how Hoffmann's reviews combine romantic metaphysical speculation with detailed, sometimes bar-by-bar analyses. There are about 3500 words of such technical writing in the original Fifth Symphony review and about 1500 words on each of the opus 70 trios, plus music examples and lengthy musical *Beilagen*. Today's rigorous musical analysts would probably characterize Hoffmann's work as mostly "description," rather than analysis proper, and they would have a point; Schenker certainly had no use for Hoffmann. But they would probably also grant that Hoffmann has some penetrating things to say especially about thematic derivations and relationships, and also that he interrupts his technical discourse with metaphorical and valuative statements only rarely—though always with calculated effect. And they should honor him, describer or analyst, whichever he may be, as a founding father of their discipline.

Hoffmann as a writer on music has his low and high styles: on the one hand music-analytical nuts and bolts, on the other great edifices of aesthetic legislation reaching up into the spirit realm. Here is a part of his conclusion to the review of the "Ghost" Trio, following his analysis of the finale (my italics):

> Notwithstanding the geniality that prevails in the entire Trio, not even excepting the melancholy Largo, Beethoven's genius is still earnest and solemn. It is as though the Master feels that man could never speak of deep, mysterious matters—even when the spirit, intimately familiar with such matters, feels itself exalted with gladness and joy—in ordinary words, but only in sublime, noble language. The dance of the Priests of Isis must be a supremely exultant hymn! This reviewer, too, is convinced that where music operates only through itself and not, let us say, towards some specified dramatic end, pure instrumental music ought to shun *insignificant facetiousness* and *trifling japes*. What a profound mind seeks, for the presentiment of joy—a joy which, coming hither from unknown regions, more glorious and beautiful than anything here in our constrained world, kindles a wondrous inner life in the heart—is a higher expression than can be imparted by mere words, which pertain only to the sphere of limited earthly feelings.[2]

While such sentiments are not unfamiliar in romantic writings about music, here they seem strangely ill-fitted to their immediate context. *Gemüthlichkeit* is not the word one would have thought of for the ghostly slow movement of this Trio, and the finale, which Hoffmann has just finished analyzing and praising for its originality, organicism and powerful stormy quality, can hardly be said to shun the *Spasshafte* (let us not presume to refer to *tändelnden Lazzi*...). To be sure, Hoffmann was always rather slow to respond to the unbuttoned side of Beethoven's genius. In his review of the Fifth Symphony, he remarks dryly that the abrupt double bass outbursts beginning the second half of the Trio may strike some people as playful, "but for the reviewer a sinister feeling was awakened."[3] Nevertheless, a warning against facetiousness in music coming hard on a discussion of the "Ghost" Trio finale seems very curious indeed, so much so as to implant the suspicion that Hoffmann may have been covertly pleading with Beethoven not to let his sense of humor get the better of him.

If I now enumerate a number of points—six, to be exact—that seem to me decidedly playful, it is not that I wish to show up Hoffmann. On the contrary, if this essay were not dedicated to Gerald Abraham, I would wish to dedicate it with respect to Hoffman's memory. My main wish is to get something down on paper about a brilliant movement which has been all but ignored by critics since Hoffmann's pioneering review. What follows will go into detail at some points, though of course it is not conceived of as a full critical study. Like Hoffmann, I shall indulge myself in some rather lengthy musical examples.

1. While Hoffmann rightly observed that Beethoven's finales tend to build up activity and pressure continuously,[4] this tendency need not be incompatible with a continuous display of high spirits in the best classical tradition for finales. The Eighth Symphony (which Hoffmann did not yet know) is a perfect example. For each of his first four symphonies—though not, as it happens, for the next two, completed just before the "Ghost" Trio—Beethoven had devised (or chosen) themes with witty or jocular features of one kind or another. The finale of the "Ghost" Trio has a decidedly amusing theme, and amusement is compounded by the way the theme is treated later in the movement.

Ex. 1

One point of wit within the theme (ex. 1, theme 1) is provided by the accompaniment motive in bars 1-2, 3-4,[5] 5-6, and 6-7. This Beethoven derived by free inversion from the opening motive in the melody, construed as starting with the first downbeat—which is indeed where the theme starts at most of its later reappearances and transformations, eliding or omitting the opening upbeat leap of a sixth. Another source of wit is the rhythmic situation. The first *fermata* comes unexpectedly soon and extends a slightly unexpected harmony; but what is most unexpected is the irregular way the harmony resolves, with the F♯ holding fast and the A♯ turning back to A♮. As an aberrant check to rhythmic continuity, a *fermata* generally sets up somewhat momentous expectations, at least in this style, and so when a *fermata* comes on a chord demanding resolution—such as, typically, the 6-4 chord of a cadenza—the music can seem to slip on a banana peel if that resolution is thwarted. Here, rather more subtly, it seems about to take a pratfall but lands insouciantly on its feet.

There is no problem about the resolution of the second *fermata;* its dominant harmony is simply prolonged in the sequel. It contributes to the whimsical rhythmic instability of the theme nonetheless, by insistently renewing the slow-down already suffered in bar 4, and by renewing it a bar early—or is it only two beats early, or even one? This second slow-down is less sudden than the first. The music seems to be getting under way by a series of very odd fits and starts.

(In the first movement of the Trio, too, the music hardly has a chance to get under way before it stops unexpectedly. No *fermata* is specified, but the opening flurry of eighths and sixteenths *all'ottava* slows down to a single high note, F♮, held by the cello all through bars 5 and 6. The effect, enhanced by a diminuendo, might be described as that of a "written-out *fermata.*" Something similar occurs also in the "Archduke" Trio, opus 97. As in the finale of the "Ghost" Trio, in the first movement the stop comes on an unexpected (implied) harmony: although in bar 5 the F♮ suggests nothing stranger than the tonic minor chord, in bar 6 it is sea-changed into E♯ by the low octave B♭ quietly set under it by the piano. F♯(E♯) and B♭ resolve to a D-major 6-4 chord. The widely-spaced hollow fifth or doubly augmented fourth in bar 6 is a wonderful and very original sonority; Beethoven does *not* add the D and G♯ which would turn it into a conventional German sixth, both because that would sound tawdry and because what he is doing is gradually building up the texture from the opening octaves through two parts to three and up. In any case, the resolution of the first *fermata* in the finale seems doubly whimsical when one remembers the rich and mysterious resolution at the analogous point in the first movement.)

2. The finale is in sonata form. Common as it may be in sonata-form movements for elements of theme 1 to return somewhere in the second group, it is hard to think of another case in which this happens just in the way it does here. Example 2 shows the situation. An overlapping *fortissimo* phrase in A major simulates the opening gesture of theme 1, sweeping its way up to a *fermata* on another slightly remote chord. This time the resolution of the held chord is normal in harmonic terms; in thematic terms, however, the sequel is not the second phrase of theme 1 but a version of the first. In other words, what had originally been a 4-bar antecedent in the tonic now appears as an 8-bar consequent starting in the supertonic, B minor.

Ex. 2

This is such a disconcerting and delightful twist that Beethoven decided to repeat the passage with yet another twist. In bars 95ff. the upward sweep leads to a stop on a different chord, whereupon the piano right hand spins out a deceptively innocent-sounding cadenza-like passage, nine bars long, leading to the antecedent-become-consequent in a very different key, the flat supertonic, B♭ major. "This [passage] must be played so light and equal that it may appear like a free improvisation," writes Czerny in his disquisition upon the correct performance of Beethoven's piano music, "*but yet so strictly in time* that the accompanists [*sic*] may come in at exactly the right moment."[6] Sooner or later *fermatas* in Beethoven themes are nearly always filled out by cadenzas or cadenza-like passages, as has happened here. There are prominent examples in both of the symphonies he had just completed: the famous oboe cadenza in the recapitulation of the first movement of the Fifth, and a cadenza in tempo for the first violins at a closely analogous point in the Sixth (bars 282-88).

In the Trio Beethoven works his way back from B♭ and F to A in a vigorous octave passage with shifting accents (not illustrated). The juxtaposition of sharp and flat regions embodied in this part of the exposition is exactly mirrored in the recapitulation, where E minor/E♭ major leads to D as previously B minor/B♭ major had led to A. And in both exposition and recapitulation the flat region is anticipated by momentary features in the bridge passages, which include *fortissimo* outbursts on F♮ and B♭ respectively.

(In the first movement of the Trio, too, flat and sharp regions had been juxtaposed, first of all in the F♮ and F♯ that we have already discussed within the first theme itself. In the first movement—as in the finale—the bridge passage in the exposition includes a *fortissimo* outburst on F♮. And as in the finale, this is mirrored in the recapitulation: it is not mirrored exactly, though, but more powerfully, since the first theme group is now extended in such a way as to lead into a long cantabile passage in B♭, which in effect crowds out the original bridge material. F♮/F♯ and B♭/♮ flicker in the trills preceding the final cadences of the exposition and recapitulation, respectively. F is also an important key area in the development section. The whole treatment of the flat regions is more searching here—more earnest and solemn, perhaps, as Hoffmann would have wished—and wittier in the finale, where Beethoven is carefully saving a punch-line for the coda.)

3. The development section of the finale is relatively short. It emerges out of an overflow of energy uncontained by the exposition, culminating in yet another *fermata,* after which the main subsection of the development applies fragmentation technique to the secondary theme (shown beginning in bars 9-10 of example 1). Basically, in large structural terms, the next and last subsection amounts to a straightforward dominant pedal, 18 bars long, preparing for the recapitulation. Seldom, however, has such a pedal at such a formal juncture been bodied out in so surprising a fashion.

The passage is illustrated in example 3. It was also singled out for illustration by Hoffmann, who noted that the triplets constitute an entirely new feature in the movement. In this version of the first theme, every musical element has been simplified. Its rhythmic anomalies have been smoothed out into steady quarters for the first four bars (with one triplet) and steady triplets thereafter, all over an ostinato in halves. Its harmonic subtleties have been cancelled out by a regular two-bar alternation of tonic and dominant harmonies. Its phrase structure has been simplified from an *a b* pattern to *a a'*; the original consequent has been dropped and a new one added which is simply a variation of the antecedent with a new cadence.[7]

The process here is nothing other than "that ancient device of theme-transformation" which is usually associated with the name of Liszt, and which Gerald Abraham once defined by reference to that music-hall science, but dimly remembered in Britain in the 1930s, "by which a black felt ring ingeniously twisted into the shapes of various characteristic hats enabled the performer to impersonate now Napoleon, now a Nonconformatist minister."[8] To this memorable definition, in which musicology draws upon chapeaugraphy, a historical corollary may be added. The nineteenth-century process of theme-transformation treats relatively brief themes within symphonies, sonatas, and so on, in one of the ways traditional for the treatment of full tunes in variation sets—not the "decorative" or ornamental way, but the

Ex. 3

"characteristic" way, by which a tune is altered in tempo, rhythm, mode, dynamics, etc., so as to register some new unexpected mood. Beethoven had always known about this way of writing variations, like Byrd and Bach before him. As early as 1802, he experimented with a set of variations consisting exclusively of "characteristic" members—they are even all in different keys: the Six Variations on an Original Theme, opus 34, a work of which he was evidently quite proud. Napoleon appears in C minor. Outside of variation sets, however, there are few examples of theme-transformation in Beethoven.[9] This one in the "Ghost" Trio is certainly one of the most striking.

For here the elegant and witty first theme of the finale has been transformed into something that is clearly intended to sound naive and rustic, and therefore by definition a little comical. Countrified strains of just this kind become a feature of Beethoven's writing rather suddenly in 1824-26, as I pointed out in my book on the Beethoven quartets. Quite like example 3 is the first little tune in the trio of the Presto movement from the C♯-minor Quartet, opus 131, in which again both the cadences after *a* and *a'* are harmonically stable—both come on tonic chords—but only the second is melodically so. Tunes of this kind are much less easy to find in Beethoven's earlier music, however; and it may come as a surprise to find almost as many in the minor mode as in the major. But of course there are two such tunes in the major in the third movement of the "Pastoral" Symphony, where they contribute to the peasant merry-making. And with the first of these, the F-major tune for oboe with bassoon accompaniment which Schindler said was meant to evoke the drowsy blunders of village musicians, we might indeed presume to refer to *tändelnden Lazzi*. The Sixth Symphony and the "Ghost" Trio offer another example of two works sketched in close conjunction which, for all their very considerable differences, share certain particular musical ideas occupying Beethoven at the time.

(Was it from the finale of Beethoven's D-major Trio, one wonders, that Brahms got the idea for the famous theme-transformation in *tranquillo* triplets shortly before the recapitulation in the finale of his D-major Symphony? A most unrustic moment.)

4. We can perhaps backtrack for a moment, just long enough to observe that the official "second theme," shown in example 4, is another rustic item quite similar in spirit to those we have been discussing, although the disposition of the cadences after the *a* and *a'* phrases is less naive than in example 3, less static and more propulsive (as makes sense for a sonata-form second theme, especially such a short one). Actually I illustrate this fragment mainly in order to illustrate Beethoven's show-off counterpoint. Notice how this theme, too, starts with an accompaniment motive in inversion, and a pretty jokey one at that, how the piano perseveres with the inversion after sashaying or dribbling past a 6-4 chord, and how very distinctly we are given to hear the characteristic motive of the *first* theme a moment later.

Contrapuntal and thematic work of this kind is sometimes taken as evidence of constructive intent and intellectual power. That surely would be too solemn a way of looking at the action here (or at the appearance of the inverted inversion motive in example 2, bars 90, 92, 94, etc.). A composer to whom counterpoint had never come easily, at first, is now able to improvise all sorts of *lazzi* with it; he is also able to convey something of his own pleasure at this new virtuosity. (The counterpoint is not literally improvised, but it was probably invented at high speed while the autograph was being written. The whole compositional process, Tyson suggests, was unusually rapid.) How seriously Beethoven took these contrapuntal appendages in example 4 seems indicated by the abruptness with which he dropped them, one and all. His second presentation of the little theme, with its chords safe in root position and its workaday piano figuration, sounds rather like a plain man's good-natured answer to the dandified airs of the first (bars 63ff.).

Ex. 4

5. *Fermatas* in Beethoven themes, as has already been remarked in connection with example 2, are sooner or later nearly always expanded into cadenzas or cadenza-like passages. But it is also true that sooner or later these *fermatas* are nearly always cancelled, too—usually later, in the coda, so that the motion of theme 1 can carry through strongly and unequivocally to a firm conclusion.[10] (Everyone will immediately think of the first movement of the Fifth Symphony as an exception. It is only half an exception, though, since the second *fermata*— the one filled in by the oboe cadenza in the recapitulation—is indeed expunged from the coda.) In the finale of the "Ghost" Trio Beethoven has in fact divested theme 1 of its *fermatas* early in the exposition and recapitulation, at bars 28ff. and 238ff., and of course also in its transformation at the end of the development section, as we have seen. Never mind; he is saving his most pointed demonstration of the theme's potential for rhythmic normalcy till the usual place, the coda. The demonstration is a double one and, needless by now to say, doubly hilarious.

The coda begins (ex. 5) with theme 1 sounding blunter than ever before, partly because the neat inversion motive has at last been put to rest. When the melody reaches high C♯ there is no *fermata* but instead an extra bar; the *fermata* is measured out exactly. There follows an extraordinary passage in which the tricky harmonic progression of bars 4-5 is slowly unpacked in *pizzicato*. Bar 374 adds a seventh to the F♯-major chord; bars 375-77 finally respell A♯ as B♭, etc.; bars 378-80 feint towards a cadence in B♭ minor—a last reference to the flat regions which were opened up in the exposition; bars 381-84 opt for a diminished seventh rather than an augmented sixth; and the D-major sixth chord of bar 5 returns, somewhat shakily, at bar 384. In four more bars we are arrived at a tonic cadence, which is not what happened but what we expected to happen the first time around.

Ex. 5

Yet one more appearance for the first theme: and Beethoven rolls out yet one more inspiration. The tune is broken up in performance bar by bar between the two string instruments, the violin bending a little low to meet the cello reaching up a little high. For him who harkens secretly, as Schumann might have said, there is a special little bonus at bar 391, a special quick smile. This is the one bar of the theme in which the instruments do not alternate; and so the high C♯, far from receiving a corona, is in this last appearance decidedly eclipsed.

The fascinating effect of the violin-cello alternations in this passage seems to be unique in Beethoven. Its humor is far less broad than that registered by the alternations breaking up the scherzo theme in the Second Symphony, for example, and is in fact hard to account for—hard and dull and flat, no doubt, as is always the case when tiresome people insist on trying to explain jokes. The alternations amuse, I think, because at this tempo they strike us as improbable and precarious; but instead of seeming gauche, they seem as elegant and funny as a pair of aerialists' flailing motions which balance them perfectly on a high wire. Beethoven tried similar thematic break-ups in his later piano trios, though in a serious and even sententious mood: see opus 70, no. 2, Allegretto, bars 51ff. and opus 97, Andante cantabile, 141ff. Then there are wonderfully imaginative examples in the late quartets: see opus 127, Adagio, 39ff.; opus 130, Andante con moto, 14ff. and Alla danza tedesca, 129ff.; opus 131, Andante, 1ff. and Presto, 149ff; opus 132, Assai sostenuto-Allegro, 23ff.; opus 135, Allegretto, 5ff. and Allegro, 54ff. The latter passage, in which yet another country-dance theme is cradled by a freely alternating accompaniment figuration, approaches the original model in the "Ghost" Trio most closely, both in technique—in rhythm, tempo, even key—and in affect.

6. We come finally to the one feature which more than any other, I think, causes the fun in this finale: its metrical ambiguity. Does theme 1 scan in more or less regular two-bar patterns, and if so do the strong beats come at the beginning of the odd or the even bars?

Such questions come up again and again in analyses of Beethoven and all other composers, and they are not always easy to resolve. In a penetrating article devoted to this problem specifically, " 'Extra' Measures and Metrical Ambiguity in Beethoven," Andrew Imbrie reaches different conclusions than did Schenker and Tovey in their metrical analysis of certain passages in the Fifth Symphony and the Piano Sonata in D, opus 10 no. 3 (a work with interesting points of contact with the "Ghost" Trio).[11] Imbrie concludes that in some cases metrical questions ought not to be resolved at all—that the composer may very well have been working deliberately with ambiguity as an expressive element of his language. Themes may not always scan the same way at all their reappearances.

In the "Ghost" finale, things seem fairly straighforward at the beginning. The *second* and *fourth* bars should be strong because of the *sforzato* and the *fermata,* among other reasons. A shade of ambiguity clouds the fifth bar, though the stress provided by the melody is offset by the bass, unchanged from bar 4; by the *seventh* bar, however, Beethoven has plunged the meter into a cheerful chaos. According to this scansion, incidentally, the *sixth* bar is strong (note the *crescendo*) and so the F♯ chord in bar 4 can be heard deceptively resolving to the subdominant in bar 6, rather than to the tonic in bar 5—a progression that surprised and amused us earlier. The rather odd C♮s play into the subdominant resolution.

This scansion is certainly forced by the rustic information of theme 1 at the end of the development section (ex. 3). The accompanying half-note ostinato starts one bar ahead of the melody, of which the *second* and *fourth* bars are made strong by the regular changes of harmony. But there is more than a suggestion of shifted accents when the tune moves from the cello to the violin. Now the change of harmony at bar 202 to a D-major 6-4 chord seems to make the *first* bar of the theme strong; the second bar is harmonically ambiguous, perhaps, but perhaps we hear it more easily as a (weak) continuation of the 6-4 than as a (strong) new dominant. And in the repeat the *first* bar (bar 206) is strengthened further by the reinforcement of the ostinato by the violin octaves. Scanned in this way, the passage brings out the recapitulation on a weak bar, thus matching the exposition.

The *forte* appearance of the theme in the coda (see ex. 5) comes out on a strong bar, but a reversal of bar-accents must take place at once, for bar 375 must clearly be strong. The scansion of the unpacking episode that follows is baffling; and by the application of a familiar critical plot which some will probably find not amusing in the least, I conclude that Beethoven meant us to be baffled and bemused by our own bafflement. A touch of unusually broad humor, for this movement, is provided by the diminution in bar 387.

The final thematic entrance in bar 388 also comes out on a strong beat (I think), but now the reversal of accents is undercut. This is a particularly delightful and witty passage. Somehow the alternation violin/cello keeps the theme's *first, third, seventh* and *ninth* bars sounding strong; there is now no *sforzato* on the second bar, and I have already suggested why the fourth sounds weaker than before. A shrewd new harmonic-rhythmic detail strengthens the *fifth* bar. Then in the continuation the *eleventh* bar gets an extra accent when the half-note ostinato returns from example 3—in itself a droll gesture in this new context.

Clearly the coda is now careering towards metrical disaster, or at least bathos! The indication *"cresc."* at bar 401 already hints at the change of accent which by 405 is a *fait accompli*. The piece ends strong. It might have been a great joke to end a big piano trio on a weak bar. But it would not have been Beethoven's kind of joke—never, not even in his most unbuttoned mood, not even in a piece that Tyson shows was composed in high fettle and at a great rate.[12]

To read through numerous commentaries on the opus 70 trios from Hoffmann's day to our own is to get a single message, though it is sometimes expressed more explicitly than at other times. Critics almost always seem to view the second trio, in E♭, as a finer work than the first, in D, and in particular they prefer the E♭ finale to the D-major. I think this view requires—how can I say?—review. Apart from its indubitably higher ranking on the scale of *Spasshaftigkeit,* the D-major finale seems to me more finely crafted than its companion. Beethoven's untamed sense of humor, so easily accepted by those Beethovenians who first cut their teeth on Tovey, may actually put off others raised up under sterner masters. Schenker, whose claim to divulge the "true content" of Beethoven's "Eroica" Symphony should never be forgotten or forgiven, could write ten pages of fine print on the finale without so much as suggesting that humor might form any part of that content. We humourists, who cherish the "Eroica" finale, can only chuckle when Nigel Fortune in *The Beethoven Companion* calls the "Ghost" finale "less arresting" than the other movements. It arrests, all right. It is Beethoven's *Musikalischer Spass* without Mozart's malice.

Notes

1. *Proceedings of the Royal Musical Association* 97 (1970-71), 1-20. There is a penetrating discussion of the first movement of the "Ghost" Trio in August Helm's *Beethoven* (Berlin, 1927), pp. 161-76.

2. E.T.A. Hoffmann, *Schriften zur Musik: Nachlese,* ed. Friedrich Schnapp (Munich, 1963), p. 130. I draw on English translations of the *Fantasiestücke* version of this passage which appear in *The Musical Quarterly* 3 (1917), 132 (Arthur Ware Locke) and Strunk's *Source Readings,* pp. 779-80.

3. *Beethoven: Symphony No. 5 in C Minor,* ed. Elliot Forbes (Norton Critical Score, New York, 1971), p. 159.

4. Hoffmann, *Schriften zur Musik: Nachlese,* p. 129.

5. The motive at this point is made explicit in the recapitulation and elsewhere.

6. Carl Czerny, *The Art of Playing the Ancient and Modern Piano Forte Works, Together with a List of the Best Pieces for that Instrument, by All the Celebrated Composers from Mozart to the Present Day, Being a Supplement to the Royal Piano Forte School, op. 500,* tr. John Bishop (London, [1846]), p. 98.

7. Another simplification is the omission of the opening upbeat leap of a sixth; but perhaps we hear that echoed in the new downward sixth between bars 194 and 195, etc.

8. Gerald Abraham, *A Hundred Years of Music* (London, 1938), p. 42.

9. I am indebted to Walter Frisch for the clarification of this and many other issues in musical analysis and criticism. Theme-transformation in the finale of Beethoven's Piano Concerto in C minor is discussed in his *Brahms and the Principle of Developing Variation* (California Studies in 19th-Century Music, II; Berkeley and Los Angeles, 1984), pp. 42-44.

10. See my article "Notes on Beethoven's Codas" in *Beethoven Studies* III, ed. Alan Tyson (Cambridge, 1982), pp. 141-59.

11. In *Beethoven Studies* [I], ed. Alan Tyson (New York, 1973), pp. 45-66.

12.   Reversal of bar accents was also, I think, Beethoven's main reason for the two compositional changes that Tyson discusses and illustrates in his *PRMA* article (note 1). In his example 3, an early version of the "fragmentation" subsection of the development (bars 165-93), Beethoven corrected the autograph so as to cut out one bar, thus assuring that the 8-bar lead-in to the "transformation" sub-section (my example 3) comes out on a strong bar, bar 185. In Tyson's example 5, from the big draft in the sketchbook which Beethoven followed when preparing the autograph, the passage leading from F major to A major near the end of the exposition (bars 117-26) was again abbreviated by one bar, in two half-bar segments.

Russians in Venice: The Visit of the *Conti del Nord* in 1782

Elsie and Denis Arnold

Venice was perforce eastwards looking. Her prosperity was built on the trade from the Middle East and beyond; she was a bulwark against the heathens, and until the last years of the republic she was still interested in links with Russia. The whole relationship with Russia came into question in the 1780s when the final setting up of embassies became a serious issue; and by a happy chance, the heir apparent to the throne, Catherine the Great's son Pavel Petrovich and his bride Maria Feodorovna, the Princess of Württemberg, proposed a visit to the Serenissima. It was to be an informal visit, preserving a *perfetto incognito*. The visitors merely asked that they be able to enjoy "tutti li divertimenti e Spettacoli del Paese."[1] But the Venetians grasped the opportunity and decided that the visitors should be entertained at public expense. So they put into operation their procedures for receiving important guests. These had been evolved throughout the years, for their first official guests could be traced back to the fourteenth century.[2] They had been so frequent throughout the eighteenth century that a routine had been established. In the distant past, the nobility had been entertained at a banquet in the Arsenale and a small sum of money for incidental expenses had been put at their disposal. Now a group of noblemen, generally of some official office, were told to make arrangements.

For the visit of the *Conti del Nord* (the *incognito* of the Russians) four very distinguished partricians were given this task. This quartet—Francesco Gritti, Piero Mocenigo, Nicolò Tron and Alvise Mocenigo—was given no concrete figure of what to spend; the official views were merely that it was necessary to have "alcune Feste di Ballo ne' Teatri, ed altri Pub[bli]ci Spettacoli,"[3] so the committee set to work with a will. The visitors were in Venice for not quite a week, from 19 to 25 January. What was packed into these few days was incredible.[4] An opera at the Teatro San Benedetto, a cantata concert at the Casino filarmonico in the Procuratie Nuove, a visit to the Arsenale followed by a grand dinner again at the Teatro San Benedetto, a bullfight in the Piazza, a regatta, the gymnastic display known as the *Forza d'Ercole*[5]—these were only some of the arranged events. Far from being truly incognito, the royalty (always an attraction for republicans) were introduced to most of the top rank of Venetian society, the ladies considering it their greatest good fortune if they could dance with the heir apparent to the throne of All the Russias.

At the end of it all, the *Conti del Nord* left for Padua and then southern Italy. The Venetians were left to count the cost—which was enormous. There were the inevitable recriminations. How had such great expenditure been incurred, one Senate committee wanted to know.[6] The committee of four produced its figures, in the greatest detail, shrugging its collective shoulders in the way all bursars do to this day. "If you want to give the visitors lavish entertainment, this is what is costs!" From this defense we can glean a great deal about the payment of musicians and how concerts and opera performances were arranged.

The opera house of San Benedetto was the first to benefit. The new opera had not yet been prepared so there were additional expenditures. The relevant entries in the state treasurer's accounts tell us what it amounted to:

	Lire
Per restauri occorso nel Teatro di San Benedetto	990.23
All'Impresario dell'Opera in San Benedetto Michiel Dall' Agata p[er] Decoraz[io]ne delle Scene, e rinovazione del Vestiario	3300
Per l'aggiunto di Otto Ballarini figurati	495
Per ricognizione adesso Dall'Agata	82.12
Acquisto Palchi	2015.18
[Decoration of the Palchi]	1869.19[7]

Indeed, the decoration and refurbishment of the two boxes had amounted to major building works; it also seems as though the opera had been lavishly produced because of the royal visitors, with the very large sum for scenery and dresses, and the additional eight dancers. In any case, the impressario Dall' Agata had gained over 8000 lire from the state towards the upkeep of the theater and the expenditure on its main production. It is not known whether there was any additional fee for "Sig[nor] Maestro Borghi Romano,"[8] who had composed the new opera seria *Arbace*.

The composer of the other *pièce de résistance* probably did better. This was the cantata called *Il Telemaco nell' Isola Ogigia,*[9] music by one Signor Mortellari, and was performed by some eighty girls from the four Conservatories. This was a usual spectacle offered by the state to royal visitors. It might be thought to be a usual piece of Venetial economy, since surely this would cost little. The girls and Conservatories would expect a tip or donation from the visitors but nothing from the state.[10] It was not without its expenses, however, as a sheet marked "nota di Spesa per la Cantata delle Figlie dei quattro Ospitali nella casa dei Filarmonici li 20 Gen[nai]o 1781 M.V." reveals:

	Lire
Copia di Musica come da Polizza No. 1	813.10
Sig[no]ri da Ponte, e Foschi assistenti a tutte le prove, e sera sud[de]tta per accordare Violini, Violoncelli, e Violoni	264
Sig[no]re Pasini, e de Mezzo Maestri di Canto alla Pietà, ed Ospedaletto	264
Vestiano a No. 82 Figlie come da Polizza No. 110	10400
Coperta No. 30 libri cantata in seta, et oro come Polizza No. 111	670
A Placa per nolo cembali, a loro accordatura, Lettorini [music stands], spese, e sua recognizione come da Polizza No. 1111	396
In Candelle, majoli, et altre piccole spese occorenti per le Figlie	148.7
Poeta	330
Al Sig[nor] Maestro Mortellari [composer]	1760
Spese fatte nelle Peote, e Burchiello per condure le Figlie alle prove a sera sud[dett]a	964
Alle Sig[no]re Cubli, e Lucovich de Mendicanti come assistenti per accordare i Violoni, Violoncelli, e Violone, e Maestro di Canto	264
All Sig[no]r D. Franc[esc]o Menegati direttore della Cantata	330
	16635.17*

[*sic* in the document; the correct total comes to 16603.8]

Ho recevuto io [il] sottosc[ritt]o il saldo del p[rese]nte C[o]nto
D. Franc[esc]o Menegatti[11]

The "Polizza No. 1" is in fact the copyists' bill which shows the scale of the operation: 43 members of the orchestra, with an average of eight pages per part. But the presentation copy for the royalty was presumably handsome in view of the cost of the binding. The singing teachers Pasini and de Mezzo (the latter was very well known in Venice) did well; they probably taught the choir. Placa, who provided the harpsichords, was one of the main dealers in keyboard instruments. Interestingly, the fee for the composer was high. 1760 lire was about 250 ducats, which although not as much as for an opera, may be compared favorably with 600 ducats for the annual stipend of the maestro di capella of San Marco around this time. By this standard, the fee of 330 lire for the poet seems low, while that to the Director of Music (Direttore della Cantata) must be one of the earliest recorded for a conductor, since it might be expected that the composer would normally have performed this task. It remains that the largest single item was the expenditure for the girls' costumes and that when this is subtracted from the total, the actual cost of the music was just over 6000 lire or nearly 1000 ducats; and this when the cost of the services of orchestra and choir themselves was nil! Did the girls eat their way through the biscuits made at a cost of 650 lire "per la Sera della Prova Generale della Cantata" recorded elsewhere in the accounts? One would like to think so.

The cantata itself is lost, although there are a few examples of such pieces still extant. If it was anything like the work provided for the visit of the King of Naples in 1791,[12] it was an *azione scenica,* virtually a short opera in two acts scored for full orchestra with three soloists and, in that work, a SATB chorus. The solo parts are florid, the choruses solidly homophonic, with a surprising amount of recitative. The cantata for the Russians was described by one chronicler as given by:

> 80 Figlie, tratte da 4 Conservatorij della Città, tutte vestite in uniforme, che divise in due ampie orchestre, chi col canto, e chi col suono di varj Strumenti formarono un gradevole trattenimento per circa un' ora, e mezza....[13]

No doubt the visitors had heard nothing like it.

Their visit to the Teatro San Samuele cost the state only 137 lire for the hire of two boxes, though as at San Benedetto the theater had to be redecorated and the republic gave help to the impresario. The dances in the Procuratie Nuove were more profitable to the musicians, the orchestra for the first of them costing 2480 lire, that at the ball in the Teatro San Benedetto 1376 lire, while the third in the Procuratie was obviously a huge affair as the entry in the accounts shows:

> Terza Festa in Procuratia compreso copie de Menuetti, Contradanze, Radoppi di Sinfonie, Composizione di No. 12 Menuetti nuovi e consueto Regalo alli Due Cappi, il tutto come appar di Polizza asistite in mia mano. Lire 3154.[14]

The *polizza* shows the bill from the "fixer" and orchestra leader Santo Trento. The orchestra for the first dance evening consisted of 36 violins, 1 cello, 4 violoni, 2 oboes, 2 flutes, 2 bassoons and 4 horns; for the second evening, 45 violins, 4 oboes, 4 horns, 2 trumpets, 8 violoni, 1 bassoon and 2 timpani players; for the third only 37 violins, 4 oboes, 4 horns, 4 violoni and 1 bassoon. We do not know the payments to the individual players, although some simple division sums show that if the total fees were split reasonably equally, then each player might go away with 5 or 6 ducats per evening—not a bad haul—though they probably earned their money, since the dances went on until the early hours of the morning at least.

The real bonanza for the orchestral players, however, was the final evening of the visit, when there was the "Caccia de Tori" on Piazza San Marco. Not that the principal expenditure was on music. The "Carri Trionfali" and the decoration of the Piazza were extraordinarily lavish, the cost amounting to 36,800 lire.[15] Of this only 2048 lire were paid to the "orchestre de suoni" which "servirono dalle Ore diecanove sino le ore sei della Notte" (2:30 P.M. until 1:30 A.M.). The actual payments to individuals are recorded in the state treasurer's accounts. They reveal an ensemble of 19 trumpets, 38 horns, 28 oboes, 5 flutes, 8 bassoons, 14 trumpets (of whom two were members of the Dragonetti family), 1 cymbals player and a tromba marina. These grand forces were divided into six, each under its own director. The typical payment for the rank and file was 110 lire, while the leaders of sets might go up to about 170 lire. And although the total of these seems to amount to more than the treasurer put into his balance sheet (the payments included those for two rehearsals at San Giorgio [Maggiore]) they still do not form a very large part of the bill for the entertainment as a whole. There were, it is true, some other minor payments. The copyist produced a bill for the parts of "due Marchie, a due orchestre con molte radop[p]i Foglie"; but it was only for 130 lire. The various directors had fees ranging from 374 lire for the principal conductor, Menegatti, to 174 lire for one of the juniors.[16]

During the rest of the celebrations, there was fireworks music for one night; the state paid compensation of 550 lire to the impresario of the Teatro San Benedetto for taking over his opera house for a banquet; the aged Galuppi presented six sonatas to the Russian princess and was rewarded with a gold box;[17] and there were other pieces of music making, including some water music as the visitors went up the Grand Canal. The guests must have departed for Padua and the south in a haze of sound; but all was not finished. At Padua they were to hear the castrato Guadagni in a part he had "created" in Vienna: the Orfeo of Gluck.[18]

These grand celebrations quickly became a legend. Printed descriptions abounded, foreigners wrote home telling of them, the books of ceremonial which the republic kept so that precedents could be established and obeyed contain massive accounts of it all. Did it succeed in its purpose? The committee of noblemen who had organized it clearly thought so. For music, they had outshone the Viennese, who had only provided an inferior opera buffa for the Russians on their way to Venice.[19] The visitors had been very impressed to see "un assemblea Sovrana di Cittadini liberi, governati solamenti dalle leggi, e non dall' arbitrio"[20] and they hoped, it was reported, to see "some of us in Russia, not just as visitors"—in other words, some political rapport was intended. Sure enough, by the end of 1782, Girolamo Ascanio Giustiniani was appointed as Minister (the title of Ambassador was not yet agreed) and he finally set off for Russia in February 1783.[21] So on that account the Venetians' massive expenditure had paid off.

Whether in the long run anyone was any the more prosperous, or whether the Venetian cause in its political ventures was more successful is open to doubt. Fifteen years later no pact or delicate feeling for the balance of power was to save the republic from invasion and demise; nor was it allowed its independence after the defeat of Napoleon. Perhaps, however, it helped to maintain the artistic links between Italy and Russia. It is surely no coincidence that the composer who did most to further the cause of opera in Russia in the early nineteenth century, Catterino Cavos, was a Venetian; nor that he went to St. Petersburg in 1798, during the reign of Pavel, the famous visitor of 1782.

The scale of expenditure on music during the visit must invite some reflection on the changes over the centuries in the Venetian republic's priorities. It had always prided itself "d' acco[m]pagnar le cose temporali con la religione," to use the words of a sixteenth-century commentator.[22] So its visitors usually attended St. Mark's for Mass or Vespers. This was not possible for the Russians, who made their devotions in the Greek Church; and it is noticeable that several of the foreign dignitaries feted by the Venetians were Protestants. Even so, the complete secularization of these celebrations comes as a little surprise to the historian of Venetian music. And a simple comparison of expenditure on secular and sacred music is even more surprising. In the 1760s we have a list of expenditure on the capella of St. Mark's,[23] and although it may have changed in detail by 1782, it was not substantially different. This shows that they spent about 1000 ducats on the main officials—maestro di capella, vice-maestro, organists—1440 ducats on the choir and 2300 ducats on the orchestra. These figures must be approximate, since there was "stiffening" for one or two great occasions and also some occasional payments to the officials for special services. Nevertheless the grand total of 4750 ducats does not seem unrepresentative. The expenditure on music during the "Russian" week is harder to compute. The figures given by the treasurer do not always add up correctly, and it is hard to classify some of the expenditures, such as that for decorations and repairs at the theater. In spite of this we can make an approximation as follows:

	Lire
Cantata	16635
Piazza entertainment	2048 (plus the rehearsals)
Balls	9398
Regatta	1186
Opera	6850
Dinner	470

36537 lire (= c. 5500 ducats)*

*[*sic* in the document; the correct total comes to 36587]

Thus this week's frenetic activities benefitted the musical profession more than the whole year's music at St. Mark's.

If it had been an isolated example of extravagant display it would seem an aberration; but it was, of course, taken as a precedent. In 1784 the King of Sweden came to Venice. He also came in *perfetto incognito* as the *Conti di Haaga,* on his way back from Rome, where the Venetian ambassador found out his wishes, which were very much on the lines of the Russians, interpreted by one official in Venice so that:

> ...il tempo della di lui dimora, tuttavolta ogn' uno di essi lusingasi di aver campo a divertirsi, come fecero allora che passarono di qui le Loro Altezze Reali Duchi del Nort.[24]

So in May there was the same round of theaters, balls, a regatta, and the annual *Fiera dell' Ascensione* in Piazza San Marco was brought forward so that the king could see this traditional festivity. The state again rented and decorated two boxes at the Teatro San Benedetto, where the opera *Ademira* of Lucchesi was given; there was a cantata, *Il Trionfo di Adria,* in a "casino" or club on the Giudecca, arranged by the Pisani family, again with girls from the Ospedaletto and the Pietà in double orchestra.[25]

We do not have the detailed figures for expenditure for this visit, perhaps because at least some of these were borne by the Pisani host; but they were clearly enormous.[26] Nor was this the final occasion of festivities on this scale. In 1791, the Grand Duke of Tuscany and his consort came. This time the arrangements seem to have been left in the hands of the Accademia Filarmonica, who clearly took the visit of the *Conti del Nord* as their model. Here the papers show that musicians again did well.[27] The leader and the "fixer" for the orchestras, for the balls, regattas and so on was paid 528 lire plus seemingly 60 ducats for five days' work (the separate items are not explained), and the rank and file all received 372 lire each for the dance music. The orchestra was 8 violins, 2 violas, 2 basses, flute, 2 oboes, 2 horns and 2 bassoons. Moreover, there seems to have been a room at one of the balls where chamber music was given, for there is a bill for 320 ducats for the "professori che suonarono Concerti, et altri che accompagnorono Concertoni, Concerti, Quartetti, Quintetti ed altro. ..." There was the usual open air music by a strings and wind band of twenty which played marches (as the copyist bill reveals); and the inevitable cantata cost 2777 lire, including a payment of 225 lire to the composer.

We know that the Serenissima had only six more years to run, and such expenditure seems like a rake's progress, the desire to *fare bella figura* overcoming prudence and economy. But this is due to our hindsight and our knowledge of the shaky economy of pre-revolutionary Venice. It must have felt very different in the heady days of the 1770s and 1780s, when Venice still seemed as solid a rock as civilization ever had. And it is worth remembering that when the dam broke, it was not the poor of Venice who rose in protest but those of France. It may be that the Venetian penchant for display and entertainment had something to do with that.

Notes

1. Venice, Archivio di Stato [hereinafter: A.S.V.], Collegio, Ceremoniali, Registro VI, fol. 4.

2. Venice, Biblioteca nazionale marciana, Cod. It. VII-707 (=7898).

3. A.S.V., Collegio, Ceremoniali, Registro VI, fol. 5v.

4. Letters of Signor Luigi Ballarini to Signor Cavalier Delfino, Vol. 1, p. 409, 25 January 1782, Venice Biblioteca Correr ms P.D. 255-b I. Modern edition: *I Conti del Nord a Venezia, due lettere di Luigi Ballarini a Daniele Dolfin Ambasciatore di Venezia a Parigi* (Venice, 1870).

5. Biblioteca nazionale marciana, Cod. It. VII-2212 (=7381).

6. A.S.V., Senato, Corti, Filza 392, entry of 16 February 1781 *mores veneto* [=1782].

7. Ibid.

8. *Notizie del mondo,* 1782, p. 48.

9. Ibid., p. 64.

10. An examination of account books where such payments might be recorded has revealed no payments of any kind.

11. A.S.V., Savio Cassiere, Busta 589.

12. Biblioteca nazionale marciana, Cod. It. VI-586 (=9866).

13. *Descrizione degli spettacoli e grandiose feste datesi in Venezia per occasione della venuta degli Augusti Conti del Nort nel mese di Gennajo 1782* (Venice: Formaleoni, 1782), p. 5.

14. A.S.V., Savio Cassiere, Busta 589.

15. A.S.V., Senato, Corti, Filza 392.

16. A.S.V., Savio Cassiere, Busta 589.

17. *Descrizione degli spettacoli,* p. 13.

18. Ibid., p. 14 ff.

19. A.S.V., Senato, Corti, Filza 392. Entry 16 February 1781.

20. Ibid.

21. A.S.V., Collegio, Ceremoniali, Registro VI, fol. 46.

22. Francesco Sansovino, *Venetia città nobilissima* (Venice: Curti, 1663), p. 493.

23. A.S.V., Procuratoria de Supra, Registro 156, fol. 96 et seq.

24. C. Malagola and G. Dalla Santa, *Il viaggio di Gustavo III Re di Svezia negli stati veneti e nella dominante, 1784* (Venice, 1902), p. 16 ff.

25. Ibid., p. 26.

26. Ibid., p. 27, where they are given as 109,000 lire or approximately 15,000 ducats.

27. Contained in A.S.V., Savio Cassiere, Busta 416.

Carl Maria von Weber in his Diaries

John Warrack

Weber kept a diary for the last 16 years of his life, that is, from 1810 to 1826. Before his journey to Vienna on 10 February 1810 to negotiate *Euryanthe* with Domenico Barbaia, he had become sufficiently worried about the deterioration of his health for him to leave a farewell note for his wife Caroline in a sealed envelope, in case he did not return, and also to make his will. The letter included the instructions, "Meine alten Tagebüchern verbrenne ungelesen." Presumably he wished to spare Caroline the references to the unmistakable nature of the encounters with girls he knew before her; but at all events, she did not burn them, and they were preserved in the family. Weber's son Max Maria made surprisingly little use of them in his biography of 1864, though they were drawn upon extensively for their invaluable details of dates of composition and other matters when Jähns came to prepare his Weber thematic catalog.[1] Jähns also set up a small *Gedenkstätte* in Hosterwitz, the little village a few miles up the Elbe from Dresden where Weber had a summer house (this is, incidentally, the only surviving Weber house apart from his birthplace in Eutin, now a café; his two Dresden town houses were both lost in the destruction of Dresden in 1945). In the Hosterwitz *Gedenkstätte,* Jähns lodged a number of personal relics that remained the property of the Weber family, also setting up in the then Prussian State Library in Berlin a *Weber-Gedächtniszimmer* in which he placed his large collection of scores, manuscripts, books and other musical materials, cataloging them with great meticulousness. The diaries eventually passed into the hands of Carl Maria von Weber's great-great-grandson, Hans-Jürgen von Weber. After the war, he left the diaries in Hosterwitz on long loan, while retaining the ownership and copyright. Still only a very few excerpts had been published, for instance in a short selection of letters and contemporary documents by Otto Hellinghaus[2] and a few in a short "Weber Reader" by the Berlin Weber enthusiast and publisher Hans Dünnebeil.[3]

Then in 1956 the Hosterwitz *Gedenkstätte* was reestablished by Franz Zapf while he was working in the Dresden Stadtmuseum; and as well as organizing the restoration of this house and the reordering of its contents (today forming an excellently arranged and charming little museum), he set himself the task of making a full transcription of Weber's diaries. He completed this in 1966, and after his death the rights to his work were acquired by the Deutsche Verlag für Musik, in Leipzig. Publication *in toto* did not seem a practicable proposition, and there for some years matters rested. The manuscripts of the diaries and Zapf's transcription were later moved to Jähns's collection in what is now the Deutsche Staatsbibliothek in East Berlin, where they are lodged with Jähns's collection of Weberiana. Only recently have plans been made for what may lead to full publication in German and perhaps partial publication in English.

The transcriptions, even though they leave certain matters unresolved, are an invaluable aid to work. Mere familiarity with nineteenth-century German handwriting is insufficient for the easy understanding of Weber's writing; its illegibility was a standing joke among Weber's friends and correspondents,[4] and later extreme haste and then exhaustion and illness caused it to deteriorate into little more than a scrawl. There are places where even Zapf had to confess himself defeated, and there is often a problem over proper names: Zapf, for instance, makes Weber refer to a *Dictionnaire de musique* by one J.J. Roupcar, obviously misreading the old German manuscript double "s" for "p" and misinterpreting the subsequent squiggles, since it is quite clear that Weber meant Rousseau. He knew Rousseau's *Dictionnaire* well, and indeed found the tune for his *Turandot* overture and incidental music in it. However, Zapf performed his task patiently and thoroughly, and anyone working on the diaries must now find his transcription essential in clearing up some obscure points, in interpreting some almost illegible passages, in identifying various forgotten Dresden characters and allusions, above all in providing a generally reliable and quickly readable typescript version of the difficult original.

It must be said that we do not have, in Weber's diaries, one of the major documents of Romanticism, journals that can be compared to, say, those of Delacroix for the insight they give us into the mind of a Romantic artist. Nevertheless, there is much here that sheds light upon Weber and his world, that documents the progress of works, that fills out a portrait of his character and attitudes, that gives glimpses of illustrious and obscure contemporaries. Not least, for those with an interest in the period, the diaries tell us a great deal about the day-to-day life of an early nineteenth-century German Kapellmeister in the detail with which Weber kept all records, and indeed about the domestic economy of the middle classes in these years, in a manner which could be of value to social historians as well as to musicologists. Weber records impressions of his friends and surroundings especially in the early diaries; latterly he was too busy to indulge in much prose, and there are stretches where they contain little more than jottings recording his rehearsals, his working on a new piece, his visit to a friend, his cash accounts. The beginning of the diaries coincides with his expulsion from Stuttgart *persona non grata* as a debtor, when he found it necessary to impose some organization on a life that had been casual and dissolute to the point of involving brief imprisonment; he was also, clearly, wasting his talent catastrophically, despite the friendly efforts of Franz Danzi to recall him to a sense of his vocation. The daily entries in his diaries were obviously to help him organize his expenditure and his professional life, and the device proved helpful enough for him to keep it up for the rest of his life.

Thus, he sums up the first year of the diaries, 1810, with what he calls a *Moralische Übersicht,* as follows. "As a new epoch of my life began for me on the 26th of February, I reckon the beginning of the year from this point. I have given this year six public concerts and played in public eight times." (There then follows a list of the concerts and works). "God has certainly caused me to struggle with many vexations and irritations, but also always brought me into the company of good men who made my life worthwhile again. I can say with calm and truth that I have become *better* over these ten months, and my sorry experiences have taught me a lesson. I have become orderly in my business affairs, and steadily industrious." The accounts show that he had arrived in Mannheim from Stuttgart with 40 gulden in his pocket, plus 25 gulden given him by the friendly police officer who had escorted him over the frontier. Out of concerts and from other receipts in the year he made 1383 gulden, and the expenditure was about 1334, so his balance was about 49 gulden, say around five pounds of contemporary English money. However, 1811 saw the annual profit standing at over 400 gulden, 1812 at over 172, and so on in an upward curve until he was eventually able to open an account with the Prague banker Ballabene in 1815 and to pay off the accumulated Stuttgart debts. This kind of prudence and efficiency is very characteristic of his whole approach to life in his reformed character, as with the detailed register of productions he kept during his Prague intendancy[5] and indeed with his whole methodical approach to the preparation of a new production in the opera house.

The diaries also provide us with a picture of the problems besetting a composer and virtuoso with no fixed post trying to make his living in the early years of the century. Useful contacts had to be sought out; much time had to be spent in antechambers; with luck, an introduction to a well-placed courtier might lead to an invitation to play for the local prince and to the permission to give a concert. All his life Weber was rather too easily dazzled by the aristocracy, and with his not inconsiderable charm he was often able to win his way into the necessary favors and, at worst, accept a setback with good grace. On 13 May 1810 he notes a problem of this kind when there was insufficient time to arrange a concert in Amorbach; the diary records that he was obliged instead to be received by the Prince at seven and after playing and supping to continue playing for the Princess's singing until nearly midnight, and what is more, the diary shows, to pay for his own linkman to light him home afterwards—yet he enjoyed himself and records what a pleasant evening it was. His annoyance is reserved for more serious upsets. Frankfurt, 16 September 1810: "In the afternoon, Madame Blanchard's damned balloon ascent, on account of which the theater opened at seven. In the evening, for the first time, my opera *Silvana,* with much applause, in spite of the scattering of the audience and in spite of the fact that it didn't go well. The drinking chorus was encored, and I was given a curtain call with the ladies, which I didn't take. Because of the late start three arias had to be cut." There are many subsequent entries giving details of how concerts and the first performances of operas were received, and of how he himself played.

It is useful also to have a note of some of the operas which Weber heard, and which were to have a formative influence on his mature style. A great deal of French opéra-comique then formed the staple part of German repertories, as more selectively it was to do in Weber's own repertories in Prague and Dresden; and we can assume that he saw and read through a good many scores, even if he did not coincide in a particular town with the work's performance. But it is good to have confirmation that he actually saw, for instance, Méhul's *Mélidore et Phrosine, Joseph,* and *Uthal,* Paer's *Camilla,* Cherubini's *Elisa,* and *Les Deux Journées,* Dalayrac's *Makdonald* (the German version of *Léhéman*), Winter's *Das unterbrochene Opferfest,* Boieldieu's *Beniowsky,* Bierey's *Rosette,* Mayr's *Ginevra,* Weigl's *Die Schweitzerfamilie,* and Isouard's *Cendrillon,* all by the end of 1812. These were the years when he was absorbing the operatic impressions that he was to put to work for German Romantic opera in his life in Prague from 1813 and eventually in his own mature operas.

There are some vivid glimpses of contemporaries. Though Weber seldom essays a full character study, he can give quite a strong impression, as in the account of his meeting with the Abbé Sterkel on 24 February 1811. "He welcomed me with priestly pathos; I had to sit down at the table opposite him and he as it were preached to me, but when he heard my name, he became rather warmer and told me the story of his life..." Without saying much, Weber leaves an impression of a dry old egoist, in sharp contrast to the warmth and generosity he perceived in Joseph Fröhlich, whose admirable work with students is reflected in Weber's enthusiastic account of the bustle of activity surrounding him and the student orchestra he conducted. Weber was also interested in the clarinetist Georg Reinhardt whom he heard playing with Fröhlich, and whose beautiful tone and execution he praised. This was shortly before he came to know Heinrich Bärmann, with whom he records he gave his first concert on 20th of December of that year, 1811. On 27 September 1812 he noted in his diary the impressions made on him by the playing of Spohr's favorite clarinetist Johann Hermstedt at an evening in Gotha. "In the evening much music-making at Spohr's. Hermstedt played twice, very nicely, a broad, somewhat hollow tone *(einen dikken, beynah dumpfen Ton).* Masters fearful difficulties, but not always attractively; many things horribly against the nature of the instrument. Also a good technique, and he has appropriated a number of violin devices which sometimes work well. But there's a lack of the consummate evenness of tone from top to bottom, and the sublimely tasteful execution, of

Bärmann." This is a useful comment to support the impression we have from the music which Weber wrote for Bärmann that he played with an elegance and a kind of flair that was quite distinct from Hermstedt's rather more traditionally German heaviness of tone. That this did not mean going to an extreme of shrillness is supported by another account of Bärmann, by Georg Sievers, who wrote in the Leipzig *Allgemeine musikalische Zeitung [AMZ]* in a report from Paris in 1818, "his tone is consummate, his *piano* is marvellously effective, and his taste is the most refined I have ever heard from a wind player: this is by means of not even the slightest overloading or shrillness of tone, both of which qualities one finds so often in clarinetists."[6]

These years of travel, 1810 to 1813, produce the best descriptive diary material, as impressions crowd in on a talented young Romantic in his mid-twenties. He always loved travel, and even when mortally sick in London he could write home to his wife Caroline looking forward with pleasure to the actual journey home to her. The fullest descriptions of the natural world are of his visit to Switzerland in 1811. For a man of slender build and small stature, lame from birth, his energy is incredible. He got up at three so as to climb Mount Rigi, hurrying so as get to the top to see the sunrise. "I arrived," he says, "very overheated, but it was pretty cold there and the fire made by our guide was very welcome. At half-past five the sun burst forth in all its splendor, having already gilded the tips of the glacier, and I was richly rewarded for my effort. One cannot describe such things." Nevertheless, one wonders whether Weber did not in fact, 15 years later, describe in music the impression this glorious sunrise had made upon him when he came to write *Oberon* and Reiza's "Ocean! thou mighty monster." Certainly these sensations of the natural world were particularly acute, for nowhere else in the diaries does he give so much space to lyrical descriptions of the mountains, the blue of the sky, the little chapels and wayside altars, the sea of clouds beneath his feet as he stood on the peaks, and the quaintness of the sensation of buying cherries and taking them onto the glassy surface of a great glacier to eat them.

The diaries also give a picture of the tumult of his private life, especially his love life, and it is probably this aspect of them that made him feel that the very jealous Caroline had better burn them unread. The references are discreet but unmistakable. Clearly he was greatly attracted to women, and attractive to them, but he was quick to berate all women when one betrayed him, as seems to have happened with great regularity. In Bamberg in March 1811 he writes of "new evidence that women are worth nothing, *all* of them," this in the course of an entry that records trouble with his future wife Caroline Brandt and someone named Bothe. He seems to have consoled himself sufficiently that day to spend the evening at the theater, seeing Winter's *Opferfest* and greatly admiring a young tenor, finishing the day inevitably in Bamberg's famous inn *Die Rose,* where E.T.A. Hoffmann used to hold court. At this period he was also giving lessons to Fanny Wiebeking, the daughter of a Munich friend, but though very fond of her there seems to have been no romantic attraction, at any rate on his side, for the references to other unhappy encounters are profuse. "Alte Liebe rostet nicht," he quotes, "old love does not grow rusty. If this were true, how happy I should be. But who can trust a woman. No one and I least of all. So I take pleasure in dreams, and rock myself in them." This longing for stability begins to grow stronger, despite his endless disappointments, especially at this time with a girl whom he refers to as Max, and whom he seems at least once to have surprised with a rival. Later, in Berlin, there was a girl he refers to simply by the initial A, who seems to have shown him much tenderness, and when words fail him to describe in actual language what took place between them, he resorts to little snatches of nonsense music. Caroline, reading these entries, could have been left in little doubt as to what was meant. The most pathetic of these affairs was described in painful detail in the diaries of the Prague years, and concerned an obviously very trying singer named Therese Brunetti. As usual, Weber found himself enchanted but also ensnared by her coquettish behavior, and made miserable by her open association with a rival, a wealthy banker. It was not until his friendship with Caroline Brandt ripened into love that he found any sense of security; and as the diaries and letters record, it took a long time for him to persuade her to accept him, for she seems to have had considerable doubts about abandoning her promising career as a singer in favor of this lame, consumptive Kapellmeister. She seems also to have been capable of behaving as capriciously in her way as all the other women with whom Weber came in contact. However, on 4 November 1817 he was able to record, in Dresden, "Early with Lina to confession and communion. Then into wedding clothes, and my Lina astonished by the necklace and shawl I gave her. At twelve we were fetched by Kleinwächter and the doctor, and at half past twelve there occurred the most important event of my life, conducted in a ceremonial and moving manner by Fr. De Very." Weber continues with a very touching account of his wedding day, and with his hopes and prayers for their future, and characteristically he winds up with a detailed list of the wedding accounts and expenses.

Caroline was probably wise to abandon her career in any case, for she was not a singer of the highest rank. She played the usual soubrette roles of the day, including Cherubino, and one report of her, in the *AMZ* of 1816, says of a visit she made to Berlin that "she pleased more for her naive, lively acting than for her singing."[7] The marriage was a very happy one, though Weber probably had a more romantic view of it than she did: she seems to have settled into the role of contented *Hausfrau* quite easily, with only the occasional flurry of unwarranted jealousy to remind Weber of the difficulties he had once had with her. Though very provident, Weber was always pleased to buy her presents when he could afford to; he paid 126 gulden for her wedding dress, a large sum for someone in his position. He was quite careful of his own appearance, too, and the accounts show him concerned to buy shoes, shirts, cravats and other items of clothing to make sure that he presented a good image to the world. They also gave a very vivid picture of German domestic economy in those years when he was setting up first a bachelor establishment in Prague, and then, with touching attention to detail, preparing a house in Dresden that would be worthy of Caroline. Another characteristic the accounts show is Weber's particular generosity to beggars: perhaps with Romantic fellow feeling for the precarious wanderer, together with a sense of religious obligation, he always gave freely even when hardly solvent; and to servants and children he was also very generous with tips and presents. Travelling presented problems and expenses that we can hardly conceive of nowadays. The trip Weber and Caroline made from Prague to Berlin from 7 to 9 October 1816 cost nearly 140 gulden, in such standard items as post fees, postillions' tips, fees for passing the city gates, porters for luggage, tips to the customs (this was a big item) and very little in the way of coffee or refreshment, nothing in the way of food, meaning that they must have taken food with them.

After Weber had settled into a full time post in Prague, and particularly after he had moved to Dresden and married, the diaries become much more laconic. There was no time for descriptions of scenery, for impressions of new friends, for accounts of how concerts or opera performances had gone except in very succinct terms. The principal exception is for major domestic matters, such as the birth of children or occasional celebrations or worries about the family illnesses, and the tragic death of their little daughter. Weber's own illnesses are meticulously detailed: he was not a little fascinated by his own health, but it is less a matter of hypochondria than a mixture of real and justified worry about the future, and of a certain Romantic fascination with sickness of a kind that would have greatly appealed to Thomas Mann. Wagner, watching Weber limping past his window in Dresden on the way home from a rehearsal, found himself associating physical disability with creative talent. The record of work done in the years when Weber was rapidly failing in health is astonishing, and the record of the diaries helps to emphasize the superhuman effort involved. The demands of the theater were extreme, especially in the frequent absence of his opposite number at the Italian Opera, Francesco Morlacchi; yet the diaries include an endless record of letters written and received, of visits made, of work done or completed, even the very rare entry *gefaulenzt,* "lazed about."

By the last period of his life, and especially on the journey to London, the entries become very terse, though the amount of activity they record is still astonishing. The effort to gather together enough resources to provide for his family if he failed to return from England shows in dozens of details—the sale of a snuffbox and a ring for 650 thalers to pay for a well-equipped carriage at 400 thalers to take him to England in comfort, the taking on of a lot more pupils on top of his other work, not to mention his own English lessons to help with the English visit and the setting of *Oberon,* yet still the free giving of alms and the generous tipping of servants. Even when the record of sickness comes to dominate the entries for days on end, there is a scrupulous attention to the efficient organization of his life and his work which was the fruit of the lesson he had learnt after the expulsion from Stuttgart. In London, the diary becomes almost unbearable to read, for though he is hardly strong enough to write more than a few words, in a script that has deteriorated into a wavering, spidery scrawl, he still records the dutiful attendances at concerts, the opera, various soirées in the great houses of London, and other obligations. Most touching of all is the contrast between the cheerful note he maintains in the letters to Caroline and the pain-wracked, frightened entries in the diary. For instance, on 17 April he wrote to Caroline saying that he was sleeping well, and that if the days weren't worth praising they weren't bad enough to grumble over either: the diary for the previous day reads: "Sunday. Worked. Spat up more blood. Very shaken by this. Cold day. Dinner at 6 o'clock with Hyrton. Ate nothing. Very ill. Bed at eleven." Again, on 28 April he reassures Caroline about his cough and his general health, but the diary records, "A good night. At 10 o'clock so ill, such constriction. O God! To Hawes's concert. Rehearsal. Dinner at home with Smart. Evening Hawes's concert. Conducted *Euryanthe* and *Oberon* overtures . . ." And so it continues, a harrowing story of a painful death fended off for as long as possible by heroic efforts, with concerts played and conducted in the face of physical collapse. The last entry was on 3 June, and Weber died early on the morning of the fifth. Together with his effects, the last of the diaries was returned to Caroline, who added a short and touching note hoping that she would manage to bring his children up well, and that they would think nothing but good of their father when first they read the diaries he had bidden her destroy for fear of distressing her.

Notes

1.   F. Jähns, *Carl Maria von Weber in seinen Werken*... (Berlin, 1871).

2.   O. Hellinghaus, *Karl Maria von Weber: seine Persönlichkeit in seinen Briefen und Tagebüchern und in Aufzeichnungen seiner Zeitgenossen* (Freiberg, 1924).

3.   H. Dünnebeil, *Carl Maria von Weber: ein Brevier* (Berlin, 1949).

4.   See the letter of 12 September 1812 written at Gotha to his Berlin friends, published in Max Maria von Weber, *Carl Maria von Weber: ein Lebensbild*, 3 vols. (Leipzig, 1864-66), 1:378, and *Sämtliche Schriften von Carl Maria von Weber,* ed. G. Kaiser (Berlin and Leipzig, 1908), p. 422.

5.   The manuscript is preserved in the Archív Státní Konservatoře in Prague; it has been published in Czech in Z. Němec, *Weberová pražska letá* [Weber's Prague years] (Prague, 1944).

6.   *Allgemeine musikalische Zeitung* 20 (1818), cols. 58-60.

7.   Ibid. 18 (1816), col. 877.

Serov and Musorgsky

Richard Taruskin

By the end of the 1860s the warring camps of Russian music—
Rubinstein/Conservatory, Balakirev/Free Music School, the Serovian
"opposition"—had become so firmly entrenched in their respective positions
and mutual antagonisms[1] that one tends to forget the atmosphere of sweet
camaraderie that prevailed a decade earlier, when the musical profession was
just getting on its feet in Russia. In Stasov's memoir on César Cui (written in
1894 to mark the silver anniversary of *William Ratcliff*), right before launching
into a typically hysterical attack on the memory of his quondam friend Serov,
the kuchkist tribune recalled this pleasant time with real nostalgia:

> Serov himself, the most noteworthy writer on music and critic of the fifties, who was then still
> forward looking and who then had a great influence on the better part of our public, made
> Cui's acquaintance with pleasure, delighted in his interesting and talented nature, his first
> experiments in composition, and, in turn, was an object of great affection, even adoration on
> the part of Cui. Nor is this hard to understand. Serov was such an animated, diverting
> conversationalist, especially when it came to music; he in those days so passionately loved all
> that was highest and best in music, especially Beethoven and Glinka; he was so enthusiastic,
> and so gifted in enthusing others; his nature contained so many truly artistic, warm and lively
> traits! So one can see why God only knows how pleasant it was for Cui and Balakirev to be in
> close contact with such a nature. And they all three got together very often (and I, too,
> belonged to that company though I was not a musician, but a longstanding friend and
> comrade of Serov's who in fact grew up with him, but was now very close to these *newly-
> arrived*, talented Russian musicians). But starting in 1858-59, things changed.[2]

That's when things changed for Stasov, to be sure, for that is when the
furious press controversy between him and Serov got underway.[3] But cordial
relations between Serov and the "newly-arrived" composers, whose circle by
now included Musorgsky as well, persisted for a while. They reached their
pinnacle during the 1859-60 concert season, when Rubinstein's Russian
Musical Society made its long-awaited bow. The precarious Era of Good
Feeling in Russian music was epitomized when both Cui and Musorgsky made
their debuts as serious composers at Society concerts under Rubinstein's baton
during this inaugural season—and were greeted with warm reviews by Serov,
who gladly wielded his considerable power as St. Petersburg's critic of record
on their behalf. Both of them were represented by orchestral scherzos

composed under Balakirev's tutelage. Of Cui's, performed at the fourth concert of the series (14 December 1859), Serov had this to say:

> In conclusion—greetings to a Russian composer who made his first appearance before the public with an extremely remarkable work. The Scherzo of César Antonovich Cui, a student of Stanislaw Moniuszko, is, in its individual way, closely related to Schumann's symphonic works with shades of something Chopinesque as well. There are hardly any vivid "effects," whether of invention or of orchestral combination, but all the ideas inhabit the noblest spheres, are combined and developed effortlessly and with a profound internal logic. In the technical workmanship of the rhythm, harmony, and orchestration, one can see knowledge and subtle planning, such as one very rarely encounters in debutants. From one who begins *thus,* one can expect *much* that is uncommonly good. Make way, make way for *Russian* musicians. There will be the most unexpected, the most heartening results.[4]

Musorgsky's Scherzo was premiered at the seventh and last concert of the season (11 January 1860), on a program that also included Meyerbeer's incidental music to his brother's tragedy *Struensee* (1846). Serov's review compared the two works in a curious—but to Musorgsky no doubt exceptionally gratifying—fashion.

> About the *Struensee* music I can't give a report this time, for I chanced to arrive late, and only caught the last two numbers from this big score. . . . Both numbers, to my taste, were very bad. And what I found especially pleasant to notice was that the antimusicality of this work of Meyerbeer's was frankly perceived by the audience. Applause, which accompanied practically every piece on the program, was almost entirely absent here.
>   And it was even more pleasant to encounter the audience's warm sympathy toward the Russian composer M.P. Musorgsky, who made his debut with an extremely good—only, unfortunately rather too short—orchestral scherzo.
>   This scherzo is not as interesting, in my view, as the scherzo of C.A. Cui, which was performed at the fourth concert, but it also revealed decided talent in a young musician embarking upon a creative career.
>   It was remarkable that this symphonic fragment by a composer as yet unknown, placed alongside the music of a "celebrated" maestro, not only lost nothing, but actually gained a great deal by comparison.[5]

Serov had also had nothing but good to say of Balakirev's compositional debut with a movement of a never-to-be-finished piano concerto in 1856. His review of the collection of songs Balakirev published in 1859 was nothing short of ecstatic. And as late as 1867 he greeted Rimsky-Korsakov's appearance on the musical firmament (with the *Serbian Fantasy*) in terms equally cordial. His opposition to the kuchka is a Stasovian myth, based on invective he directed at Balakirev and at Cui only after huge provocation, mainly engineered by Stasov himself.[6]

How, then, did Musorgsky feel toward Serov? That seems an easy enough question to answer, since Musorsky's letters are full of condescension toward the older composer, and in *The Sideshow* (*Raek,* 1870) he derided Serov without mercy. But one must bear in mind the circumstances. The letters dealing with Serov were mostly addressed to Musorgsky's seniors within the kuchka—Balakirev, Cui, and Stasov—who by the early sixties were united in their envious hostility to the critic, and, after *Judith,* to the composer as well. Stasov, moreover, was the dedicatee of *The Sideshow,* in which Serov was lampooned alongside Stasov's other enemies real and imaginary: Famintsyn (who had successfully sued Stasov for libel), Rostislav (Serov's most enthusiastic exponent in the press), Zaremba (acting director of Rubinstein's Conservatory) and the Grand Duchess Elena Pavlovna (Rubinstein's patroness). It was Stasov who inspired, nay, practically *commissioned* this "musical pamphlet," as a retort to what he perceived as a concatenation of "hostile elements" that were threatening the kuchka and also, especially, as an insult to Serov, whom Stasov by now regarded with a fanatical, well-nigh paranoiacal hatred. But Stasov can speak for himself; here is how he described the circumstances surrounding *The Sideshow* in his 1881 biography-necrology of Musorgsky:

> The man who stood at the head of the hostile camp, Serov, had long since ceased being the progressive human being, musician, and critic he had been in his youth. He was now writing bad operas, aimed at pleasing the coarse crowd. Long since frozen in the enthusiasms of his youth, he was maintaining that after Beethoven further symphonies were unthinkable and therefore with blind fanaticism attacked Franz Schubert and Schumann (whom he deemed a mere "demi-musician"), Berlioz, and Liszt. The summit of operatic music, he thought, was Wagner and his half-baked *Tannhäuser* and *Lohengrin,* and then he began dragging *Ruslan and Ludmila* through the mud, asserting (in 1868) that within five years that opera would lose the stage. On the occasion of Wagner's concerts in St. Petersburg, in 1863, he had written on his behalf the most monstrous puffs, claiming that Wagner had "brought whole worlds into being." In his musical critiques he was ever puffed up with himself, groundlessly captious, petty, and feebly impertinent, always going after personalities. In 1866, giving the public a press report on the performances of *Ruslan* in Prague under M.A. Balakirev's direction, I said that Balakirev and his talented fellow innovators made up a *"moguchaia kuchka,"* a mighty little bunch. Serov seized upon this expression and started persecuting the Balakirev party with it, as a derisive epithet. Serov's cohorts in hatred of the new musical trend, Messrs. Laroche, Zvantsev etc., rejoiced in the nickname and began using it like an expletive. They found in it, apparently, great wit and profundity. When in 1867 Berlioz was in Russia (for the second time), constantly surrounding himself with talented representatives of the New Russian School, Serov (who, by the way, had constantly attacked Berlioz in his journal *Muzyka i teatr*) was beside himself with annoyance. Such a personality and such writing about music (Serov's former personality and writing were as far from the latter as heaven from earth, so much had he changed!) could not but be antipathetic and even somewhat contemptible to the talented group. Among the "mightly little bunch," in reaction, Serov and his comrades were a constant topic of conversation. César Cui wrote very often about them in his gifted and brilliant polemical articles, in which he, over a period of many years, gave voice not only to his personal opinions, but to those of the whole group and in particular its chief, Balakirev. Combat seethed ever more bitterly, until one day in 1870 I advised Musorgsky to enter the fray once more with the same scourge of musical satire he had already tested with so much talent in *The Classicist* [*Klassik,* 1867].[7]

Stasov continues with a few half-hearted sallies at the other exhibits in Musorgsky's sideshow, but by now he is out of steam and soon goes on to other things. It is clear that the motive force behind the piece was Stasov's neurotic vendetta against Serov. And it is equally clear that Musorgsky's aim in composing the piece was to indulge his beloved confident and mentor, to vent Stasov's spleen rather than his own. As he reported in a letter to Vladimir Nikolsky, he had given the manuscript to Stasov with a dedicatory letter containing a line of scripture: "Of thine own we have given thee" (I Chronicles 29:14).[8] Stasov's passionate invective—and the very fact that he went after Serov (already a decade deceased) at such length and with such gusto in a piece ostensibly dedicated to the memory of Musorgsky (as he later would do in the piece cited above, ostensibly devoted to Cui) betrays the uncontrollability and unassuageability of his hatred—amounts to a fairly comprehensive bill of kuchkist indictment against Serov. It is mostly absurd, the most absurd of its elements being the perfectly ludicrous exaggeration of his rival's power and prestige. Serov led no camp in the 1860s, and it is especially risible to find him cast as mentor to Laroche, one of the foremost public detractors of Serov's operas. Stasov also had his facts quite wrong on the origin and progress of his unfortunate coinage, *moguchaia kuchka*. He had made it up not in connection with Balakirev's Prague activities, but in connection with "Mr. Balakirev's Slavonic Concert," a festive affair performed before an audience of delegates to a Pan-Slavist congress in 1867. Serov, whose music was conspicuously snubbed on this occasion, had ample provocation (given his natural cantankerousness) to deride the "little bunch" that would have no part of him, and loudly to dissociate himself from it. This he did in an article in *Muzyka i teatr* called "The Elephant and the Fly," which was much discussed by everyone, including Musorgsky, as we shall see. As for the other, more serious snub—when Serov was not invited to the testimonial dinner tendered Berlioz on his birthday (his last, on 11 December 1868) by the Russian Musical Society—this was Stasov's own doing, engineered through Balakirev, who was then enjoying his brief tenure as conductor of the Society's concerts, and also through the sick, enfeebled Dargomyzhsky (in his last month of life), its vice-president, who signed a letter Stasov drew up in answer to Serov's protest.[9] But neither the insult itself nor Musorgsky's taunting allusion to it in the text of *The Sideshow* could gratify Stasov sufficiently to quell his anti-Serovian mania. Not even Serov's sudden death did the trick. To the end of his life, Stasov's blood would boil and his pen run out of control at the thought of him. For no one, it would seem, had ever made Stasov feel quite so inferior as this former friend whose heinous crimes had been, first, to best Stasov in the *Ruslan* debate and, second, to achieve resounding success as composer in his own right.

But all of this was Stasov's *idée fixe,* not Musorgsky's. Feuding with Serov was a favorite pastime of the kuchka's "older generation." The newer members—Musorgsky, Rimsky-Korsakov, Borodin—had little to do with it, understood it poorly, found it distasteful and burdensome.[10]

Though it is hard to imagine that Musorgsky never met Serov, nothing ever passed between them that anyone, whether participant or onlooker, saw fit to record. That Musorgsky's personal feelings had little to do with either the text or the music of *The Sideshow* can be seen from the case of Zaremba, whom he mocked in 1870 and in whose house he lived (with Rimsky-Korsakov) in 1871. As for Serov, what *The Sideshow* chiefly reveals is how thoroughly Musorgsky had learned Serov's *Rogneda* (just as Musorgsky's forced derisive letter to Balakirev on Serov's *Judith* seven years earlier had shown how attentively he had listened to that opera).

The one epistolary reference to Serov that passed between Musorgsky and another member of the younger generation of kuchkists is contained in a letter to Rimsky-Korsakov (15 July 1867), in which Musorgsky advises him to remove a passage from *Sadko* reminiscent of the Witch in *Rogneda*. At the end of the letter Serov crops up again, in connection with "The Elephant and the Fly."

> My friends in St. Petersburg have written me about the sixth issue of Serov's paper. In this number he went after Mily and impugned his education. Well, Serov is no one to talk: some fine educated musician, he, who thought up a High Priest for Perun in a Russian epic and who plants pilgrims in the Kievan bush. And as for the music, from the historical point of view it's lower even than Verstovsky [i.e., in *Askold's Grave*]; at Vladimir's feast he throws in a current tavern song and dancing girls—just as though Vladimir were Holofernes. But Serov really had a field day with Cui: on account of Cui's remark (an entirely tactless remark) that in the Slavonic Concert nothing of Serov's was played, this author of two five-act operas writes: *a diplomatic regret, but in vain*.... How do you like that "diplomatic"? Too bad César was so tactless. They tell me we all caught it in this issue—and so it must be; on account of this Serov must hate us with a holy vengeance.[11]

So there we have Musorgsky's attitude. When all is said and done, after the *pro forma* defense of Balakirev and the predictable sniping at *Rogneda* (stale news, parroted dutifully from long-since-published articles by Cui and Stasov[12]), Musorgsky sounds a note of regret—genuine (unlike Cui's), not feigned. Where Balakirev and Cui gleefully abetted Stasov's vendetta, Musorgsky and Rimsky could only watch disconsolately from the sidelines, cluck their tongues at one another and prepare to "catch it." And Musorgsky caught it not only from the "other camp." It was probably because he expressed his honest reaction to an unreasonable Stasov at the *Judith* premiere that Stasov shrieked to Balakirev that Musorgsky seemed "a perfect idiot."[13]

Serov and his work interested Musorgsky as deeply as they did Rimsky.[14] To paraphrase Satie's famous sally about Ravel and the Legion of Honor, Musorgsky rejected Serov but all his works accepted him. And his contemporaries were quick to notice. Laroche, whose reviews of *Boris*

Godunov were as trenchant as they were ambivalent, made the most of it. "Mr. Musorgsky is more a follower of Dargomyzhsky than the other members of his circle," he observed, "but by a strange combination of circumstances that was stronger than the composer, in places of massive and colossal character he often falls into *Serovshchina*."[15] Laroche's catalogue of Serovianisms in *Boris* is long. Some of them can be accounted for merely by the fact that Serov had set the sole Russian precedent for grand historical opera by the time of the composition of *Boris* (though by the time of the premiere, Rimsky's *Pskovitianka* had reached the stage). But by no means can all of them be so written off. And some are quite astonishingly specific, testifying not only to the accuracy of Laroche's observations, but to the acuity of his ear.

In the introduction to the Coronation Scene (the pealing bells) Laroche discerned an echo from the Introduction to the first act of *Rogneda* (ex. 1). And the characteristic, now famous "proto-octatonic" chord progression of Musorgsky's bells (oscillating between dominant sevenths with roots a tritone apart, preserving a common tritone) was anticipated in the royal hunt from the same opera (ex. 2).[16]

1. *Rogneda,* Introduction to Act I (Moscow: A. Gutheil, n.d. [ca. 1885], p. 2)

INTRODUCTION.
Largo lugubre.

2. *Rogneda,* from the Royal Hunt, Act III (p. 138)

3. a. *The Power of the Fiend,* Eriomka's song to the balalaika, Act
   III (Moscow: Muzyka, 1968, p. 243)

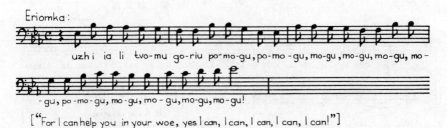

Eriomka:

uzh i ia li tvo-mu go-riu po-mo-gu, po-mo - gu, mo-gu, mo-gu, mo-gu, mo-

- gu, po-mo-gu, mo-gu, mo - gu, mo-gu, mo-gu!

["For I can help you in your woe, yes I can, I can, I can, I can, I can!"]

b. *Boris Godunov,* the "clapping game," Act II (vocal score, ed.
   Lamm [Moscow: Muzgiz, 1931], p. 173)

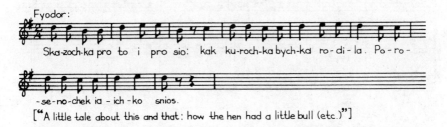

Fyodor:

Ska-zoch-ka pro to i pro sio: kak ku-roch-ka bych-ka ro-di-la. Po-ro-

-se-no-chek ia - ich -ko snios.

["A little tale about this and that : how the hen had a little bull (etc.)"]

4. *Rogneda*, the Pilgrim Elder's recitative, Act III (pp. 119-20)

Ex. 4 (continued)

The dance songs in the Terem Scene (the Nanny's song of the gnat, the "clapping game") reminded Laroche of the Jester's songs in the second and third acts of *Rogneda* as well as of Eriomka's songs in *The Power of the Fiend* (the Shrovetide song in act 2 and the song to the balalaika ["Pomogu-mogu-mogu-mogu-mogu"] in act 3). This was a particularly injurious "charge," since among the "models" cited was the very "current tavern song" that had called forth so much kuchkist vitriol, including Musorgsky's letter to Rimsky-Korsakov. And it had been parodied in *The Sideshow* to boot! The reference to Eriomka, however, carries conviction. Not only must this dark character have appealed strongly to Musorgsky ("this Russian Bertram" he called him in a letter to Stasov),[17] but the timing was right. *The Power of the Fiend* was premiered posthumously in April 1871. Musorgsky revised his Terem Scene and added the dance songs in August of the same year.[18] In any case, the kind of folk-derived ostinato patter song one finds in the "clapping game" had Russian operatic antecedents only in Serov (ex. 3).

Boris's monologue at the center of the Coronation Scene Laroche compares with the Wanderer's recitative in *Rogneda,* act 3 (ex. 4). And the offstage chorus of monks in the Cell Scene, Laroche avers, was inspired by the mourning chorus for Ruald in the same act of Serov's opera (ex. 5). The critic sums up: "The general decorativeness and crudity of Mr. Musorgsky's style, his passion for the brass and percussion instruments, may be considered to have been borrowed from Serov." And then, no friend to either party, he twists his knife: "But never did the crudest works of the model reach the naive coarseness we note in his imitator."[19]

5. *Rogneda,* the Pilgrim's Funeral Chant, Act III (pp. 182-83)

ЗАУПОКОЙНЫЙ ХОРЪ СТРАННИКОВЪ.

„Боже прости его, грѣшную душу пріими"

Long as Laroche's list is, it could be considerably extended. And his conclusion, purged of its malice, could be considerably strengthened. For the similarities between Musorgsky and Serov as creative personalities were fundamental, and their common creative penchants numerous. Our next witness will be Musorgsky himself. His well-known letter to Balakirev on *Judith* has been much analyzed. Gerald Abraham, with characteristic acuity, has described it as a "weak attempt at exculpation" after Stasov blew up at his younger colleague's "idiocy" at the premiere.[20] With the single exception of the act 1 finale, which Balakirev himself had mildly praised when shown the score by Serov in 1861 in a last act of good will, Musorgsky dared not actually praise the opera or any of its parts. But even the passages chosen for blame show at least what interested him in *Judith,* and they make a revealing list. Holofernes's act 4 delirium, for example, is singled out for special scorn:

> Holofernes, dead drunk, starts having hallucinations. . . . What a broad field for a musician, this feasting sensualist-despot, how interestingly might his hallucinations have been portrayed in the orchestra. But there is nothing of the sort—just banal French melodrama with Wagnerian howls from the violins.[21]

So it would seem that Boris Godunov's hallucination—one of the very few episodes in the first version of Musorgsky's opera that did not come from Pushkin's play, and which is chiefly "portrayed in the orchestra"—was prompted by the wish, as it were, to set Serov straight. And so one might boldly extend Professor Abraham's just but cautious observation that Serov's scene suggested Musorgsky's "dramatically, not musically."[22] The musical suggestion was there, too, precisely in what Musorgsky found lacking in Serov's achievement.

There is another conspicuous example of Serov having planted an idea in Musorgsky's mind as it were by omission rather than commission. The younger composer, writing to Balakirev, pointed with approval to a melody that accompanied the pacing of the elders at the raising of the curtain in act 1, typically Serovian in its tortuousness and angularity (ex. 6). But Musorgsky called attention to what he regarded as a "serious dereliction":

> This phrase, which portrays the predicament of the people lying exhausted upon the stage, is dropped with the beginning of the elders' recitative. I would have continued it, added some juice, and upon its development, upon the progress of this phrase, I would have constructed the elders' declamation.[23]

And do he did, exactly, for Pimen's monologue in the Cell scenes.

The one literal plagiarism from *Judith* in Musorgsky's works, however, is found neither in *Boris* nor in *Salammbô,* but in the concert chorus after Byron, *Porazhenie Sennakheriba* (*The Destruction of Sennacherib,* 1867), which treats of the same subject matter as Serov's opera: the war between the

6. *Judith,* opening of Act I (Moscow: A. Gutheil, n.d. [ca. 1885], p. 8)

Assyrians and the Hebrews. Undoubtedly because of this congruence, Musorgsky copied Holofernès's "War Song" from act 4 of *Judith* in the first theme of the chorus. It is something one cannot imagine Musorgsky doing consciously, yet the parallel is so obvious that one has to wonder how it escaped not only Musorgsky's notice, but that of his fellow kuchkists as well. For had they noticed, they would scarcely have "permitted" it! (ex. 7).

But interesting as all these specific points and parallels may be—and the list could be extended further still, to include Serov's enharmonic third relations, particularly the progressive reidentification of a given pitch as root, third, fifth, and seventh, such as we find in the fanfares in Musorgsky's Coronation Scene, which reflect such typically Serovian passages as the harp arpeggios in the Introduction to act 1 of *Judith* (ex. 8)—they are neither as interesting nor as important as the general aesthetic and dramaturgical parallels. Here we really see how indispensable a precursor Serov was for Musorgsky. Asafiev put it rather loftily and abstractly when he observed that "their paths were not at all far from one another . . . in the predominance of all that was *characteristic* over the generalizing and the harmonious."[24] What he meant was that Serov provided a spiritual source for some of the most basic tenets of Musorgsky's aesthetic credo—traits, as a matter of fact, which rather set him apart from his kuchkist elders Balakirev and Cui: his contempt for "beauty," his harmonic empiricism, his preoccupation with pathological psychology and its unvarnished, unflinching representation. One is almost tempted to say that what Musorgsky "got" from Serov was realism itself. So much of what one is apt today to regard as characteristic of Musorgsky and of Musorgsky alone can be found in embryo in Serov's work, and the opera to look to first—Asafiev recognized this—is neither of the ones referred to by Laroche (and by a host of such lesser critics as Mikhnevich, Rappaport, and Solovyov),[25] but *Judith.* There one finds more than the orientalism of *Salammbô,* which Musorgsky dismissed with a shrug when asked why he had never finished that first operatic attempt.[26] One also finds such patently "Musorgskian" devices as the fragmentation of the chorus, extreme harmonic "ugliness" in the interest of expression (and vocal ugliness, too, to the point

7. a. Holofernes's "War Song" (A.N. Serov, *Judith* [Moscow: Gutheil, 1885], pp. 264-65.

    [We cross the torrid steppe! The air breathes fire!]

    b. *The Destruction of Sennacherib* (M.P. Musorgsky, *Polnoe sobranie sochinenii,* ed. P.A. Lamm, vol. VI [Kalmus reprint: vol. XXI], pp. 56-57.

    [Like a pack of famished wolves, the enemy has attacked us.]

8. *Judith,* Introduction to Act I, reduced to block formation from harp arpeggios over pedal (pp. 4-5)

where even Cui was offended),[27] and above all, an austerity amounting almost to asceticism in the dramaturgical plan (the Assyrian acts excepted, as one must except the Polish act of *Boris*). Some of this was developed further in Serov's later operas (the jeering of the Pecheneg prisoners in *Rogneda* as noted by Abraham,[28] the "murder chords" in *The Power of the Fiend*), but Musorgsky's reaction to *Judith* was fresh and as yet relatively unprejudiced. He acknowledged it to be "the first seriously treated opera on the Russian stage since [Dargomyzhsky's] *Rusalka*,"[29] and he could only have been kindly disposed at this point toward the work of the critic who had welcomed his own debut three years earlier.

When Musorgsky next heard from Serov as composer for the stage, it was not with *Rogneda* itself but with the Preface to the libretto, published in September 1865, over a month before the premiere. This ringing, bellicose manifesto on behalf of "dramatic truth in tone" and against all " 'conventional' beauty"[30] is so close to Musorgsky's own creative aspirations (as he began to state them only later in his letters) that one easily imagines him, in different circumstances, hugging its author to his breast and bestowing upon Serov the epithet he accorded Dargomyzhsky: "great teacher of musical truth."[31] But St. Petersburg musical politics decreed otherwise, and Musorgsky joined the kuchkist chorus of gleeful abuse. It was all too easy to point up the gap between Serov's lofty preachments and his at times risibly inadequate practice. But still, Musorgsky's ears remained open to the harmonic barbarities of the sacrifice to Perun, the naturalism of the choruses and, occasionally, of the declamation.[32] Serov's Christian Elder (see ex. 4), though compared by Laroche with Boris Godunov, was rather a natural prototype for Pimen. It seems Cui agreed, for how else is one to account for his odd hostility toward the Cell Scene in *Boris*? He must have sensed the kinship between Musorgsky's "choppy, unmusical recitatives" and Serov's.[33]

As for *The Power of the Fiend,* no opera set a more powerful precedent for *The Fair at Sorochintsy*. Musorgsky's Fair scene, with its vendor's cries set contrapuntally against a continuously developing orchestral backdrop, ineluctably evokes Serov's Shrovetide fair (ex. 9). But beyond that, and beyond

Eriomka, there is the matter of folksong recitative. The whole concept so flies in the face of Musorgsky's practice (not to mention his theorizing) from *Marriage* to *Khovanshchina,* yet figures so prominently in *The Fair,* as to send one off in search of explanations. A comparison at random with Serov's recitatives in the earlier acts of his Ostrovsky opera suggests a compelling one (ex. 10).

9. a. *The Fair at Sorochintsy,* opening of Fair Scene, Act I
    (Moscow: Muzyka, 1970, p. 7)

b. *The Power of the Fiend,* Shrovetide Scene, Act IV (p. 264)

10. a. *The Fair at Sorochintsy,* Act I, sc. i (pp. 24-25)

[--"Do you think you can approach my daughter just like that? Just like that?" --
"Bah, it's Solopii himself! Hello old pal! Hello, Pan Cherevik!"]

b. *The Power of the Fiend,* Act II (pp. 137-38)

["Now you leave off greiving, at least for today!" -- "What a spell you've cast on me!"]

This was an aspect of Musorgsky's work his contemporaries could not judge, for *The Fair* remained an unknown quantity (apart from a few excerpts) until the second decade of this century. By then, of course, the realist ferment in Russian music had long since died down, and so had Serov's once mighty reputation. So no one seems to have drawn the perfectly obvious connections between Musorgsky's opus posthumum and Serov's.

But by now they should elicit no surprise. Musorgsky and Serov were kindred spirits who by rights should have been allies. Only the vagaries of musical politics, in which Musorgsky's role was a passive one, kept them apart in life and in conventional historiography. Laroche was already of the opinion that Serov "would have considerably softened his wrath at the *'moguchaia kuchka'* had he lived to see the production of *Boris Godunov,* [for] in the person of Mr. Musorgsky he would have found a composer who not only fulfilled but even exceeded" his own Gluck-derived operatic ideals.[34]

"Amazingly, no one up to now has said so yet among us," wrote Stasov in 1883, "but Perov and Musorgsky represent in the world of Russian art an astonishing parallel. It seems to me that anyone who will take the trouble to look into these two personalities will come to the same conclusion."[35] A century later, it is time to recognize that if we change the first letter of the painter's name to an *S,* Stasov's provocative assertion holds good.

Notes

1. For an introduction to the tumultuous world of St. Petersburg musical politics, see Robert C. Ridenour, *Nationalism, Modernism and Personal Rivalry in Nineteenth-Century Russian Music* (Ann Arbor, 1981). Ridenour places a healthy emphasis upon the last element in his triad, and this should be held in mind cantus-firmus-like when considering relations between Serov and the "elder" members of the moguchaia kuchka, Balakirev and Cui.

2. V.V. Stasov, *Izbrannye sochineniia* [Selected Works], vol. 3 (Moscow, 1952), p. 396.

3. For the details of this war of words, see my "Glinka's Ambiguous Legacy and the Birth Pangs of Russian Opera," *19th-Century Music* 1, no. 2 (November 1977), 142-62. (Relations between Stasov and Serov were also severely complicated by the former's affair with the latter's sister, Sophie DuTour; see the introductory article by A.A. Gozenpud and V.A. Obram to the voluminous Stasov-Serov correspondence in *Muzykal'noe nasledstvo* [Musical heritage], vol. 1 [Moscow, 1961], p. 77.) In 1858-59 Stasov interfered strenuously with the continued development of good relations between Serov and the "newly-arrived" Balakirev and Cui, as can easily be seen in the 14 letters from Serov to Balakirev published by A.S. Liapunova in *Sovetskaia muzyka* [Soviet music] (May, 1953), pp. 68-75. The correspondence is regular and extremely cordial through 1856 and 1857; then it suddenly breaks off after 9 February 1958. The only one to follow, dated 1 March 1859, begins thus: "If *Monsieur Cui bono* cannot attend my lectures [i.e., Serov's ill-starred venture of 1858-59 at St. Petersburg University on "Music from the Technical, Aesthetic and Historical Points of View"] because the Stasovs [i.e., the brothers Vladimir and Dmitri] have forbidden him, that certainly doesn't surprise me (Poles [!] love to submit)." And it ends even more ominously: "How can I persuade you that it is neither wise nor right to make an enemy for oneself out of someone who could be a strong ally." Little need be added to account for the break between Serov and the kuchka. Stasov's meddling accounts for it all. It is all the more remarkable, then, how long Serov strove to maintain his relationship with Balakirev and Cui, e.g., in the critiques discussed in note 6 below.

4. A.N. Serov, *Izbrannye stat'i,* [Selected articles], vol. 2 (Moscow, 1957), pp. 612-13.

5. Ibid., pp. 616-17.

6. Serov's review of Balakirev's debut is reprinted in Serov, *Izbrannye stat'i,* vol. 2, pp. 542-43 (the conclusion: "Mr. Balakirev's talent is a rich find for our nation's music"); his review of Balakirev's collection of songs, in *Izbrannye stat'i,* vol. 1 (Leningrad, 1950), pp. 339-42. At the conclusion of the latter review Serov sounded an avuncular note that may have rankled a bit: "It remains to wish Mr. Balakirev the maximum possible ardor and strength of will in embarking on a career so difficult as that of a composer of music! A Russian musician must remember at all times that fame, esteem, and money are not for him. For all these things to materialize as in a dream, one needs, besides talent (which hardly matters), first of all not to be Russian, even if born in Russia." These lines, however, were written out of bitter personal experience, and express above all Serov's anti-Semitic envy of Rubinstein. Anti-Semitism is even closer to the surface of Serov's review the same year of Balakirev's first Overture on

Russian Themes, where he commiserates with the composer because his name is not Balakirstein. Such remarks could only have gratified Balakirev, whose anti-Semitism, if anything, surpassed Serov's. But the avuncular note was also intensified in this review, where Serov complained of Balakirev's inability to sustain the sonata form: "His Overture . . . is not yet a complete work of art; the general impression the piece makes is unsatisfactory, it seems to lack wholeness of form, roundedness; . . . in the overall sequence of events one wants something a bit different, and the central development section (the *Mittelsatz,* to speak technically) is not clearly enough carried through" (*Izbrannye stat'i,* vol. 2, pp. 585-86). (The ostentatious and redundant use of jargon is, by the way, entirely characteristic of the pre-*Judith* Serov, whose insecurities about his own lack of training peep through everywhere.) All this smacks of effrontery, and one begins to understand the uncharacteristic and apparently calculated pedantry with which Balakirev, in turn, reviewed the first act of *Judith*—a gratuitous insult that infuriated Serov and made final the split between him and the "older generation" of kuchkists. That Serov never lumped the whole kuchka (as we understand the term today) together is evident from the cordiality with which he treated Rimsky-Korsakov to the end of his life. The *Serbian Fantasy* review is in *Izbrannye stat'i,* vol. 2, p. 617. Serov lived to review one more Rimsky-Korsakov composition, the "symphonic picture" *Sadko*—once in Russian in his own *Muzyka i teatr* (no.14, 1867) and once in French for the *Journal de St.-Pétersbourg* (no. 279, 1869). In this second, very late review, animosity toward the senior kuchkists at last shows through: "Mr. Rimsky-Korsakov, alone among his whole party, is gifted with an enormous talent—settled, remarkable, profoundly appealing. Amid his ill-starred entourage he shines as a diamond among cobblestones. . . . Now here is a musical picture that really deserves its name, not merely arrogates it, like the pitiful potpourri of Mr. Balakirev [i.e., "1000 Years"], with all its doomed pretension. . . ." (*Izbrannye stat'i,* vol. 2, pp. 627-28). Just how much *Sadko* impressed Serov was revealed by Vasily Vasilievich Bessel, the music publisher, at a testimonial dinner tendered Rimsky-Korsakov on 17 December 1900, the thirty-fifth anniversary of his debut. When it came his turn to toast the jubilee, Bessel "informed us that when A.N. Serov came into his store after a rehearsal at which *Sadko* was played, he replied to Bessel's question how he liked that composition, after a moment's reflection: 'This is how much—after the very first page of that fantasia I was ready to go down on my knees, it impressed me so much.' And that was the proud and puffed-up Serov!" (V.V. Yastrebtsev, *Nikolai Andreevich Rimsky-Korsakov: Vospominaniia,* vol. II [Leningrad: Muzgiz, 1960], 262.) Given the nature of the occasion, we can assume that Bessel was exaggerating a bit. But at the very least, all these pronouncements about Rimksy-Korsakov show that Serov was careful to distinguish between kuchkist generations. It is one of our contentions here that we ought to do the same in treating his relations with them.

7.   Stasov, *Izbrannye sochineniia,* vol. 2, pp. 202-3. *Klassik,* according to a note on the autograph, was "an answer to Famintsyn's remarks on the heresies of the Russian School" (M.P. Musorgsky, *Literaturnoe nasledie,* vol. 2 [Moscow, 1972], 182).

8.   Musorgsky, *Literaturnoe nasledie* [Literary Heritage], vol. 1 (Moscow, 1971), p. 114.

9.   For Stasov's side of the story, see his "Liszt, Schumann and Berlioz in Russia," in Vladimir Stasov, *Selected Essays on Music,* trans. Florence Jonas (New York, 1968), pp. 167-68.

10.   As Rimsky-Korsakov put it in his memoirs: "Serov's relations with Balakirev, Cui, and Stasov in former days (prior to my appearance on the musical horizon) are a puzzle to me to this day. Serov had been intimate with them, but why the break occurred is unknown to me. This was passed over in silence in Balakirev's circle. Snatches of reminiscences about Serov, chiefly ironical, reached me in passing. A scandalous story, of unprintable nature, was circulated about him, and so forth. When I came into Balakirev's circle, the relations between

Serov and that circle were most hostile. I suspect that Serov would have been glad to make up with the circle, but Balakirev was incapable of conceding it" (*My Musical Life,* trans. Judah A. Joffe [London, 1974], p. 70). Say, rather, Stasov was incapable.

11.   As a matter of fact, Serov did not go after "them all," only after those who gave him cause. See the commentary to the letter by Mikhail Pekelis (*Literaturnoe nasledie,* vol. 1, p. 295), where "The Elephant and the Fly" is described. Serov originally used the term *moguchaia kuchka* in the sense in which Stasov originally used it: to refer to those composers of the younger generation whose music was performed at Balakirev's Slavonic concert. This bunch included Rimsky-Korsakov, but not Musorgsky.

12.   Cf. Cui's review of *Rogneda* (*Sanktpeterburgskie vedomosti* [St. Petersburg news], no. 292, 1865), and two articles of Stasov: "Arkheologicheskaia zametka o postanovke 'Rognedy'" [Archeological note on the production of *Rogneda*] (*Sobranie sochinenii* [Collected Works], vol. 3 [St. Petersburg, 1894], pp. 184-88) and "Verit' li?" [Would you believe it?] (*Izbrannye sochineniia,* vol. 1 [Moscow, 1952], pp. 147-51). The latter is given practically in full (in English translation) in my *Opera and Drama in Russia* (Ann Arbor, 1981), pp. 128-31.

13.   Letter of 17 May 1863. A.S. Liapunova (ed.), *M.A. Balakirev i V.V. Stasov: Perepiska* [Correspondence], vol. 1 (Moscow, 1970), p. 203.

14.   For evidence of Rimsky's sympathetic interest and its effect on his work, see *Opera and Drama in Russia,* pp. 113-18.

15.   *Golos,* no. 29, 1874.

16.   Of course, this harmonic relationship pervades much Russian music and can be traced before *Rogneda* (e.g., Balakirev's Overture to *King Lear* [1859], as Rey Longyear points out in *Nineteenth-Century Romanticism in Music* [2nd ed., Englewood Cliffs, 1973], p. 222). But Laroche was certainly right in tracing the oscillation effect to Serov.

17.   *Literaturnoe nasledie,* vol. 1, p. 121.

18.   In 1871, too, Musorgsky composed the Scene at the Fountain, and a rather improbable echo of *Vrazhya sila* may lurk there as well. At least Rimsky-Korsakov thought so. On September 29, 1897, not long after he finished work on his first redaction of Musorgsky's opera, he pointed out the resemblance to his disciple Yastrebtsev, who duly entered it in his diary. According to Rimsky, this phrase in the Pretender's monologue—

A. *Boris Godunov,* ed. Lamm (Moscow, 1928), p. 262
     ["I will take her up with me onto the royal throne"]

—was subconsciously inspired by the notorious drunkard's song in the fourth act of *Vrazhya sila,* which itself was a reworking of the folksong *Kapitanskaia doch', ne khodi guliat' v polnoch'* (Lvov-Pratsch, no. 61), on which so much of the music in Serov's opera was based.

B. *Vrazhya sila* (Moscow, 1968), p. 280
     ["Copper coins jingle, order us into the tavern"]

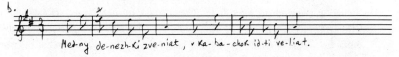

(See V.V. Yastrebtsev, *Nikolai Andreevich Rimskii-Korsakov: Vospominaniia,* I [Leningrad, 1959], 472-73.) But while the Serov snatch cited by Rimsky certainly did turn up in his own *Snegurochka* (as the composer, with characteristic candor, also acknowledged in his conversation with Yastrebtsev), Musorgsky's phrase is perhaps more plausibly a derivation from the Pretender's leitmotive, a more nearly literal citation of which immediately precedes it in the Fountain monologue:

C. *Boris Godunov,* loc. cit.
    ["I will raise her up, my precious, before the whole Russian land, (I will take her up, etc.)"]

19.   *Golos,* no. 44, 1874. The list of borrowings is drawn both from this article and the one cited in n. 15.

20.   "The Operas of Serov," in Jack Westrup (ed.), *Essays Presented to Egon Wellesz* (Oxford, 1966), p. 174. Abraham continues, "his true reaction to *Judith* was to begin his own *Salammbô* five months later."

21.   *Literaturnoe nasledie,* vol. 1, p. 68.

22.   *Essays Presented to Egon Wellesz,* p. 177.

23.   *Literaturnoe nasledie,* vol. 1, p. 65. Here Musorgsky has put his finger on one of Serov's most exasperating musical habits, one which we might call (borrowing a favorite term of Russian/Soviet critical jargon) "stifled symphonism." Arresting ideas begin in the orchestra and develop at times considerable momentum, only to be abandoned the moment a voice is heard. Examples abound in *Judith's* duet with Avra in act 2.

24.   Boris Asafiev, *Izbrannye trudy* [Selected works], vol. 3 (Moscow, 1954), p. 40.

25.   Cf. Abram Gozenpud, *Russkie opernyi teatr XIX veka* [The Russian operatic theater in the XIX century], vol. 3 (Leningrad, 1973), p. 94.

26.   "We've had enough of the Orient in *Judith.* Art isn't a pastime, time is precious." Nikolai Kompaneisky, "K novym beregam" [Toward new shores], *Russkaia muzykal' naia gazeta* [Russian musical gazette] (1906), quoted in Jay Leyda and Sergei Bertensson, *The Musorgsky Reader* (New York, 1947), p. 67.

27.   "In the entire fourth act what we hear from Mr. Sariotti [in the role of Holofernes] is not singing at all, but raucous bellowing. If Mr. Serov were really aspiring to this, then he probably would not have written a vocal part, but merely indicated 'Holofernes declaims hoarsely.'" But as Cui himself realized, "Mr. Sariotti is . . . singing and acting on Mr. Serov's instructions." For more on the vocal style of *Judith,* including more of Cui's review, see my "Opera and Drama in Russia: The Case of Serov's *Judith,*" *JAMS,* vol. 32, no. 1 (1979), pp. 114-17.

28.   *Essays Presented to Egon Wellesz,* p. 180.

29.   *Literaturnoe nasledie,* vol. 1, p. 64.

30.   The Preface is given practically in full in *Opera and Drama in Russia,* pp. 88-90.

31.   Two of Musorgsky's naturalistic songs of the late sixties—*Kolybel'naia Eremushki* ("Yeriomushka's Cradlesong," 1867) and *S nianei* ("With Nanny," the first of the *Nursery* cycle, 1868) bear dedications to Dargomyzhsky in these terms.

32. See *Opera and Drama in Russia,* pp. 119-20, for some specific instances of Musorgskian borrowing from *Rogneda.*

33. See his famous review of the *Boris* premiere, still unreprinted and untranslated in full (*Sanktpeterburgskie vedomosti,* no. 37, 1874).

34. G.A. Laroche, *Sobranie muzykal'no-kriticheskikh statei* [A Collection of music critiques], vol. 2 (Moscow, 1922), p. 116.

35. This is the opening of "Perov i Musorgsky," one of Stasov's finest essays, whose title prompted my own. It was first published in *Russkaia starina* (May 1883), pp. 433-58, and is reprinted in V.V. Stasov, *Izbrannye sochineniia,* vol. 2, pp. 132-52. Vasily Grigorievich Perov (1834-82) was one of the *peredvizhnik* painters ("The Wanderers"), whose highly individualized Daumieresque "types" have often been compared with Musorgsky's realistic songs of the sixties.

A Fiasco Remembered:
Fiesque Dismembered

Hugh Macdonald

Lalo's *Fiesque* is a fine opera which has never been performed. The overture
and certain extracts were played in the composer's lifetime but it has never
reached the stage. From the beginning the work was dogged by mischance, and
it eventually suffered the most humiliating of fates, being chopped up into tiny
morsels and fed to the hungry maws of later works. In the creative slumber of his
last years Lalo picked over one of his best scores like a vulture feasting on its
own offspring. Yet the original opera survives vigorous enough to merit at least
brief attention and one day, one may hope, a stage premiere.

The story of its composition and non-performance was a well-known
Parisian scandal, much discussed at the time and a cause of one of Lalo's many
bouts of discouragement. His career began propitiously in the 1850s with some
songs and chamber music but he had produced very few recent works, and
nothing of substance, when in 1867 the Minister of State announced a
competition for a new opera. Lalo was 44, essentially unknown as a composer,
though familiar as the viola player of the Armingaud Quartet. In 1865 he
married a pupil, Julie Besnier de Maligny, and we may perhaps attribute his
commencement of the work on 2 May 1866[1] to the encouragement and ease the
marriage afforded: *Fiesque* was eventually dedicated to his mother-in-law,
Mme J.B. de Maligny. Much of it may have been completed when the
competition was announced in 1867, and it was certainly ready for submission
by August 1868. His librettist was Charles Beauquier (1833-1919), a well-
known politician of the Left, to whose credentials we shall return. We have no
details of their collaboration which was never continued after *Fiesque*. Forty-
three[2] operas were submitted; they were examined by two juries, one for the
scores and one for the librettos. Among the composers on the panel Benoit was
by far the most distinguished.[3] By June 1869 a short list of five operas had been
drawn up: *Le Magnifique* in one act, by Jules Phillipot; *La Coupe et les lèvres,*
in five acts, by Gustave Canoby; *Fiesque* in three acts, by Edouard Lalo; *La
Vierge de Diane,* in one act; and *Roger,* in three acts, the composers of the last
two not being identified in the jury's report since scores were submitted

pseudonymously (Lalo's motto, from Montaigne, was "Qui ne lutte, ne choit"). After three votes the prize was awarded to Phillipot's *Magnifique,* with Canoby's opera coming second, despite being judged "impossible au théâtre" (in the commission's own words), and Lalo's third; *Fiesque* was reported to be an "ouvrage également, consciencieusement et savamment écrit par les auteurs du poème et de la musique."[4]

Although with hindsight it is easy enough to ridicule such strange judgments, it is nonetheless hard to imagine that either Phillipot or Canoby, whose names have effectively disappeared from the pages of history (the latter was a pupil of Halévy), could have composed operas with even a fraction of Lalo's vitality and invention. Beauquier's record as a radical and the opera's republican tone may have weighed against him in those declining days of the Second Empire; Lalo was not supported by any musical notabilities. A correspondence opened in *L'Art musical* in which Paul Lacome, himself a composer who might well have been an entrant in the competition, pointed out the folly of any competition which could produce a one-act curtain-raiser as a winner: "On ne fait courir les poneys corses avec les grands chevaux anglais," he commented.[5] A month later a correspondent complained that the director of the Théâtre-Lyrique, Pasdeloup, being also on the jury, was thereby prejudiced against complicated and expensive works.[6] Pasdeloup's first season as director had been unfortunate, with lawsuits on his hands and the rapid emergence of anti-German feeling directed at his performance of *Rienzi.* Beauquier, with his politician's nose, scented scandal and wrote formally to Camille Doucet, director of theater administration, protesting at Pasdeloup's inclusion on the jury and at the exclusion of other theater directors. He knew full well that Pasdeloup had not been named when the juries were officially drawn up the previous year, and demanded the cancellation of the competition. Lalo publicly dissociated himself from this protest in a letter to the *Chronique musicale* on 1 September 1869, yet although Beauquier's move won no official response, the winning opera was not staged until 1876 when four performances at the Opéra-National-Lyrique produced the coolest reception from audience and critics. By that time Lalo was considerably more prominent, but whether he attended *Le Magnifique* or not is not recorded.

Fiesque came near to production on two occasions. Perrin, director of the Opéra, in the twelvemonth between the announcement of the results and the outbreak of the Franco-Prussian War, expressed an interest, but how far his plans went it is hard to say. A better prospect came from the Théâtre de la Monnaie, Brussels, so often the scene of important premieres of French operas in this period, where the director, Vachot, even announced a cast (11 February 1872) for a forthcoming production. For quite unconnected reasons Vachot shortly afterwards tendered his resignation, with the effect that his successor, Avrillon, was under no obligation to pursue his predecessor's plans. Despite Gounod's entreaties *Fiesque* was dropped.

Lalo showed some confidence that a performance might be arranged in Germany. Presumably before the outbreak of war he had had a German translation made by Levysohn and a vocal score engraved at his own expense, with both French and German texts. This appeared in February 1872 over Georges Hartmann's imprint.[7] In the same year certain fragments were heard in Paris. Lalo's wife sang Léonore's *Air* (no. 18) on 27 January 1872 at a concert given by the Société Nationale,[8] and the Entr'acte before act 2 (no. 7) was heard as an *Intermezzo* arranged for ten instruments in a concert given on 30 January that year by the Société Classique de Musique de Chambre. Shortly afterwards, on 8 December 1872, this same piece reappeared as the first of four movements in the orchestral *Divertissement* eventually to be one of Lalo's best-known works. This was the beginning of the long process of dismemberment on which Lalo was now embarked, for once this pretty movement was known in its new setting it became harder for its original version to make its way in the world. Subsequently the movement was published in its reduced scoring as the first movement of the *Aubade.*

In 1873 there were a number of concerts in Paris featuring parts of *Fiesque*: the overture, on 6 April and 4 May; Léonore's *Air* (No. 18) once again, on 4 May; and two scenes at the Odéon on 10 April—a part of no. 5 under the title *Invocation pour la patrie* was arranged for soprano and chorus, and the final scene of act 2 (no. 13) was heard as *Scène de la conjuration.*[9] With the provision of a *fortissimo* ending in place of the previous *pianissimo,* the overture was published by Durand, Schoenewerk et Cie in 1875[10] and performed again at the Concerts du Châtelet on 23 January 1876. It was also given two performances by Hans von Bülow in Glasgow in December 1877. Lalo was sent a program.[11]

Fiesque seems then to have lain undisturbed in Lalo's bottom drawer for some ten years. His muse was fertile, and new works were produced with regularity without drawing on old ones. When, exactly, the carving up of *Fiesque* began it is hard to say, since precise dates of the smaller works have not yet been established. All the evidence points to a major decline in Lalo's capacity for original creation around 1883, *Le Roi d'Ys* having probably been finished (though not scored) by 1881. Most of the works attributed to the last ten years of his life (1883 to 1893) were adapted from earlier pieces, the most notable exception being the lacklustre Piano Concerto of 1889. In 1886 he composed his Symphony in G minor, large parts of which were based on *Fiesque,* including the motto theme in all four movements, the whole of the scherzo and most of the material of the slow movement. An *O Salutaris* was published, metamorphosing the love duet in act 2 (no. 11) into a religious hymn; similarly the triumphal march in act 3 (no. 23) became, of all things, a *Litanies de la Sainte Vierge* for women's chorus and organ.[12] One song (in no. 5) was published separately as *Humoresque,* and a duet (no. 4) as *Au fond des*

halliers, with different words. The first part of no. 10 was pressed into service in
Le Roi d'Ys for its premiere in 1888.

The most substantial reworkings, however, were made for the two
dramatic works which preoccupied Lalo in his last years when the eventual
acclaim won by *Le Roi d'Ys* spurred him to new undertakings he no longer had
the physical strength or the inspirational resources to fulfil. These were the
choral pantomime *Néron* staged at the Hippodrome on 28 March 1891 and the
opera *La Jacquerie* of which Lalo only lived to "compose" one act, the
remaining three being supplied by Arthur Coquard. This was published by
Choudens in 1894 and staged in Monte Carlo in 1895, two years after Lalo's
death.

Of *Néron* there survives a manuscript vocal/piano score not in Lalo's
hand[13] containing stage directions for a mimed spectacle in which only the
chorus sang words. *Fiesque* was the major supplier, but themes from the
Symphony and *Le Roi d'Ys* appear, also adaptations of two songs, *La Zuecca*
and *La Fenaison,* both first published, like the Symphony, only in 1887. Not a
note of *Néron* was new. In the scenario by P. Milliet, devised unashamedly as a
grand spectacle, Nero's life is sensationalized in three scenes: the first shows
Agrippina plotting to murder Britannicus. She forces a slave to take the poison
first. Nero enters to a paean of praise followed by Britannicus. Agrippina pours
the poison for Britannicus, and though his mistress Junia attempts to intervene
Britannicus dies. Junia then repulses Nero's attentions and takes refuge with
the Vestal Virgins, while Flavius who had protected her reveals that he is a
Christian. A cross appears in the sky. In fury Nero orders Flavius and the
Christians to be thrown to the lions. There follows an orgy with a sequence of
ballets and a bacchanale.

In scene 2 a gladiatorial combat in the Circus is presented, followed by a
duel on horseback. Finally the Christians are led in. On the stroke of a tam-tam
the trap opens... The stage directions fall silent at this point, but the
Hippodrome's public would expect real lions. Scene 3 opens with a moonlit
street scene, purely for contrast, followed by another orgy of drinking and
debauchery interrupted by the burning of Rome, the death of Nero, the
massacre of his women, and the triumphal entry of Galba.

La Jacquerie has a rather more serious claim on our attention. The
libretto, by Edouard Blau (librettist of *Le Roi d'Ys*) and Simone Arnaud, is a
historical drama based on the Jacques rising of 1358. The starving peasants are
ordered to find a dowry for the Comte de Sainte-Croix's daughter Blanche.
Jeanne, a widow, explains that her son, Robert, has gone to Paris to seek his
fortune. Guillaume, the peasant leader, stirs the men up to sedition. Robert
suddenly returns with a tale about an unknown girl of noble birth he met in a
convent. The Count arrives with his daughter Blanche and a baron whom the
Count has chosen as her husband. Needless to say, Blanche, when left alone,
reveals that she does not love the baron but an unknown young man whose

wounds she once tended in a convent. The curtain falls on Robert's sudden appearance and their horrified recognition of each other.

Coquard's remaining three acts complete this somewhat predictable tale of violence, misunderstanding, and religion cast very much in the Scribe mould. Coquard's music is an acceptable copy of Lalo's style without, it seems, any direct borrowing, even from the music of act 1. Lalo wrote little new music, but had to contrive more recitative and linking sections than were necessary for *Néron*. The nature of Coquard's collaboration leaves some doubt as to the true extent of Lalo's original work on the opera.

Charles Beauquier, the librettist of *Fiesque,* was a radical député for Doubs for thirty years. He had numerous publications seized by the police and was said to be a frequent duellist. He had no experience in opera, but had, however, published a book in 1865 grandly entitled *Philosophie de la musique* in which certain commonplace observations about music are set forth at considerable length. Beauquier called himself a "guerrillero de philosophie" being more politician than philosopher; furthermore he firmly declared himself to be neither musician nor scientist. He had much to say on the effects of music upon animals and on the relationship between music and morality, but his grand conclusion, unveiling "ce qui constitue l'essence de la musique," is a hollow disappointment. How Lalo came in contact with this man is not known. After the *affaire Fiesque* was over, Beauquier published yet another tract on the earlier subject: *La Musique et le drame: étude d'esthétique* (1877), a hot blast against Wagnerism in the aftermath of Bayreuth's opening. Beauquier defended the high level of disbelief in romantic opera and the necessarily second-class nature of libretto writing, calling attention to the craft that keeps the action moving while allowing lyrical elaboration and balances simple with complex, ensembles with solos, cavatinas with recitatives, and so on. Most surprising is his hostility to rhyme, since the libretto of *Fiesque* is full of rhyme and since Beauquier was clearly a disciple of Scribe in his treatment of the libretto and in versification; like Scribe he was content with standard vocabulary and doggerel meter:

> Eloignons ces présages
> Qui glacent mon coeur en feu!
> Pourquoi craindre les orages
> Quand le ciel est si bleu!

It was surely Beauquier, not Lalo, who chose the subject, strongly identifying with its republican message. This was Schiller's early drama *Die Verschwörung des Fiesco zu Genua,* based on the conspiracy in 1547 led by Giovanni Luigi Fiesco, count of Lavagna, against the Doria family, Doges of Genoa. This Fiesco was a descendant of the Jacopo Fiesco familiar from

Simone Boccanegra (though that opera was not then known in France). Apart from its political message the play had the advantage of being of a type and by an author successfully adapted by many other composers, but it had not been treated thus before. Conspiracies generally make good operas since male-voice ensembles and suspicious rendezvous are frequent. At the same time it required no unusual level of disbelief, by the standards of mid-nineteenth-century opera, and mixed great national upheavals with personal conflicts of love and loyalty in a manner familiar to habitués of the Opéra in the 1860s. Schiller's play required little knowledge of previous events and few improbable confrontations, with a forward momentum that leads to a grand climax in the final act. Its five acts and 75 scenes include numerous characters and subplots that were readily discarded, so that Beauquier's libretto offers a skillful reduction into broad streams of action, using the chorus to replace the great number of named conspirators and giving little space to the Doria opposition. Schiller himself acknowledged the prolixity of his first version when he reduced it to fifty-nine scenes.[14] Beauquier follows Schiller closely in the opening scenes and departs more freely from him in later acts, especially in his treatment of the women. He also attributes Gianettino's murder to Verrina, not Borgonino. Three conflicts are interwoven with some skill: (1) The Fiesco party, republicans, are entrenched against the ruling Dorias; (2) Fiesque's wife, Léonore, is jealous of his involvement with Julie, daughter of Andreas Doria; (3) Verrina, the old republican fanatic, though a supporter of Fiesque, is deeply distrustful of his ambition and fears that he simply craves absolute power for himself.

Schiller helpfully summarized his main characters as follows:

Fiesque, "Count of Lavagna, leader of the conspiracy, a young, slim, handsome man of 23, proud of bearing, friendly and dignified, courtly and smooth, but also artful." Tenor.

Verrina, "republican conspirator. Sixty years old, grave, serious and gloomy," not unlike Beauquier himself in later life, one imagines. He is a humorless fanatic like Marcel in the *Huguenots* and naturally a bass (requiring over two octaves).

Léonore, Fiesque's wife. "A lady of 18, pale and delicate, refined and sensitive, attractive but not dazzling, a wild melancholy in her countenance." Soprano.

Julie, countess (princess in the opera), daughter of Andreas Doria, the Doge, and sister of Gianettino Doria. "Twenty-five years old, large and ample, proud and coquettish, her beauty spoiled by bizarrerie, striking but not pleasing, a malicious mockery in her appearance." Soprano.

Beauquier may not have intended the opera to reproduce these characters as Schiller offers them, but it is striking how strongly we are invited to support the Fiesco faction. Julie is clearly not sympathetically drawn, her father is not seen at all and her brother only once. The Doria party is an unseen enemy throughout the opera.

The following scene-by-scene summary of *Fiesque* is divided into three parallel commentaries. First in each case is a synopsis of the action with a reference to the Schiller scene or scenes on which it is (often very loosely) based. Second is a commentary on the music, and third a record of the later use Lalo made of the music of each scene.

No. 1. *Overture* (also termed *Introduction* and *Prélude*)

Was it accident or mockery that led Lalo to open his opera with an abrupt *fortissimo* Tristan chord? The second bar resolves it into a diminished seventh, and the third confirms the tonality of E flat. The overture is based on two themes from the opera, the love duet (no. 11) and the conspiracy chorus (no. 13) in a simple form: A (in E flat) - B (in G flat) - A (in E flat, varied) - B (in E flat), maintaining an Adagio 3/8 throughout. Lalo originally gave a quarter-note pulse of 66, changed it to 60 in the vocal score, and ended up with 52 in the printed full score. The published score has a briefer *fortissimo* ending for concert use.

Act 1, Scene 1—An Anteroom in Fiesque's Palace

No. 2. (Schiller I/1). *A ball is in progress. Léonore and her attendant ladies are masked. A brisk dance is being played offstage. Léonore is in a melancholy mood, distressed by Fiesque's obvious passion for Julie, the Doge's daughter. Her ladies comfort her. All leave.*
     Most of Léonore's music is in recitative, sometimes very passionate and expressive; the chorus always sings in breezy rhythms. Léonore has a set-piece song "Amour, amour, ton souvenir" in simple melodic style, followed by a fiery outburst of passion and anger, calmed by the chorus.
     [The off-stage music anticipates the *Choeur dansé* later in the act (no. 5). It became the main theme of the scherzo of the Symphony. The choral interjections were also used as a secondary theme in the same movement. Léonore's song was not reused but her opening recitative reappears as Agrippina's opening recitative in scene 1 of *Néron;* to the fiery second part she forces poison upon a reluctant slave later in the same scene.]

No. 3 (Schiller I/2). *Gianettino Doria (his only appearance) enters with the Moor Hassan, both masked. Gianettino engages Hassan to kill Fiesque for 100 sequins. Hassan extracts a promise of 300 sequins before agreeing to do so.*

Hassan is treated as a comic figure; the bargaining for more money is not in Schiller and is conducted in a jolly 6/8, after the manner of *Robert le Diable.* Gianettino's music is more ponderous and menacing.

[The menacing music accompanied Agrippina's poisoning of Britannicus in scene 1 of *Néron,* then Nero's repulsed advances upon Junia, also Nero's order to throw the Christians to the lions in the same scene. The light Allegretto 6/8 which accompanies the bartering dialogue was transformed "comme une marche funèbre" for the removal of Britannicus's corpse!]

No. 4 (Schiller I/4). *Julie enters, followed by Fiesque. Gianettino points to Fiesque, then he and Hassan leave. Julie is afraid of Léonore's jealousy, but Fiesque declares his passion. As proof of it Julie demands the portrait of Léonore that Fiesque wears round his neck. He gives it. Julie gives her own portrait in return. The scene closes in a love duet. They go out.*

The opening exchange is accompanied by a brilliant web of rushing figures in 12/8, occasionally broadening into a full texture. Lalo's harmonic and orchestral gift is at its most brilliant here. The love duet chooses C major and 4/4 but is full of warmth and expressive chromatic detail. Servières rightly draws attention to its departure from the prevailing Gounod style of the 1860s. Schiller made no further dramatic capital out of the exchange of portraits, for they are not mentioned again.

[Fiesque's first strong declaration of love became Junia's lament over Britannicus's body in scene 1 of *Néron.* The C major love duet was published in 1887 as *Au fond des halliers,* with different words by André Theuriet, though still a love duet. Lalo rewrote the closing page.]

Act 1, Scene 2

No. 5 (Schiller I/7). *A curtain rises to reveal the ballroom crowded with masked dancers. After a choral dance, a group in black masks, including Verrina, is on the left. Léonore and her friends, also masked, are on the right. Verrina approaches Léonore and together they lament the sufferings of Genoa and Fiesque's apparent desertion of their cause. Fiesque approaches. His mood is frivolous and he simply proposes wine and dancing to enliven the company. "What is that black arm-band?" he asks Verrina. "In mourning for my mother, our country!" is the reply. Fiesque sings a gay song with choral interjections, acclaiming the life of pleasure. Verrina is unmoved. After Fiesque moves away, Verrina resumes the lament. Fiesque and Julie approach, to suspicious mutterings from the conspirators. The choral dance is resumed.*

This is one of the great scenes of the opera, constructed as an arch form, with the brilliant choral dance at the beginning and end. The lament is a fine musical idea, made more striking by its bare two-part texture against an inner dominant pedal. Its later return is amplifed by cries of "Liberté!"

Ex. 1

Fiesque is rather crudely portrayed here as a man of fickle jollity, his music being abrupt and self-consciously frivolous. His set-piece song, though, is a potential show-stopper, to be compared perhaps with "Questa o quella" as an invitation to carefree merriment. Verrina of course maintains his sombre, fanatical tone.

[The choral dance, in E major, already heard offstage at the beginning of the act, is the main material of the scherzo of the Symphony, where the key of E jars somewhat with the G minor before it and the B flat after. It was written in 3/8 but renotated in 6/8 in the symphony, a revision that Berlioz also made with the carnival music of *Benvenuto Cellini* when he adapted it in the *Carnaval romain* overture. Lalo had played under Berlioz's direction in the 1840s and may well have modelled this scene on Berlioz's. The lament, in E minor, became the trio section of the same scherzo. Both scherzo and trio are said to have figured originally in a youthful symphony offered to Pasdeloup and rejected.[15] If this is so, the *Fiesque* version would have been a vocal adaptation of an instrumental original and the Symphony a salvage of the original. The lament also appeared twice in *Néron,* firstly as a double chorus of Christians and pagans in scene 1, secondly to accompany the entry of the Christians into the arena in scene 2. That scene is introduced by Verrina's threatening declaration before the resumption of the choral dance, "Si nos malheurs ne doivent pas finir, mieux vaut mourir." Fiesque's song in praise of the gay life was published as a separate song under the title of *Humoresque,* the chorus parts being omitted, with no reference to the ailing opera from which it had been extracted.]

No. 6 (Schiller I/9). *All have left the stage except Fiesque. Hassan approaches to warn him that his life is in danger. Handing him a list of proscribed names Hassan prepares to stab him. But Fiesque, seeing Hassan in a mirror drawing a dagger, disarms the assassin. Pressed to reveal his paymaster, Hassan gives Gianettino's name and admits the reward of 300 sequins. Fiesque then offers him a thousand sequins to work for him instead. Hassan is at his service. He is engaged to go about the city to pick up gossip about the Dorias and test the feelings of the people. A duet closes the act.*

Hassan's comic-villainous character is sustained with a staccato motif on clarinets and bassoons in octaves heard throughout the scene. A fragment of it punctuates a striking series of chords as Hassan craves Fiesque's mercy:

Ex. 2

Ex. 2 (continued)

Hassan's offer to be of service, advertising his nefarious gifts, is a lively aria in 6/8, F-sharp minor, and the closing duet in C minor/E flat similar in character. The scene is thus rather long for the action it carries.

[Neither the aria nor the duet appear to have been used in later works. The opening part of the scene, including Hassan's attempt to assassinate Fiesque, was used for the gladiatorial combat in scene 2 of *Néron.*]

Act 2, Scene 1—A Public Square in Genoa

No. 7 *Entr'acte. Flower-sellers move among the crowd.*
    After a sombre introduction Lalo writes an enchanting ballet movement worthy of Delibes or Bizet, with a fluffy melody typical of the best French ballet music:

Ex. 3

The movement is ternary with a somewhat earnest sustained theme for a middle section.
    [This is the best-known music from *Fiesque.* The main melody (ex. 3) was drawn from a *Sérénade* for piano published in 1864. Lalo rescored it for 10 instruments in 1872 under the title *Intermezzo* and did a second rescoring, for full orchestra, when he used it as the first movement of the *Divertissement,* also in 1872. The chamber version reappeared as the first movement of two in the *Aubade* in 1887.[16] In *Néron* it was a ballet in which Venus repulsed Vulcan during the orgy at the end of act 1. The sombre introductory 14 bars were also the opening of scene 3, to evoke a moonlit street.]

No. 8 (Schiller I/10 and II/4). *Hassan draws the people into conversation. Pretending that a rich relative has died, he offers to buy wine for everyone. When they grumble about the oppression they suffer under the Dorias, Hassan tells them that Gianettino has abducted Verrina's daughter. At this news they reject Hassan's offer of drink and call instead for vengeance.*
    Hassan remains locked into triplet rhythms, 6/8 and 3/8, with a lively pace throughout the scene. The writing for the men's chorus is admirable, always urgent and vital, introducing at the end the "vengeance" rhythmic motif:

Ex. 4

    [The first part of this scene became the music for the *combat équestre* in scene 2 of *Néron.* The vengeance cry was adapted as a coda in 4/4.]

No. 9 (not in Schiller). *Verrina appears and echoes the crowd's cry for vengeance. Tumult is audible off-stage. Verrina rages in fanatical fury against the oppressors. The chorus is roused to a high pitch of frenzy in support. Hassan congratulates himself on his success. The women pray for victory. Verrina vows to avenge his daughter's dishonour. The curtain falls.*

The music of this scene is masterly throughout. Dramatically it resembles conspiracy scenes in *Guillaume Tell* and *Les Huguenots* but the music has unique vigor and force, particularly in the choral participation. The interplay of chorus and orchestra is particularly striking, with the rhythmic "vengeance" figure prominent throughout. Verrina's entrance is tremendously dramatic, worthy of Verdi, and the free arioso of his opening lines is strongly punctuated by threatening bass lines and accented orchestral interjections. The main movement is a driving Allegro con fuoco in A major. No French composer in the 1860s, not even Bizet, was writing music as powerful as this.

[In *Néron* Verrina's entrance music was used for the release of the lions in the Circus in scene 2—with the addition of a tam-tam and some minor alterations. The choral Allegro was the central section of Galba's triumphal entry at the end of scene 3.]

Act 2, Scene 2—A Room in Fiesque's Palace

No. 10 (Schiller II/19 and III/2). *Fiesque, alone, recalls his love for Léonore. Then he recounts how a vision of glory has fired his ambition; he dreams of power and of becoming Doge, acclaimed in triumph by the people.*

The two parts of this solo scene are clearly contrasted: tenderness and nostalgia followed by martial splendor. Lalo creates a delicate murmuring for the background to Fiesque's main melody "Dans le livre de mes amours" and a finely shaped line for the tenor voice. The music tautens as his thoughts turn to his public ambition and the key moves from G, through chromatic steps, to D. The motif dominating the second part is curious in its closeness to the "vengeance" rhythm, but seems designed more to reflect the drive of his ambition:

Ex. 5

The gradual build-up and repetitive rhythms are reminiscent of Smetana's style at its most vigorous. The scene has great scope for a fine tenor, and matches the quality of the previous scene. As Servières pointed out, it is dramatically equivalent to Jean's dream of glory in act 2 of *Le Prophète,* although the musical treatment is quite different.

[Lalo excerpted this scene for separate performance, although no such performance has been traced. The autograph full score of the opera contains two autographs here, the second entitled "Le Rêve de Fiesque" with fuller scoring. There is also an autograph vocal score[17] transposed down a tone into F with the vocal part on the bass clef; an altered modulation takes the second section down two tones into C, and the conclusion is changed to end in a brilliant *fortissimo* rather than a *diminuendo* as Fiesque sinks in thought, as it is in the opera. A second manuscript vocal score (not autograph)[18] gives the scene transposed down a fifth to C (with the conclusion in G) for baritone, although the vocal part is still notated on the treble clef.

[The Andantino section is the only part of *Fiesque* to find its way into *Le Roi d'Ys.* It appears there as a love duet for Mylio and Rozenn in act 3 scene 1 to the words "A l'autel j'allais rayonnant." Servières, again citing Marcel as his source,[19] states that it was put in at the request of the tenor Talazac when there was not time to compose a new duet. Perhaps it was Talazac who had sung the scene in an earlier concert performance. The adaptation as a duet works extraordinarily well.

[The chromatic passage that links the two parts of the scene recurs twice in *La Jacquerie,* the first part of *Fiesque* to be used in that opera. It is first a chorus of peasants, complaining of their distress and second the announcement of Guillaume of a meeting place in the forest where the rebellion is to be launched.]

No. 11 (Schiller III/3). *As Fiesque sits lost in thought Léonore enters. She upbraids him for his neglect. He protests that he loves her still, despite her doubts. Admitting that Julie is the cause of her unhappiness, he promises to avenge Léonore's sufferings within two days, without explaining what form that vengeance will take. Her hopes are restored and a love duet ensues. They leave.*

Léonore's plaintive Andantino cantabile "J'avais rêvé" is a touching expression of her sorrowful character. Fiesque's reassuring responses and the references to Julie are carried forward in a swift, bouncy passage that seems intended to remind us of his frivolity. The love duet (already used, with the introduction of the scene, in the overture) approaches Mendelssohn's style with a somewhat relaxed sweetness as if Fiesque is unable to participate with conviction. Léonore closes the scene with some attractive but perfunctory decorations on the melodic line.

[In *La Jacquerie* the theme of Léonore's Andantino is used to express the widow Jeanne's maternal feelings for Robert. The closing duet of this scene was published as an *O Salutaris,* opus 34, for women's voices and organ[20] where the Mendelssohnian style is surprisingly appropriate.]

No. 12 (Schiller III/4). *Hassan is pleased with his work. Julie has engaged him to poison Léonore, but he expects to make twice as much money by reporting this plot to Fiesque. Exit.*

A unison theme, staccato as usual for Hassan, opens and closes a scene which has good momentum and contrast without any formal sense of aria. This is clearly a vehicle for a good comic actor, without whom this further scene for Hassan would seem one too many.

[In *La Jacquerie* the staccato theme announces the arrival and later the exit, of the villainous and oppressive Comte de Sainte-Croix and his retinue, in striking contrast to its essentially humorous function in *Fiesque.*]

No. 13 (Schiller II/17 and 18). *The picture scene. Verrina enters with three conspirators, Borgonino, Sacco and Romano. Romano is a painter, and a page brings in his picture of Virginius slaying his daughter Virginia. They are anxious to know if Fiesque is serious in their cause or not, so when he comes in they ask his opinion of the painting. Virginius, a plebeian, killed his daughter to keep her from Appius Claudius, a decemvir, a situation similar to Verrina's rage at Gianettino for his abduction of his daughter. Fiesque admires Virginia's beauty. Verrina is furious at his casual response, but Romano gives him the painting. Fiesque pauses for a moment then suddenly declares Romano's art to be mere artifice: Romano merely paints great deeds while he, Fiesque, is a man of action. He reveals his plans for insurrection. Verrina is overjoyed and the five men join in an ensemble of defiance. The curtain falls.*

This is one of the most elaborate scenes of the opera, abundant in musical ideas but without fixed movement or tonality until toward the end. Fiesque is at first represented with the light, flitting figures that express his frivolity. One or two well-defined figures animate the accompaniment throughout. Verrina's vehement outburst "Il ne dormait pas, le lion," is resoundingly reinforced when the others join in, but the following broad unison "Plus de crainte," already heard in the overture, is too strongly Meyerbeerian, with an exaggerated dotted rhythm over a broad 9/8 pulse. The A minor Allegro that concludes the scene has much more individual character even though its function as curtain music is obvious. With excursions into A and F (major and minor) the tonality of the scene is predominantly E (major and minor), the key associated with Verrina throughout the opera.

[Fiesque's declaration of his plans, a highly dramatic moment over tremolo strings, was used in *La Jacquerie* for Guillaume's insurrectionary appeal to the peasants, "Tes petits enfants sont sans pain!" preceded and followed by the heavily syncopated F minor Allegro which in *Fiesque* merely follows it. Verrina's "Il ne dormait pas, le lion" became Guillaume's "Courbe le front, courbe le dos," with a degree of development of the motif unknown in *Néron.*]

Act 3, Scene 1—A Courtyard in Fiesque's Palace

No. 14 (Schiller IV/1). *Borgonino places sentinels on guard, leaving instructions that anyone may enter but no one may leave, on pain of death.*
    A sombre introduction presents a theme on oboe and cor anglais over a timpani roll:

Ex. 6

This has a heavy tragic mood dispelled when the curtain rises. The same theme is transformed into a jaunty Allegretto as the sentries are posted. Borgonino's menacing orders are punctuated by angular recitative figures of savage force.
    [The slow introduction, transposed up into E minor, served as prelude to the *Invocation pour la patrie* (the "lament" section of no. 5, in act 1) when it was played at the Odéon in 1873. It then became the opening passage of the Symphony in which example 6 is treated as a motto with dramatic reappearances in all four movements. Despite its prominence in that work, Lalo used it as the introductory music to the first scene of *Néron*. The Allegretto version of the same theme became the music for Britannicus's processional entry and Nero's hypocritical greeting. After Britannicus's death and the removal of his corpse, the same theme is heard, perhaps intended ironically, if any such subtleties are permitted in a score so manufactured as that of *Néron*. Borgonino's gruff recitative was given to Agrippina, seething with hatred, early in scene 1 of *Néron*.]

No. 15 (Schiller IV/2-5). *Three groups of conspirators enter, one group at a time, each challenged by the sentries. They join in a conspirators' chorus.*
    The entry music is full of atmosphere, in stealthy march rhythm, but the unaccompanied chorus is disappointing, especially when compared with some well-known examples of the genre in earlier operas (especially in *Rigoletto* and *Ballo in Maschera*). It relies almost entirely on abrupt changes of dynamic and contrasts of staccato and legato, homophonic throughout.
    [The entry march recurs as the scene in *Néron* scene 1 where Agrippina asks Locustus for poison with which to dispatch Britannicus; it also appears for Locustus's exit.]

No. 16 (Schiller IV/6). *Fiesque appears and exhorts his conspirators to be ready on the word "patrie"; a bell will sound when combat is to be joined. Verrina is uneasy about obeying Fiesque's orders and begins to suspect his ambition. All join in a chorus of enthusiastic defiance.*

The conspiratorial tone is sustained with short abrupt phrases and a marching pulse preserved for some time. The men's chorus is vehemently enthusiastic, constantly interjecting "Aux combats!" and the like. Despite its energetic forthright style and Verrina's exaltation, another conspiratorial chorus at this point seems supernumerary. The verse here is less than the best.

[This is the first scene in the opera from which no borrowings appear to have been made.]

No. 17 (Not in Schiller). *Léonore appears and all fall silent. Fiesque orders all the conspirators to leave. She is alarmed by all these preparations. He urges her to be calm and instructs her to hide, since a woman is due to arrive shortly. Fiesque goes out.*

Léonore appears on a dramatic diminished seventh from the chorus, and example 6 is heard behind her questions. The brief scene is in recitative throughout.

[No borrowings.]

No. 18 (Not in Schiller). *Léonore, left alone, guesses that it must be Julie who is due to arrive. Her aria expresses her uneasy premonitions and her longing for the restoration of Fiesque's love.*

Recitative followed by an aria in two parts, Andante then Agitato, make up a classic solo scena. Lalo's harmonic style is at its most assured and characteristic, with an expressive line supported throughout by apt orchestration and concluding in a rapt and tranquil C major. Léonore has more depth of character than any other figure in the drama.

[Lalo's wife performed this scene twice in 1872 and 1873, transposed down a fifth. Lalo's original version transposes the music up a semitone from the beginning of the Andante from C into D flat.[21] The whole scene was used in *La Jacquerie* at the conclusion of act 1 where Blanche, left alone, laments her dilemma of loving a stranger when she is betrothed to another. Over the existing accompaniment is superimposed a tolling bell to fine effect.]

No. 19 (Not in Schiller). *Léonore hides on hearing the approach of Julie preceded by a servant, who instructs her to wait and then leaves. To divert herself Julie sings a song in praise of coquetry and the cynical advantages of winning others' admiration. But then she admits this is simply to keep her spirits up; in truth she does suffer the pangs of love.*

Suddenly we enter the world of opéra comique with some couplets in the style of Auber or Offenbach. Julie admits these are not her true feelings as if to point out that this is not Lalo's true style, a transparent manipulation of the operatic medium.

[Despite its clearly popular manner Lalo seems not to have reused this *Chanson* at all. The original version of this scene was a tone higher, in B minor.[21]]

No. 20 (Schiller IV/12 and 13). *Fiesque arrives. Julie rebuffs his endearments in alarm and suspicion. In a duet Fiesque wins her confession of love. She is still frightened of betrayal. Fiesque, hurt, starts to leave. Julie calls him back begging for his forgiveness. Suddenly he turns on her and tells her that he has never loved anyone other than Léonore, whom he then reveals in her hiding place. He also produces the phial of poison Julie gave to Hassan. Julie explodes with cries of rage. In a closing trio Léonore perceives the truth about Julie, supported by Fiesque, while Julie threatens vengeance. Cannonfire is heard. Fiesque tells Julie that the Dorias' rule is doomed. Soldiers lead her away as the curtain falls.*

The light tone of the preceding scene throws the high dramatic and musical intensity of this one into relief. Lalo's invention is at its finest and the interplay between recitative and lyricism matches the alternation of calm and agitation as the relationship between Fiesque and Julie swings in the balance. The recitatives are abrupt and always pointed with some thematic development of interest. They interleave more stable sections as follows: Recitative (B flat)— Duet (B Flat and A flat)—Recitative—Solo (Julie) (F sharp)—Recitative— Trio (B flat minor and major). The tonality eventually returns to its initial B flat. The duet section is in two parts, the slower second part introducing a chromatic expressive phrase of great beauty:

Ex. 7

This leads into an A flat section, "Je t'aime avec ivresse," which is not only superbly melodic but is also original in structure. Fiesque sings his stanza alone (with no trace of irony in his blandishments), then Julie replies with some unaccompanied and disconnected figures acknowledging her surrender. When Fiesque resumes his melody her line turns out to be a counterpoint to it, eventually leading to her adoption of the melody herself:

Ex. 8

Her solo in F sharp, over throbbing triplets, is another passionately expressive line, apt for such an outpouring of feeling:

Ex. 9

Fiesque's sudden rebuff is all the more hurtful and abrupt. When Léonore is revealed there follows a trio, the first part of which, in the minor, is typical Lalo in its regular emphatic chords on the second beat and its reminiscence of the "vengeance" rhythm (ex. 4). The tempo broadens into a 9/8 in the major; Léonore and Fiesque sing in sweet concord while Julie's angular line stands out. A final dramatic recitative closes this magnificent scene.

[The Symphony, *Néron* and *La Jacquerie* all pillaged this scene, especially the slow movement of the Symphony. Its main melody is based on example 9 with much use of the final B-flat trio and a quotation also of example 7. Their sequence is much altered and developed but the movement as a whole is an interesting reworking of this movement, supported by the Symphony motto theme, example 6. In *Néron* the violent recitative which supported Léonore's emergence from hiding is used, outrageous though it may seem, for the release of lions from the trap in the Circus scene, followed as a conclusion to scene 2 by the dramatic recitative that closes the scene in *Fiesque*—appropriately violent without doubt. For *La Jacquerie* Lalo took the F-sharp theme (ex. 9) with the extension it had acquired in the Symphony and used it for Robert's narration at the moment when he recalls waking in a convent to find himself tended by this unknown girl of celestial beauty. It is immediately followed by the A-flat theme (ex. 8) which had escaped service in the Symphony, now transformed from 6/8 to 4/4 with no loss of character.]

Act 3, Scene 2—Genoa Harbour, with the Sea and Vessels Beyond

No. 21 (Schiller V/7). *In the darkness all is confusion. Men miscellaneously armed rush hither and thither, with Hassan among them doing well for himself. Looting, pillage, murder and fire are all around.*

    A single one-bar rhythm, repeated innumerable times, evokes the bustle and confusion. Apart from Hassan's interjections the scene is choral throughout. The women are directed to be dressed as men, not for dramatic reasons but to provide a mixed choral sound. The rhythmic monotony is broken by a final Allegro in 6/8 in Lalo's most virile manner.

    [With the cut of one of Hassan's stanzas and its responding line for the chorus, this movement served for the debauchery scene in scene 3 of *Néron,* followed by the burning of Rome, the death of Nero and the massacre of his women. The choral lines were retained for the most part, beginning "Venez, venez, c'est l'heure."]

No. 22 (Schiller V/13). *Borgonino and Verrina enter. Borgonino reports Fiesque's victory and the liberation of Genoa. Fiesque has been proclaimed Doge. Verrina has killed Gianettino.*

    Violent recitative fills this very short scene.

    [No borrowings.]

No. 23 (Not in Schiller). *The crowd pours in and acclaims Fiesque and Léonore in a triumphal march. A deputation of senators presents him with the keys of the city. Fiesque and Léonore exchange tender words.*

    The triumphal hymn is for double chorus in antiphony, joining together for the closing bars. The music then recalls Fiesque's dream of power in act 2, scene 2 (no. 10) as his dream is realized. Fiesque's exchange with Léonore appropriately recalls their love duet (no. 11).

[The triumphal march was adapted as *Litanies de la Sainte Vierge,* for three-part female chorus and organ.[22]]

No. 24 (Schiller V/16 and 17). *Fiesque asks Verrina why he stands apart from the jubilation. Verrina replies that he can play no part in the celebration of power and affirms his loyalty to the old Fiesque, not to the new. Fiesque dismisses Léonore and all the people. Alone together, Verrina implores Fiesque to renounce his new-won office. Fiesque is displeased but offers his hand in friendship, which Verrina defiantly refuses. As Fiesque turns to go Verrina proposes an act of clemency to inaugurate his reign: Fiesque should free the galley slaves on board the ships. "Tell them they are free," replies Fiesque. But Verrina persuades him to go on board in person. After a final plea for humility, which Fiesque ignores, Verrina follows Fiesque on to the gangplank and suddenly hurls him into the sea. At his cries the crowd rushes in only to hear from a defiant Verrina: "Il est mort! Vive la patrie!"*

Lalo's final scene leaves no overwhelming sense of musical peroration, being mostly in short sections with abrupt changes of tempo and mood. There is dramatic tension, with constant menace in Verrina's music and the habitual variety in Fiesque's. A single bass theme, with which Verrina is often in unison, provides the main recurrent material. As they step on to the gangplank the rhythm of Fiesque's dream of power (in no. 10) returns in a big *crescendo* to the point where Verrina throws him over; its similarity, whether accidental or deliberate, to the "vengeance" motif is now made tellingly clear as Verrina's defiance finally thwarts Fiesque's ambitions. Verrina's murder of Fiesque was Schiller's invention; the historical Fiesco fell into the sea accidentally.

[No part of the scene was borrowed in later works.]

One may compare *Fiesque* favorably with both Meyerbeer's and Gounod's operas which at the time of its composition were in highest favor in France, and also with his later work, including *Le Roi d'Ys.* That opera's long popularity (now waning) was well deserved, but there is no less freshness of invention or dramatic tension in *Fiesque.* Against the few scenes which disappoint (nos. 15, 16, 19, 21) must be set the greater number of scenes of magnificent quality (nos. 4, 5, 7, 9, 10, 20) whose total neglect is lamentable and whose humiliating and undignified adaptation for *Néron* and *La Jacquerie* was worse than oblivion in that they implied under-valuation on the composer's part, as though he was dismembering his work out of pique and discouragement. The style is predominantly vigorous and four-square with emphatic rhythms and a fondness for scherzo metres, 3/8 and 6/8. Lalo rarely adopts the willowy French style associated with Gounod, Fauré, and

Massenet, for he represents the more red-blooded streak in French music. His harmony is strikingly assured and resourceful, derived, like Tchaikovsky's, from Schumann with frequent chromatic alterations that never approach the more fluid chromaticism of Wagner, largely because the rhythmic pulse is strong. His characterization is successful with the women's roles, especially Léonore, but the pleasure seeking Fiesque, whose motives and intentions are never entirely clear, is a less convincing character relying largely on extrovert singing. Verrina, as a gloomy monomaniac, is scarcely ambiguous but scarcely original either. He has a regular series of chords, including the recurrent French sixth, to identify him, and certain rhythms are used, as we have seen, to link the action at different points.

Fiesque's failure in the 1868 *concours* turned Lalo's mind back to instrumental composition at an apposite moment, since Saint-Saens's encouragement and the foundation of the Société Nationale afforded new opportunities in the concert hall which he eagerly seized. But it was success in opera which he craved and which eluded him until the tardy acclaim of *Le Roi d'Ys* at the age of 65. The poor reception of the ballet *Namouna* in 1882 contributed to the rapid decline of inspiration soon after; the criticism that *Namouna* was the work of a "symphonist," which he took to be a term of abuse, particularly riled him. It is perhaps fortunate that *Fiesque* has survived at all; once it had been carved into pieces it might have suffered the fate of Berlioz's *Les Francs Juges* of which only those parts survive which were not taken up in later works. But then Berlioz came to regard the opera as flawed, whereas Lalo, we may permit ourselves to guess, held his *Fiesque* in high enough esteem to hope that one day it would attract serious attention and receive even a portion of the admiration it deserves.

Notes

1. The date is found on the autograph vocal score, F-Pn (Conservatoire MS 1399). The autograph full score of the whole opera is in the library of the Stiftelsen Musikkulturens främjande, Stockholm, to whose staff I wish to express my thanks. This manuscript lacks the Overture, which was detached for publication and is now in F-Pn (Conservatoire MS 1400).

2. This is the number given in most sources, although Pougin in the Fétis *Supplément* says that 52 composers entered.

3. *Revue et gazette musicale,* 15 November and 20 December 1868.

4. Ibid., 27 June 1869. An account is also given in Georges Servières, *Edouard Lalo* (Paris, 1925). *Roger* may have been the two-act opéra comique *Roger Bontemps* by Jean-Jacques Debillemont, played at the Fantaisies-parisiennes on 18 March 1868. The composer of *La Vierge de Diane* is unidentified.

5. *L'Art musical,* 8 July 1869, p. 251.

6.   Ibid., 12 August 1869, p. 292.

7.   The proofs of the vocal score, with Lalo's corrections, are in F-Pn (Conservatoire Rés.1978). The score was reissued by Durand, Schoenewerk et Cie in 1875 with the plate number D et Cie 2163, though there can have been little demand for it and surviving copies are rare. See below, note 10, for the date of this issue. I am greatly indebted to Mr. Richard Macnutt for the loan of his copy of the Hartmann issue.

8.   She sang it transposed down a fifth, in F. Lalo's autograph score of this transposition is in F-Pn (Conservatoire MS 1401).

9.   Lalo prepared new scores for both these scenes, to be found in F-Pn (Conservatoire MS 1391).

10.   This date is given by Servières, op cit., p. 31. The plate number D et Cie 2162 adjoins that of the reissued vocal score (2163) and the full score of the *Symphonie espagnole* (2165), issued in 1875. The autograph full score of the overture, showing the altered ending, is in F-Pn (Conservatoire MS 1400).

11.   *Musiciens peints par eux-mêmes,* ed. Marc Pincherle (Paris, 1939), p. 167.

12.   Servières, op cit., p. 109, gives the *O Salutaris* the date 1886 and the *Litanies* a publication date of 1876 (Hartmann). No Hartmann edition has been seen, however, whereas the work was certainly issued by Heugel. In view of other borrowings from *Fiesque* the *Litanies* may well belong to the last years. The opus number (34) suggests a date for the *O Salutaris* as early as 1884.

13.   F-Pn (Conservatoire MS 8412).

14.   See *Theatre-Fiesko,* ed. Hans Heinrich Borcherdt (Weimar, 1952).

15.   Servières, op. cit., pp. 38 and 112, cites an article by B. Marcel in the *Depêche de Toulouse* of 27 April 1892 as his authority. He also cites (p. 124n) a letter from Lalo to himself of 25 October 1887 asserting that two youthful symphonies were destroyed, although "certain fragments were re-used."

16.   It is often said that all of the *Divertissement* was intended as ballet music for *Fiesque,* but there is no reason to connect any movement other than the first with the opera.

17.   F-Pn (Conservatoire MS 5043-2).

18.   F-Pn (Conservatoire MS 5043-1).

19.   Servières, op. cit., p. 70; see note 15.

20.   See above note 12.

21.   Both earlier and published versions are found in F-Pn (Conservatoire MS 1399), Lalo's autograph vocal score of the whole opera.

22.   See above note 12.

Dramatic Time and Music in Tchaikovsky's Ballets

Roland John Wiley

In "The Essence of Russian Music," one of the first of many essays which Gerald Abraham has contributed to the bibliography of required reading for students of that repertoire, he writes of the dramatic aspect of Russian opera. It tends to be somewhat disjointed, he observes, and in the finest Russian operas

> ...we find only the sketchiest outline of a plot, no drama of development, but a brilliant series of stage pictures, sometimes highly dramatic in themselves, sometimes not at all so, detached and apparently almost disconnected yet cumulatively most effective in their presentation of an exuberantly vital whole.[1]

A Philistine might state the case more bluntly, pointing out that Russian opera, as a rule, does not observe the unities—that a work like *Boris Godunov* or *Prince Igor* is involved with more than one strand of action, changes setting freely, and advances the time frame of the action without regard for the audience's ignorance of what has happened in the periods not represented on stage.

Granted that Russian composers felt no obligation to comply with the "Aristotelian" precepts set forth in 1570 by the Italian humanist Lodovico Castelvetro, such a criticism misses the mark for another reason. It fails to recognize that the so-called unities, whatever their reputation as an ideal, are difficult to observe and if observed can lead to inartistic results. Carl Dalhaus hints at this possibility when he writes:

> "Unity of Time" and "Unity of Place [Raum]"...condition and mutually support each other. The unity intended by the dogma signifies, properly speaking, unobtrusiveness, neutrality, or even indifference to place and time, [and] in the extreme, "placelessness" and "timelessness." In contrast, a change creates an emphasis; and every transformation of one moment governs at the same time the mindfulness of another. A change of place [Ortwechsel]—provided it means something and is therefore a characteristic and not some indifferent scenery change—makes conscious a lapse of time, and on the contrary colors the feeling that time has passed, the impression given out by one place; the space [Raum] seems no longer to be the same even when it is the same; and through the transformation, real or imaginary, it moves forward instead of remaining a neutral background.[2]

The very act of changing time or place, then, brings with it the realization that time has passed; breaking the unities emphasizes an awareness of time. This phenomenon mitigates to some degree the disjunctions of Russian opera because, like any other artwork, opera imposes a particular conception of time onto an audience. From beginning to end the artwork moves at its own rate(s), typically not the same rate as that of normal clock time.

"Time is a phenomenon of the style of a work of art," writes Dmitri Sergeevich Likhachev in a discussion of literary genres,

> But time is also represented: it is an object of representation. The author can represent a short or long interval of time, he can cause time to pass slowly or rapidly, and he can represent it as flowing continuously or intermittently and sequentially or non-sequentially (i.e., regressing to an earlier stage or "getting ahead of himself," etc.). He can represent the time of the work [as] being closely linked to general historical time or out of touch with it and locked within itself, and he can represent the past, the present, and the future in diverse combinations.[3]

If time may be employed imaginatively by the creator of literary works, it offers even richer possibilities to the composer. The propensity of music to affect our sense of time in a song or an opera, normally the result of a slower than natural delivery of the text, is axiomatic. The additional expressivity that music brings compensates for the loss of naturalistic effect.

Musicologists have begun to analyze time. Reinhard Strohm, for example, has explained how Wagner, in *Tannhäuser*, represents "two complete and uninterrupted time cycles simultaneously: that of the day and that of the year."[4] Whatever Wagner's disdain for "Aristotelian" rules, the result betrays a concern for the unity of time. Like Likhachev, Strohm sees the representation of time as susceptible to changes in rate. And Wagner, Strohm points out, addresses the problem of filling-in the action between acts 2 and 3 by a long orchestral piece, "Tannhäuser's Pilgrimage," in which the "music functions as a slow-motion picture giving the whole of the pilgrimage...."[5] In effect, Wagner here uses music to create continuity, to describe action essential to the story but not otherwise taken up in the opera (though Tannhäuser will sing about his pilgrimage later in act 3), and to compress a long period of dramatic time into a few minutes of clock time.

In *Die Meistersinger von Nürnberg* he does this again. Of all Wagner's works, this one perhaps most carefully observe the unities: there is one central action, the wooing of Eva; the entire opera is set in one locale, Nuremberg (though in a number of places within Nuremberg), and takes up a little more than a day.[6] The prelude to act 3, like that of *Tannhäuser*, compresses a long stretch of dramatic time into a few minutes of clock time: it tells us Sachs's thoughts as he reads through the night. There is an additional detail here not present in *Tannhäuser*. The clock time of this prelude, when added to that of the intermission between acts 2 and 3, is proportionate to the amount of dramatic time that separates the arrival of the Night Watchman after the riot from David's arrival home the next morning after delivering Beckmesser's shoes. Dramatic time and clock time are not yet the same, but they are, from the end of act 2 to scene 1 of act 3, proportionate to one another. The speeding up and slowing down of dramatic time by means of music varies within narrower limits in *Die Meistersinger* than in Wagner's other works: the first note of the act 1 prelude sets dramatic time in motion at a rate and consistency that follows through to the end and even accounts for intermissions.

These observations, which at first seem unrelated to ballet, in fact provide models for the study of Tchaikovsky's use of time in *Swan Lake, Sleeping Beauty,* and *Nutcracker.* Indeed, these works illustrate a range of responses to dramatic time that embraces both Russian opera's disjunct series of stage pictures and Wagner's efforts to establish temporal continuity. Two issues in Tchaikovsky's ballets are of special interest: the parallel relationship between disjunction (or conjunction) in dramatic time and musical articulation, and the use of music to represent time.

Swan Lake is Tchaikovsky's *Meistersinger* as regards unity: there is one central action, Siegfried's betrothal; the entire ballet is set in one locale (though in two places within that locale, the castle and the lakeside), and the narrative takes up a little more than a day, beginning late one afternoon and ending the following evening. This work exemplifies Tchaikovsky's simple but effective method of coordinating temporal and musical articulations, which employs two principles. First: if the action of an interior act continues the action at the end of the preceding act without a noticeable disjunction in dramatic time, the musical articulation at the beginning of the interior act is gentle and nondisruptive, such as to confirm or enhance the effect of unbroken continuation.

Act 1 of *Swan Lake* takes place at the party celebrating Siegfried's coming of age. At the end, a flock of swans passes overhead, and Siegfried leaves in pursuit. Tchaikovsky accompanies these occurrences with the first statement of the celebrated "swan" theme. As act 2 begins, the swans alight on the lake; presently Siegfried and his companion arrive. Tchaikovsky stresses these parallel situations by repeating the "swan" theme and by giving it a new continuation. In particular the softness of the opening of act 2—a harp arpeggio above quiet tremolo strings—enhances the effect of unbroken dramatic time between the acts. The intermission has also played a part. The lake is nearby (or so one justly presumes, if the hunters reach it soon enough to spend most of the night there); the time of the intermission plus that of the instrumental introduction of act 2 constitute, as does the parallel situation in act 3 of *Die Meistersinger,* a period of clock time proportionate to the amount of dramatic time that has passed between the acts—in this case, the time Siegfried would require to find his way from the party to the lake.[7]

Act 2 ends at dawn by the lakeside; act 3 begins later in the day at a ball in Siegfried's palace. The intermission between them should last about as long as the first intermission, but it represents a considerably longer period of dramatic time: Siegfried has not just returned home, but has in addition passed most of the day. Tchaikovsky responds to this situation by invoking his second principle: to match a break in the continuity of dramatic time with an emphatic musical effect. He begins act 3 of *Swan Lake* with two measures of solo tympani at the dynamic level *forte*. This sudden, powerful explosion of sound immediately reorients the audience's perception of dramatic time. The strength of the musical articulation galvanizes the listener's attention to the present moment in the drama and bridges over whatever dramatic time remained unaccounted for by the intermission.

In act 4 the action again takes place by the lakeside at night. Siegfried has again made his way there from the castle "during the intermission," and arrives only after the swans have made their appearance in an initial number. And Tchaikovsky again begins the act with an unobtrusive musical effect, as he had the beginning of act 2. To the likenesses of setting and music between these acts, then, we may add the similarity in the treatment of musical articulation with respect to dramatic time.

Sleeping Beauty is Tchaikovsky's *Boris Godunov* or *Prince Igor,* that is, a brilliant series of stage pictures. The parallel is not fortuitous and may be more telling than any parallels *Sleeping Beauty* might have with *Swan Lake* and *Nutcracker* on the basis of genre. With respect to time, *Sleeping Beauty* is a tale or *skazka,* a literary type in which, Likhachev points out, the traditional unity of time representation is considerably violated. Many of the points he goes on to elaborate apply directly to the adaptation of the *skazka* to the ballet:

> The tale tells of the past—of things that happened once upon a time and place....
>
> The time of the tale is closely bound to the composition. Time is often mentioned in the tale, but it is measured from one episode to another, beginning at the last event: "in a year," "in a day," "the next morning." A break in time is a break in the development of the composition....
>
> The time of a tale always moves sequentially, in one direction, and never returns. The story is always moving ahead. This is why there are no static descriptions in the tale. Whatever descriptions of nature there may be are made in passing and continue the development of the action....
>
> The tale ends with an "absence" of events—prosperity, death, feasting.... The achievement of well-being marks the end of the time of the tale. The time in question is inseparable from the composition, the events, and the narrative itself. When the story is ended, so is the time.[8]

The action of *Sleeping Beauty* starts at no particular time and ends about 121 years later. That act 3 is set in the gardens of Versailles and that Apollo, in the apotheosis, appears in the guise of the Sun King, are topical elements of the libretto that do not affect the characteristics of dramatic time. The sense of the narrative is more general than that; it is of things that happened once upon a time and place.

The long period of time that separates one episode from the next—baptism, courtship and crisis 20 years later, deliverance 100 years after that, and marriage after another (unspecified) period—precludes the integration of intermissions into a conception of continuous dramatic time. It is therefore no surprise that every act of *Sleeping Beauty* opens with a powerful, attention-galvanizing musical articulation of the kind that opened act 3 of *Swan Lake*. Every act constitutes a re-beginning that requires the instantaneous adjustment of the audience's time perspective.

But time in *Sleeping Beauty* involves more than overcoming the disjunctions between the acts. A study of the work reveals some of the most extraordinary temporal conceptions to be found anywhere in Tchaikovsky's *oeuvre*. These conceptions are at once unusual and perfectly appropriate to the genre and libretto.

The dances of the fairytale characters in act 3 originate in long sanctioned traditions of divertissement. They add nothing to the narrative (being performed by the guests invited to the wedding of Aurora and Désiré); none except the pas de deux of the wedding couple involves a character who has appeared in the story before. The temporal effect is precisely what Likhachev perceives in the ending of a *skazka*—prosperity, feasting, the absence of events. The achievement of well-being in act 3 of *Sleeping Beauty* literally marks the end of dramatic time. There is no sense of progression in this act even though it contains almost an hour of musical and physical movement. The convergence of balletic tradition and narrative inaction makes this act the longest passage of clock time in *Sleeping Beauty* in which Tchaikovsky modifies the progress of dramatic time.

It is not, however, the only such passage, nor the most striking. For this we must turn to act 2, no. 19, the symphonic entr'acte "Le Sommeil," the first 95 measures of which represent Florestan's sleeping kingdom. This magnificent piece is striking in part because it lacks any practical function. It is not a cover for scene changes (an entr'acte intended for this purpose was cut from the production in the week before the first performance), nor is it an accompaniment for any stage action.[9]

Nor can it be argued that the entr'acte represents the compression of dramatic time in a manner comparable to the one observed in "Tannhäuser's Pilgrimmage" or even the beginning of the second act of *Swan Lake*. In the first place, the dramatic time has already jumped forward to the period of Désiré's life by the beginning of act 2, some 10 musical numbers before the entr'acte. In the second place, there is no action to summarize in *Sleeping Beauty* at this point: *nothing has happened* in Florestan's castle for a hundred years.

And yet there is a point. On the most accessible level, the somnolence of Florestan's court is being presented here as a simple tableau vivant which shows us the moments just before the return to life.[10] If this were all, the piece would seem to be a static description of the kind Likhachev excludes from the *skazka.* The music immediately and repeatedly tells us that the entr'acte is more. The principal tonality (before Désiré and the Lilac Fairy enter) is C major, expressed by cadence and by the pedal note C, which sounds somewhere in the orchestra throughout. C major was the destination of a breathtaking modulation in act 1 at the very moment when the Lilac Fairy plunged Florestan and his court into slumber.

Tchaikovsky also composes much of the entr'acte on themes recalled from the earlier acts: the opening theme sounded as Florestan's kingdom was frozen into sleep, the culminating action in the rivalry of Carabosse and the Lilac Fairy; following this are the melodies associated directly with the good and evil sisters. If the entr'acte unfolds in the key of slumber, the themes are associated with the forces that had vied for Aurora's life. These themes, however, are not merely restated: they are transformed. In particular the sleep motive has lost the imperious quality, the majesty and power it had before, and all vestiges of malice and brutality have been removed from the music of Carabosse.

If the entr'acte has no practical function, if it is not being used to compress time and so to enhance temporal continuity, what is its purpose? The thematic transformations offer a clue, in that the contentiousness between the Lilac Fairy and Carabosse, which took the form of strident clashes in the prologue and act 1, has been reduced to naught. Carabosse's mischief in particular is now but an echo. Far from being a static description within the *skazka,* the entr'acte is a description of stasis, which also serves as a commentary on the workings of time on the conflicts of a century earlier. It does not so much represent time as describe its effects. To the extent that the entr'acte slows the flow of dramatic time, it is like the divertissement in act 3. But it does contribute to the narrative, and in addition the musical effect is much different from that of act 3. Here Tchaikovsky comes as close as he ever does to those extraordinary moments elsewhere in Russian music (such as Ratmir's aria in act 3 of *Ruslan and Ludmila* and the beginning of *In Central Asia*) that unfold in a rarified temporal dimension where the movement of the notes paradoxically creates a sense of non-movement.

Given the citation of an "eastern" work of Glinka and one of Borodin as parallels to Tchaikovsky's entr'acte, the reader might be tempted to pursue some connection with the Russian composers' often fabricated orientalisms. The subject matter of *Sleeping Beauty* tends to discourage such a pursuit, to say nothing of Gerald Abraham's apt conclusion that "the oriental element in Russian music is purely external and decorative."[11] Tchaikovsky, moreover, can make less claim to musical orientalism on the basis of his bloodlines and his artistic predilections than his nationalist colleagues. A worthier speculation might be that Tchaikovsky's remarkable effects of stasis in *Sleeping Beauty* originate in his own cultural heritage, which through Orthodoxy embraced Byzantine concepts of escaping time. Aurora escapes time in her hundred-year sleep, the fable escapes it in the divertissement. Indeed, the story of this ballet is French chiefly in the language of its prior literary source.

To understand Tchaikovsky's use of time in *Nutcracker* we must know the action of the ballet as set forth in the original libretto, a scenario rarely followed in modern revivals. The first scene of act 1 begins at the Christmas party in Silberhaus's home. The godfather of Silberhaus's children, Councillor Drosselmayer, gives them a nutcracker, which young Fritz breaks and his sister Clara consoles. When all have retired, Clara comes downstairs to check on the nutcracker. Midnight sounds; an army of mice invades; the Christmas tree grows to immense proportions. The toys come alive and try to defend themselves against the army of mice. This failing, the Nutcracker engages the mouse king in single combat; when the latter gains the advantage, Clara throws her slipper at him and thereby saves the situation. The army of mice is routed, the Nutcracker, now a handsome prince, leads Clara over to the Christmas tree and they are lost in its branches.

In the second scene, a forest of fir trees in winter, snow begins to fall and gradually turns into a blizzard.

Act 2 takes place in Confiturembourg, the land of sweets. The Sugar Plum Fairy awaits Clara and the Nutcracker. When they arrive, Clara is hailed for having saved the Nutcracker from death. In celebration of his safe return, a lavish divertissement is performed.

As drama, *Nutcracker* is unusual if not flawed. While events without causes and the unmotivated shifts in setting between scenes contribute to dramatic weakness, the problematical aspects of the ballet are more easily perceived by analyzing the use of time.

The story shifts aspect rather awkwardly in the middle. It begins as a simple narrative and ends as a *skazka*. Soon after the second act begins, a sense of well-being is achieved, and events stop; the ballet conveys that mythical aura and relatively indistinct "once upon a time and place" that characterized *Sleeping Beauty*. Ending in this way does not, however, make the audience any less aware that the work began in a far more mundane setting, and that the sense of disjunction, typical of the *skazka* and needed to accomplish such a radical shift in locale, is absent. In act 1, moreover, the librettist takes pains to make the audience specifically aware of time. The wall clock is an important property. According to the instructions Tchaikovsky received from the balletmaster, it sounds at nine o'clock, again when Drosselmayer arrives, and again at midnight. The children, in addition, are given leave to stay up until ten o'clock in their own pas de deux.

From act 1 to act 2 we move from time to timelessness. This shift in perspective would not be so disturbing if the librettist had invoked some simple device, such as a dream, to justify the magical occurrences that begin when Clara goes downstairs to check on the nutcracker. Neither published libretto, balletmaster's plan, nor Tchaikovsky's instructions refers to any such device. Nor is the music, which in *Nutcracker* follows the stage action more closely and continuously than in Tchaikovsky's other ballets, allowed to exercise its ability to alter the rate of dramatic time. Especially relevant in this regard is the quiet articulation at the beginning of act 2, where Tchaikovsky again, as he had in *Swan Lake,* quotes the music at the end of act 1 to insure the least possible disruption of dramatic time. The score is disturbingly continuous and conjunct here and at other points where a sense of disjunction would be warranted and even desirable, such as the beginning of act 1, scene 2, where both a new place and time are represented on stage without the least assistance from the score. As matters stand, the miraculous events and sweeping changes in landscape happen too quickly to be credible, even granting the most liberal exercise of theatrical illusion. They are dramatic strokes on the scale of those in *Sleeping Beauty,* but they are not separated by intermissions and are not coordinated with appropriate musical articulations.

What we find in Tchaikovsky's ballets are examples of how the study of time can enrich our understanding. The beginning of a useful classification based on time may be perceived in *Swan Lake* and *Sleeping Beauty,* a classification that permits comparison across genre boundaries. In the case of *Sleeping Beauty,* as in Russian opera, an understanding of dramatic time mitigates the negative effect of features otherwise construed as faults. The issue in *Nutcracker* is not so much classification as analysis—devising methods that help us identify the work's dramatic infelicities. The study of time need not be restricted to philosophical musings and intricate semiotic calculation; like the study of harmony or formal pattern, it can be part of our first approach to an opera or a ballet.

Notes

1.   *Studies in Russian Music* (London, n.d.), p. 14.

2.   *Wagners Konzeption des musikalischen Dramas* (Regensburg, 1971), pp. 29-30.

3.   "Time in Russian Folklore," *International Journal of Slavic Linguistics and Poetics* 5 (1962): 79, 74. For a more comprehensive discussion of this topic (and but one title in an imposing bibliography on the subject of time in the artwork), see Likhachev's *Poetika drevnerusskoi literatury* [Poetics of old Russian literature], 2nd ed., expanded (Leningrad, 1972).

4.   "Dramatic Time and Operatic Form in Wagner's *Tannhäuser,*" *Proceedings of the Royal Musical Association* 104 (1977-1978):5; see also Kenneth G. Chapman, "Siegfried and Brünnhilde and the Passage of Time in Wagner's *Ring,*" *Current Musicology* 32/1981:43-58.

5.   Strohm, "Dramatic Time," pp. 6-7.

6.   Act 1 of *Die Meistersinger* takes place in the afternoon, act 2 from early evening to the middle of the night, and act 3 most of the next day. The shortness of the night is explained, of course, by the fact that the action of act 2 takes place on Midsummer's Night, the shortest night of the year.

7.   When Marius Petipa and Lev Ivanov revised *Swan Lake* for a production in St. Petersburg, they combined acts 1 and 2 into one larger act. In doing this they implied more strongly than had the original collaborators the proximity of the party and the lake, and thus increased unity of place. With the intermission now gone, the two playings of the swan music changed the basis of perception of dramatic time, in that the time required for the journey of Siegfried was now expressed (as in "Tannhäuser's Pilgrimage") by music alone, with its ability to compress dramatic time. In short, dramatic time was no longer perceived directly in its analogy to clock time; it came to be *represented* by music.

8.   "Time in Russian Folklore," pp. 86-88.

9.   The cadence at measure 95 sets off the first part of the entr'acte from the second, at the beginning of which stage action recommences with the arrival of the Lilac Fairy and Désiré. Their coming marks a striking change in the music, which takes on a sense of forward progress commensurate with the resumption of progress in dramatic time.

10.   Even though *Sleeping Beauty,* strictly speaking, proceeds in the manner of a *skazka* (that is, without returning to the beginning), the powerful symbolic undercurrents of meaning in the tale—Aurora-Dawn, and the stages of her life, which include a springlike reawakening—give the story a strong cyclic sense.

11.   "Oriental Elements in Russian Music," in *On Russian Music* (London, n.d.), p. 80.

Tchaikovsky and Chekhov

David Brown

All his life Tchaikovsky was a voracious reader. His tastes were wide; periodicals, both on current issues and historical matters, biographies and novels by native and foreign authors—all provided the fare of his daily reading. Among foreign writers, the English novelists Dickens and Thackeray especially commanded his respect and gratitude, while his reading within the literature of his own country was avid and wide. But though his own fame would have gained him easy access to the presence of many leading figures in Russia's literary world, he seems to have had little direct contact with any of them. He did, while still only a student, chance to meet Dostoevsky at a social gathering, but there seem to have been no further personal encounters. Much more important was his early relationship with Alexander Ostrovsky, the leading Russian playwright of the 1860s. Tchaikovsky met him in January 1866, immediately after arriving in Moscow to take up his first appointment as teacher of musical theory in what was imminently to become the Moscow Conservatoire. Ostrovsky provided Tchaikovsky with the subject of his first opera, *Voevoda,* and was even persuaded by the composer in 1867 to write part of the libretto. Turgenev is known to have come into Tchaikovsky's life when he attended the première of Tchaikovsky's First String Quartet in March 1871, and especially during the 1870s he was one of the composer's favorite authors. Since Turgenev lived mostly abroad, meetings would have been difficult, but Tchaikovsky deliberately declined to take such opportunities as did present themselves. As he explained to his patroness, Nadezhda von Meck, when she demanded to know of him why he did not call on Turgenev in Paris in early 1879: establishing new acquaintanceships was always a torment to him. But by now there was a deeper reason. Direct contact with an author could bring disenchantment, for the reality of the man might prove to fall sadly short of the image which could be conjured from his creations. Tchaikovsky had discovered this all too painfully when he had met Tolstoy in Moscow late in 1876. It was wonderful to sit beside this colossus of Russian literature during a performance of Tchaikovsky's own First String Quartet, and to see him reduced to tears by the Andante Cantabile, but the mundane streak, even pettiness, which Tolstoy exposed in his subsequent conversations with

Tchaikovsky so badly smeared the latter's image of the great writer that for some years Tolstoy's work suffered in his estimation. They never met again, nor did Tchaikovsky ever attempt to encounter the novelist face to face, preferring to allow his esteem for the man to recover itself through readings of his works.

It is not so surprising, therefore, that the direct contact Tchaikovsky had towards the end of his life with the young Anton Chekhov should have been only brief. Yet this relationship with a man who became one of Tchaikovsky's favorite authors is of much interest, especially since it might have produced a direct effect upon the composer's own work. As for Chekhov, who viewed Tchaikovsky as one of the greatest ornaments of the Russian scene, it was a matter of profound pride that Tchaikovsky should have had such faith in his talents as to entertain the idea of a collaboration.

Chekhov had been contributing to humorous journals for some years before he came to Tchaikovsky's notice. His first published work appeared in 1880, while he was still a very junior medical student in Moscow, and during the next few years he produced a vast quantity of humorous sketches which gave him much popularity with a lowbrow readership, and through which he developed his skill as a writer. In the mid-1880s he was able to place his work with two established St. Petersburg dailies, the *Peterburgskaia gazeta,* (The Petersburg Newspaper) and *Novoe vremia,* (The New Times) and this enabled him to exploit further the more serious vein which had been opening up in his work, and also brought him to the notice of a more discerning public such as that to which Tchaikovsky belonged. "Yesterday I was utterly enchanted by a *Chekhov* story in *Novoe vremia,*" he wrote to his brother Modest on 20 April 1887 O.S., providing the first indication that he was acquainted with Chekhov's work.[1] "He has great talent, hasn't he?" he added, suggesting perhaps that his knowledge of the writer's work extended beyond this particular story, and was wide enough for him to discern a rising star of some magnitude. Also present at this reading aloud was Tchaikovsky's close friend, Nikolai Kashkin, who believed that Tchaikovsky had forthwith written a letter of congratulation to Chekhov.

The work in question had appeared only two days earlier; later revised and reprinted with the title *Pis'mo* (The Letter), it is the tale of a humble deacon who, observing that his son is not conducting his life according to the strict code in which he had been brought up, asks his pompous clerical master to devise a stern letter of reproof. After being persuaded against sending the letter by a poor and less-than-perfect priest, who advises instead that he should extend forgiveness, the father finally decides to dispatch it after he has added a gossipy, open-hearted postscript which annihilates any effect the exhortation might have had. Tchaikovsky's enthusiasm is easy to understand, for it is a simple tale with many human resonances—of a father whose affection for his son in the end ingenuously transcends his paternal disapprobation, of a disorderly priest whose instinctive humanity is greater than that of his self-righteous superior, and of a son whose worst fault seems to have been a determination to live his life according to his own beliefs.

Tchaikovsky's personal acquaintance with Chekhov followed at the end of the next year. By then Chekhov had come to know Modest Tchaikovsky, and at the latter's St. Petersburg home on 14 December 1888 O.S., he was introduced to the composer himself to discover that their admiration was mutual. Though there seems to have been no further personal contact for nearly a year, Tchaikovsky continued to delight in Chekhov's stories as they were published. And as their quality continued to improve, Tchaikovsky's estimate of their creator continued to consolidate. "Have you read anything by Chekhov?" he asked Yulia Shpazhinskaia, wife of the dramatist Ippolit Shpazhinsky, who had provided the libretto of Tchaikovsky's most recent opera, *Charodeika* (The Enchantress). Yulia had separated from her husband, and had plunged into a long period of deep depression from which Tchaikovsky had tried to draw her by encouraging her literary inclinations. Chekhov could be an excellent stimulus to her creative talents, he thought. "In my opinion this young writer promises to become a very major literary force," he continued in his letter of 9 January 1889 O.S. "Would you like me to send you collections of his short stories (he doesn't write large pieces)?"[2]

Meanwhile Chekhov's own veneration of his country's leading composer had reached such a pitch that he longed to express his feelings in public terms. "Dear Pyotr Ilich," he wrote on 12 October 1889 O.S.,

> This month I am going to begin printing a little collection of my own stories. These stories are tedious and boring as is autumn, their tone is monotonous, and artistic elements in them are closely entwined with medical ones. Nevertheless this has not prevented me from daring to turn to you with a very humble request: permit me to dedicate this little collection to you. I very much wish to receive a favorable reply from you, in the first place because this dedication will afford me great pleasure, and secondly because it will gratify at least a little that deep feeling of respect which impels me to remember you daily. The idea of dedicating this anthology to you was sown in my head as far back as that very day when, while dining with you at Modest Ilich's, I heard that you had read my stories.
>
> If, together with your assent, you would also send me your photograph, then I shall receive more than I'm worth, and I shall be happy to all eternity. Forgive me for troubling you, and allow me to wish you all the best.
>
> Yours sincerely,
> A. Chekhov[3]

Though Chekhov still did not enjoy anything like equal fame in Russia, Tchaikovsky was delighted by the writer's proposal. "Just think, Chekhov has written to me that he wants *to dedicate to me* his new collection of stories," he wrote to Modest four days later, "I have called on him to say thank you."[4] Indeed, two days before, he had hastened to respond to Chekhov's request for a signed portrait, and to make good any deficiency in the oral expression of thanks he had already given to Chekhov when he had made an unannounced call on the writer:

> Dear Anton Pavlovich,
>   I enclose my photograph, and earnestly beg you to entrust yours to the messenger.
>   Did I adequately express my gratitude for the dedication? I think I did not, and so I will tell you again that I am *deeply touched* by your kindness.
>   I press your hand warmly.
>
> > P. Tchaikovsky[5]

Chekhov did more than was requested, sending not only an inscribed photograph, but also a volume of his own stories. "I am very, very touched, dear Pyotr Ilich, and I give you boundless thanks," he wrote in the covering letter,

> I am sending you both a photograph and a book, and I would send you the sun, too, if it belonged to me.
>   You left behind your cigarette case. I am returning it to you. Three cigarettes are missing; these were smoked by the cellist, the flautist and the teacher.
>   I thank you again, and allow me to remain your heartfelt, devoted,
>
> > A. Chekhov[6]

The inscription in the book, a second edition of *Rasskazy* (Stories) printed earlier that year, is revealing: "To Pyotr Ilich Tchaikovsky, from his future librettist: 14.X.89 A. Chekhov." The unexpected visit on which Tchaikovsky had left behind the cigarette case and had discussed an operatic collaboration had taken place earlier that same day, as Chekhov excitedly reported next day to his friend Alexei Suvorin, the wealthy publisher and proprietor of *Novoe vremia.* "Yesterday Tchaikovsky called on me, which made me very proud—in the first place because he's a great man, secondly because I love his music passionately, especially *Onegin.* We want to write a libretto."[7] This was to be based on Lermontov's "Bela," the first part of his novel *Geroi nashego vremeni* (A Hero of our Time). However, there was going to be no time for the moment to pursue further this proposal, as Tchaikovsky had to tell Chekhov on 20 October O.S. Feeling he needed in some way to match the unexpected gift of the book he provided Chekhov with a subscription for Moscow's most important concert series:

> Dear Anton Pavlovich,
>   I am sending you a ticket for the *symphony concert series of the Rus*[sian] *Mus*[ical] *Soc*[iety]. I am terribly glad that I can be of some little service to you. I cannot deliver it myself, for all this week is being swallowed up in preparing for the first concert and in looking

after our guest *Rimsky-Korsakov* [who was to conduct this concert]. God grant that next week I shall be able to talk with you as I would like.

Yours,

P. Tchaikovsky.

I would point out that the ticket can be used by anyone, if you so wish.[8]

It might have seemed from this sudden, concentrated exchange of letters and with the prospect of creative collaboration in the offing, that a new, intimate friendship was about to begin in the lives of the two men. But it was not to be. Tchaikovsky had engaged in such brief, fervid (if ambivalent) relationships before—for instance with Tolstoy in 1876, as we have noted, and with Balakirev when they had reencountered each other in the autumn of 1884, on which occasion Tchaikovsky earnestly attempted to catch from Balakirev something of the strength of that despotic bigot's own religious faith. The close contact with Chekhov likewise ceased as abruptly as it had begun. How seriously Tchaikovsky entertained the idea of a Lermontov opera with Chekhov as his partner is difficult to say. According to Chekhov's brother Mikhail (as reported by their sister Maria), it was Tchaikovsky himself who had put forward the suggestion; he had even specified which voice should be used for each role, also insisting (characteristically) that there should be no marches or processions. Yet all his life Tchaikovsky was running up against subjects which briefly inflamed his interest and then sank from sight. There were some immediate attractions to the opera composer in this story of a tragic relationship between a young Russian officer and a native girl from the Caucasus. It afforded ample opportunity for love music and also for a harrowing death scene. But other aspects of Lermontov's tale would have been less amenable, and one suspects that "Bela" would never have been written, even if Tchaikovsky had not, within a couple of months, committed himself to set Modest's libretto based on Pushkin's "Pikovaia dama." As for the subscription ticket, Chekhov found he was able to have only limited personal use for it, and his sister Maria seems to have derived the greatest benefit from it.

In the spring of 1890 the volume dedicated to Tchaikovsky was published, and Chekhov confirmed his estimate of the composer in a letter to Modest:

> I am prepared day and night to mount a guard of honor at the porch of Pyotr Ilich's house—I revere him so much. If we're talking of ranks, then he now occupies in Russian art the second place after Lev Tolstoy, who has long occupied the first (I allot the third to Repin [the painter], and award myself the ninety-eighth). I have long harbored an impertinent wish to dedicate something to him. This dedication, I thought, would be a partial, minimal expression of that great critical opinion which I, as a writer, have formed about his magnificent talent, and which, because of my lack of musical gift, I cannot set down on paper. Unfortunately I have had to fulfil my dream through a book which I do not consider my best. It is made up of especially gloomy psychological studies and bears a gloomy title, such that my dedication must be little to the taste of Pyotr Ilich himself and his admirers.[9]

Chekhov need hardly have apologized. Despite its forbidding title, *Khmurye liudi* (Gloomy People), the book collected together ten of Chekhov's best published tales to date. There was "Kniaginia" (The Princess), "Volodya," "Spat' khochetsia" (Sleepy), "Pripadok" (The Seizure)—above all, "Skuchnaia istoriia" (A Dreary Story), that harrowing study in senescence in which a distinguished but now sick medical professor reflects cheerlessly upon an outwardly successful life and career and tries to cope with approaching death— a literary achievement of psychological penetration the more extraordinary considering its author was still in his twenties. Chekhov was much given to self-deprecation, but Tchaikovsky was delighted with the dedication, while Chekhov's assessment of him, duly reported by Modest, touched him deeply. "You can't imagine how pleasant I find *Chekhov's* words about me," he wrote back to his brother. "I'll write to him when I've returned a little to normal."[10]

Though Tchaikovsky must quite certainly have written, no letter survives, and it does not appear that the two men met face to face at this time. Tchaikovsky spent the first four months of 1890 in Italy, and by the time of his return to Russia, Chekhov had set out on his one-man sociological expedition to Sakhalin Island off the eastern coast of Siberia, which took him away from Moscow for the rest of the year. On his return he began to manifest a violent dislike of Moscow, and spent as much time away from it as he could. Tchaikovsky certainly continued to read devotedly new Chekhov stories as they appeared. "What a delightful piece!" he was moved to exclaim to Modest after reading "Gusev" in the Christmas 1890 number of *Novoe vremia.*[11] Then, on one of his excursions to Moscow in November 1891, he received his last letter from Chekhov and wrote his own final letter to the author. Tchaikovsky's is of interest not only because its terms confirm that his regard for Chekhov and his work remained strong, but also because it is yet another proof of the kindness which Tchaikovsky was always prepared to extend to young people to whom he could be of service. His sexual condition of course precluded any family life of his own, but the joy he found in the company of his sister Sasha's offspring when they were children was boundless. To others outside the family he provided material support; several students were funded through their studies with the help of his money, others were given practical help in various ways, and advice was always readily forthcoming when Tchaikovsky judged the cause to be good. In this instance Chekhov was applying to Tchaikovsky on behalf of a young professional musician.

> I have a cellist-friend Marian Semashko, a former student of the Moscow Conservatoire. He is a splendid chap. When he knew that I was acquainted with you, he asked me more than once to intercede with you on his behalf: was there not a place suitable for him somewhere in the capitals or provinces (Kharkov, for instance) or abroad, and if there was, then would you be so kind as to use your influence on his behalf? Knowing from experience how wearying such requests can be, I held back for a long time from troubling you, but today I decided to do so, and I beg you to be magnanimous and forgive me. It both grieves and annoys me that

such a good worker as Semashko is hanging about without a serious occupation, and he begged me so plaintively that I had not the strength to resist him. Nikolai Dmitrievich Kashkin knows him well.

I am alive and well, and am writing a lot but printing little. My extensive story "Duel," will soon be published in *Novoe vremia,* but you don't need to read it in the paper; I'll send you a book [containing it] which will come out at the beginning of December. *Sakhalin* [Chekhov's report on his expedition] is not ready yet.

Again I apologize for troubling you.

Sincerely esteeming you and infinitely devoted,

A. Chekhov[12]

Tchaikovsky had already met Semashko; he was, in fact, the cellist who had smoked one of the cigarettes left behind by Tchaikovsky when he had visited Chekhov the previous year. As expected, Tchaikovsky's response to Chekhov's appeal was immediate; the advice was generously set out, sound and practical, and firm in demolishing any tendency to hubris on the part of Semashko:

Dear, much respected Anton Pavlovich,

Having received your letter yesterday, I wanted to reply forthwith, but then thought that before saying anything to you about *Semashko* (whom I do know, though not enough to have an authoritative opinion about him), it would be better to enquire about him among people who did know—and because I was going to a concert and must see a lot of professional musicians—this seemed an excellent occasion for this. From everything which was said to me about him and which I myself know of him, I have come to the conclusion that Mr. Semashko, thanks to his good technique, application and love of work, might become a good orchestral player. But for some reason I completely fail to understand, he has turned down a proposal that he should join the orchestra of the imperial theaters. He will be visiting me imminently, and this question will be cleared up. If for some family, or some other special circumstance he does not wish to work in Moscow, then I can, of course, give him a recommendation for St. Petersburg—but, whatever the case, this will have to be postponed until next season. If he wants an open recommendation from me, then I will willingly give him one, but I simply cannot myself know where there are vacancies for cellists, and he must have—and does indeed have—means of finding out in other ways. But if he considers employment as an orchestral player is unsuitable for him, then there's absolutely nothing I can do for him. You cannot live by giving concerts, and what cellist, however highly gifted, can live by orchestral playing unless he also gives lessons—which, moreover, are few and far between? *Karl Davydov,* the king of all cellists of our time, played for many years in the orchestra of the Italian opera in St. Petersburg, and it never entered his head that he was demeaning himself by doing so. If Semashko considers such employment beneath his dignity, then this is very strange and very unwise. However, I know nothing definite about this, for I am writing to you before I have seen him. Whatever the case, I promise to show a genuine interest in him.

How glad I am, dear Anton Pavlovich, to see from your letter that you are in no way angry with me, for I did not really thank you for the dedication of *Gloomy People,* in which I take immense pride. I remember that during your expedition [to Sakhalin], I was always going to write a long letter to you, even attempting to explain which particular qualities in your talent so captivated and bewitched me. But there was not the time for it—and, above all, *I had not got it in me.* It is very difficult for a musician to express in words what and how he feels in regard of this or that artistic phenomenon.

And so, thank you for not complaining about me. I am awaiting "The Duel" impatiently, and of course I shall certainly not follow your advice to wait until December, although I warmly thank you in advance for the book. God grant that during this visit to Moscow we shall be able to see each other and have a chat.

I press your hand warmly. Sincerely devoted to you,

P. Tchaikovsky[13]

It is very doubtful that the meeting took place, even though Tchaikovsky remained in Moscow more than a fortnight longer. It is impossible to escape the suspicion that he did not really want to meet Chekhov face to face—that, as with Tolstoy, he preferred to think of him through his works. As for Chekhov, his detestation of Moscow drove him in March 1892 to shift his headquarters to Melikhova, some fifty miles away, thus making meetings with Tchaikovsky yet more impracticable.

It may seem strange that two men whose arts were in some respects so different should have felt such attraction to each others' creations. After all, one of the things so striking about Chekhov is his objectivity. The range of character and treatment in his literally hundreds of sketches and short stories is prodigious; yet his ability to get inside the skin of every conceivable type of humanity, to note its behavior and to accord it every type of treatment, from the outrageously comic to the poignantly serious, shows a virtuoso range which few writers can match. Tchaikovsky, by contrast, seems to have been intensely subjective, preoccupied with the projection of a personal, inner world. True, he could on occasion view this world with some detachment, as in works like his first three suites or the Serenade for Strings, and in his rococo pastiches he even time-travelled to impersonate himself in eighteenth-century terms. Yet even in these apparent negations of his most personal self, there is no real hint of a creative personality other than his own, while the relative failure of most of his operas is evidence enough of his inability to penetrate beneath the skin of another character unless that character displayed some trait or emotion shared by Tchaikovsky himself. Yet Tchaikovsky and Chekhov did possess one fundamental quality in common: a deep and very basic humanity. Reading Chekhov, Tchaikovsky could revel in sharply observed projections of ordinary human nature which are mostly affectionate, even when satirical, and compassionate, even when bitingly critical. Hearing Tchaikovsky, Chekhov could respond to a composer whose music always nourished the emotional needs of his listener, and which sometimes addressed these needs with a force which, though perhaps disconcerting, afforded an experience of a searing personal relevance. Just how deep and wide was Chekhov's understanding of Tchaikovsky's music is impossible to say. His own capacity to reproduce it seems to have been limited to tapping out tunes with one finger on a piano. Yet of the truthfulness in his enduring admiration there can be no doubt. On 25 October 1893 O.S. Tchaikovsky died at Modest's home in St. Petersburg. Two days later Chekhov telegraphed Modest. "The news staggered me. It is a terrible anguish. I loved and revered Pyotr Ilich very deeply, and I am indebted to him for much. You have my heartfelt sympathy."[14]

Notes

1. P. Tchaikovsky, *Polnoe sobranie sochinenii; literaturnye proizvedeniya i perepiska* [Collected Works; Literary Works and Correspondence], 17 vols. (Moscow, 1953-81) [subsequently referred to as *TLP*] 14:95.

2. *TLP* 15a:27.

3. A.P. Chekhov, *Pis'ma v 12 tomakh* [Letters in 12 volumes] (Moscow, 1974-) [subsequently referred to as *CP*] 3:259.

4. *TLP* 15a:201.

5. *TLP* 15a:198.

6. *CP* 3:262.

7. *CP* 3:264.

8. *TLP* 15a:202.

9. *CP* 4:39-40.

10. *TLP* 15b:108.

11. *TLP* 16a:14.

12. *CP* 4:285-86.

13. *TLP* 16a:249-50.

14. *CP* 5:240.

Dvořák's Visit to Worcester, Massachusetts

John Clapham

When Dvořák visited England for the second time, as guest of honor at England's oldest music festival, the Three Choirs Festival at Worcester, he can have had no inkling of a curious coincidence that the future held in store for him. With commissions in his pocket for a symphony for the Philharmonic Society, a cantata for Birmingham and an oratorio for Leeds, he was well aware how firmly his music had taken root in England, and his future prospects there seemed excellent. There was speculation at this time that he might undertake a concert tour in the United States. Dudley Buck, the American composer, had put forward this suggestion when he met the composer in London, and V.J. Novotný, Dvořák's travelling companion, gained the impression that his friend was beginning to favor the idea. Nevertheless nothing came of Buck's suggestion. Almost seven years elapsed before the Czech composer received so generous and comprehensive an offer from New York that he knew he could not possibly reject it and must signal acceptance. It was this wonderful opportunity which made the coincidence possible.

Mrs. Jeannette M. Thurber's telegram to Dvořák reached him in June 1891 when he returned from Cambridge. It simply enquired: "Would you accept position Director National Conservatory of Music New York October 1892 also lead six concerts of your works." A letter followed giving more details, and stated that the salary would be $15,000 a year. It also spoke of 10 concerts, but it became clear later that four of these would be the students' choral and orchestral concerts, which Dvořák would be expected to conduct. The six public concerts, at which he would present his own compositions, remained a vital feature of Mrs. Thurber's contract regardless of whatever changes Dvořák decided he must press for in other areas. Her primary concern was to engage an internationally famous musician to add luster to her National Conservatory while the fourth centennial of the discovery of America was being celebrated. In her view the publicity she would gain for her institution, with Dvořák as a teacher of composition, an advocate of his own music, and above all a figurehead for the National Conservatory of Music of America, fully justified the tempting salary she was offering.

Dvořák's two-year contract stipulated that the maximum number of public concerts in one year was to be six, that they were to be arranged by Mrs. Thurber in New York or in other cities, and were to take place within the eight-month academic year, 23 September to 23 May, of each year. It was agreed that any concert taking place at Chicago during the World's Fair would not be regarded as one of the six. If concerts took place in other cities besides New York, Mrs. Thurber would defray any travelling, hotel and hire of carriage expenses. Should Dvořák be approached with an offer of a public engagement, he was obliged to refer the matter immediately to Mrs. Thurber. And finally, although it was stated that the programs of these six concerts were to consist solely of Dvořák's compositions, in practice this came to mean that it was possible for him to conduct one or more of his own works in a program that included music by other composers, which in that case would be directed by another conductor.[1]

Mrs. Thurber arranged for Dvořák to make just five public appearances within this framework during his first year in America. Had she wished she could have increased the number to six. However, having had a serious disagreement with Emma Juch, who was to be the soprano soloist in the *Stabat Mater* in both New York and Brooklyn during February 1893, Mrs. Thurber prevented her director from appearing on the same platform with her. And when the Apollo Club of Chicago invited the composer to conduct his *Requiem Mass* on 11 April 1893, Mrs. Thurber, for reasons that are not clear, withheld her consent. He was able to present the *Te Deum* for the first time and direct his *Triple Overture (In Nature's Realm, Carnival* and *Othello)* at his inaugural concert on 21 October 1892; he directed the *Requiem Mass*'s public rehearsal "for the workers" and public performance "for the wealthy and intelligentsia" at Boston on 29 and 30 November; he conducted the Sixth Symphony in D major in a New York Philharmonic Society program on 17 December; and when the Church Choral Society of New York, under Richard H. Warren, presented *The Spectre's Bride* on 6 April 1893, Dvořák, conducting the Symphony Society, opened the proceedings with his *Hussite* Overture.

In only one of these concerts, the inaugural concert, was it incumbent on Mrs. Thurber to bear the cost involved, the expense of engaging a choir and orchestra and the hire of the hall, together with other incidental and miscellaneous items. Even while the United States and Mrs. Thurber personally were reeling under a formidable financial crisis, we must assume that she could have continued as before during Dvořák's second year of office, without involving herself in any expense, by seeking engagements for her Director in programs arranged by other bodies. For we notice that despite the nation's troubles, concerts continued very much as before. It is therefore strange that she provided Dvořák with only one outside conducting engagement during his second year. It seems unlikely that the occasional adverse comments levelled by critics at his conducting could have weighed at all heavily with Mrs. Thurber. She is much more likely to have noticed with considerable satisfaction the enthusiasm of audiences whenever her Director presented his own music, and felt a glow of pride at the reflected glory it brought to her National Conservatory.

Dvořák was first given news of this single engagement he was being offered while he was on holiday, enjoying the tranquility of the little Czech settlement at Spillville in northeast Iowa. In a letter dated 19 August 1893, Mrs. Thurber wrote to him as follows:

> Dear Dr. Dvořák,
> The secretary of the Worcester Festival has written requesting that you conduct yr. 149th Psalm and Hussite Overture the 28th September. In yr. absence I have written giving the consent of the National Conservatory.
> I suppose that you will have no objections. Kindly write me if the above meets with yr. approval—by return mail if possible—and with kind regards to all,
> Yours very sincerely,
> Jeannette M. Thurber[2]

This letter would have reached Dvořák more than a week before he set off on his trip to Omaha and St. Paul. Judging by what Dvořák has to say in his reply, he appears to have written the following undated answer about a week before the end of August:

> Spillville
> Winnesheik Co
> Iowa
>
> To Mam: J. Thurber
> Dear Madam
> I am very pleased to see *Worcester* and I only wish to know about the rehearsals.[3]
> I think only one rehearsal will do, supposing Chorus and Orchestra are well prepared and so I will be there on 27 of Septbr one day before the performance.
> We stay here only 3 weeks and then we go to Chicago to see the exhibition and I hope to be back in New York 24. of Septbr.
> Meanwhile I remain
> sincerely yours
> Antonín Dvořák

It did not become generally known for a little while that the composer intended to be present at the 36th annual Music Festival at Worcester, Massachusetts, for we find that the American correspondent of *The Musical Times* (H.E. Krehbiel), writing on 11 September, named the principal artists who were being engaged to appear, listed the main works to be performed and provided details about the choir and orchestra, without making a single reference to Dvořák or his compositions.[4] After visiting Buffalo and Niagara, the entire Dvořák family arrived back in New York less than a week before the composer was due to depart for Worcester.

Dvořák, described by a local newspaper[5] as "a pleasant-faced rubicund, well-built man" who "in his street clothes looked much like a prosperous sea captain on shore leave," made the journey to Worcester on 27 September, but arrived too late to hear Vladimir de Pachmann play Chopin's F minor Concerto and Lilian Nordica sing extracts from Mendelssohn's *Loreley* at the afternoon concert. Between this and the concert performance of *Samson and Delilah* in the evening, a journalist from the *Daily Spy* questioned him about his views on music in America. But because of Dvořák's lack of fluency in the English language, all the journalist could glean was that Americans "have yet to grow more enthusiastic about music and its study before they can come up to the European standard," after which Dvořák added with a smile: "That fault is growing less every day."

Not wishing to admit defeat, the *Daily Spy* made another attempt at interviewing Dvořák next day, and judging by their success they must have found an interpreter. The composer praised the performance of *Samson and Delilah* and spoke enthusiastically about the superb artistry of Madame Carl Alves, who sang the part of Delilah. His one complaint was that the orchestra of sixty, drawn from the Boston Symphony Orchestra, was overbalanced by the 500-strong chorus, a fault which he found in all American choral work. He continued as follows:

> Such faults as the one I just mentioned are incidental to a new country like your America, where there is a little musical knowledge. It is a very big place, but it has very little music. See this orchestra; it is all German. So are the orchestras of New York and Chicago. Everywhere a good orchestra here is an orchestra of Germans. Why? Because you Americans have not enough music in you at present, not enough musical culture to support anything first class.
>
> It was so in England, 15 or 20 years ago. But those German orchestras so educated the English public, that now Englishmen are filling the places of the Germans, and the music is not poorer than before. So it will be here after twenty years, and what I am trying to do is to educate a little part of the American people.
>
> My work is entirely at the New York Conservatory, with now and then a visit to some other city. I have three classes a week in composition, two in orchestral practice and one in chorus singing. I have little time or inclination for what is called society; I prefer to spend my leisure with my wife and six children. They need all the time and thought I have to give.
>
> It seems to me American men are quite wanting in musical enthusiasm, and that is one reason why music here is so poor and scarce. The women are better; they love it and have talent. But the men only want it for a pastime. They want always money, more money. In Europe there is too much music; here, not enough. And what you have you bunch into a little time and then you have nothing left for the rest of the year. There is too much music here for one week; and through the winter you will have little to make up for it.[6]

This plain speaking by Dvořák was far more than the *Worcester Evening Gazette*'s critic was prepared to stomach, and led to the following extremely bitter reply:

One hardly knows which to admire the more—Mr. Dvořák's ignorance or his impertinence in his absurd comments upon the state of music in America, for both are colossal. If the orchestras are chiefly composed of Germans, this is chiefly because the Germans are clannish and combine quietly against other nationalities. America can supply good orchestral players if places could be found for them, and in certain departments it is necessary to send to France for competent men. When he talks about music being "poor and scarce" in this country, he talks as foolishly as bumptiously. He has as much to learn as to teach if the *Spy* correctly reports him.[7]

The critic's extreme fit of anger affected his sense of judgment over the performances of Dvořák's music. In summing up the Psalm, he said: "One can hardly conceive of a greater volume and vigor of sound as emitted by the same number of singers and players. It was one tremendous roar and rush of tumultuous tone, excited and hurried on by the urgent and imperative baton of the leader." And he described the *Hussite* Overture as "scarcely less than a rage of battle and madness of triumph."[8]

As far as we know, the *Gazette*'s critic was the only one who took strong exception to the *Spy* interview. The interview came to the attention of none other than Philip Hale, arbiter of musical taste in Boston. He reproduced the greater part of Dvořák's remarks for the benefit of regular readers of his Sunday column in the *Boston Morning Journal* on 1 October 1893 beneath the subheading "Dvořák tells hard truths in Worcester," and preceded this with the succinct comment: "The following extracts from the *Spy* are of present and permanent interest."

We must certainly assume that what Dvořák is reported to have said reasonably accurately represented his impressions at that time. They were the outcome of his personal observations, coupled with what he had been able to glean in conversations with musicians and others with whom he was in personal contact. Yet they are in the nature of first impressions, made by one who had spent eight months in New York and paid only fleeting visits to Boston and Chicago. As a musician he had been brought up in a completely different environment, in close touch with leading and long-established musical centers in the heart of Europe. He was now transported into a new country which had no chance at all of developing comparable musical traditions, and had to resort to sending her sons to Europe if they were to receive an adequate musical education. He was well aware that Mrs. Thurber had entrusted him with the task of commencing to sweep away America's deficiencies by creating a new American school of composition, from which the country's future music tradition, as she thought, would spring. Understandably he probably felt it would be unhelpful if he were to gloss over the immense gulf that separated the conditions in which music was fostered in the Old and the New Worlds.

Nevertheless, on getting to know and understand the people of America better during the next year or so, Dvořák shifted his ground to some extent. Having presented his views in a somewhat crude, off-the-cuff manner at Worcester, he reassessed them carefully and more positively, taking care at the same time to exercise rather more tact. This came about as the result of an invitation to contribute a long article on "Music in America," in collaboration with E. Emerson, for *Harper's Magazine.*[9] If he still considered that the ladies of America were more enthusiastic about music and more talented in that direction than the gentlemen, he refrained from saying so. He was particularly impressed, as a foreigner, by "the unbounded patriotism and capacity for enthusiasm of most Americans." He admitted he had been ruffled earlier on by what he had regarded as the excessive enthusiasm of his students, whose determination to probe to the root of their musical problems led them well beyond the bounds of their capacity to understand. Later he became convinced that this was an asset, and was able to say: "I have come to the conclusion that this youthful enthusiasm and eagerness to take up everything is the best promise for music in America." It was essential that their enthusiasm should be suitably channeled, for he said:

> Only when the people in general begin to take as lively an interest in music and art as they now take in more material matters will the arts come into their own. Let the enthusiasm of the people once be excited, and patriotic gifts and bequests must surely follow.

Mrs. Jeannette N. Thurber and Henry Lee Higginson had set a splendid example by founding the National Conservatory of Music and the Boston Symphony Orchestra respectively; but unless other equally public-spirited men and women were to show a similar generosity and vision, music in America would remain the Cinderella of the arts. Given the right institutions and conditions, he believed that American music was bound to flourish.

For many years the Worcester Music Festival had been directed by its chorus master, Carl Zerrahn. In this instance the fare that he offered, and which as we have noted Dvořák considered too much for one week, included *Miriam's Song of Victory* by Schubert, Henry Smart's *Bride of Dunkerron,* Schumann's Second Symphony, a Cello Concerto by Davidoff which Alwin Schroeder played, Goldmark's Overture *In the Spring, Samson and Delilah,* the extracts from Mendelssohn's *Loreley* and the Second Chopin Piano Concerto, already referred to, Beethoven's Eighth Symphony, Jules Jordan's *Jael,* the two Dvořák works, a Macdowell Suite, a Symphony in B flat by Haydn and *Judas Maccabaeus.* In addition the seven concerts included a wide range of solo vocal and instrumental items by the numerous artists who had been engaged.

Philip Hale, apparently, wrote some fascinating program notes for *Samson and Delilah,* but did not appear in person at the Festival. Nevertheless he expressed his approval of the display of fashion—it was reported that Lilian Nordica wore a creation by Worth designed for her appearance at the princess of Wales's garden party at Marlborough House not long before—and the directorate let it be known by means of a polite hint that they would welcome it if the audience donned full evening dress. "Why," Hale enquired, "should not the people at a festival array themselves in festival attire? Surely the Muse does not disdain such flattering attention."[10] According to the *Evening Gazette,* "The stocky, sturdy Dvořák seems not to fit the formal dress precisely," a dig which led Philip Hale to remark: "There are men whom it is hard to associate with evening dress. Dvořák is one of them. The great rugged *Naturmensch!* What has he to do with thoughtfully prepared cravat or carefully cut swallowtail? Ten to one his inclination when leading his "Husitzka" overture was to conduct in his shirt-sleeves, that he might enjoy the greater freedom."

Mechanics Hall was very well filled for *Samson and Delilah* and for the Thursday afternoon concert in which Nordica and Pachmann delighted their audience, who on each occasion were roused to a high pitch of excitement and enthusiasm. Judging by the account of the concerts given in the *Worcester Daily Telegram,* the audience seems to have risen to an even greater pitch of excitement at being so richly rewarded by hearing *Praise Jehovah* (Psalm 149) and the *Hussite* Overture directed by the celebrated composer himself. The Psalm, however, was not entirely faultless. At the rehearsal the chorus discovered that Dvořák's tempi differed from those to which they had become accustomed, and during the performance there was one moment when the basses failed to understand the composer's intention. Nevertheless this did nothing to diminish the unrestrained enjoyment of those present, as can be seen from the *Daily Telegram*'s account of the proceedings. Their critic appears to have been swept along by the mounting tide of warm-hearted, effusive popular feeling by which he was engulfed. This is what he had to say about the performance:

The Psalm had never been heard in Worcester, and it was at once accepted by the audience as a valuable addition to classic music of the didactic or serious order. Everybody knows the Psalm who is familiar with his Bible. It is a theme of praise—exultant, triumphant, redolent of harp and timbrel and dance and song, and Dvořák has given it a remarkably fine setting. His music is even brilliant. It certainly is broad, strong and impressive and well sustained throughout.

The chorus excelled itself in the performance. Almost all that was wanted of it was pure and sustained volume and unison, and the chorus gave both with right good will. Dvořák wielded his baton in a vigorous, snappy way, that brought the best work out of both chorus and orchestra. Both bodies threw themselves with enthusiasm into the performance and when Dvořák laid down his staff of office and when he nodded his head to the chorus with satisfaction, and when he clapped Kneisel[11] on the back, and waved his arm towards the rest of the instruments, as much as to say, "You boys have done magnificently," a remarkable thing occurred. The audience burst into a cheer. There could be no possible mistake about it. There it was—a clear, palpable roar.

Of course audiences have cheered before in Mechanics Hall. One memorable audience cheered itself hoarse not very long [ago] over Governor McKinley in the same building. But when fashionable Worcester, in its fashionable finery, gets excited enough to yell, it may be taken for granted that something has happened. The members of the chorus took up the refrain, and Dvořák must have felt it the proudest moment of his life as he stood before the throng and received such a tumultuous tribute to his genius.

He bowed and bowed till he bowed himself off the platform, but still the enthusiastic uproar continued, till Dvořák came back again to pay his respects. Even then the tumult continued, and once again the composer of the 149th Psalm had to return to the scene of his triumph and bow again. The excitement produced by Dvořák's Psalm did not evaporate the whole evening. It vented itself in encores. Probably never before was there such a voracious audience in Mechanics Hall. They encored everything on the program without regard to its merit, and the probability is that if one of the soloists had come out and sung "After the Ball," they would have encored that too, instead of casting a brick at the singer.[12]

Having experienced the effusiveness and warm-heartedness of the Worcester audience, and fulfilled his engagement, Dvořák must have returned to New York on the midnight train, feeling a glow of satisfaction and gratification at the reception that had been accorded to him and his music.[13]

Notes

1. A facsimile of Dvořák's contract with Mrs. Thurber appears in Merton Robert Aborn, *The Influence on American Culture of Dvořák's Sojourn in America,* Ph.D. diss., Indiana University, 1965 (Ann Arbor, 1966).

2. This letter, formerly in the possession of Dvořák's heirs and quoted with their kind permission, is now in the Czechoslovak State Collection of the composer's works. Dvořák's visit to the Worcester Festival is discussed in Raymond Morin's *The Worcester Music Festival,* 2d ed. (Worcester, 1976), but has been overlooked by all his biographers.

3. This letter is quoted by the courtesy of Merton Robert Aborn.

4. "Music in America," *The Musical Times and Singing-Class Circular* 34 (1893):611.

5. *Worcester Daily Spy,* 28 September 1893.

6. Ibid., 29 September 1893.

7. *Worcester Evening Gazette,* 29 September 1893.

8. Ibid. The report on this concert was reprinted in the *Gazette*'s allied weekly newspaper *Aegis and Gazette* for 7 October 1893, but the critic's sharp reaction to the *Spy*'s interview was omitted.

9. *Harper's New Monthly Magazine* 90 (Dec. 1894-May 1895):[428]-434. The reprint in S. Morgenstern's *Composers on Music* (New York, 1956) is abridged.

10. *Boston Morning Journal,* 1 October 1893.

11. Franz Kneisel, concertmaster of the Boston Symphony Orchestra and leader of America's foremost string quartet. The Kneisel Quartet gave world premieres of the String Quartets in F major, Op. 96, and A-flat major, Op. 105, and also the String Quintet in E-flat major, Op. 97—a record unequalled by any other chamber music group.

12. *Worcester Daily Telegram,* 29 September 1893.

13. The author is indebted to the Librarians of the Worcester Collection and the Reference and Research Librarians at Worcester Public Library for their kind and much valued assistance.

Sibelius and Balakirev

Edward Garden

Although Sibelius was coy about admitting the effect of influences on his style, like every other composer he was, naturally enough, influenced by others. Finland was part of the Russian Empire until the end of the First World War, and the comparative proximity of popular resorts on the South Finnish coast, and Helsinki itself, to the capital St. Petersburg ensured that there was a good deal of intercourse (even if Sibelius's musical education outside Finland took place in Central Europe rather than in Russia). The importance of the influence of Russian composers on Sibelius has been mentioned by various writers, from whom may be cited Gerald Abraham and Robert Layton. In his admirable "Master Musicians" book on Sibelius, Layton draws attention to a "striking correspondence between the second group of the first movement of Tchaikovsky's *Souvenir de Florence* and the figure at bar 84 of Sibelius's slow movement [First Symphony]."[1] Abraham thinks that the influence of Tchaikovsky on this symphony, referred to by other writers besides Layton, is "entirely absent,"[2] stating elsewhere that the composers to whom he is susceptible here are "Borodin, Grieg, and Bruckner."[3] That he had studied Borodin's First Symphony in E flat is certain, since, as Abraham points out, in the first movement of his Second Symphony (1902) Sibelius "adapts to his own ends the structural principle" of the initial movement in the Borodin work,[4] which proved to be of seminal importance for the Finnish composer.

Layton also remarks that the first subject group of the Legend *Lemminkainen ja saaren neidot* "includes a theme distinctly reminiscent of Balakirev's first symphony, full of tenderness and warmth."[5] He refers to the opening of the first subject of the first movement of the Balakirev work, whose notes are identical with the Sibelius figure he cites. Indeed, some of the guises in which Sibelius dresses his theme later in the work seem to resemble quite closely the manner in which Balakirev treats his theme in the symphony. Yet this must surely be fortuitous, since Sibelius wrote this particular Legend—the first of four—in 1895, revising it in 1897.[6] Though Balakirev had extemporized his symphony to his circle in St. Petersburg in the 1860s, and according to Rimsky-Korsakov had written down in manuscript about one-third of the first movement,[7] he did not complete it until 1897; the first performance was in

1898, and it was published in 1899. Therefore, while Rimsky-Korsakov, who had heard Balakirev extemporizing the symphony in the 1860s, was considerably influenced by it in his Third Symphony in C major (1873, revised 1886), it does not seem to be possible to trace any direct influence of Balakirev on Sibelius in this particular case, which exemplifies the risk inherent in reading too much into such apparent resemblances.

Nevertheless I do think that, just as Sibelius had in his Second Symphony learnt from the methods employed by Borodin in his First (composed, by the way, under the strict guidance of Balakirev), so Sibelius was to take Balakirev's First Symphony in C major as a starting point for his Third Symphony in the same key. As far as dates are concerned this would be possible. Sibelius began his C major Symphony in 1904, and it is not unlikely that he knew the Balakirev work, published five years previously. The first subjects of Balakirev's first and last movements—the latter being the folksong *Sharlatarla from Partarla* given to the composer by Rimsky-Korsakov—bear a certain resemblance to one another. I quote them, together with the opening of the first subject of Sibelius's first movement:

Ex. 1

It is not so much a similarity of actual notes—which is to say the least tenuous—as the similarity of style which is immediately striking. The recurrent nature of the themes, almost endlessly repeating themselves without seemingly getting anywhere very important, is common to the Balakirev and Sibelius examples, together with the urgent rhythmic vitality and the apparently commonplace nature of the themes. It is the distinguished way in which the composers develop the themes that matters. In Balakirev's finale his theme is contrasted with two others (one of which has Finnish origins), and in the course of time all three occur together in an elaborate fresco of sound. The first movement theme is also treated with much elaboration, split up into pieces, subjected to diminution and augmentation, heard in imitation and so on. Just before the end of the movement the first five notes are augmented into whole notes—eight times the value of the original quavers—in D flat major; C major has merely been a base for Balakirev to wander from at will, and comparatively little of the movement is in that key. It is quite otherwise with Sibelius. The rhythmic vigor of his theme soon engenders a sense of inexorable progression, and although other ideas are generated by the main theme there is, as Layton has remarked, "no excess of flesh in this vital, athletic body of a movement."[8] In contradistinction to the constantly modulating Balakirev, Sibelius remains firmly in C major until his second subject is reached. The theme bears some resemblance to Balakirev's second subject:

Ex. 2

a. Sibelius (exposition)

b. Sibelius (recapitulation)

c. Balakirev

Balakirev's theme goes on turning in upon itself while slowly descending in pitch, while Sibelius' continues at the same pitch, but with altered decoration, until the melody is eventually taken over by the relentless onward thrust of continuous sixteenth notes. Once again it is not the melodic similarity (which is nevertheless more obvious here) but rather the repetitively wandering nature of both themes, so well contrasted rhythmically with their respective first subjects, that is particularly noticeable.

The overall forms of the first movements of the Sibelius and Balakirev C major symphonies are quite different. Balakirev's scintillating, continuously developing, mosaic-like structure, based on an initial *largo,* makes only nominal obeisance to sonata form. As for the Sibelius, one cannot do better than to quote Gerald Abraham once again: "In clearness and simplicity of outline, it is comparable with a Haydn or Mozart first movement.... Nevertheless the organic unity of the movement is far in advance of anything in the Viennese classical masters; and even the general architecture is held together in a way that had classical precedents but had never before, I think, been so fully developed."[9]

From similar ostensibly prosaic foundations, then, the two composers have produced totally different edifices. In his work, Sibelius was able to cut and to prune, to reduce his material to the bare minimum while at the same time creating one of the most masterly movements of the early twentieth century. Balakirev, on the other hand, produced one of the most elaborate first movements in the history of the symphony, though his elaboration is unlike the typical amplifications which were occurring in symphonies being composed in central Europe at the time. Both these fine symphonies have one other thing in common, however. They are unaccountably neglected.

Notes

1. Robert Layton, *Sibelius* (London, 1965), p. 30. Another Tchaikovsky work which anticipated Sibelius in a general way was the Symphonic Ballad *The Voyevoda,* published posthumously in 1897. In this work, Tchaikovsky's "sometimes interminable sequences have been translated into long *ostinati,* often over pedal points, and the whole lay-out of the score, including much use of divided strings and some singular wind-writing, reminds one of Sibelius, as does the depiction of the snowy landscape and the icy finger of death postulated by the story on which the ballad is based." See Edward Garden, *Tchaikovsky* (London, 1973; reprinted 1976, 1978, 1984), p. 149.

2. Gerald Abraham, *A Hundred Years of Music,* 4th ed. (London, 1974), p. 259.

3. Gerald Abraham, *The Concise Oxford History of Music* (London, 1979), p. 805.

4. Ibid. Sibelius averred that he did not know this Borodin symphony when he was writing his *First* Symphony.

5. Layton, op. cit., p. 67.

6. The work was withdrawn and revised again in 1939. But unless Balakirevan traits occur in this last version which are not to be found in the earlier ones, there can be no direct influence of the Balakirev symphony here.

7. N. Rimsky-Korsakov, *Letopis' moei muzykal'noi zhizni* [Chronicle of my musical life], 8th ed. (Moscow, 1980), p. 57.

8. Layton, op. cit., p. 39.

9. In *Sibelius, a Symposium,* edited by Gerald Abraham (London, 1947), p. 22.

Alexander Skriabin and the Russian Renaissance

Martin Cooper

Through the whole of nineteenth-century Russian literature there runs a strong vein of apocalyptic, messianic feelings and beliefs, which had shown themselves clearly in Russian Orthodoxy at least since the seventeenth century and had entered secular life unmistakably during the last ten years of Alexander the First's reign (1815-25).

If the westernizing, rationalizing party in the social, political, religious, and artistic debates of the nineteenth century clearly descends from Peter the Great, their Slavophile opponents drew their strength not only from the instinctive nationalist conservatism of the unenlightened or uneducated, but also from the strong mystical, irrational vein that marked the greatest of the Russian writers, endowing Gogol, Dostoevsky, and Tolstoy with a unique insight into human nature in general and particularly into the conflicting tensions and forces that gave Russian life its uniquely explosive character. These writers were in a double sense prophets: that is to say, they both "spoke out" the often unpalatable truth and foresaw, in many instances with extraordinary clarity, the future. Even the lyric poets, Pushkin and Lermontov, had uncanny glimpses of future events, as early as the third decade of the century. Lermontov's poem *Prophecy* for instance opens with the words, "The year will come, Russia's black year, when the tsar's crown will fall; the crowd will forget its former love for him, and death and blood will be the food of many."[1]

Throughout the nineteenth century the *intelligentsia*—a Russian word for a specifically Russian phenomenon—played a unique and increasingly important part in Russian life. They had both the obstinate vitality of a gifted minority conscious of having reason on their side, and the nonconformist *esprit de corps* engendered by persecution. Their moral strength lay in an altogether extraordinary capability for self-sacrifice. Where they differed from the huge majority of their countrymen, and introduced what often seemed an unmistakably foreign French—or more often German—note into their writings, was in their complete freedom from that "instinctive hatred of dry and rigid thinking... and that desire to supersede logic," which the poet Alexander Blok regarded as characteristic of all Russian literature.[2]

Each decade of the nineteenth century in Russia marked a change of character, sometimes amounting to a change of front, in the opposition that the intelligentsia presented to the autocratic government and to those social abuses which the vast majority of the country accepted passively, as at best "the established order" or at worst as incurable conditions of Russian life, a double legacy from Byzantine caesaro-papism and Tartar oppression. It was not until the increased political and police pressures of the eighties had increased the numbers and raised the hopes of the active social and political revolutionaries that the intelligentsia began to divide into two camps. On the one hand the politicals had little interest in the arts except as instruments of social and political propaganda; and on the other stood the aesthetes, a new phenomenon and a tiny but gifted clique for whom politics represented an irrelevance or an interruption in their search for "hitherto unknown possibilities of experiencing the ecstasy of Dionysian inspiration, irrespective of the realities to which the experience was related" (Viacheslav Ivanov). The interests of those of the non-political wing of the intelligentsia were religious inasmuch as they were anything other than purely aesthetic; and to be an aesthete, a "mystic" or a "seeker after God" had become by 1900 an accepted fashion. "A belated rationalist or positivist could scarcely hope for success even in his love affairs. Just as in the forties only an idealist or romantic could be sure of success in such matters; in the sixties a materialist or rationalist; in the seventies a 'populist,' who had offered himself, as a sacrifice for the liberation of the 'people'; or in the nineties a Marxist."[3]

The chief fields in which these new attitudes first showed themselves were philosophical or religious thought and poetry; painting and music showed their influences rather later. Vladimir Solovyov (1853-1900) formed a bridge between the worlds of philosophy and religion, which the extreme anti-intellectualism and otherworldly emphases of Russian Orthodoxy kept unusually far apart. A brilliant career opened with his essay on *The Crisis in Western Philosophy* (1874), followed by his first lectures at Moscow University, on *The Defense of Metaphysics*. Journeys to London and Paris, and later to Egypt, confirmed an already strong religious bent, which soon showed itself unmistakably in his *Lectures on God-Manhood;* but his public address asking for mercy on the murderer of Alexander II (1881) effectively closed any hopes for an official career in Russia. In the last year of his life Solovyov published *Three Speeches,* dedicated to the memory of Dostoevsky, in one of which he depicts with astonishing power and premonitory brilliance the coming of Antichrist, a pendant to the legend of the Grand Inquisitor in *The Brothers Karamazov.* Apocalypse for Solovyov was not only a revelation of the end of history, and a "Last Judgment": it also implied the nearness of an "end" within history itself, a judgment upon history within the historical framework. And in fact the whole of the art, literature, religion, and philosophy of Russia during these last 25 years of the Tsarist regime is deeply colored and influenced by this often mute, but increasingly vocal awareness of belonging to a society under sentence of death yet big with new life. Berdyaev has described the atmosphere of these years in Russia as "a state of expectancy, a passive, mystical trembling before the future" and Russians as consciously or unconsciously expecting "a revelation as well as a revolution."[4]

Solovyov's mysticism centered around the figure of Sophia, or Divine Wisdom, a reintroduction of the feminine element into the conception of deity and, like many earlier attempts of the same kind, easily and insensibly identified with the figure of an individual human woman, with strong erotic overtones. The poets were, in fact, not slow to borrow this mystical feminine figure, which we find in the early poems of Andrei Bely and Alexander Blok as the Unknown Woman *(Neznakomka)* or the Beautiful Lady *(Prekrasnaia Dama).*[5] Solovyov's concern with the gnostic, illuminist elements in Christianity provided a fragile and uneasy link with the movement of renewal within Russian Orthodoxy; and both found expression at the meetings of the Moscow Philosophical Society, under its president Prince Sergei Trubetskoy, author of another quasi-gnostic *Study of Logos,* who frankly expressed a dislike of abstract rationalism and opened the society to mediums, "mystics," and occultists as well as bona fide philosophers. "Never before were Russians so acutely aware of the illimitable unknown surrounding human life," writes Berdyaev,[6] "of the mystery and the terrifying abyss with which man is faced." But he goes on to say that this very awareness became in many cases a pose, and that words such as "mystery" and "abyss" became catchwords hiding a growing emptiness. The underlying instinct in every case was escape from reality into that state of ecstasy *(ekstasis),* or standing outside the self, that has always been the aim of illuminism and has invariably attracted the charlatan and the mentally unbalanced as well as the artist and the genuine religious seeker. This search united the often dissimilar members of the movement which called itself "The New Religious Consciousness" *(Novoe religioznoe soznanie),* centered in St. Petersburg round the poet Dmitri Merezhkovsky and his wife Zinaida Gippius and associated with the periodicals *Novy Put'* (The New Way [1903-04]) and later *Voprosy Zhizni* (Questions of Life). Merezhkovsky was a man of very consciously European culture, a friend of the Decadent poets who imitated Verlaine or Verhaeren in the 1890s and then of the Symbolists. He and his wife surrounded themselves with an atmosphere of "magical sophistication" and proclaimed a cultural cosmopolitanism, a religion of "the sanctity of the flesh" diluted with the gnostic sectarianism of Rudolf Steiner's anthroposophy, which had a large following among Russian intellectuals in the years between the first abortive revolution of 1905 and the outbreak of war in 1914.

One of the moving spirits among the poets, Viacheslav Ivanov, was aware of the dangers of extreme subjectivity and individualism and advocated the development of "symphonic" consciousness and "symphonic" culture, not the "togetherness" *(sobornost')* of Khomiakov or its extension in Solovyov's thought but something nearer to Wagner's *Gesamtkunstwerk.* Viacheslav Ivanov was a classical scholar who identified Christianity with Dionysianism (that is to say, ecstatic experience) and opposed "organic" culture (synthesis) to the "critical" culture (analysis) initiated by the eighteenth-century Enlightenment. After the 1905 revolution he was associated with Yuri Chulkov in a movement preaching mystical anarchism and "non-acceptance of the world"; and it is perhaps not without significance that both men were eventually associated with Fascism, a movement that had a root in common with these elitist Russian cults in the uncritical and often uncomprehending admiration of Nietzsche. The characteristically gnostic identification of the redeemer-figure of Prometheus with Lucifer and Satan formed a link between the Satanism borrowed by Russian poets of the 1890s (Valery Briusov, Fyodor Sologub) from Huysmans and the different yet closely related concepts of the man-god, or superman, in Rudolf Steiner and Skriabin. It would be almost possible to construct a history of the whole renaissance of Russian art and thought between the last years of the nineteenth century and the outbreak of war in 1914 from a scrutiny of the periodicals which supported, and did propaganda for, the movement. The place of *Novy Put'* and *Voprosy Zhizni* has already been mentioned in connection with religious or philosophic thought; but in the field of literature and painting a far more important role was played by *Mir Iskusstva* (The World of Art), published between 1899 and 1904. The editor, Sergei Diaghilev, was interested primarily in visual art and professed the same cosmopolitan artistic ideals as Merezhkovsky and Gippius, who both contributed to the journal. In fact Diaghilev was a successful organizer of art exhibitions for nearly ten years before he organized the first of the historic seasons of Russian opera and ballet in Paris (1907-8). French influence was very strong from the beginning. There were articles on Puvis de Chavannes and on the French Impressionist painters, on Whistler and Beardsley and on Wagner's conception of art; and whole issues were devoted to exhibitions held in Paris, Dresden, and Berlin. The links with the Vienna Secession and with the Munich School were even stronger; and it was only in the very last issue that Gauguin, Van Gogh, and Cézanne were discussed. *Mir Iskusstva* was in fact a powerful organization of Western aesthetic sophistication, and it is a surprising fact that it received support from the private purse of Nicholas II, considering its device of "art for art's sake," which can have made little appeal to the overwhelmingly naive or philistine personalities of court circles. How restricted the appeal of such an organ of opinion was at that time in Russia is eloquently suggested by the average circulation of *Mir Iskusstva*—just over 1,000 in a country of some 180 million.

In the year that *Mir Iskusstva* came to an end (1904) there appeared a new journal, *Vesy* (The Scales) which for the next five years was the acknowledged organ of the Symbolist movement, largely under the control of the poet Valery Briusov, who published the work of Balmont, Bely, Viacheslav Ivanov, and Blok, and their French models. The pioneer stage of the Symbolist Movement was over by 1905, and during the next four years (*Vesy* ceased publication in 1909) the separatist strains within the movement began to assert themselves.

As often happens, music during these years (1895-1905) in Russia seemed oddly impervious to the new ideas and interest in the other arts. Among the older composers, Rimsky-Korsakov paid an unexpected tribute to both Neo-Orthodoxy and the fashionable pantheism in his opera *The Legend of the Invisible City of Kitezh and the Maiden Fevronia* (1907); and attempts were even made to claim Rimsky's *Koshchei the Deathless* (1902) as a "decadent" work on the grounds of its advanced harmony. The composer himself, however, rejected Petrovsky's original version of the libretto on the ground that "the subject was treated in the decadent manner."[7] What is more probable is the suggestion that in the figure of Koshchei the composer symbolized the much hated Chief Procurator of the Holy Synod, Konstantin Pobedonostsev; and possibly the ubiquitous but intangible figure of Revolution in the *Buria-Bogatyr* (Storm Knight). Vladimir Belsky, the author of the librettos of Rimsky-Korsakov's *Sadko* and *Kitezh,* also adapted from Pushkin the texts of *The Legend of Tsar Saltan* (1900) and *The Golden Cockerel* (1909). In act 2 of *The Golden Cockerel*[8] Belsky invests the Queen of Shemakha's lines with a "sultry sensuality" which disturbed the composer and reminds one commentator at least of the language of the Symbolist poets Balmont and Briusov. Belsky also tried to interest Rimsky-Korsakov in an opera based on Byron's *Mystery of Heaven and Earth;* but although he was working on this as late as 1906, in June of that year he dismissed the idea as "unreal nonsense." However, it was only a very short time before a Russian composer of the younger generation was engaged on a far more ambitious "mystery," and had chosen to write just that "music of the spheres" to which Rimsky-Korsakov preferred, as he wrote to Belsky, "what belongs to Russia and the people."

The composer was Alexander Nikolaevich Skriabin, born in 1872 and certainly the most original of the three contemporaries who together formed the brightest hopes for Russian music in the 1890s and the first years of the present century. Of the other two, Sergei Rakhmaninov (b. 1873), though as brilliant a pianist as Skriabin, was temperamentally a conservative and content to continue in his compositions the line of Tchaikovsky. The third, Alexander Glazunov (b. 1865), was gifted with an extraordinary facility which gave him an easy mastery of traditional forms; but of real originality he showed little trace, and his copious output is almost wholly academic in character. Skriabin, whose pianist mother died in his infancy, was brought up by an adoring aunt and grandmother, and while still at the Cadet School in Moscow began his musical studies. Rakhmaninov was his companion in Zverev's pianoforte class, and after his entry into the Moscow Conservatory (1888) he worked with Arensky, Taneev, and Safonov, who was to play a large part in propagating Skriabin's music after the composer himself largely abandoned the pianoforte for conducting. In 1891 Skriabin won the Gold Medal and was taken up by the Maecenas-publisher Mitrofan Beliaev, who arranged concert tours in Western Europe for the brilliant young pianist. Between 1895 and 1897 these tours took him to Germany, Switzerland, Holland, France, and Italy; and after his marriage in 1897 he settled in Paris for five months (November, 1897). In the following year he became Professor of the Pianoforte at the Moscow Conservatory, a post which he held for five years.

The compositions of these early years are very strongly reminiscent of Chopin, and more rarely Liszt. All conceived for the piano and cast in the small forms (preludes, etudes, impromptus, and mazurkas) favored by Chopin, they are characterized by a consciously exquisite, perfumed delicacy of harmony and phrase which had its counterpart in the composer's personal appearance, to which he paid great attention. They also reflect, in their often extreme brevity and emotional concentration, the poetry which the new generation of Russian poets was translating from the French (Baudelaire and Verlaine, Rimbaud and Mallarmé, in particular) or imitating in their own language. The cult of the artificial and the rejection of actuality for a dream-world of the artist's own creation is echoed in countless poems by Briusov[9] and Merezhovsky. In Sologub this pride and isolationism reach the most grandiose proportions, and his language was certainly not lost on the young Skriabin:

> I am the god of a secret world,
> the whole world exists only in my dreams[10]

and in another place:

> I created heaven and earth
> and will create anew a gleaming world[11]

At the same time the Baudelairean worship of Evil, fundamentally a protest against the bourgeois narrow and restricted conception of Good; the concern with death rather than life; and the interest in erotic perversion, as the supreme flaunting of both Nature and conventional "virtue," earned for these poets with the tiny group of people who read—or more often read about—their poems the title of Decadents, which they avidly accepted.[12] Whether Skriabin at this time had close friends among the Decadent poets or not, his early music chimes with at least the majority of their obsessions. The suggestion of diabolism, in particular, enters his music through Liszt, though he was not in fact to entitle a work "Poème Satanique" until much later.

Many of Skriabin's early pieces, for all their superficial similarity to Chopin, are nearer in spirit to the miniature mood-poems of Verlaine and his Russian imitators, Briusov or Sologub. A good instance dating from as early as 1894 is the tenth of the *Twenty-four Preludes,* in C sharp minor. Only 20 bars long, it contains a single idea: a semitone interval, descending in the accompaniment and ascending in the melodic cell round which it is constructed. On the other hand dynamic and expressive marks are frequent, from *pp* to *sff* and *fff,* with careful accentuations and *ritenuto, rubato* and—already characteristic—one of the *pp* bars marked specifically *con anima.* This is in fact even more an expressionist than an impressionist miniature, and the whole Russian art movement of these days was in fact oriented towards Munich and Vienna rather than Paris. When Skriabin visited Paris in 1896, in company with Beliaev, he met "Decadent" society for the first time. In speaking later of his Parisian experiences to Leonid Sabaneev, he said comparatively little about music, but more, of leading "a very corrupt life" and of "trying everything"; and his drinking had been noticed earlier even in Russia, where the standard was high. But if Sabaneev's memory is to be trusted, the most important discovery linked in the composer's mind with this visit was psychological—that, for him at least, "the creative act is inextricably linked to the sexual. The creative impulse has all the signs of sexual stimulation in my own case...and maximum creative power is inseparable from maximum eroticism." He quotes the case of Wagner, and accounts for the difference between *Tristan* and *Parsifal* by the decrease in the composer's sexual vitality.

After his marriage in 1897 Skriabin spent five months in Paris with his wife, but from 1898-1903 he held the post of Professor of Pianoforte at the Moscow Conservatory; and the restraint that this put upon his travelling may have played a part in turning his mind towards orchestral composition. He had already written a piano concerto at the time of his marriage; and there now followed a symphonic poem (1896-99, unperformed), *Rêverie* (1898), Symphony No. 1 (with choral finale, 1899-1900), Symphony No. 2 (1901-02), and Symphony No. 3 (*Le Poème Divin,* 1903). In these works Skriabin showed himself, like the contemporary painters of the Russian avant-garde, more under German than French influence. Just as the painters of the *Mir Iskusstva* circle turned to the Vienna Secession, to Böcklin and the Munich painters rather than to Paris, so Skriabin's use of the orchestra was determined by the examples first of Liszt and Wagner and then of Richard Strauss. The text of the finale to the First Symphony, though painfully conventional in expression, is in fact a hymn to Art as an instrument of personal salvation entirely in the spirit of the "aesthetes." Exactly when Skriabin began to attach a mystical, quasi-religious significance to this music is impossible to say. It is significant that the only occasion on which his music was discussed in the columns of *Mir*

Iskusstva (1899) the writer (Alexander Koptiaev) found evidence even in the harmless piano concerto to show that "the cult of ecstasy . . . is his religion" and in the B flat minor Polonaise the marks of "morbidity and mannerism."

The Evenings of Contemporary Music organized in St. Petersburg in 1901 had little or no effect on Skriabin's development. Of the composers whose music was introduced into these programs—Debussy, Dukas, Fauré, Chausson, d'Indy, Roussel, Schoenberg, Reger, Wolf, and R. Strauss—the only two who can be said to have exercised any influence on Skriabin are Strauss and, purely pianistically, Debussy—the Russian element in whose own music Skriabin was inclined to exaggerate.

It was certainly not until Skriabin gave up his post at the Moscow Conservatory and moved with his wife and family to Switzerland that philosophical-mystical ideas came to dominate his music, giving an extraordinary stimulus to his creative powers. Although there is no evidence that he read theosophical literature at this time, or indeed ever considered himself a theosophist in the sense of being a follower of Blavatsky (he seems not to have read her *La Clef de la Théosophie* at least until 1905), he certainly attended the meetings of the second session of the International Congress of Philosophy in September 1904 at Geneva, where he heard a lecture on "Panpsychism." At this time the thinker who influenced him most was Nietzsche, whose conception of the Superman was the exact obverse of Vladimir Solovyov's doctrine of god-manhood which played an important part in Russian religious thought of the day. Solovyov himself was well aware of this affinity and discussed it in an article published in *Mir Iskusstva* (no. 12) in 1899 on the grounds that "The first task of any intelligent criticism of an error is to determine the truth that it contains and misrepresents."

Skriabin shared Nietzsche's aristocratic conception of art and contempt of the common herd; and the philosophic aphorisms which he wrote during 1904-6 (translated by Oskar von Riesemann with the significant title *Prometheische Phantasien*) are entirely in Nietzsche's vein.[13] The titles of the Third Symphony's three movements—*Luttes, Voluptés, Jeu divin*—represent three cardinal points in Nietzsche's philosophy; the warrior-virtues, the sacredness of unashamed physical delight, and the supreme value of the dance as an activity for its own sake—"play" in the widest sense of the word. The Third Symphony *(Le Poème Divin),* finished in 1904 and performed in May 1905 in Paris by Nikisch, represents a transitional stage in Skriabin's development. Musically it is still conventional, resembling a cross between a Lisztian tone-poem and the traditional symphony, whose forms are for the most part preserved. There are passages of wholetone harmony, but not much more than are to be found in contemporary works by Rimsky-Korsakov; and for the most part the alternation of heavily chromatically altered harmony with the would-be sublime simplicity of diatonic passages follows exactly the practice of Liszt. The three movements each pass into the other without a break, and together form a triptych representing the process of "redemption," which was, in differing forms, the overriding concern of Skriabin's whole life.

The most noticeable features of the *Poème Divin* are the monotony of the music, due to its reiterated ideas, and a sense of strain arising from the composer's desire to invest it with greater significance than in fact, simply as music, it possesses. This is clearly reflected in the many marks of expression, which are often in ludicrous disaccord with the passages they mark. Thus, in the first movement, we find a passage of B flat major repeated chords and arpeggios marked *de plus en plus triomphant* and another of hackneyed chromatically descending sixths marked *écroulement formidable;* similarly *divin, monstrueux, sublime,* and *terrifiant* are repeatedly used, and the marking which seems most suited to describe the character of the whole is the frequent *grandiose,* with its suggestion of contrivance and actual performance that falls below conception. Here again, the similarity to Liszt is striking; and this grandiosity has in each case prompted the acusation of charlatanry. Stravinsky was nearer the truth when he described the *Poème Divin* as "a severe case of musical emphysema"; and it may well be that Stravinsky's own severe insistence on the Apollonian, objective aspect of art was rooted in a reaction against the excesses of the "Dionysian" artists among whom he grew up in the last years of Imperial Russia, and of whom Skriabin was the musical leader.[14]

Before *Le Poème Divin* was finished, Skriabin was deeply involved in the literary text of his next major work, *Le Poème de l'Extase.* In this the form is clearly copied from Nietzsche's *Also sprach Zarathustra,* but the language is that of contemporary Russian poets and especially Konstantin Balmont, a slightly older contemporary and an extraordinarily gifted translator of Shelley, Blake, Coleridge, Tennyson, Wilde, Whitman, and Poe, as well as poetry in many other languages. In 1903 Balmont published a book of poems called *Da budem kak solntse* (Let us be like the sun), whose cover showed the Promethean figure of a naked man with ruffled hair and outstretched arms, lilies at his feet and roses on either side, the *kak* of the title decorously veiling his genitals. The language and many of the ideas of the poems in this volume are strongly reminiscent of Nietzsche and very close to those of Skriabin's *Le Poème de l'Extase.* Here we find, for example, in *Prazdnik svobody* (The Festival of Liberty) such lines as "I am the sudden break. / I am the playing thunder. / I am the transparent stream. / I am for all, but belong to no man."[15] Images of light recur throughout these poems, and there is a "Hymn to Fire" which ends with the lines, "O spirit of soaring matter/ striving towards the bastion of heaven / I long for Death to dawn on me in a white, undimming radiance."[16] In the same volume the equation of the artist not only with Prometheus but with the Devil is common, and the whole apparatus of vampires, sabbaths, gargoyles, incubi and succubi is used. The idea of the artist as creator and demiurge, the identification of consciousness with creation,[17] and of artistic creation with the sense of triumphant ecstasy and bird-like escape to an upper air, run through all these poems and they are the basic ideas of *Le Poème de l'Extase*. Skriabin runs the gamut of words compounded from the roots *krylo-* (wing) and *lyot* (flight), *pian* (intoxication), *tvor* (creation), *laska* (caress), *tain* (secret), *chud* (miraculous), and *rad* (joy). All these ideas and their verbal derivatives play a large part in the poems not only of Balmont but of his younger contemporaries Blok, Bely, and Briusov.[18] In Skriabin, however, the most striking feature is the positive, life-affirming, Nietzschean *Lebenslust (zhazhda zhizni, zhizniradost')* that from the period of the Fourth Piano Sonata (1903) heavily outweighs the drooping, despairing, "decadent" note predominant in the early miniatures. This was a conscious reaction on the part of Skriabin, who was impatient of Tchaikovsky's and Rakhmaninov's music and of Chekhov's writing, because he felt that theirs was an art that could not "uplift," but could only depress. Even as a teacher, he insisted first of all on playing that was intoxicating *(upoitel'naia);* and it is significant that while his music remained within the limits of tonality, and even later, he preferred the major mode, or at least its suggestion, to the minor.

The enormous final cadence of *Le Poème de l'Extase* is in fact a dominant to tonic in C major, the tonality of Wagner's *Meistersinger* that is an affirmation of the same *Lebenslust* only terrestrial rather than cosmic in character. Even the diabolism of the *Poème Satanique* is no more than a theatrical contrivance and was explained as such by the composer as "the apotheosis of insincerity," an idea wholly in accord with his admiration for Oscar Wilde and the Russian Symbolists' proclamation of the "art of lying" *(iskusstvo lzhi).*[19] Skriabin's deification of Will and Desire, which he learned from Schopenhauer and Nietzsche, was the exact opposite of Solovyov's Christian teaching and his conception of *sobornost',* community, a kind of apocalyptic togetherness with panerotic overtones. In these ideas we find the beginnings of what became after Skriabin's eventual return to Russia in 1910 a mental disequilibrium so severe, and an inability to distinguish the world of external reality from that of his private imagination so absolute, that it led him at least to the brink of insanity. Skriabin's creative career may perhaps reasonably be divided, as Clemens Christoph von Gleich has suggested,[20] into seven-year periods that Rudolf Steiner regards as significant in all human lives. The first two of these seven-year periods are his childhood, and during the third he is learning the musician's craft, as performer and composer. Between the ages of 21 and 28 (1893-1900) he gradually develops his musical personality, outgrowing the strong early influence of Chopin and widening his interest from the piano to the orchestra. The fifth seven-year period (1900-7) is marked by the growth of the composer's extra-musical interests and sense of mission, and ends with *Le Poème de l'Extase,* and during the sixth and final period (*Prometheus* and the last five piano sonatas) the personal sense of messiahship prompted Skriabin to develop a new musical language, based on an arbitrary rather than scientific harmony that in fact restricted the character of his music, although it enhanced its individuality.

What in fact was the nature of Skriabin's growing obsession? It was neither theosophical, at least in the conventional sense, nor Nietzschean, though it had points in common with both. It was in the first place the proclamation of a religion of art, or a fusion of art, philosophy, and religion into a new gospel of which Skriabin himself was at first the preacher and later something more—prophet, messiah, even (in the terminology that he borrowed from Sologub and Balmont) god. In the volume of poems which Balmont published in 1909 and which Skriabin particularly admired, we find the lines, "I am God incarnate / marked by a starry countenance, / all other gods cannot be counted / but there is no other God."[21] This, as far as it can be said to mean anything, is a claim to be the creator of a solipsistic universe, a claim prompted primarily by a desperate desire to reject the world of objective "reality." Every catastrophic event of these years strengthened the impulse of these Russian artists to proclaim the coming of the end; not only the defeats of the Russo-Japanese War or the revolution of 1905, but the Messina earthquake of 1908 prompted cries of despair. "In the face of the raging elements," Blok wrote in that year, "the haughty flag of culture is lowered. . . . Every promoter of culture is a demon, coursing the earth and devising wings in order to fly away from it."[22] Skriabin differed from the poets and thinkers in his positive belief that his music contained the magic spells which would in the end dissolve the universe as we know it and usher in a new world. "The tortured universe awaits a miracle," he wrote, "awaits the last great Act of Fulfilment, the act of union between the male Creator-Spirit and the Woman-World." Unlike the large majority of mystics (or rather gnostics) Skriabin did not identify himself with the passive role in this mystical union. He speaks of the first principle of the universe indifferently as creator, god, death, or new life; and what he means in each case is the principle of spirituality, creating and working through the world of material phenomena. The two polarities of this universe were not Good and Evil, which he saw as merely two complementary exhibitions of Energy, but the principles of Activity and Passivity; and he identified himself with the active principle, the principle of creation. Just as Solovyov's Sophia, or Divine Wisdom, all too easily became identified with the "Unknown Woman" or the "Lovely Lady" of the poets, or even with an individual woman, so Skriabin's metaphysical principles of Activity and Passivity all too easily took on an overtly sexual connotation, and his claim to embody the active principle deteriorated into a mystical sensuality.[23] The *Poème de l'Extase* is in fact a celebration of this mystical sensuality, a hymn to sexuality with a very thin metaphysical veneer. As late as 1905 the projected title had been *Poème Orgiaque,* and we know from Sabaneev that, after the experiences of the composer's visit to Paris with Beliaev in 1896, the creative act was, for him, "inextricably linked to the sexual." Even if we did not have such markings as *"avec une volupté de plus en plus extatique,"* there is plenty of internal musical evidence to suggest erotic connotations in the themes that suggest stretching or writhing bodies, sections of breathless flight and pursuit followed by triumphant capture and submission, rhythms that repeatedly suggest the periodicity of orgasm voluptuously interrupted. There are mounting, thrusting trumpet themes and alluringly hesitant or beckoning phrases which have clear parallels with male and female sexual attitudes; but it is the general atmosphere of the music, the sum of these individual characteristics that has the unmistakable nature of erotic fantasy.

A far stronger piece written simultaneously with *Le Poème de l'Extase,* and connected with it both verbally and musically, is the Fifth Piano Sonata. This carries as a motto a quotation from the text of the *Poème de l'Extase:* "I summon you to life, hidden impulses! Drowning in the dark depths of the creator spirit, timorous germs of life, I bring you boldness!" In the sonata the erotic element, which is overwhelmingly strong in the orchestral *Poème de l'Extase,* forms only one of several elements. In fact the *languido* and *accarezzevole* markings in the introduction to the main *Presto con allegrezza* suggest hesitations and caresses that are not so much those of lovers but rather the exchanges between the creator and his half-formed creations, as in Skriabin's motto. The *Presto* itself, which opens with a tense *pianissimo,* is a magnificent example of a style of piano-writing liberated from Chopin's influence and entirely original. The cross-rhythms (4/4 against a disjointed and syncopated 6/8; ex. 1) take on an obsessive character, while the leaping staccato chords give the music a vertiginous quality that the composer was never to achieve in his orchestral writing. The imperious trumpet-calls which were to appear increasingly in all Skriabin's music after this date, clearly suggest the summons of creation, the call to existence; and their combination with the langorous second subject, introduced by a passage where the composer's marking *con una ebrezza fantastica* is for once no exaggeration, is purely musically a superb conception. Even more important as a distinction between the Fifth Sonata and the *Poème de l'Extase* is the harmonic language. The orchestral work is marked by an overwhelmingly "dominant" atmosphere, with seventh and ninth chords following closely on each other and often combined with a tonic-dominant pedal. The Fifth Sonata, on the other hand, is the first of Skriabin's works not to end with a chord on the tonic; and we find already the so-called "Promethean" chord—a six-note chord constructed of fourths, two augmented, one diminished, and two perfect (e.g., C–F sharp–B flat–E–A–D). This chord is transposable and therefore gives what are in effect twelve "sound-centers," which Skriabin came to use freely but persistently. The origin of this harmonic change in Skriabin's music (which can be traced back at least as far as the fourth-dominated Fourth Sonata of 1903) is empirical rather than scientific and therefore resembles Debussy's quasi-systematic use of the

Ex. 1 Piano Sonata No. 5, *Presto con allegrezza*

whole-tone scale rather than Schoenberg's invention and scientific application
of serialism.

Although a doctrinaire in the sphere of his own religious-philosophical
outlook and opinions, Skriabin was wholly intuitive as a composer; and if in
fact the works written after the Fifth Sonata become increasingly atonal in
harmony, this was largely because the composer believed that a new language
should be elaborated for the Final Mystery, the work to which all his music
after *Prometheus* (1911) approximated. The non-musical language for this
imagined rite was elaborated by Skriabin with the help of Emil Sigogne, a
theosophist in Brussels where Skriabin moved with Tatiana Schloezer in the
autumn of 1908. In June of that year the financial side of Skriabin's existence,
which had always been precarious despite his own hard work first as performer
and then as composer, and the assistance first of Mitrofan Beliaev and then
Margarita Morozova, was transfigured by the visit of Sergei Koussevitzky. An
enormously rich wife enabled Koussevitzky to found his own music-publishing
firm, and to start a series of Koussevitzky Concerts. Skriabin not only accepted
a soloist's fee of 1,000 rubles a concert from Koussevitzky; he also interested his
new patron in the project of the Final Mystery, in which Koussevitzky at once
bought rights, in addition to offering the composer an annual sum of 5,000
rubles for the next five years. In these fairytale circumstances it is hardly to be
wondered at if the borderline between dream and reality became even more
confused in Skriabin's imagination. The cover of *Prometheus,* the "poem of
fire," which was begun during a visit to Russia in the first part of 1909, shows a
fire-and-lotus encircled lyre, with a man's face poised in the middle, above an
altar marked with the Star of David and bearing seven candles which rise, like
lyre-strings, to a sun. The imagery is characteristically heterogeneous,
theosophy possessing an accretive, assimilative power which gives it the
attraction and the weakness of all gnostic systems.

As in the Fifth Sonata, the erotic element occupies a secondary place to
the magical in *Prometheus*. The material is all derivable from the opening
"Promethean" chord, with the muted horn's summons which, like many of
Skriabin's themes, circles round a central pivot (ex. 2).

Ex. 2.   *Prometheus, Lento brumeux*

The character of this theme suggests a comparison with the spells *(zagovory)* or incantations that form a considerable part of Balmont's *Firebird (Zhar Ptitsa)* poems of 1907, in which one whole section is entitled "Soothsaying" *(Vorozhba)*. The vocalizing wordless chorus that Skriabin employs in *Prometheus* had already been used by Debussy in *Sirènes,* the third of the orchestral *Nocturnes* first performed in Paris in 1901. The solo piano part which plays an important role in the score also serves to clarify the work's formal structure. As in his earlier orchestral works, Skriabin preserves in broad lines the traditional arrangement of exposition, development, recapitulation, and coda; but, as in *Le Poème de l'Extase,* the micro-structure of the music depends entirely on the transformation and free combinations of thematic material; and it is this rather than the broader architectural lines that gives this music its quasi-oriental, wholly un-architectural character. The atmosphere of *Prometheus* is less oppressive than that of *Le Poème de l'Extase,* partly owing to the presence of the percussive piano but even more to the greater variety of ideas and the more astringent and adventurous harmony. That adventure is restricted, however, within the limits of the fourth-based "Promethean" chord, which heavily flavors the whole work and all that Skriabin was to write in the next four years; and if we compare the orchestral writing of *Prometheus* with that of such contemporary works as Ravel's *Daphnis et Chloë,* Debussy's *Ibéria,* or Strauss's *Der Rosenkavalier,* it is clumsy, even amateurish in character. To the end of his life Skriabin remained before all else a composer for the piano; and although his last piano sonatas (nos. 6-10) move obsessively within a narrow range of musical ideas, the presentation of these ideas on the keyboard was unquestionably new and original.

The most original feature of the score of *Prometheus* is the inclusion of a color element, in the form of a *clavier à lumières.* This represented a first step in the direction of that symphony of all the senses—"a musical phrase ending in a scent, a chord that resolves into a color, a melodic line whose climax becomes a caress"—of which Skriabin dreamed. Rimsky-Korsakov believed in a system of equivalents between tonalities and the colors of the spectrum, but his equivalents were not the same as Skriabin's; and the idea is in fact arbitrary, and no more than a poetical fancy like Rimbaud's sonnet on the colors of vowels—"A noir, E blanc, I rouge, U vert, O bleu." The line which appears in the score of *Prometheus* as *luce* is written in two parts, to which a third is very occasionally added.[24] The upper of the two parts is identical with the root of the sound centers produced by the transpositions of the "Promethean" chord. Thus, although the bass of the opening chord (see ex. 2) is G, the root is A, and A appears accordingly in the upper line of the *luce* part. The lower of the two parts consists of long-held "notes" resembling pedal-points, and although the progression of these seems to follow roughly a whole-tone scale, it appears more probable that Skriabin had in mind a generalized color scheme that was to form an overall background to the individual changes of color determined by the harmonies.

Skriabin was not alone either in his insistence on the close link between music and color, or in his belief that the traditional language of his art was now exhausted. Another Russian, some five years his senior, was coming to very similar conclusions at exactly the same time, also in Western Europe. Vasily Kandinsky had abandoned his legal career in 1896, at the age of 30, and joined another Russian émigré, Alexei Yavlensky, to devote himself entirely to painting. In 1902, Kandinsky joined the Berlin Secession, and during the next six years he travelled extensively in Europe and the Near East before settling in Bavaria. In 1909, he formed the New Artists' Association, whose second exhibition (1910) was introduced by an article in which Kandinsky adumbrated a highly spiritualized conception of painting freed from conventional "content." Skriabin himself might have written the words, "The communication of what is secret—by means of a secret—is not that the content?" In fact between 1909-12, Kandinsky was under the influence of Rudolf Steiner, whose anthroposophical lectures he attended; and both Steiner and Blavatsky receive friendly mention in his long essay *Concerning the Spiritual in Art* (*Über das Geistige in der Kunst,* 1912, English trans., New York, 1946).[25] Kandinsky does not in general use apocalyptic language, but in his adumbrations of an abstract art, freed from the domination of the subject matter, we again find words that Skriabin could well have written: "When we remember that spiritual experience is quickening, that positive science, the firmest basis of human thought, is tottering, that the dissolution of matter is imminent, we have reason to hope that the hour of pure composition is not far away. The first stage has arrived."[26]

The imminent dissolution of matter celebrated and brought about by a great Mystery in which music—his music—should play the chief part was the belief that inspired Skriabin ever more exclusively during the last 10 years of his life; and when this dream became more remote, he too began to speak of a "first stage" or Introductory Action. Kandinsky twice mentions Skriabin in his essay. On the first occasion he couples his name with that of Debussy, finding in the music of both an alternation between "internal" and "external" beauty, which he compares unfavorably with Schoenberg's exclusive concern with "internal" beauty (Schoenberg was at this time associated with Kandinsky who, with Munter, Kubin, and Franz Marc, had withdrawn from the New Artists' Association and founded "Der Blaue Reiter"). These artists were consciously aiming at applying to painting the principle that Verlaine and Mallarmé had already applied to poetry—*"reprendre à la musique son bien":*

> Music is found to be the best teacher...the art which had devoted itself not to the reproduction of natural phenomena, but to the expression of the artist's soul and to the creation of an autonomous life of musical sound.... The painter naturally seeks to apply the means of music to his own art; and from this results that modern desire for *rhythm* in painting, for mathematical, *abstract construction,* for *repeated notes* of color, for setting color in motion, and so on.[27]

There is a direct reference to *Prometheus* in the second passage of *Über das Geistige in der Kunst,* where Kandinsky foresees a new dance-theater in which the traditional language of mime will be replaced by another able to "arouse finer spiritual vibrations." This dance-theater will combine musical, pictorial and dance movements.

> Skriabin's attempt to intensify musical tone by a corresponding use of color is naturally an elementary attempt presenting one of many possibilities.... The tortuous paths of the new world will lead through primeval forests and over bottomless chasms, toward icy peaks, with the same unfailing guide—the unchanging principle of internal necessity.[28]

As in Skriabin's own writings, we find in Kandinsky too the imagery of the Russian Symbolist poets, for whom nature existed only in its most violent or extreme forms. Polar imagery is particularly common in Blok,[29] who uses it as a symbol. In Kandinsky's early painting there was a combination of revolutionary pathos with introverted emotion. The sophisticated fairy-tale illustration—a parallel to Rimsky-Korsakov's *Kashchei* and Stravinsky's *Firebird*—plays a part in his significantly named *Poésies sans paroles,* where "a popular balladic element is mixed with the conscious curves of an Aubrey Beardsley" (H.K. Rothel). Even as a student, however, Kandinsky had found the subject matter of a painting more of a disturbance than a help; and when in 1910 he started a series of pictures which he called *Improvisations,* he used riders, cupolas, swords, goblets, and women as so many emotional tokens, visual counters, or symbols, very much as the Symbolist poets used their images. The Munich *Jugendstil* may have contributed something to his iconography, but it was Wagner's *Lohengrin* that opened his eyes not only to a new world of color but to a magical, theurgic conception of art very like that of Skriabin:

> I saw all my colors; they stood before my eyes. Wild, almost crazy lines drew themselves before me.... I realized that art in general is much more powerful than I had thought, and that painting could develop the same kind of powers that music possessed.[30]

The correspondences between color and sound that Kandinsky gives in his essay seem no less arbitrary than those of Skriabin or Rimsky-Korsakov, and they reveal associations that may seem strange to musicians. We may accept that the shades of blue, from pale to dark, correspond to a timbre scale descending from the flute, through the cello and doublebass to the organ; but what are we to make of the identification of orange with the sound of the church-bell (tolling Angelus) or "the *Largo* of an old violin"? And to compare violet with the timbre of English horn or bassoon seems to argue an inability to make the precise musical distinctions which alone give these systems anything more than a vague and fanciful character.

Nevertheless, there is a real parallel between Kandinsky's gradual abandonment of the object and increasingly confident use of "abstract expressions" and Skriabin's abandonment of traditional tonality and use of a strictly atonal language based at first on the superimposed fourths of the "Promethean" chord, but in his very last works moving away even from this sheet-anchor. But whereas Skriabin was anxious to attach an extra-musical meaning to his music, Kandinsky was very aware of the dangers inherent in the "poeticizing" that abstract painting seemed to invite in the spectator. He would certainly not have welcomed the title that Skriabin's theosophical friend Podgaetsky gave to the Ninth Piano Sonata—"the Black Mass"—or written of the Tenth as the composer himself was to do: "My Tenth Sonata is a sonata of insects. Insects are born from the sun...they are the sun's kisses.... How unified world-understanding is when you look at things this way...."[31] Much nearer Kandinsky's conception of art were Skriabin's comments, as reported by Sabaneev, on the five preludes of opus 74, his last music, written in 1914. Here he claimed to have written music that "is like a crystal, for the same crystal can reflect many different lights and colors." With less than a year of life before him he spoke, with unconscious prophecy, of death and quoted his favorite Balmont "there must be no trace of fear about it. It is the highest reconciliation, a white radiance."[32] The last piano works contain a large proportion of movements in which this transparent, radiant quality is suggested by the high pitch of the music and the use of bell-like chord ostinatos. As early as *Désir,* opus 57, no. 1, he had hardly used the bass clef, and the first of the *Poèmes* of opus 71 is high-lying with *pianissimo* triad sequences against ninth chords. If his earlier dance pieces, like the *Caresse dansée,* opus 57, no. 2, often have a self-conscious *art nouveau* character and suggest the world of Loie Fuller or Isadora Duncan, the Sixth and Seventh sonatas contain passages in which a vertiginous dance-flight is announced or interrupted by the trumpet calls or trombone summonses that had played an increasing part in his musical vocabulary from the time of the *Poème de l'Extase* and the Fifth Sonata. After Skriabin returned to Russia in 1910, he was the center of literary and artistic attention. Among the writers nearest to him were Briusov, Bely, Merezhkovsky, Baltrushaitis, Balmont, and Viacheslav Ivanov, whose latest

(1909) collection of essays *Po zvezdam* (In the Stars) included characteristic pieces on "Nietzsche and Dionysus," "The Poet and the Crowd," and "Wagner and the Dionysian Dream." The volume of poems that he published in 1911 under the title *Cor ardens* was a particular favorite with Skriabin, and contains a "Praise of the Sun," "Solar Psalm," and "Firebearers" that echo exactly the "Promethean" obsessions of the composer.

Of his fellow-musicians Skriabin was much more critical. He had no use for Rakhmaninov's or Medtner's music and could see nothing in the early works of Prokofiev's that were apearing at this time in Russia. He met Stravinsky in Switzerland in 1913; and although Stravinsky wrote to him in admiration of the seventh sonata, Skriabin could find in his music nothing more than "a mass of insolence and a minimum of creative power." The two men had in fact almost nothing in common. Nor does he seem to have showed any interest in the feeble Vladimir Rebikov, whose *Mélomimiques* and *Tableaux musico-psychologiques* had caused some stir some years earlier and whose *Alpha and Omega* (1911) had a fashionable cosmic libretto which might have caught Skriabin's attention. The painter who might have interested him was the Lithuanian, Chiurlionis, who called his works sonatas and his exhibitions concerts; but Skriabin dismissed him as a dreamer who did not wish his dream to become reality. He seems to have known nothing of Kandinsky.

After a triumphal concert-tour down the Volga organized by Koussevitzky in the spring of 1910 the two men quarreled bitterly, and it was to England that Skriabin now turned to implement his dream of the Mystery. In March 1914 he began a successful series of concerts in London and the provinces, in the intervals of which he got in touch with the Theosophical Society and bought a plot of land near Darjeeling, the proposed site of the Preliminary Action of the Final Mystery. But in London he suffered for the first time from the boil on his lip which a year later was to cause his death in Moscow.

Berdyaev characterized as "a false sophiological romanticism" the attitude to life of Blok and his fellow poets, and what he says of them is even truer of Skriabin. "They saw false dawns and mirages in the desert," wrote Berdyaev, "but never saw the real dawn. In their tragic fate is reflected the lie at the heart of this whole way of life, this whole current in Russian spiritual life and literature. . . . The revolution came in literature before it came in life."[33] And so, although the so-called Russian Renaissance of these years produced new schools, the blossoming was as short-lived as it was brilliant. All these artists suffered from the fact that theirs was the art of a tiny minority, completely out of touch with the realities of the everyday life surrounding them and alien in every way to the spirit of pity, compassion, and humanity which has been the hallmark of all the greatest art in Russia. If the circumstances of rootlessness and dependence on Western European models gave this movement its thin-skinned and hectic character, the strong anti-intellectual and messianic vein in the Russian character opened the door wide to excesses easily exploited by the mentally unbalanced as well as by charlatans. *Voprosy Zhizni* consciously aimed at bringing about a rapprochement between the cultural and the social movements, between the aesthete poets and thinkers and the liberal-radicals, whose drab moral respectability and exclusive concern with political stringencies reflected none of the changes taking place in Russian culture. That rapprochement was never made; and while the politicals went on to achieve eventually the revolution for which they were working, the lack of all moral decisiveness and the inability to choose and to act condemned the artists, with very few exceptions, to a vague aestheticism and romanticism. When the greatest of them, Alexander Blok, spoke apocalyptically of "self-intoxication by the passionate whirlwinds of revolution," he failed tragically to distinguish between a spiritual revolution which was also a revelation, and what were to be the hard realities of 1917.

Notes

1.   Nastanet god, Rossii chernyi god. / kogda tsarei korona upadet, / zabudet chern' k nim prezhniuiu liubov' / i pishcha mnogikh budet smert' i krov'.

2.   A. Blok, "The People and the Intelligentsia," in *The Spirit of Music* (1908; English translation, London, 1946), p. 36.

3.   Nicholas Berdyaev, *Dream and Reality* (London, 1950), pp. 141-42.

4.   In his review of Bely's *Reminiscences of Aleksandr Blok,* published in *Sophia,* (1923).

5.   Vechnaia zhenstvennost' nyne / v tele netlennom na zemle idet,/ v svete nemerknuvshchim Novoi Bogini / nebo slilosia s puchinoiu vod [The Eternal Feminine today / wanders the earth in incorruptible form. / In the undimmed radiance of a New Goddess / heaven is united with the watery abyss.]

6.   Berdyaev, *Dream and Reality,* p. 162.

7.   Conversation with Tiumenev quoted in A.A. Gozenpud, *Rimsky-Korsakov: Issledovaniia, materialy, pis'ma* [Research, materials, letters] (Moscow, 1953), p. 24.

8.   Ibid., p. 250.

9.   Sonnet (1892): Mne malo istiny, / mne malo prostoty, / sozdal ia v tainykh mechtakh / mir ideal'noi prirody. / Chto pered nim etot prakh / stepi, i skaly i vody [I care little for truth or simplicity / In my secret dreams I have created / a world of ideal nature / compared with which this is dust and ashes, the steppes, the cliffs and waters.]

10.   Ia—Bog tainstvennogo mira, / ves' mir v odnikh moikh mechtakh.

11.   Ia sozdal nebesa i zemliu, / i snova iasnyi mir sozdam.

12.   For the whole subject see Georgette Donchin's *The Influence of French Symbolism on Russian Poetry* (The Hague, 1958).

13. Between 1901-3 Skriabin was engaged on the libretto for an opera with a Nietzschean *Übermensch* as protagonist. According to Schloezer this figure personified the active, male principle dominating the crowd (and the Tsaritsa, who impersonates the Eternal Feminine or passive principle) by "the vibrations of his will." Fragments of the text read exactly like the fantastic "library" plays that the Symbolist poets wrote in poor imitation of Maeterlinck, e.g., Balmont's *Three Dawns—the theater of Youth and Beauty.*

14. Yet Stravinsky's early works were strongly colored by this art. There are clear evidences of Skriabin's influence in *Fireworks* (1908) and even *Firebird* (1910), and the poems of Balmont played an important part in his early life. He set two—*The Flower* and *The Dove*—in 1911, and took the text of the cantata which he dedicated to Debussy—*Zvezdoliki* [The Star-faced One], 1911—from a collection of poems that Balmont published in 1909, *Zelenyi Vertograd,* a great favorite with Skriabin. The title of *Firebird* comes from Balmont's collection *Zhar Ptitsa* (1907), a volume chiefly concerned with old Slavonic deities and rites and containing many poems in the form of spells. It is significant that one poem in this collection is entitled *Prazdnik vesny* [Spring Festival] which may have suggested the title, and the character, of *Le Sacre du printemps* [Vesna sviashchennaia]. The whole "Scythian" movement [*Skifstvo*] in Russian art, which is comparable to the Celtic Revival in England at the same time, was absolutely alien to the cosmopolitan Skriabin, though it prompted Prokofiev's aborted ballet *Ala and Lolly* (which supplied the music for the *Scythian Suite*). *Skifstvo* was chiefly represented in painting by one of the *Mir Iskusstva* artists, Nicholas Roerich, whom Diaghilev commissioned to do the sets of *Le Sacre du printemps.*

15. Ia vnezapnyi izlom Ia igraiushchii grom Ia prozrachnyi ruchei Ia dlia vsekh i nichei.

16. O dusha voskhodiashchei stikhii / stremiashcheisia v tverd' / ia khochu, chtoby belym, pomerknuvshim svetom, zasvetilas' mne Smert'!

17. Particularly tempting in Russian where the two words have only a single letter different: *soznanie* (consciousness)—*sozdanie* (creation).

18. Briusov's mock-medieval *conte, The Fiery Angel,* which Prokofiev used for an opera, contains many of the diabolist, sadistic, and generally morbid traits common to all these poets in different degrees. It was first printed in the Symbolist magazine *Vesy* in 1907-8. Prokofiev set poems by Balmont and Gippius (Merezhkovsky's wife) and the title *Suggestion diabolique* (1909) explains itself. The title of *Sarcasms* (1912) was suggested to the composer by Nuvel and Nurok.

19. Cf. Briusov's lines addressed to Balmont, "Ia v tebe liubliu / chto ves' ty lozh'" [I love in you / the lie incarnate].

20. Clemens Christoph von Gleich, *Die Sinfonischen Werke von Alexander Skrjabin* (Bilthoven, 1963), p. 80.

21. *Zelenyi Vertograd:* Az esm' Bog vochelovechennyi / zvezdolikost'iu otmechennyi / vsekh drugikh bogov ne schest' / no inogo Boga nest'.

22. Blok, "Nature and Culture" (1908), published in *The Spirit of Music,* pp. 50-51.

23. Vasily Rozanov had already developed a religion of very much this type, and Rasputin was to use a similar doctrine in order to obtain a hold over the Tsaritsa and members of the court. Readers of Norman Douglas's *South Wind* will remember the character of the mystical Russian sensualist, a Messiah sharing many traits with the historical character of Gurjiev, whose *All and Everything* contains claims to secret knowledge, gnostic illuminism, and oriental mysteries often similar to those made by Skriabin. Balmont too wrote in *Zelenyi Vertograd* (1909): "V sonme vostochnykh / dal'nykh nebes / v migakh urochnykh / v

zvenakh / chudes, / byl / ia, khodil ia, / meda vkusil / ia, / sveta ispil ia, / snova / ischez"[I was in the Eastern throngs / of the distant heavens, / in the uttermost moments / in the links of wonders, / there I was, there I wandered, / I tasted honey, / I drank the light, / again I vanished].

24. Cf. Clemens Christoph von Gleich, *Die Sinfonischen Werke,* p. 71.

25. Kandinsky was not a whole-hearted believer. "Skeptical though we may be regarding the tendency of the theosophists towards theorizing and their excessive anticipation of definite answers in lieu of immense question-marks, it remains a fundamentally spiritual movement...a strong agent in the general atmosphere, presaging deliverance to oppressed and gloomy hearts." This search for *redemption,* which ran through all Wagner's work, was transferred in this last phase on to the cosmic plane, one on which Russians felt particularly at home. It is worth noting that in 1909 the painter Mondrian became a Theosophist, and that in the same year W.B. Yeats, the chief poet associated with the Celtic Revival which had much in common with *Skifstvo,* was writing seriously, if not very sympathetically, about the Dublin theosophists, whose language is reflected in many of his poems.

26. V. Kandinsky, *Concerning the Spiritual in Art* (New York, 1946), p. 68.

27. Ibid., p. 40.

28. Ibid., p. 82.

29. Cf. a poem written by Blok in September 1909:

> Beri svoi cheln, plyvi na dal'nii polius
> v stenakh iz l'da—i tikho zabyvai
> Kak tam liubili, gibli i borolis',
> i zabyvai strastei byvalyi krai.
> I k vzdragivaniiam medlennogo khlada
> ustaluiu ty dushu priuchi,
> chtob bylo zdes' ei nichego ne nado
> kogda ottuda rinutsia luchi.
>
> [Take your boat, plunge to the distant pole
> With its walls of ice—and gently forget,
> how there men loved, died and fought...
> and forget the old world of the passions.
> And mid the shudderings of the slow-moving cold
> teach your tired spirit,
> that *here* she needs all but nothing
> when the rays come streaming in from *yonder.*]

30. Kandinsky, *Concerning the Spiritual in Art,* p. 46.

31. Leonid Sabaneev, *Skriabin,* 2d ed. (Moscow, 1923), p. 122.

32. See p. 28, fn. 16.

33. *Sophia* (1923).

Tovey's Prose: "Emotion Ratified by Design"

Paul S. Machlin

Anyone who studies music of the nineteenth century sooner or later—and almost always sooner—encounters the work of Gerald Abraham. With the publication of *The Concise Oxford History of Music* (1979), his audience has doubtless considerably widened; it's probably not hyperbole to claim now that anyone at all who takes a serious interest in the music of western civilization cannot avoid reading something he has written. My own first encounter occurred as an undergraduate, when I read *A Hundred Years of Music.* A few years later, I had the good fortune to participate in a seminar on Wagner which he taught at Berkeley in 1968-1969, the year he held the Ernest Bloch Professorship there. (It must have been in some ways an astonishing year for him: this was the era of People's Park and other such student "disturbances," a time in which the normal routine of campus life was constantly interrupted. Each quarter, because of a new crisis or dispute, one was presented with the same moral dilemma—to attend or not to attend classes. However, there was never any question, even among the most political of us, of skipping Professor Abraham's seminar.)

Since that time, I have visited and corresponded with him often, seeking advice on all kinds of research problems. He has responded with unfailing generosity; indeed, as his published work has illuminated crucial concepts for me, so his letters have consistently guided my own work in the right direction. I remain deeply grateful for his substantial support at important junctures in my career, as well as for his material assistance and encouragement, and I am especially glad to have this opportunity to acknowledge the extent of my debt to him.

*   *   *

The critical malady of our age is an indifference to sheer creativeness as a thing—of power and of pleasure—in itself. In its itch to correlate and laminate and explain, current criticism has half-lost the instinct to respond and enjoy. Worse, in its obsession over what makes the clock tick, it all too often fails to notice whether it tells the right time.[1]

Sir Donald Francis Tovey repeatedly emphasized that music should be understood and appreciated through listening; analysis derived from the score was useful for him only insofar as it reflected what he had heard. Thus he writes as much to explain his intuitive perceptions rationally to his reader (the "naive listener") as to analyze compositional processes. We may share his reactions to a certain work or find flaws in his description, but in either case, what impresses us in his best writing is the vitality of his response and the conviction that music's most important function is to provide a profound emotional experience.

A central component of that experience for Tovey is the recognition of moments of great intensity in music combined with an understanding of how they have been prepared. Because such moments often occur at important structural points, a sensitivity to them also enhances the listener's comprehension of the work. It is crucial to Tovey that his reader gain a clear understanding of the construction and function of these climaxes and of the passages which prepare them. He takes pains, therefore, to discuss them in detail, and in assessing their inherently dramatic quality, he captures in prose the essence of his emotional response to the music.

One such gesture of concentrated force occurs at the recapitulation of the first movement of Beethoven's Symphony No. 9 in D minor, and Tovey characterizes it with illuminating clarity:

> The present catastrophic return now reveals fresh evidence of the gigantic size of the opening. Hitherto we have known the opening as a pianissimo, and only the subtlety of Beethoven's feeling for tone has enabled us to feel that it was vast in sound as well as in spaciousness. Now we are brought into the midst of it, and instead of a distant nebula we see the heavens on fire. There is something very terrible about this triumphant major tonic, and it is almost a relief when it turns into the minor as the orchestra crashes into the main theme, no longer in unison, but with a bass rising in answer to the fall of the melody.[2]

This description constitutes more than a simple narration of musical events; the prose itself approximates the course of Tovey's response to the music. The adjectives and expressive phrases convey a sense of the power behind the recapitulation: "catastrophic ... fresh ... gigantic ... vast ... heavens on fire ... terrible ... triumphant ... relief ... crashes ... " By employing elements of contrast, visual imagery, suggestive verbs and adjectives, even alliteration, Tovey explicates the drama of this moment in the music, particularly in his characterization of the major tonic as both "terrible" and "triumphant." The passage excites him and leaves him awed, and he effectively communicates that same series of sensations, convinced we must share them upon hearing the music.

When Tovey responds immediately and profoundly to a piece of music, then, his prose is energetic, fluent, "terse"—to use one of his own accolades— and attuned to the music he discusses. But he is also capable of paragraphs which are diffuse and unclear, incorporating extensive digressions and abstruse analogies. I suspect that such weakened writing reveals at best a lukewarm appreciation for the music in question, in spite of Tovey's nominal defense of it. This suspicion obviously reflects a speculative and subjective reading of his prose, and in some instances it directly contradicts his stated opinion. Nevertheless, because the vitality of Tovey's writing often provides an unmistakable clue to the degree of his enthusiasm for the music he discusses, it is difficult to believe that a piece excites his imagination if the prose he uses to describe it is lackluster.

The essays "Franz Schubert" and "Brahms's Chamber Music" will serve to illustrate this thesis. Tovey responds strongly to Schubert's music, but cannot always justify or explain it as fully and logically as he would like. On the other hand, he defends Brahms's early chamber music because it follows principles of composition of which he approves; except for his discussion of a few of the late works and the Piano Quartet in C minor, opus 60, however, his enthusiasm seems somewhat forced. Tovey's difficulties in formulating these two critiques arise in part from his well-defined notions of correct and appropriate compositional procedures, particularly concerning sonata form movements (where he rarely hesitates to distinguish between "right" and "wrong"). For example, although he disdains the concept of sonata form as an inflexible model ("There are people who talk *a priori* nonsense about the sonata forms, as if these forms were stereotyped moulds into which you shovel your music in the hope that it may set there like a jelly"[3]), he maintains that certain aspects of its shape are inviolable, "fixed":

> Now, the sonata forms... depend largely on the balance and distinction between three typical organic members; an exposition, a development, and a recapitulation. Of these, the most delicate is the recapitulation, on which the symmetry of the whole depends... The real fixed points in the matter are: that there is at the outset a mass of material clearly establishing the tonic key; that there then follows a decisive transition to another key; and that in that other key another mass of material completes the exposition. In any case, the exposition asserts its keys in order to maintain them.[4]

Such guidelines are perhaps broad enough in Tovey's mind to escape classification as "*a priori* nonsense," yet despite their generality, he must occasionally revise them when discussing Schubert's music: the flexibility and unpredictability of Schubert's forms often confound Tovey's expectations.

When Tovey approaches Schubert's instrumental music, the underlying tensions between his intuitive sense of Schubert's greatness and his profound respect for principles Schubert disregards begin to emerge. One difficulty concerns Schubert's handling of recapitulations. Tovey maintains that "there is no surer touchstone of Schubert's... treatment of form than the precise way in which [his] recapitulations differ from [his] expositions."[5] Thus, he dismisses Schubert's literal recapitulation in the first movement of the Quintet for Piano and Strings in A major (D. 667, the "Trout") as "a mere copyist's task" and "wrong."[6] But he again warns the reader against preconceived assumptions about form: "the *a priori* theorist is not less wrong who regards extensive recapitulation as ʌ weakness in the classical schemes."[7] This apparent equivocation serves Tovey's didactic purpose well; it allows him to except "the extreme case where an exact recapitulation is all that is required"[8] from his general criterion that recapitulations should not duplicate expositions. In fact, such symmetry (which, as we have seen, is a crucial consideration for Tovey) can be achieved through either a literal or free recapitulation. "The true conception of this musical symmetry," he remarks, "is thus essentially dramatic."[9] In other words, the effect produced by the return of the familiar music must be made striking or arresting in some way (i.e., "dramatic"), whether or not the music is an exact repetition of the exposition. The return must engage the listener emotionally; if it does, then the purposes of symmetry and balance have been served, and the composer has succeeded. Given Tovey's continual admonitions against accepting a priori postulates, this piece of inductive reasoning hardly comes as a surprise. It does, however, make it difficult for us to take seriously his claim that certain principles are "fixed."

To support his argument, Tovey cites two works, one of which—the first movement of the Piano Sonata in B♭ Major, D. 960—represents an "extreme" instance in which an exact recapitulation is justified. He acknowledges that Schubert's technique of generating doubt as to the moment when the recapitulation begins—a method that should disrupt the overall balance of the movement—results in a compelling transitional passage. Indeed, it is precisely this ambiguity which necessitates a literal restatement of the opening part of the exposition: only the exact resemblance of this music to the exposition identifies it unequivocally as the recapitulation.

> The frivolous theme itself begins to gather energy in the course of the development. It originates a dramatic passage which begins picturesquely and rises from the picturesque to the sublime. When the calm has become ethereal a distant thunder is heard [measure 195]. That thunder had been twice heard during the opening of the movement. At present the key (D minor) is not far from the tonic. The main theme appears softly at a high pitch, harmonized in this neighboring key. The distant thunder rolls again, and the harmony glides into the tonic. The theme now appears, still higher, in the tonic. An ordinary artist would use this as the real return and think himself clever. But Schubert's distant thunder rolls yet again, and the harmony relapses into D minor. The tonic will have no real weight at such a juncture until it has been adequately prepared by its dominant. The theme is resumed in D minor; the harmony takes the necessary direction, and expectancy is now aroused and kept duly excited, for a return to the first subject in full.[10]

Despite Schubert's unorthodox procedure, then, Tovey discerns genuine aesthetic merit in the dramatic situation created by the music, and he uses metaphor and language to convey his sense of the drama's progress. The phrase "distant thunder" captures the slightly ominous effect of Schubert's trill in the bass register. The verbs "glide" and "relapse" evoke the frictionless yet peculiarly unsettling quality of the harmonic shifts into and away from the tonic. The explanation that the second statement of the main theme, even though it appears in the tonic, cannot serve as the beginning of the recapitulation, identifies the source of Schubert's quiet suspense. And finally, in an observation which concludes his description of this passage, Tovey suggests that the transition, apparently because it supplies the necessary dramatic symmetry, eliminates the need for a varied recapitulation: "Accordingly this return is one in which transformations would be out of place; and so Schubert's recapitulation of his first subject is unvaried until the peculiarities of his transition themes compel the modulations to take a new course."[11]

On occasion, Tovey's conflicting attitudes toward Schubert's music surface consecutively in his prose. He notes, for example, that Schubert's second subjects[12] often begin in a "quite unexpected key, remote from that in which [they are] going to continue";[13] this procedure doesn't follow Tovey's model, but he readily accepts its validity in certain contexts (the String Quintet in C major, D. 956, and the Symphony in C major, D. 944, among others). He goes on, however, to criticize Schubert's gestures following the statement of the second subject because they violate one of his own most basic assumptions about the nature of sonata form (i.e., the separation of the "three organic members"):

> And Schubert's ways of bringing the unexpected key round to the orthodox one are thoroughly masterly. The trouble begins after this problem is solved. Then Schubert, feeling that the rest of his exposition must not be less spacious than its enormous opening, fills up most of what he guesses to be the required interval with a vigorous discussion of the matter already in hand. Even if the discussion does not lead him too far afield, it inevitably tends to obliterate the vital distinction between exposition and development....[14]

The noticeably abrupt shift in perspective here ("...masterly. The trouble...") reveals again the conflict between Tovey's intuitive response to the music and his distrust of Schubert's method. And unlike his description of the B♭ major sonata transitional passage cited earlier, Tovey fails to provide a detailed explanation of how the composer achieves the "masterly" transition to the expected key. Thus, while he stresses the satisfying nature of this musical event, he ignores the technique behind it, and concentrates on what he perceives as shortcomings.[15]

In more extreme instances of this conflict, doubt and admiration seem almost to wrestle for syntactical control. This dual reaction to Schubert's music manifests itself by Tovey's expressing enthusiasm and skepticism simultaneously:

> Since the indiscretions of Schubert's expositions, though they may spoil the effect of his developments, do not prevent him from almost always developing magnficently, and sometimes faultlessly, we may say that up to the end of the recapitulation Schubert's energy stands the strain of his most impracticable designs.[16]

> The enormous sprawling forms of the typical Schubert finales are the outcome of a sheer irresponsibility that has involved him in little or no strain, though he often shows invention of the highest order in their main themes.[17]

The criticism in these passages is directed at structural elements, apparently because Tovey disapproves of their extent: "indiscretions...impracticable designs...sprawling forms...irresponsibility." At the same time, he commends the quality and beauty of the music itself: "developing magnificently...invention of the highest order in their main themes." This surprising mix of praise and criticism underscores Tovey's ambivalence toward Schubert's aesthetic success. His reluctance to credit Schubert without reservation suggests a resentment of what he perceives as the composer's ability to achieve beauty without any evidence of an effort to be concise.

In the end, Tovey attempts to resolve his conflicting responses by trusting his intuition, favoring Schubert over technical considerations. With a disarmingly simple stroke he interprets Schubert's "wrong" procedures as a progressive move away from traditional structures and toward a new, superior form.

> But when we find (as, for instance, in the first movement of the great C major Symphony) that some of the most obviously wrong digressions contain the profoundest, most beautiful, and most inevitable passages, then it is time to suspect that Schubert, like other great classics, is pressing his way towards new forms.[18]

Tovey's offhand alignment of Schubert with "other great classics" strengthens the positive tone of his assessment. Further, his association of "profound" and "beautiful" with "inevitable" provides him with the means to express approval of important but unusually structured aesthetic events. For if he can assert that a musical gesture, effect, or result (to use his terminology) which attracts him is in some way inevitable, he absolves himself of the need to justify it according to his own principles. Even if the gesture violates those principles, he can still praise the passage which leads to the arresting moment.

Later in the essay, Tovey focuses again on Schubert's recapitulations, especially in regard to the second subject:

> When Schubert's instrumental works are at their best his handling of the recapitulation...is of the highest order of mastery where the original material permits. He shows an acumen not less than Beethoven's in working out inevitable but unexpected results from the fact that his "second subject" (or his transition to it) did not begin in the key in which it was destined to settle.[19]

This comment also includes the codeword "inevitable" and compares Schubert favorably to a composer who clearly may be numbered among the "other great classics"—Beethoven. Tovey intends the comparison to shore up his none too analytical defense of Schubert. His repeated use of "inevitable" functions in a similar way: whether "wrong" and inevitable or "unexpected" and inevitable— a neatly paradoxical construct in both instances—the invocation of inevitability signifies that the musical result justifies the procedure, whatever its form. Thus although Tovey cannot always reconcile Schubert's music to his expectations concerning shape and structure, he nevertheless recognizes its greatness and is moved by its power, and the buoyant quality of his prose throughout the essay provides ample evidence of his genuine enthusiasm for Schubert's musical "results."

Examining "Brahms's Chamber Music," we confront the opposite phenomenon. Tovey admires this music precisely because it follows structural principles crucial to his conception of proper form. But because his writing often lacks the energy and eloquence so apparent in "Franz Schubert," he fails to convince us of the emotional power of the chamber music, except in the case of the Piano Quartet in C minor, opus 60, and a few of the late works. A subtle gauge of Tovey's attitude towards Brahms's early chamber music appears both in his introductory paragraphs and in the opening commentary on the B major trio, opus 8. Instead of concentrating on Brahms's music, he includes lengthy discussions of Beethoven, Mendelssohn, and Schumann, as well as substantial references to Mozart and Wagner. There is a diffuse and unfocused quality to the prose: he attempts to define "sense of motion" with an arcane and elaborate analogy involving the automobile (a reference which reappears shortly thereafter, in a jocular aside involving "road-hog composers"[20]). And he considers questions of instrumentation, especially the combination of piano with strings, pizzicato playing, and the relationship between form and instrumentation. Some of these matters may not be entirely peripheral, but they receive a disproportionate amount of attention from Tovey, while he avoids meatier questions of structure, harmony, and so forth. Even when he approaches these more germane considerations, however, his tone is oddly negative. Compare, for example, the description of the transitional passage in Schubert's Piano Sonata in B♭ major, D. 960, cited earlier with the following (a reference to the opening theme of opus 34a):

> The fact that the semiquaver figure is a diminution of the previous theme is an item of high aesthetic value, but does not constitute the "logic" of Brahms's exposition. Any other semiquavers that fitted the harmony and kept within the rhythm might be substituted without destruction to the real scheme. But close up those gaps in the rhythm...and mishandle the process to the close on the dominant, or drift in some other direction, and all the thematic connexions in the world will not put sense or life into the drama you have stultified.[21]

This is backhanded praise at best, for Tovey seems less concerned with what Brahms actually accomplished (having decreed that the original semiquaver figure composed by Brahms is superfluous for purposes of form) than with potentially disastrous alternatives. Further, after he begins the survey proper, with what seems an unnecessarily lengthy scrutiny of the opus 8 trio, given the space accorded the later, more important works, Tovey often veers away from the music in his attempts to explicate it:

> The finale is unique in chamber music in being a strict fugue with a free middle section and a da capo. The most official of "Brahmins" used to call this "the crabbed and canonic finale." It would have done their souls good to have it proved by experiment that their musical schooling had made them really hate all fugues as Byron hated Horace, and that they would have automatically talked of the "sublime poetry in which severest art is used but to conceal art" if this fugue had been introduced to them as by Bach. With later composers the noses of such critics are in the air.... [22]

Somehow, one feels that Tovey must be working hard to develop such passages. Perhaps the necessity for examining works which he does not find immediately stimulating prompts him to make such erudite allusions and witty analogies. These asides may amuse, but it is difficult to avoid wondering if they are meant to disguise a lack of genuine interest. Tovey labors to sustain the conviction that the early chamber music is exciting and inventive, but we remain unconverted by his efforts.

However, a distinctly new tone emerges in the discussion of the Piano Quartet in C minor, opus 60. Suddenly, the energy that pervades Tovey's writing on Schubert appears. Significantly, he describes the treatment of the first theme in the development of opus 60 as "Schubert-like" and that of the second subject as "Schubertian."[23] By the time he has reached opuses 99-101, Tovey's language again includes highly charged emotional terms, as he responds more intensely to the music.[24] His commentary on these late works is often quite brief, but it is consistently acute and to the point.

Perhaps, then, it is not entirely fair to cite Tovey's flagging prose in the first half of "Brahms's Chamber Music" as evidence of disenchantment with all of this oeuvre. Still, not until two-thirds of the way through the essay, with the description of the Piano Quartet, opus 60, does the tone of Tovey's prose achieve an unforced enthusiasm. Not surprisingly, the separate article on opus 60 in *Essays in Musical Analysis* confirms its significance for him. He begins that analysis by commending the work's terseness (praise reserved for opuses 99-101 in "Brahms's Chamber Music") and proceeds to discuss its tragic impact.

This digression into the essence of tragedy in music, although brief, provides a clue to Tovey's aesthetic principles in general. He emphasizes that "true tragedy"[25] involves conflicting feelings of sympathy for the victim and admiration for "the destiny that brings the catastrophe to pass,"[26] and contrasts this view with that of "popular and hurried criticism...[which prefers] mere misery as something far more pathetic..."[27]—by implication, false tragedy. This same distinction between what Tovey calls "true and false art"[28] animates John Ruskin's analysis of the grotesque in art in *Modern Painters*—a passage cited by Tovey when he describes the finale of Schubert's Symphony in C major, D. 944, as "an example of grotesque power."[29] To clarify his definition, Ruskin contrasts two images of a griffin: "a piece of true grotesque from the Lombard Gothic and of false grotesque from classical (Roman) architecture."[30] Of course, Ruskin's specific terminology would not be appropriate for Tovey, but both critics consistently strive to establish "right" and "wrong" as viable critical concepts. Indeed, the parallel is still more profound; Ruskin articulates the difference between right and wrong by referring to the two opposing forces which shape the true and false griffins:

> Now observe how in all this, through every separate part and action of the creature, the imagination is *always* right. It evidently *cannot* err.... So it is throughout art, and in all that the imagination does; if anything be wrong it is not the imagination's fault, but some inferior faculty's, which would have its foolish say in the matter ... and it is not therefore wonderful that it should never err; but it is wonderful, on the other hand, how the composing legalism does *nothing else* than err.... And another notable point is, that while the imagination receives truth in this simple way, it is all the while receiving statutes of composition also, far more noble than those for the sake of which the truth was lost by the legalist.... So that taking the truth first, the honest imagination gains everything ... but the false composer, caring for nothing but himself and his rules, loses everything.... [31]

We know Tovey admired this passage; surely he found in Ruskin's "honest imagination" and "legalist" identical twins for his "naive listener" (to whose uncorrupted ears sonic design will be apparent) and "professional" (the analyst whose rigid notions of form hamper his ability to discern real aesthetic value).

This critical method—the juxtaposition of absolutes—obviously appeals to Tovey. It reinforces his unbending stance early in the opus 60 analysis, providing a point of departure for his defense of the work as a whole. However, much of the "analysis," as he readily admits, involves simply quoting certain themes and motives. One might again suspect that his admiration is not entirely spontaneous, except that he cites the second subject as "unique in the history of musical form."[32] Tovey has already emphasized that second subjects are of special concern to him, and a unique treatment of one would be certain to arouse his interest. In opus 60, the second subject consists of a theme and variations, yet this radical departure from a balanced structure apparently produces none of the agony generated by Schubert's "indiscretions." On the contrary, Tovey finds Brahms's use of this scheme in the recapitulation especially intriguing; he abandons his theme lists to praise Brahms's procedure in explicit, relevant terms:

> It will be remembered that this second subject was a set of variations: which implies that its framework is exceptionally simple and recognizable. That being so, Brahms takes his advantage in the recapitulation and surprises us by three totally new variations. With any

other form of second subject the result of this freedom in recapitulation would be chaos; but here, where there is, *ex hypothesi,* only one theme, and that designed for variation, an exact recapitulation would be a contradiction in terms. The surprise is, therefore, inevitable and artistic.[33]

Tovey's suggestion that freedom in recapitulation produces chaos may, on the face of it, appear inconsistent with his contention in "Franz Schubert" that literal recapitulations, except under unusual circumstances, are wrong. In discussing Schubert, however, Tovey concentrates on first subject material in the recapitulation, while for the analysis of Brahms's opus 60, he focuses on the second subject. And in any case, it is not Tovey's compositional dicta that carry weight in his essays but the exceptions he makes to them: a literal recapitulation becomes necessary in Schubert's B♭ major Piano Sonata in order to restore the musical symmetry disrupted by a premature appearance of the first theme in the tonic. And in Brahms's opus 60, the freedom in recapitulation which Tovey characterizes as normally unacceptable succeeds because the intrinsic nature of the musical material requires a nonliteral—that is, varied—restatement.

Thus, what governs Tovey's enthsiasm for a work of Schubert or Brahms rests more in its dramatic potential or in a coherent logic unique to the individual work than in the fact that it adheres to predetermined analytical rules. For one whose critical apparatus was so firmly rooted in the Victorian era, it seems an oddly contemporary value. Nonetheless, passages in the music of both composers which simultaneously surprise Tovey and satisfy his requirements of inevitability, however he may articulate those requirements, become for him a touchstone of high aesthetic merit and profound emotional content. Certainly, such passages inspire Tovey to write energetically, imaginatively, and persuasively.

In concluding his discussion of Brahms's opus 60 in *Essays in Musical Analysis,* Tovey praises art in which "emotion is ratified by design, and design vitalized by emotion...."[34] This phrase strikes me as having an arresting relevance to Tovey's most incisive writing—his own finest work of art. For if the source of his urge to write lies primarily in his emotional response to a piece of music—a response which he articulates through a special and often very convincing use of language—I can think of no better way to suggest the particular quality of his best prose than to call it, too, "emotion ratified by design."

Notes

Work on the original version of this essay was completed during the summer of 1977, when I was a participant in Professor Joseph Kerman's National Endowment for the Humanities Summer Seminar for College Teachers. An abbreviated form of that version was presented at the February 1979 meeting of the New England Chapter of the American Musicological Society.

Following their first citation in a footnote, the titles of certain sources are abbreviated as follows: "Brahms's Chamber Music": "BCM"; "Franz Schubert": "FS."

1.   Louis Kronenberger, "Introduction" to Lord Byron's *Don Juan* (New York, 1949), p. ix.

2.   Donald Francis Tovey, "Beethoven: Ninth Symphony in D minor, op. 125—Its Place in Musical Art," *Essays in Musical Analysis,* vol. 2 (London, 1972), p. 18.

3.   Ibid.

4.   Tovey, "Franz Schubert," *The Main Stream of Music and Other Essays* (Cleveland, 1959), pp. 118, 120.

5.   Ibid., p. 118.

6.   Ibid. This recapitulation is actually varied in one or two details; Daniel Coren, in his article "Ambiguity in Schubert's Recapitulations" (*Musical Quarterly* 60, no. 4 [October 1974]: 571) disputes that Tovey's assessment represents an accurate characterization of Schubert's procedure.

7.   Ibid.

8.   Ibid.

9.   Ibid.

10.   Ibid., pp. 119-120.

11.   Ibid., p. 120.

12.   Tovey vociferously objects to the term "second subject" both in this essay ("FS," p. 120) and elsewhere ("Some Aspects of Beethoven's Art Forms"). Yet he consistently uses the term, and there seems no reason to try to replace it here.

13.   Tovey, "FS," p. 121.

14.   Ibid.

15.   Having offered one such analysis, Tovey may feel any further technical discourse is unnecessary. In fact, he later goes out of his way to be sensitive to the needs of his naive listener, declining flatly to supply technical information: "To describe these results would be too technical a procedure . . . " ("FS," p. 126). And he further magnifies—by implication—the importance of the listener's intuitive reactions by suggesting that "it is no *mechanical* matter to sift 'right' and 'wrong' from Schubert's instrumental forms" ("FS," p. 122, italics mine).

16.   Tovey, "FS," p. 126.

17.   Ibid., p. 127.

18. Ibid., p. 122. Tovey buttresses this claim with the observation that "the fruition of Schubert's new instrumental forms is to be found in Brahms, especially in the group of works culminating in the Pianoforte Quintet, op. 34" ("FS," p. 123). In his lengthy and thorough two-part study, "Schubert's Sonata Form and Brahms's First Maturity" *(19th Century Music* 2, no. 1 [July 1978]: 18-35, and 3, no. 1 [July 1979]: 52-71), Professor James Webster pursues the ramifications of Tovey's claim, providing substantial support for it through detailed analyses of works of both composers. Prof. Webster points out that "characteristically, however, Tovey never spelled out this relationship in detail . . . " (*19th Century Music* 3, no. 1:52).

19. Ibid., p. 126.

20. Tovey, "Brahms's Chamber Music," *The Main Stream of Music and Other Essays* (Cleveland, 1959), p. 223.

21. Ibid., p. 239.

22. Ibid., p. 247.

23. Ibid., pp. 253, 254. Prof. Webster also notes these references to Schubert (*19th Century Music* 3, no. 1: 54, footnote 10).

24. See especially the discussion of the Clarinet Quintet, op. 115 ("BCM," p. 266 ff.).

25. Tovey, *Essays in Musical Analysis; Chamber Music* (London, 1972), p. 204.

26. Ibid., p. 203.

27. Ibid., p. 204.

28. Ibid., p. 203.

29. Tovey, *Essays in Musical Analysis,* vol. 1 (London, 1972), p. 210.

30. John Ruskin, *Modern Painters,* vol. 3 (London, [1906]), p. 97.

31. Ibid., pp. 101-3.

32. Tovey, *Essays in Musical Analysis; Chamber Music* (London, 1972), p. 206.

33. Ibid., p. 208.

34. Ibid., p. 214.

Some Letters of Pavel Chesnokov in the United States

Miloš Velimirović

Following the death of Professor Alfred J. Swan on 2 October 1970, parts of his library and personal archive were donated by his widow in 1973 to the Alderman Library of the University of Virginia. The archive contains letters addressed to Swan from a large number of persons. It should be noted at the outset that Swan's own letters are missing, since he had the habit of writing in longhand and not making copies. Moreover, the most valuable correspondence in the archive—the letters to Swan from Rakhmaninov and some from Medtner—has already been published by Swan himself.[1] Among the remaining letters, not all are of interest to musicologists; this writer intends to publish those that do contain information pertinent to musicological studies.

It is appropriate, indeed, that this archive is at present assembled at the University of Virginia where Swan started his teaching career in the United States and where he taught from 1921 to 1923, and where he also completed and saw through publication his book on Skriabin. Except for brief biographical entries in a few of the standard dictionaries, no biographical study of Swan is available. It is to be hoped that at least parts of his autobiography (still in manuscript) may eventually be published, since his life and his associations with numerous important persons present a fascinating picture of a composer, teacher, and scholar of our time.

Among the letters addressed to Swan are a group of nine from the Russian composer Pavel Grigorievich Chesnokov, whose name is well known to enthusiasts of Russian church music. These letters date from 1933 to 1936. It may be inferred from their texts that others also existed, but have not been preserved. Since these letters reveal rather interesting aspects of the inner turmoil and problems experienced by a composer of church music living in the Soviet Union in a period of great tensions, they are published here with a few annotations and comments.

It is worth noting that to this day, no monograph of any kind has been printed in the Soviet Union about Chesnokov. The only study devoted to his musical compositions is an American doctoral dissertation of relatively recent date by Professor Harry Elzinga.[2] Biographical data about Chesnokov are scanty and scattered in various publications.[3] He was born on 24 October 1877 (O.S.) in Voskresensk near Moscow. He started his studies at the Moscow Synodal School in 1884, at age seven, and graduated as a choral conductor in 1895, obtaining a gold medal at the time. While there he studied with the distinguished scholar and connoisseur of Russian church music, Stepan Vasilievich Smolensky.[4] It seems that Chesnokov may have taught for a while at the Synodal School and at other schools. In the period 1895-99, he took composition lessons from Sergei Taneev. Having already become established as a composer of both secular and religious choral works, Chesnokov enrolled in the Moscow Conservatory in 1913 where he studied composition and conducting with Mikhail Ippolitov-Ivanov and instrumentation with Sergei Vasilenko,[5] graduating in 1917 just as he was about to turn forty years of age. After the Bolshevik Revolution, Chesnokov appeared publicly as a choral conductor, and he seems to have been a member of a committee for music publishing. From 1920 to his death on 14 March 1944, he was a faculty member at the Moscow Conservatory where he taught choral conducting. His activities as a composer had considerably diminished, as it appears that before 1917 he had published at least 45 opus numbers, yet his total output does not go beyond opus 55 (so far as can be ascertained at present).

Chesnokov's religious choral works were being published in the United States at least from 1913 in adaptations by N. Lindsay Norden for the "Russian Church Music" series.[6] While the frequency of performances of works by Chesnokov in the United States is difficult to determine, there is no doubt that the late Archibald T. ("Doc") Davison performed some of them with the Harvard Glee Club in the 1920s and 1930s, and that at least two of Chesnokov's works were published in the Concord Series of choral works with which Davison was associated. In fact, he arranged one of Chesnokov's hymns for publication in 1935.[7]

In the absence of concert programs conducted by Alfred Swan, it cannot now be stated how many of Chesnokov's works were accessible to Swan or how often he may have performed them. That Swan did conduct performances of Chesnokov's works is quite certain, as references in their correspondence corroborate this point.

When and why Swan first established contact with Chesnokov remains unknown at present. One may surmise that with the normalization of diplomatic relations between the U.S.A. and the U.S.S.R. in 1933, a Russophile like Swan may have felt that the time had come to reestablish some links with the land in which he was born and in which he received his schooling. As far as I can determine at this time, Swan was not yet interested in the scholarly study of Russian liturgical chant but was primarily active as a teacher and conductor of Russian musical compositions. Perhaps he wanted to obtain more works for performance with his choir (the number of Chesnokov's works available in this country was barely a dozen at that time). On the basis of the wording in the earliest extant letter from Chesnokov to Swan in the Swan archive, there is an implication that Chesnokov had written earlier to Swan, but no earlier letter has survived. At any rate, the facts that may be established suggest that in the Spring of 1933, Swan sent money to Chesnokov. The composer's reply, dated Moscow, 2 July 1933, constitutes the first surviving letter; it reads in English translation:

No. 1

Very esteemed Professor Swan,
Yesterday (on the first of July) I received the money which you sent me. I express to you my great gratitude for it; it was most timely. I am awaiting your answer to my first letter with great interest. I somehow feel that fate will link us for a long time. I clasp your hand and cordially wish you all the best.

Devotedly yours, P. Chesnokov

It may be surmised that Chesnokov was not the one to initiate this correspondence and that a still earlier letter by Swan must have been mailed, but, as already indicated, Swan did not keep copies of his own letters.[8] Some four-and-a-half months later, Chesnokov wrote the second extant letter to Swan; dated 22 October 1933, it reads:

No. 2

Very esteemed Alfred Alfredovich,
    Thank you for your kind letter and the information about the choir. For twelve years it has been my lot to direct an amateur chorus. It's a very good and enjoyable occupation because the participants come voluntarily out of love for it. I have devoted my life to choral music and have been working in this area for thirty-eight years already. I have written a great many choral compositions, especially religious ones. I estimate about 500, and about 100 secular. But my central work, my lifework itself, I consider the book that I completed in December 1930. I had been writing it for exactly thirteen years. It is entitled "The Choir and its Direction" [Khor i upravlenie im] and the subtitle is "Choral Conducting and Choral Management." The size is 437 pages in large format, tyepwritten. I have three copies of the book. It was twice examined by Muzgiz [the state music publishers] in Moscow and twice ... rejected. The reason—it is 'apolitical'. I was told both orally and in writing: "a very good, valuable book, of which there are none in the area of choral literature. But in the U.S.S.R., to write apolitical books is not allowed." So my poor book is left dangling in the air. What a pity. It is needed by all choral directors and advanced choral singers. This has been said to me by Moscow choral conductors and by students in the Choral Department at the Moscow State Conservatory to whom I have read and am still reading my book in the form of lectures. But what can one do? I hope that the time will come when people will remember my poor book.
    I have sat down to start copying a whole series of my choral works to send to you.
    I sincerely wish you everything good. Give my warm greetings to your choir.

Cordially yours, P. Chesnokov.

The contents of this second letter raise a few interesting points. Chesnokov's mention of directing an amateur choir for 12 years remains unclear for the moment. It is known that he was teaching at the Conservatory from 1920. It is also recorded that from 1917 to 1922 he conducted one of the state choirs, and that from 1922 to 1928 he headed the Moscow Academic Capella. Neither of these would seem to qualify as an "amateur" group, but perhaps Chesnokov was involved in yet another group not mentioned in the brief accounts of his life found in available encyclopedia entries. His reference to having been working for 38 years indicates that he was counting the time since his graduation from the Moscow Synodal School in 1895, when he started his activities as composer and conductor. His estimated number of musical compositions appears to be higher than that found in the available biographical sketches. The mention of his book is only the first of several that will follow. I shall anticipate developments by pointing out that Chesnokov's book was eventually published in Moscow in 1940, with a second edition published posthumously in 1952, and even a third edition in 1961.

In the absence of the envelopes in which Chesnokov's letters were mailed, it is unclear whether he was writing to Swan in Europe, where Swan spent part of the Summer of 1933 and while in Paris met Michel Ossorguine [Mikhail Osorgin][9] for the first time—a meeting which may have been a turning point in Swan's orientation and his interest in the sources of Russian Chant. At any rate, in the summer of 1934, after obtaining his long-awaited M.A. degree from Oxford and having visited the Valaam Monastery on Lake Ladoga on the border of Finland and the Soviet Union, Swan was moving in the direction of studying Russian chant. At that time, he must have received a copy of Chesnokov's typescript, which Swan intended to translate into English with the hope of finding a publisher for it in the U.S.A. Almost a year elapsed before the next preserved letter from Chesnokov, dated 14 October 1934, which reads:

No. 3

Dear Alfred Alfredovich,

I am quite disturbed by your silence. Since the 13th of July I have not had a bit of news from you. Write both the good and the bad. I'll be waiting impatiently.

An unpleasant thing happened here in connection with my book. In [19]31 when I in my gullibility submitted the book to the so-called Muzgiz for the second time, it was given to three people to read. The book was rejected for the same reason about which I wrote you earlier (its being apolitical). But one of these people (about the others I don't know), a teacher at the Moscow State Conservatory (I won't mention the name for now), made use of the book... At the moment he has already submitted three chapters for publication... Even from this brief communication you can see how essential it is to publish my book, so as to unmask its plagiarizers. Write to me more often and in more detail.

With regard to the score of *Boris Godunov*, although I've made inquiries, I still do not know if it's possible or not. In this affair you've got to be careful. A proposal may reach you from one of the people at "Mezhdunarodnaia kniga." Hold off if you receive such a proposal and write me in detail. But I'm making inquiries and I'll give you a final answer in the next letter.

In any case, dear Alfred Alfredovich, write to me, tell me about the book, and, in general, keep in touch with me. I am so alone. Then suddenly, somewhere beyond the Ocean, I have a friend. A friend whom I have never seen, but whom I have grown to love and in whom I sense the fulfillment of one of my life's dreams.

Here, at the end of September and in the first days of October, there were concerts by the American Westminster Choir, under the direction of Mr. Williamson. I went to three concerts. Great technical skill, suppleness, and a great many effective and varied tone qualities. But the more elementary aspect of the choral sound was not irreproachable (the most important elements, especially the intonation). But I must say that the Americans have shaken us up thoroughly and pretty well put us to shame... At the present, we do not have a single choir that might be called exemplary. The classics, ours as well as Western ones, are not being performed. We are subsisting on contemporary trash and a repertory of "whatever you wish." There are no "a capella" choirs at all. And this in the heart of Russia—in Moscow! And yet it is not so long ago that our Synodal Choir amazed Vienna with its "a capella" singing. Please give your choir my most cordial greetings. [The photograph of your] choral group is always in front of me and I feast my eyes on it. With all my heart, dear Alfred Alfredovich, I wish you good health and complete success in your endeavors.

Cordially yours, P. Chesnokov.

On the verso of the sheet is the address in Chesnokov's handwriting and it reads:

Moskva 17, Bol'sh. [Bol'shaia] Yakimanka 17, kv. [kvartira] 2
Chesnokov, Pav. Grigor'evich

The sadness of the situation in which Chesnokov found himself is evident from the tone of his letter, which contains some interesting references. The point about the manuscript being submitted to readers is, of course, a normal procedure for any publishing house, and although I believe I have been able to identify one of the readers[10] it remains for Soviet colleagues to reveal the others, especially the one who seems to have "emulated" Chesnokov in writing a book.

In the absence of data about Swan's activities in Swarthmore and Haverford, one can only surmise that he may have contemplated the possibility of obtaining performance rights and orchestral parts for the staging of the original version of Musorgsky's *Boris Godunov,* which only a short while earlier had been published by P. Lamm.[11]

The mention of the Westminster Choir refers to the first American group to visit the Soviet Union after the resumption of the diplomatic relations between the two countries. This tour and the preparations for it are amply documented in contemporary press reports, especially in *The New York Times* and in *Time* and *Newsweek* magazines.[12] The first concert in Moscow took place on 30 September 1934, and a report from Moscow indicated that at the request of Soviet officials the Choir was to give two additional concerts in the factories, one of which was to be broadcast to the U.S.A. on 6 October of that year.

The most stunning part of the letter are the comments about the absence of choirs in Moscow and the sentimental lament about the time before 1917 when Russian choirs had sung outside of Russia. Six weeks later, Chesnokov wrote the following letter, dated 28 November 1934:

No. 4

Dear Alfred Alfredovich,

I have to answer two of your letters at once: one of 28 October and one of 6 November (although I already basically answered the first one). "Having gone hungry" (i.e., having not received any answering letters for 3 months), I read your letter of 28 October quite greedily. (By the way, I had predicted a long time ago and even wrote on my calendar the date when I would receive your answer. It was the 14th of November. And so at 11 A.M. on the 14th of November, I was given your letter of 28 October). The second letter I received on 18 November.

As I value your time, I shall do my best to answer the first letter briefly (I have numbered it as No. 9).

In fact, as stated above, I already answered that letter. Now I want to comment on what can be sensed between the lines. It seems I've already written about it, but right now, briefly and to the point, in a few resolute words: I am happy that I have acquired in you a real friend! They say that one of the ancient sages pronounced the clever saying: "Save me, O Lord, from my friends, and I'll save myself from my enemies." At present I am receiving not a few confirmations of this at first glance rather strange saying. This you shall see below. But in you I have perceived and found a TRUE friend. In order not to be [thought] ill-founded I cite an excerpt from a letter (received the other day) from an old "gloomy" friend of mine known for his exceptional fairness.

"Until now I remained silent on all of your inquiries about what I know concerning certain ticklish questions; I simply didn't want to answer because I didn't wish to distress you and disillusion you about people, in particular about his opinions about your book which, had he really wanted it, would have been printed long ago. But now, after this much, I must give you my opinion about his role in its [i.e. the book's] downfall, that he too rejected it I haven't the slightest doubt. Here's that 'fine fellow's' opinion of your book as stated by him somewhere in Moscow and repeated here (Leningrad) in a private conversation: 'Passé, passé, and again passé. It's a sin to print such things at this time of paper shortage.'"

The "fine fellow" is my deferential pupil and bosom friend. Not once does he pass through Moscow without paying me a visit. Until this very moment I loved that man with all my sincere and open heart. True, it has seemed to me in recent years that in certain word choices, in the pronouncement of viewpoints and opinions not characteristic of him, in not quite sincere yet carefully concealed facial expressions and movements (and from whom?— from me, who perhaps does not always comprehend with the brain, but inevitably, and even against the will, with the feelings)—that my "fine fellow" has been to a considerable extent infected with egotism and careerism. I didn't imagine anything bad. On the contrary, I helped him in every way. But I could never have imagined that my bosom friend would play "such" a role in the affair of the realization of my life's dream . . . I've gone on too long and am probably boring you. That I have written this at all is only because I wanted to let you know what I have been going through emotionally and also to impress upon you how important it is to publish the book in America. Its publication will destroy all this slinking around in the dark and give me complete satisfaction. After this I can hurry on to other work in this direction with renewed strength. My book is technical. And I am more and more drawn to writing a book "On the Artistic in Choral Performance." But I can't get going. not having yet "lifted in my arms" the child whom I had brought up and coddled for fifteen years.

I could talk on and on about this, my "sore" spot, so I'll stop.

––––––––

Having received and read your second letter, I—forgive me,... wept... There was so much warmth and cordiality in it. Whatever will be, will be... but I have found a friend and that shall never be obliterated from my heart!

About *Boris,* I've already written you. In a few days I'll make some final decision on that question and take some decisive steps.

As for my past life, I think that in each subsequent letter I'll enclose a separate sheet about it. Thus in some 4-5 letters I can briefly lay out my autobiography.

It is a great honor for me that you sometime inform your choir about me. Please express my deep gratitude to the choir for mailing the picture. I can't help it but feel the most sincere sympathy for your choir as a performer of some of my works. Once again, please convey to the choir my cordial greetings and gratitude.

I'll be writing you much, dear Alfred Alfredovich, about myself and about everything. And don't you forget me. My cordial affection for you,

P. Chesnokov.

Without access to Chesnokov's archive (assuming he saved the letter he quotes) it is impossible to guess who informed Chesnokov of the events or who the "fine fellow" might have been. The mention of the photograph of Swan's choir refers to the picture mentioned in the previous letter. It is interesting to note that Chesnokov numbered Swan's letter of 28 October 1934 as "no. 9" indicating clearly that they had corresponded for some time.

Chesnokov's next letter is dated 9 May 1935 and in the intervening five-and-a-half months Swan apparently found a helper to translate Chesnokov's book typescript. Swan must also have informed the composer about the business side of publishing, which seems to have baffled Chesnokov as can be seen from his next letter:

No. 5

Dear Alfred Alfredovich,

Your letter of 22 April cheered me up and encouraged me immensely. I am very glad that you will nonetheless look over the translation. That is a full guarantee of the correctness and accuracy of the translation. It would be very good if the book were prefaced by your foreword, even if it were short, in which you would recommend it to the American public. Your view of the book is a correct one: the book is not of passing interest, rather "with time, the need for it will continue to grow." Thus, the book will have some kind of a small history of its own, and in that history you shall occupy one of the most honored places.

With regard to the financial side of the publication, I don't understand a thing about it and rely entirely on you. I admit that the question interests me as I am an impractical man, who even now is not in good financial order (at least in comparison with my colleagues at work). At the same time, I am not counting on establishing myself financially by means of the book. I should be glad if this matter gave me the opportunity to improve some aspects of my life and the lives of my family. Oh well, that question I place entirely in your hands. I shall be quite satisfied even with a little bit. Most important, and the greatest thing for me will be that my offspring of so many years will see the light of day!

I shall be waiting impatiently for your news about this matter and for your letters in general, which give me great cultural satisfaction.

———

Thank you: my health and general condition are fine. Of course there are a few concerns: life is a sea and without some waves it cannot exist. But all of these trifles, simply waves but not a storm.

As for you, dear friend, there is lots of big news, at least for me: a year's leave, a trip to Europe, the completion of a big job! The last interests me especially. If it isn't a secret do share it; give me a chance to rejoice for you and with you.

Poor Mr. Davison! How awful that he has such a difficult illness. But I imagine that in America medicine can work miracles and he will be helped.—I had already answered his kind letter with a letter no less kind and was expecting more news from him. But now, I understand. What a pity! Where is he now? I would very much like to send him my sympathy.

I shall be waiting impatiently for your news.

I wish you good health and all success in your work and in everything.

With cordial devotion and profound thanks to you,

P. Chesnokov

The mention of Swan's forthcoming year-long trip to Europe implies that Swan must have written to Chesnokov of his plans, though we don't know to what extent he spelled them out. As his interest in studying Russian church music and its origins kept growing, Swan travelled during that year (1935-36) to Jerusalem (encountering Johann von Gardner for the first time), Belgrade (where he met Kosta Manojlović) and Vienna (where he met Egon Wellesz and tried to understand the problems in the study of Byzantine Chant).[13] The year 1935 also marked the initial publication of the series "Monumenta Musicae Byzantinae," and this too may have served as an additional stimulus to Swan to start investigating Russian church music. Swan revisited Ossorguine and Rakhmaninov in that period and travelled to Estonia where he collected folk songs before returning to the U.S.A. Judging by the dates of the remaining letters from Chesnokov to Swan, it is clear that they maintained their correspondence during Swan's travels.

The reference to Mr. Davison toward the end of the letter refers to Archibald T. Davison of Harvard University,[14] whom Swan must have mentioned in his letters to Chesnokov. Swan and Davison met in the summer of 1925. This writer has kindly been informed by Professor A.T. Merritt, at present retired, of Harvard University, that he recalls very well how in the 1930s Davison conducted Chesnokov's works with the Harvard Glee Club. Professor Merritt has also been kind enough to confirm that about then (i.e., the academic year 1934-35) Davison learned of his [first] wife's cancer and that he himself became ill and incapacitated for a time. Chesnokov's reference to "Poor Mr. Davison" can only mean that Swan wrote of Davison's illness to Chesnokov.

Through Professor Merritt's good offices, Davison's widow (presently Mrs. David Humez) examined her deceased husband's files and found a letter from Chesnokov dated 18 January 1935, which seems to be the letter

18. I. 35.

Dear Professor Davison.
I was really happy to receive your kind letter. It is very encouraging for me to learn that you appreciate my compositions. Having heard of you and your splendid chourus. I should be glad to hear of the methods of your work and your repertoire.
Cordially yours
P. Tschesnokoff.

Plate 1.   Facsimile of Chesnokov's letter to Archibald T. Davison of
Harvard University

Chesnokov was referring to in his just cited letter.[15] Curiously, Chesnokov's letter to Davison is written in English (see the facsimile) and reads:

> Dear Professor Davison,
> I was really happy to receive your kind letter. It is very encouraging for me to learn that you appreciate my compositions. Having heard of you and your splendid chourus [sic], I should be glad to hear of the methods of your work and your repertoire.
>
> Cordially yours,
> P. Tschesnokoff

Davison's letter to which Chesnokov refers was not available to this writer. The mention of "having heard of you" clearly suggests that Swan must have mentioned Davison's work to Chesnokov. As far as is known at present this is the only letter of Chesnokov's addressed to Davison and, besides the letters to Swan, the only other letter of Chesnokov's in this country, not to mention that it is also his only letter so far known in English.

Meanwhile, Swan's endeavors to have Chesnokov's book on choral conducting translated into English and published in this country apparently ran into problems. Simultaneously Chesnokov appears to have continued with his efforts to have his book published in Moscow, as one may infer from the next letter to Swan dated 31 July 1935:

No. 6

Dear Alfred Alfredovich,

Forgive me for not having answered for so long your, as always, dear, kind, good letter.

As for the book, looking at it objectively, it seems that it will be published in Russian and in several other languages because it is the elementary truth. You see, the book's thirteen chapters are thirteen works that have implications for the future, for all thirteen chapters are general summaries of that great choral science which will be called: choral directing—choral conducting. It was not by chance that some instinct prompted me to use the title, "The Choir and its Direction." What does that mean? It means that I only pose the question and outline briefly, in summary, the guideposts along which the question will be resolved in creating a choral science. I am told, "Nowadays that is already common knowledge." But in the first place, show me the books from which this has become common knowledge (is there really much that is common knowledge?), and in the second place, it is no wonder, because I have openly been preaching the principles of this book for fifteen years both at the Moscow State Conservatory (lectures) and during all kinds of business with choirs. I am not after all taking out a patent on this as if it were some kind of invention of mine. I say: "if there is no such book as mine, then publish mine because it—and as far as I am concerned there is no doubt—is needed." Why should a young and talented conductor torture himself for twenty-five years, arriving slowly and torturously at "the creation of the world with his own mind"! Give him P. Chesnokov's book and he will master it in the course of a few months and can then go forward building that science about which we dream.

I thank you cordially dear Alfred Alfredovich, that you are not abandoning my offspring. Please, forgive the fact that the book takes so much of your precious time and gives you so much trouble.

I salute you as my true friend and wish you good health, contentment, and success in all of your good work.

With cordial affection, P. Chesnokov

Perhaps because of his trip, there seems to have been an interruption in Swan's correspondence, as may be inferred from the next of Chesnokov's letters in which he states that Swan's last letter was dated 7 June, i.e., that it was written before the just cited letter from Chesnokov. Chesnokov's new letter to Swan is dated 2 October 1935.

No. 7

Dear Alfred Alfredovich,

For a rather long time, dear friend, you have not given me the joy of one of your letters; the last one was dated the 7th of June.

But I am patient—and shall wait. And I was very intrigued by your "detailed letter about myself" which you promised to write. Indeed, as a matter of fact (forgive me for the indiscreet questions), why did you go to England for such a long time? How did you tear yourself away from your choir and orchestra? The reason, obviously, is a very important one, and I would like to know what it is.

My life goes along quietly. It seems that there is nothing worth mentioning except for two small events. The first one: on the first of September of this year, quietly, at home, I ... drank a jigger of vodka on the occasion of the fortieth anniversary of my activity as a conductor, composer, and teacher. Second, at the end of September I submitted to Muzgiz (State Publishing House) eight Russian folk songs for a cappella chorus with soloists. They promise to include it in the publishing plan for 1936. I was delighted by that: I'm glad it's in the 1936 plan and not the one for 1946, since I won't live that long.—Well, and how is my long

Проф. П. ЧЕСНОКОВ

ХОР
И
УПРАВЛЕНИЕ ИМ

Пособие
для хоровых дирижеров

Глубокоуважаемому
профессору
Альфреду Альфредовичу
Сванн
— на добрую память —
от сердечно преданного автора.
П. Чесноков.

25. X. 40.

ГОСУДАРСТВЕННОЕ МУЗЫКАЛЬНОЕ ИЗДАТЕЛЬСТВО
Москва 1940 Ленинград

Plate 2. Title-page of Chesnokov's book with his dedication to Prof.
Alfred Swan (Music Library of the University of Virginia).

suffering little book? Any word? Will the publishers condescend to it, those barbarians of the human race!? Do write, my dear Alfred Alfredovich, my "paternal" heart throbs, thirsting for news!

Well, and now permit me to wish you, with all my heart, my dear friend, good health, above all else, and then complete success in all of your good deeds and undertakings.

I pray for God's blessings upon you.

With cordial affection, P. Chesnokov

Among the interesting points in this letter Chesnokov appears to be unaware of the practice of "sabbatical leave," questioning how one could "tear oneself away" from work with a choir and orchestra. The rather pathetic description of Chesnokov's celebration of the fortieth anniversary since his graduation, and with no mention of family, suggests a picture of a lonely dreamer indulging in a drink on a special day in his life. One month later Chesnokov wrote again, in a letter dated 8 November 1935:

No. 8

Dear Alfred Alfredovich,

Finally I received that long-awaited letter from you. Now I fully understand the reasons for your long silence: the work which tore you away from your familial nest, is enormously interesting and truly does not allow wasting much time on letters.

But, all the same, don't forget about me. In connection with the work that you have undertaken, I consider it indispensable to tell you the following:

The "Synodal School of Ecclesiastical Chant" in Moscow, where I studied from age seven to eighteen, was headed by a prodigious musician, a profoundly educated man and the first expert in the field of ecclesiastical chant—Stepan Vasilievich Smolensky [1848-1909]. St.[epan] Vas.[ilievich] reformed the Synodal School to such an extent, placed scholarship at such a high level, provided for the Synodal Choir so well with its celebrated conductor Vas[ily] Serg[eevich] Orlov [1856-1907], that the School began graduating the best choral conductors, and the superb performances of the choir compelled all composers to write works for the church, thereby giving birth to a "new direction" in church music. (Being director of the Synodal School and Choir, St. Vas. was at the same time a professor at the Moscow State Conservatory, teaching the "History of Ecclesiastical Chant." His pupils include: S. Rakhmaninov, Yu[ri] Sakhnovsky, Glière and others.)

Moreover, this very same St. Vas. Smolensky, besides his great work in the School and with the Choir, also collected old manuscripts of church music. For this purpose, he was often sent by the [Holy] Synod on journies to monasteries and abbeys, from which he gathered his main materials. He collected about two thousand manuscripts, and each manuscript is a thick book in wooden bindings covered with leather. His profound knowledge in this area permitted him to *describe* each manuscript in complete detail. He succeeded in penetrating quite deeply into the past, reaching, apparently, back to the eleventh century.

In the first months of the revolution, when St. Vas. was no longer among the living, the School and the Choir were liquidated and the library of ancient church music manuscripts, according to hearsay, was thrown into the basement of the Moscow Historical Museum...

I advise you to double-check this information with the Moscow People's Commissariat for Education (Moscow, Chistye Prudy, Narkompros). If it is true, then you are most welcome here in Moscow. Here you will find enormous amounts of material on the questions which interest you, and you will relate to the world the colossal labors of St. Vas. Smolensky, my dear unforgettable teacher—friend.

As a matter of fact, I have decided to dedicate my book—and I am endlessly grateful to you for all your troubles with it—to his memory. The dedication should read as follows: "To the unforgettable memory of a dear teacher-friend Stepan Vasilievich Smolensky." As for the dedication to the memory of P.A. Petrov, please transfer it from the book to the "Manual for the Choral Singer."

You have brought me much joy with the news from Belgrade. I felt great moral satisfaction. But it seems to me that it would not hurt my performers abroad to remember occasionally that the composer who lives in Moscow is far from being brilliantly well-off materially speaking...I shall be very glad and eternally grateful to you if work on publication of my book begins in Belgrade as well.

Please forgive the thought which I concluded with three dots, but here [i.e., in the U.S.S.R.] a composer's performance rights are strictly observed.

And with that, dear Alfred Alfredovich, permit me to wish you, with all my heart, good health, spiritual peace, and the most complete success in the interesting and important work that you have undertaken.

Do not forget me, Write.

With cordial affection, P. Chesnokov

It appears obvious that Swan's letter, to which Chesnokov was replying, must have been written during Swan's stopover in Belgrade. It is also obvious that Swan revealed to Chesnokov the purpose of his trip in search of sources for the history of Russian church music. Chesnokov's reminiscences about his teacher Smolensky are touching and show the high esteem in which Smolensky was held for his dedication to the study of Russian Chant.

As for an identification of some of the names, Orlov was one of the greatest Russian choral conductors at the turn of the century and from 1901 was the director of the Synodal School.[16] The less well-known Sakhnovsky was a conductor and music critic, an activity which he continued to practice after the events of 1917.[17] The collection of manuscripts from the Synodal Library is presently located in the State Historical Museum in Moscow where, as far as we are aware, they are well kept and accessible to scholars.

Chesnokov's dedication of his book to Smolensky appears in the first Russian edition of 1940.[18] We were unable to identify P.A. Petrov who is also mentioned as the original dedicatee. Swan must have written to Chesnokov that his works were sung in the churches of Belgrade, and it is not only a point of moral satisfaction for the composer, but since the payment of royalties for performances was strictly observed in the Soviet Union, Chesnokov makes a nice point, hoping that he may receive royalties for foreign performances as well.

In the early months of 1936 Swan was in Vienna, studying with Egon Wellesz and becoming acquainted with the methodology that he hoped to apply in studying Russian Chant.[19] Swan's correspondence suffered because of the time devoted to his work with Wellesz and the last extant letter from Chesnokov to Swan, dated 20 May 1936, reads:

No. 9

Dear Alfred Alfredovich,

Finally I received your letter of 1 May '36. Your fermatas are rather long, dear friend, rather long! True, it is not you who are to blame, but our common disease—busy-ness. I advise you to use my rule of life as a guide: always hurry, incessantly, but...as slowly as possible.

The business with the book is moving along; but the department is following my above-mentioned rule too closely. The chief of the Music Publishing House decisively rejected putting the fugue by Berezovsky into the book: "because of that fugue," he said "Glavlit might cut out the whole book, then all is lost." He decided to take out the fugue and its verbal analyses without substituting anything else. The sixth chapter of part one will suffer, but what to do?! Apparently, matters with the book are even more distressing where you are concerned. You are right that I was correct when I proposed that you take on the translation and editing yourself. You need not return the book to me since I have two more copies. Of course, if you shall have absolutely no use for it, then return it—better it "rest in peace" in my hands as I shall—more than anyone else—treat it with tenderness as if it were my own child, my own blood.*

[Footnote by Chesnokov:]

*If you wish, during the Summer in my free time I'll compile and send you a full description of my book after my final editing. The point is that the book now has a somewhat different form as (three parts) some 93 pages have been eliminated from the book, some things have been changed and abridged, etc.

In June my songs are due to appear in print, a copy of which I shall send to you immediately. This is my first appearance in print in all the time since the revolution. Henceforth I shall not stop: I shall publish something each year. During the writing of the book I completely forgot about myself as a composer. Now it is necessary to fill in that gap. Yes, and I want to write!

In the summer I think I shall write a small manual: "An Essay on Elementary Training in the Rudiments of Music." It will use a new hitherto never utilized principle. There shall be three short parts: pitch (mastery of intervals without rhythm), rhythm (mastery of rhythmic formations without pitch) and melody (joining together of the mastered pitches with the mastered rhythm). And only C major and A minor, since everything in C major remains the same in D major. In studying each element of melody separately, it seems to me, I shall significantly facilitate the process of musical literacy. One of the stipulations of this "mini-course" [*kursik*] in the rudiments of music will be ideally exact intonation, therefore, crack shots ["in intonation" implied; the Russian *"stroevye strelki"* makes a pun on *stroi* = (*mus.*) pitch] will be utilized here as thoroughly and completely as possible. Do you bless Pavel, the Lord's servant, in this work? I shall try, then we shall see. At first, of course, they'll ridicule it, but in some twenty years, perhaps, they'll publish it.

Well, in the meantime, dear Alfred Alfredovich, I wish you good health, spiritual peace, and all success in your good work.

Always hurry, incessantly, but...as slowly as possible.

And do not forget your sincere and warmly affectionate friend P. Chesnokov.

The point about the fugue by Berezovsky[20] mentioned in this letter is a curious one, since the fugue did appear in the book as published in 1940 in Moscow, but without text! This fugue is the concluding (fourth) movement of a Sacred Concerto for four voices by Berezovsky under the name "Ne otverzi vo vremia starosti" (Do not reject me in my old age). The third and fourth movements of this concerto are available on a recording issued in Bulgaria (Balkanton BXA 1333, side 1, band 3) that contains works performed during the Symposium on the Beginnings of Slavic Music held in Sofia, Bulgaria, in October 1971. Furthermore, the complete concerto by Berezovsky is currently available in an instrumental rendition on a Soviet recording, *Russian Music of the 18th Century,* performed by the "Baroque" Chamber Ensemble (Melodiya, C-04695-6, side 1) from which the text is missing and not even mentioned in the notes on the record jacket.

In the absence of the original typescript of Chesnokov's book (Swan's copy has not been located, if indeed he ever received it back from the person who was supposed to translate it), it is impossible to ascertain now how much of Chesnokov's original text was eliminated in the published version.

Chesnokov's statement that the publication of his songs in 1936 was the first time his works had been published since the 1917 revolution does not seem to be entirely correct, since the Music Library of the University of Virginia owns a copy of an edition of Chesnokov's choral works published in 1926.[21] A thorough investigation of the catalogs of Soviet publishing houses is needed to establish the exact sequence of Chesnokov's publications after the evolution. Whether Chesnokov ever wrote his intended "mini-course" on the rudiments of music remains unknown at present.

At this point, on the basis of Swan's archive, the correspondence between Swan and Chesnokov comes to an end. Chesnokov's endeavors to see his book in print did finally bear fruit, and the volume was published in Moscow in the fall of 1940. Swan's library contains a copy of that first edition inscribed to him from the author. It sounds the coda to their interchange just before the turbulent events of World War II interrupted the more or less normal conditions for correspondence. Chesnokov died in Moscow in 1944, not having witnessed the two later editions of his book nor having read the praises bestowed on him as one of the great composers of church music, as recently as 1978 in the *Bol'shaia Sovetskaia entsiklopediia.*[22] It is curious to note that the only known research on Chesnokov and his music should have been done as a doctoral dissertation in the U.S.A.

Notes

1. "Rachmaninoff: Personal Reminiscences," *MQ,* 30 (1944), 1-19, 174-191; "Das Leben Nikolai Medtners (1880-1951)," *Musik des Ostens,* 4 (1967), 65-116; for Swan's biography, see *New Grove,* vol. 18, p. 396.

2. Harry Elzinga, "The Sacred Choral Compositions of Pavel Gregoryevich Chesnokov (1877-1944)," Ph.D. Diss., Indiana University, 1970. This writer wishes to express his thanks to Prof. Elzinga for loaning a copy of his dissertation and giving insights into its points.

3. Ibid., chapter 2, pp. 55-60; oddly enough Chesnokov is not listed either in *MGG* or in *New Grove.* There is a brief entry in *Baker's Biographical Dictionary of Musicians,* 6th ed. (1978),

p. 1727; there is a good entry in *Muzykalnaia Entsiklopediia,* vol. 6 (1982), col. 216. See also brief entry in the 2nd ed. of *Bolshaia Sovietskaia Entsiklopediia,* vol. 47 (1957), p. 229, and a more expanded entry in the 3d edition, vol. 47 (1978), p. 118. We did not have access to the 2d and 3d editions of Chesnokov's book which contain biographical essays. There are scattered bits of data in *Vospominaniia o Moskovskoi Konservatorii* [Reminiscences about the Moscow Conservatory], (Moskva, 1966), pp. 551 and 582, and facing p. 117 there is a good photograph of Chesnokov from earlier years; also *Muzykalnaia zhizn' Moskvy v pervye gody posle Oktiabria* [The musical life of Moscow in the first years after October] (Moskva, 1972), pp. 17, 19, 44, 159 and 163; another interesting bit appears in *Glazunov, pisma, stat'i, vospominaniia* [Glazunov, letters, articles, reminiscences] (Moskva, 1958), p. 369, involving Chesnokov as conductor in 1922; also *Istoriia russkoi sovetskoi muzyki* [History of Russian Soviet Music], vol. 1 (1956), pp. 9 and 103, and vol. 2 (1959), pp. 102-4.

4.   Cf. *New Grove,* vol. 17, p. 242; also *Muzykalnaia Entsiklopediia,* vol. 5 (1981), cols. 114-15.

5.   On Vasilenko (1872-1956) see *New Grove,* vol. 19, pp. 560-61; also *Muzykalnaia Entsiklopediia,* vol. 1 (1973), cols. 683-685; about Ippolitov-Ivanov (1859-1935) see *New Grove,* vol. 9, p. 291 and *Muzykalnaia Entsiklopediia,* vol. 2 (1974), cols. 561-562.

6.   On Norden see *Baker's...*, p. 1241; The series "Russian Church Music" was published in New York by J. Fisher from ca. 1913 to 1919. Cf. *New York Public Library—Dictionary Catalog of the Music Collection,* vol. 21 (1964), p. 51; see also 14 works by Chesnokov in that series listed in the same catalog, vol. 6, p. 424.

7.   Davison arranged the hymn "Salvation belongeth to our Lord," words adapted by E.B.G., music arranged by A.T.D[avison]. In the Concord series of scores, # 947, Boston, E.C. Schirmer, 1935. See the *Boston Public Library—Dictionary Catalog of the Music Collection,* vol. 19 (1972), p. 78.

8.   There is a personal archive of Chesnokov preserved in Moscow in the State Central Museum of Musical Culture [Gosudarstvennyi Tsentralnyi Muzei Muzykalnoi Kultury], named after Glinka. According to *Lichnye fondy v gosudarstvennykh khranilishchakh* [Personal collections in the state archives], published by the Lenin Library, vol. 2 (Moscow, 1963), p. 296, this collection has the signature *F.36* and contains 267 archival units dated from 1891 to 1944.

9.   As far as we could determine Ossorguine is not listed in any reference resources. Some information about him is available in Swan's article "On the Quest of the Sources of Music" in the *Russian Orthodox Journal* (published by the Federated Russian Orthodox Clubs, Wilkes-Barre, Pennsylvania), vol. 33, no. 10 (February, 1960) pp. 9-13 and 26, with a photograph of Ossorguine on p. 12. There are more than 40 letters from Ossorguine to Swan dating from 1934 onward in the Swan archive at the University of Virginia.

10.   That one of the readers was Boleslav Yavorsky is incontrovertibly ascertained by the note in *B. Yavorsky, Tom I—Stat'i, vospominaniya, perepiska* [B. Yavorsky, Vol. 1—Articles, Reminiscences, Correspondence], ed. I.S. Rabinovich, 2d ed. (Moskva, 1972), p. 667; the text of fn. 14 appended to the calendar of Yavorsky's life refers to the period of his activities in Muzgiz (the State Music Publishing House). About Yavorsky see *New Grove,* vol. 20, pp. 572-73; also *Muzykalnaia Entsiklopediia,* vol. 6 (1982), cols. 608-10.

11.   Lamm's edition appeared in 1928; cf. about Lamm in *New Grove,* vol. 10, p. 424 and any study about Musorgsky.

12.   The Westminster Choir was founded in 1921 by John Finley Williamson who conducted these performances in the Soviet Union. About him see *Baker's...*, p. 1895. The tour to several European countries and to the USSR was quite an event at the time, and we find a

series of notes about in *The New York Times* for 1934, starting with preliminary announcements on 14 Jan., p. 30; then 5 April, p. 25; 6 May, p. 18; 15 July, 2nd sect., p. 6; and 26 August, 2nd sect., p. 6. On 30 September, on p. 31 there is a report from Moscow about the first concert held on the preceding day in the Moscow Conservatory in the presence of the U.S. ambassador W.C. Bullitt. The report also announces the additional concerts and the impending broadcast. The Choir returned to New York by 1 November, as a report on the next day in the newspaper (p. 26) indicates. *Time* (11 June, 1934; p. 26) and *Newsweek* (1 September, 1934; p. 35) have basic stories but no actual reports about the concerts in the USSR.

13.   See the article cited in n. 9, *above*, pp. 12-13.

14.   Cf. *New Grove*, vol. 5, p. 283 and *Baker's...*, p. 387.

15.   Professor Merritt's letters to this writer dated 10 and 24 April, 1974. The latter also contained a note from Mrs. Humez and a xerox copy of Chesnokov's letter. This writer wishes to express his thanks to both Prof. Merritt and Mrs. Humez for their kind assistance in this matter.

16.   About Orlov see *Muzykalnaia Entsiklopediia*, vol. 4 (1978), col. 103.

17.   About Yury S. Sakhnovsky (1866-1930) see ibid., cols. 869-70; About Glière, ibid., vol. 1 (1973), cols, 1014-16 and *New Grove*, vol. 7, pp. 433-34.

18.   In the letter to Swan Chesnokov's dedication reads in Russian: "Nezabvennoi pamiati dorogogo uchitelia-druga Stepana Vasil'evicha Smolenskogo" which we have translated as "To the unforgettable memory of a dear teacher-friend Stepan Vasilievich Smolensky." In the published book, on page 2 the dedication, however, reads in Russian: "Pamiati nezabvennogo uchitelia-druga...." which slightly changes the emphasis as its translation reads: "To the memory of an unforgettable teacher-friend...."

19.   See note 13 above; there are some 10 letters from Wellesz to Swan in the Swan archive, the earliest dating from 1936.

20.   This refers to Maksim Sozontovich Berezovsky (1745-77), about whom see *New Grove*, vol. 2, p. 523, and *Baker's...*, p. 347, and *Muzykalnaia Entsiklopediia*, vol. 1 (1973), cols. 419-20.

21.   The score in question is Chesnokov's opus 52, *Tri russkikh pesni* [Three Russian songs] of which the University of Virginia library has only the score of the second, entitled *Luchinushka–dubinushka*. On the title page it is clear that the work was published in Moscow in 1926.

22.   See the reference listed in note 3 above.

Prokofiev's Correspondence with Stravinsky and Shostakovich

Translated from the Russian by
Natalia Rodriguez and Malcolm Hamrick Brown

Introductory Remarks and Notes by
Malcolm Hamrick Brown

The collection of correspondence assembled here in translation includes all the communications known at present (1984) from Prokofiev to his Russian colleagues Stravinsky and Shostakovich. Likewise, it includes all the known ones from Shostakovich to Prokofiev. Stravinsky's communications to Prokofiev, on the other hand, are represented by only two letters—the sole ones available for inclusion in our collection. The extent of Stravinsky's correspondence with Prokofiev will remain a mystery so long as private collectors remain silent and national libraries or archives continue to maintain closed collections whose contents are neither accessible nor even listed in open card catalogues (the latter situation prevails with respect to one or another of these three composers in two known cases, the Bibliothèque Nationale in Paris and the Central State Archives of Literature and Art in Moscow). Still, the few letters we have brought together here nevertheless shed important new light on the personal and professional relationship Prokofiev had with each of these other Russian composers, with whom he was continually being compared throughout his creative life.

Photocopies of Prokofiev's original communications to Stravinsky served as the basis for our translations of this part of the present collection. Mr. Robert Craft was kind enough to make the material available, and we have identified and acknowledged each item in our end notes. The originals of these are now owned by the Paul Sacher Foundation of Basel, Switzerland, purchaser of the Igor Stravinsky archive from the composer's heirs in 1983.

The location of the original of letter no. 10, Stravinsky to Prokofiev, is unknown at present. The published version, which appears in translation in Vera Stravinsky and Robert Craft's *Stravinsky in Pictures and Documents* (New York, 1978), was made from a draft copy of the letter kept by Stravinsky and now also owned by the Sacher Foundation, which has kindly granted permission for us to republish the letter here.

The originals of all of Shostakovich's communications to Prokofiev included here, as well as the original of letter no. 1, Stravinsky to Prokofiev, are preserved in Moscow's Central State Archives of Literature and Art, where they are catalogued as part of the Prokofiev Collection, *fond* 1929.

The whereabouts of Prokoviev's original communications to Shostakovich are unknown, if, indeed, they have survived. Shostakovich himself confessed to Mira Mendelssohn-Prokofiev that, sad to say, no Prokofiev material whatsoever had been preserved in his personal archives—a fact, he said, that caused him no little grief (see M.G. Kozlova's notes accompanying her publication of the Prokofiev-Shostakovich correspondence in *Vstrechi s proshlym,* Installment 3 [Moscow, 1978], p. 253). The ever meticulous Prokofiev, however, kept file copies of virtually all of his personal and professional correspondence, and his copies of his communications to Shostakovich are preserved in *fond* 1929 at the Central State Archives.

As a young man, Prokofiev began cultivating the habit of using abbreviations in handwriting to conserve time and energy. By the late 1920s, he had arrived at his characteristic method of abbreviation—the omission of many vowels. When carried to extremes, as Prokofiev was wont to do on occasion, this practice causes considerable difficulty for the reader of his handwriting, regardless of the fact that his cursive hand is generally clear and precise. We have tried in our translations to preserve something of the visual effect of Prokofiev's writing, always taking care to abbreviate, however, only those words abbreviated by Prokofiev in the original Russian.

We have also striven for literalness in translation, but not at the price of idiomaticity. We never intended, however, to make the translations read as if their texts were originally written in English. By staying as close to the Russian as we could, we believe we have preserved the authentic tone of each of the three writers, which, by itself, reveals much about their individual characters and personalities—Prokofiev, often trying to strike a note of jocularity even when dealing with serious matters; Stravinsky, more solemn and astringent; and Shostakovich, sometimes blunt, yet guarded, though given at moments to heartfelt declaration.

1. *Stravinsky to Prokofiev*[1]

Ambulant, 12 May 1915

[Dear Sergei Sergeevich,]

I send you my cordial greetings and hopes to see you soon, dearest fellow! When do you expect to arrive? Diaghilev and Massine[2] are here.

How awful, Scriabin's death![3] I simply can't get over it!

I had wanted to read in detail about this horrible loss in the newspapers Rech and Petrograd, but instead of what I was interested in, I stumbled into a sea of the usual journalistic stupidities (see Karatygin's[4] article on odd-numbered overtones, which is entitled, "In Memory of Scriabin"—hear, hear! even with all my harsh criticism of Scriabin I've been professing through it more respect for him than Karatygin with all his overtones) and trivialities. . . .

Someone told me that an article about my Wedding [*Svadebka*] appeared in the Birzhevye,[5] rather sensibly put together—did it perchance come from you?[6] I'd appreciate your sending the article (it appeared, I'm told, at the end of March or the first of April our style[7]).

Hope to see you soon. I clasp your hand.

Your I. Stravinsky

2. *Prokofiev to Stravinsky*[8]

3 [16] June 1915
Petrograd

Dear Igor Fyodorovich,

Your kind postale-ka [i.e., *carte postale*[9]], which reached Petrograd in less than a month, made me very happy. I received it just having returned from hearing your symphony,[10] which was not at all badly played by Malko[11] in Sestroretsk. I got great pleasure from the 2nd movement and from much in the finale. It was extremely well received by both the public and the press.

I'm sad to say that it's been necessary to postpone my trip, but I just don't see any way to make it before the end of our June, because during this time the question about my military service is finally supposed to be decided, and I can better facilitate settling it here than from a distance. In any case, in a month I'll be in your affectionate embraces. Meanwhile, I'm enthusiastically caught up in writing the ballet,[12] which goes easily, happily and persistently. Leafing through Russian folk-songs opened up to me lots of interesting possibilities.[13]

I didn't see the article in Birzhovka about the Wedding, and it was not my handiwork. I gave Derzhanovsky[14] information [about it], on the basis of which he slapped together an article for Muzyka,[15] what's more, giving the impression that he had just returned from the first performance. The Rus. Mus. Gaz.[16] reprinted it in an adaptation of its own that was just as obtuse as the gazette itself. I sometimes see Benois,[17] Nouvel,[18] and the aged Nourok.[19] I didn't play the sketches of The Buffoon [*Shut*] for them, and I shan't. A few days ago Karatygin and I played the Rite [*Vesna sviashchennaia*] and Petrushka 4-hands. During the latter, Alexander Nikolaevich [Benois], in a transport of enthusiasm, shouted, waved his hands, and explained to the audience what was going on on stage.

Well, for now I embrace you fondly. Greetings to Sergei Pavlovich,[20] Massine, and the Khvotchinskys.[21] If you have connections with the Rus. Mus. Pub.[22] and you still feel kindly toward me, try to arrange a match between me and them. They are continuing their business activity, I understand.[23] I have a whole bunch of manuscripts, including a 2nd concerto, but Jurgenson[24] tries to Jew me down,[25] haggles, and has become positively loathsome to me.

Take care.

Your SPrkf

3.   *Prokofiev to Stravinsky*[26]

23.VI.1918 [Nara, Japan]

My dear Igor Fyodorovich,

I am living in Nara midst Buddhist temples and sacred deer, and I send you from here my affectionate greetings. I am to give several concerts in the Imperial Theater in Tokyo, and in August I expect to travel over to New York. It would be most elegant on your part were you to drop me a line there to general delivery. I have sent you many postcards during these past years but don't know if they got through from Russia. I shake your paw.

Greetings to Sergei Pavlovich. I wrote him c/o the Rus. embassy in Madrid.

Your S. Prokofiev

4. *Prokofiev to Stravinsky*[27]

10 December 1919
c/o Haensel & Jones[28]
33 West 42
New York, USA

Dear Stravinsky,
   I'm happy to let you know about the following. Yesterday, your Pribaoutki were performed for the first time in America. A very talented singer, Vera Janacopulos,[29] sang, approaching them lovingly and singing them excellently, except, perhaps, for Kornila ["Uncle Armand"], which is too low for her voice. It was a great success; all four pieces were encored. Quite a lot of the audience was laughing, not sneeringly but merrily. Fokine[30] and I were sitting next to each other and hurrahed with all our might. The orchestra played well, setting about its task with interest; only perhaps the viola and double bass were grumpy, while for the flutist, on the contrary, "the whole ocean was no more than knee deep,"[31] since he had already played the Japanese Lyrics.[32] I went to the rehearsals and tried to explain what wasn't clear. What I personally liked most of all were (1) the instrumental close [*otygrysh*] in Kornila (Ob + Cl) where, with the brilliance of a true alcoholic, you portray in the clarinet the gurgling of a bottle; (2) all of Natashka, especially the last 5 bars with the delightful muttering in the woodwinds; (3) all of the Colonel, especially the chirping of the oboes and the wonderfully successful climax on the woods "pála, propála, popá poimála"[33]; (4) lots in the last one, especially the beginning of the last instrumental episode [*otygrysh*] (Cl. sol-la♮, Cor. ang. 1a♭ marvelous! insolent!).
   I send you my most cordial greetings and best wishes. I'll be very happy to hear just a word.

Your SProkofiev

5. *Prokofiev to Stravinsky*[34]

Tia Juana, 22 Dec. 1920

[Dear Igor Fyodorovich]

   Having been baked[35] by the hot sun, I embrace you from Mexico. In a month or a month-and-a-half I hope to head for Europe and embrace you in person.

SProkf

6.   *Prokofiev to Stravinsky*[36]

[1920s]

Dear Igor Fyodorovich,

   I came by to shake your paw, because on Wednesday morning I go to London.
   If I don't succeed in catching you before my departure, then, accept my affectionate greetings.

Your SProk

Monday, 12:30 p.m.

7.   *Prokofiev to Stravinsky*[37]

66, rue de Sts Pères
[Paris, 1920s]

Dear Igor Fyodorovich,

   For God's sake explain the following to me:
   What does the sign —($\bar{f}$) mean *for stringed* instruments? Is it portamente [*sic*], as for the p.f. [pianoforte] or woodwinds,—or the opposite—a very sustained note? For example

Cello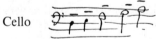

Is this supposed to be played

or rather, is it to be played, as one musician explained to me

   i.e., presumably that the sign — for the strings indicates legato with different bowings. An affectionate kiss. Don't be too lazy to drop me a line.

Your SPr.

Дорогой
          Игорь Фёдорович,

Объясните мне, ради Бога, следующую вещь:
Что означает знак — (p̄) у струнных инструментов? То ли portamente, что для ф.-п. или духовых инструментов, — или наоборот — очень выдержанную ноту? Напр.

Cello:

Надо ли это сыграть

или же, как мне объясняли один музыкант, — это надо сыграть

Т.-е. якобы знак — у струнных означает ведато на разных смычках. Кратко что дую. Не поленитесь черкнуть строчку. Ваш С Пр

Letter 7. *Prokofiev to Stravinsky.* Photocopy of the Original.

8. *Prokofiev to Stravinsky*[38]

18, rue Troyon
Paris XVII
29 Nov. 1926

Dear Igor Fyodorovich,

    Please be so kind as to tell me the address of the company that taught you how to drive an automobile. As it happens we have taken up residence someplace in the neighborhood and would like to make use of the proximity. Cordial greetings from us both.[39]

Your
SPrkfv

9. *Prokofiev to Stravinsky*[40]

[?Paris; 17 June 1932?]

Our very best wishes. I embrace you warmly. Prokofieff.

10. *Stravinsky to Prokofiev*[41]

[?Paris; 20 December 1933]

Dear Seriozha:

    I send this clipping, which appeared recently in the Paris newspapers. I suppose that your interpretation of your joke in the album of the Warsaw woman had another character than the one given to it by these unknown-to-me slanderers in the newspapers. Surely it cannot have been your intention to laugh at me as a pianist—for, after all, I play only my own compositions—or even as a conductor. My hand, drawn in the album, both plays and conducts, and not so shamefully, I think, that people might make stupid and nasty fun of me. No doubt many people object to my activity as a performer, but it is the only way to avoid the grimaces of other interpreters of my music.

Devotedly and with love,
Igor Stravinsky

11.   *Prokofiev to Stravinsky*[42]

Paris, 21 Dec 1933

Dear Igor Fyodorovich,

I very much appreciate the spirit of friendly indulgence with which you've taken this press clipping, the appearance of which caused me no little grief. It's high time to forget the period to which it relates—what you said then about my music and what I wrote in ladies' albums. The news-hack who dug up and paraphrased this misconceived witticism has done no great service, for that any shadow should fall between us would be the purest indecency.

I warmly embrace you. Your new work interests me very much.

Your SPrkfv

[*Madame Lina Prokofiev, a firsthand observer over many years' time of her husband's friendship with Stravinsky, has testified that there was indeed no lasting shadow cast over the relationship of the two composers as a consequence of Prokofiev's joke. During the Stravinsky centennial-year celebrations in 1982, Madame Prokofiev had occasion to write her recollections about Stravinsky and Prokofiev, and we are pleased to publish them here for the first time. Having been reminded of Prokofiev's witty but barbed remark at Stravinsky's expense, Madame Prokofiev then wrote a second letter, filling in some of the details surrounding the incident and providing additional insight from her perspective into the characters of the two composers. This second letter is also published here for the first time, both of the letters with the kind permission of Madame Prokofiev. Her recollection of the date when the incident occurred—"approximately 1926"—suggests the possibility that the reporter happened across Prokofiev's witticism only some years after the original event—a possibility that gains credence in the light of Prokofiev's words to Stravinsky: "It's high time to forget the period to which it relates—what you said then about my music and what I wrote in ladies' albums."*]

MY RECOLLECTION OF THE RELATIONSHIP BETWEEN PROKOFIEV AND STRAVINSKY

I have often been asked by people, especially by musicians, "what was the relationship between Prokofiev and Stravinsky?"--a most subtle question, indeed.

Never have I heard Prokofiev speak of Stravinsky in a way that would have offended him, whereas some of the comments made in one of the Stravinsky-Craft books about Prokofiev were not very flattering--and, moreover, not true. In his personal letters to close composer friends, Prokofiev would analyze the new Stravinsky works that he had just heard, but purely in professional terms, never speaking about Stravinsky himself.

It has been said that at a certain period, their relationship "cooled considerably," but there has been no clarification about "what happened," because nothing had happened, actually. At least, I do not know of any such incident. It seems to me that the only way this "mystery" might be solved is to publish the offending letter from Prokofiev to Stravinsky, if such a letter exists. The issue of a quarrel between the two men has been very much exaggerated; it never took place!

A certain mutual attraction existed between them, but never a profound friendship. Prokofiev was always very much interested in new works by Stravinsky and listened to his music attentively and with great respect. When they met, Prokofiev would ask him about specific passages in certain works. I remember very distinctly, as I was present, when Prokofiev asked Stravinsky whether he necessarily composed at the piano, because Prokofiev himself did not. Stravinsky replied that he always composed at the piano. He spoke about his belief that sitting at the piano, his fingers touching the keys, produced by means of the contact a stimulus which led to the creation of a theme, which he would then jot down on the music paper on the table to his left. Stravinsky would also ask Prokofiev about certain passages in Prokofiev's works--in other words, they would exchange ideas about professional matters.

They saw more of each other during the Diaghilev period, and also when they were together with their respective families in France. Stravinsky came several times to our apartment in Paris, for lunch or dinner, sometimes with Vera. When we were spending the summer at the Château de la Fléchère, Culoz, Ain, in 1929, Stravinsky and his sons Theodore and Soulima visited us on their way to the Lac d'Annecy, where they were spending the summer. We, in turn, paid them a visit there and saw all the family. I remember his mother, a small, rather severe little old lady, before whom Stravinsky seemed not at his usual ease. We took several photographs on these occasions, some of which I still have. Ansermet and Piotr Souvchinsky, our mutual friends who were there as well, are also in the snapshots.

Stravinsky did have, at times, a slight air of superiority, perhaps not really intended, which could rub Prokofiev the wrong way. There might also have been an unconscious incompatibility, which unfortunately occurs sometimes between artists who both have very strong personalities. Nevertheless, their personalities were so very dissimilar. They were both profoundly Russian, but in totally different ways. They were both also extremely meticulous, again in different ways.

Paris. August 31st 1982

Lina Prokofieff

Lina Prokofieff

Photocopy of Mme Prokofiev's Original Typescript.

Stravinsky and Prokofiev

10 February 1983

After having written my article on the relations between Stravinsky and Prokofiev and looking back on those early years of our married life, I did not mention a certain episode which took place approximately in 1926.

At that time, Stravinsky gave a concert in Warsaw and played his own piano concerto. After the concert, a certain Mme Grossman, who was a representative of Pleyel pianos and also active in the Warsaw Philharmonic Orchestra Society, gave a reception. After each concert of that calibre she would give a reception for the honoured guest of the concert. During the reception, she asked Stravinsky to write in her guest book. He drew on one page, the outline of his hand. Several weeks later, after a concert, Prokofiev was the guest of honour at this lady's reception. Whilst looking through the book, he suddenly saw the drawing of Stravinsky's hand, which amused him, and as the opposite page was blank, he wrote the following remark — "When I begin to learn to play a wind instrument, I will then draw my lungs." He wrote that like the mischievous big boy that he was, (but he never meant it to be an insult.)

When he told me about it, I immediately told him that one cannot say such things and least of all write about it, because there will always be people who will enjoy taking it the wrong way. After that, he promised he would show me for censorship, all his witty remarks.

This incident would have been forgotten, but unfortunately a French journalist, having seen the album, immediately wrote about it in an article to his newspaper. Of course somebody showed it to Stravinsky who, from the correspondance that followed and the letters he wrote to Prokofiev, showed that he really took it very much to heart and Prokofiev felt very badly about his reaction (because he had never intended to hurt him). It was just a spontaneous, prankish action. During his years at the Conservatory, he was known as a teaser. His wit was his defence as his colleagues were mostly twice his age. In fact, that is why I did not mention it in my first article. Thinking it over however, I felt it my duty to give a first hand account of the whole story as it will undoubtedly be mentioned in the future.

Of course, if the journalist had not seen and spoken of it, the incident would have been forgotten, but they enjoyed making a mountain out of a molehill.

They both had their weaknesses. Prokofiev had this prankishness and Stravinsky had a sufficient touch of loftiness to react bitterly to every remark — unharmful as it might be.

If this was the reason for this so-called misundertstanding over which so much ink was wasted, was it really worthwhile to make such a rumpus about an episode over which the two corresponded and straightened it out between themselves.

Of course Prokofiev was too much of a tease and did things without thinking and Stravinsky was too touchy, seeing harm when it was not really meant. It was a sort of overlapping of extreme reaction in both directions.

Lina Prokofieff

12.   *Prokofiev to Stravinsky*[43]

Paris, 10 Oct 1934

Dear Igor Fyodorovich,

I'm sending you a ticket to Pasdeloup[44] where my Symphonic Song[45] will be done on Saturday at 5:00 p.m. I very much want you to hear it. Won't you also come to the dress rehearsal, on Saturday, too, at 9:00 a.m.? They'll probably start with the Sym. Song, and I'll have a second score.
Cordial greetings and a hug.

Your SPrkfv

13.   *Prokofiev to Shostakovich*[46]

Moscow, 5 June 1938

Dear Dmitri Dmitrievich,

. . . I finally heard your 5th[47]—true, under rather dismal circumstances: it was at Sokolniki[48]—locomotives were tooting in the distance, an accordion was whining away in the park, and the mosquitos were biting savagely. But Stasevich[49] brought along the score, and I tried to fill in what I couldn't manage to hear. I liked many places in the symphony very much, although it became clear that they're not at all praising it for why it ought to be praised.[50] Nevertheless, it's good that they're praising it, for after all those "warmed-overs" being fed to us by our comrade composers, the appearance of something really fresh is heartening. They'll eventually figure it out properly.
May I fault you in one detail? Why so much tremolo in the strings? Just like Aida. But that's, of course, easy to correct, if your point of view coincides with mine.

Sincere greetings,
Your SP

14. *Shostakovich to Prokofiev*[51]

14.I.1941. Leningrad

Dear Sergei Sergeevich,

... I recently heard Stasevich perform your Alexander Nevsky. Despite a whole series of wonderful moments, I didn't like the work as a whole. It seems to me that artistic norms of some sort have been breached in it. There's too much physically loud, illustrative music. It seemed to me in particular that many sections end before they get started. The beginning of the battle [on the ice] and the entire song for low female voice made a powerful impression on me. Unfortunately, I can't say the same thing about the rest of it. Nevertheless, I'll be immensely pleased if the work receives a Stalin Prize.[52] For despite its shortcoming, this work deserves more than many another candidate.

The Sixth Sonata is magnificent. From beginning to end. I am very glad that I managed to hear it twice, and am sorry that it was only twice.

I clasp your hand warmly,
D. Shostakovich

15. *Shotakovich to Prokofiev*[53]

4.V.1942. Kuibyshev.

Dear Sergei Sergeevich,

I take this occasion to send you greetings and best wishes.

While in Moscow, I had the good fortune to become acquainted with War and Peace.[54] Unfortunately, the acquaintance was rather cursory and hurried. The profound impression [of it] has remained with me. I won't try to make an analysis. But it seems to me that the first four scenes are absolutely magnificent. While playing through them, I gasped with delight, going over some of the spots several times, which delayed full acquaintance: there wasn't time to play through it all. Everything that happens before the Battle of Borodino makes a very strong impression. The scene of the French in Moscow was less satisfying. However, I won't set that down categorically, since my acquaintance was cursory.

I warmly clasp your hand
D. Shostakovich

P.S. I would appreciate it if you would drop me a line. My address: Kuibyshev oblastnoi. Violonovskaia 2a, Apt. 2. Tel. New ATS 2-22-73.

My wife sends you greetings,
D. Sh.

16.   *Prokofiev to Shostakovich*[55]

Tbilisi, 24 May 1942

Dear Dmitri Dmitrievich,

Thank you very much for the kind letter. Your opinion about War and Peace made me extremely happy: I was not at all sure if you would like my opera. Shlifshtein[56] arrived in Tbilisi for a while in February and gave me the score of your 7th, which I held in my hands for all of three minutes. It was your original manuscript on Istanbul paper, but all sort of music was being played around me while I was holding it, and I could only take a fancy to parts of the general outline, not getting to the heart of the matter. Then we caught radio broadcasts of performances in Kuibyshev and Moscow, but not satisfactorily, and we even went to the directorate of the local radio to find out why. So, the pleasure of becoming acquainted with your symphony still lies ahead. Not too long ago, Gauk[57] played the 5th here, not at all badly, considering the somewhat motley character of the local orchestra.

In a few days I'll be moving to Alma-Ata, where I'll be awaiting a letter from my opera backer—the Committee [on Art Affairs]—with recommendations for revisions; meanwhile, I'm orchestrating those scenes that the recommendations apparently bypass.[58] By all means write me at the following address: Kazakhsakaia SSR, Alma-Ata, Central Kino-Studio,[59] addressed to me.

What are your plans? What are you working on?

I warmly clasp your hand. Cordial greetings to Nina Vasilievna.[60]

Your SP

17.   *Shostakovich to Prokofiev*[61]

[Moscow, 23 April 1948]

Dear Sergei Sergeevich,

From the bottom of my heart I congratulate you on your birthday. I wish you health, happiness, and many years of work in the fullness of your great talent to the glory of our beloved musical art.

Shostakovich

18.   *Shostakovich to Prokofiev*[62]

12.X.1952.Moscow

Dear Sergei Sergeevich,

Warm congratulations on your wonderful new symphony. I listened through it yesterday with great interest and enjoyment from first to last note. The Seventh Symphony has turned out to be a work of lofty accomplishment, profound feeling, and enormous talent. It is a genuinely masterful work. I am not a music critic, therefore I shall refrain from more detailed comments. I am simply a listener who loves music in general and yours in particular. I regret that only the fourth movement by itself was played as an encore. The whole thing should have been played. For that matter, new works ought to be played twice officially, and the third time for an encore. It seems to me that S.A. Samosud[63] performed the Seventh Symphony superbly.

I wish you at least another hundred years to live and create. Listening to such works as your Seventh Symphony makes it much easier and more joyful to live.

I warmly clasp your hand. Greetings to Mira Alexandrovna.[64]

Yours. D. Shostakovich

12 X 1952 Москва.

Дорогой Сергей Сергеевич. ...

...

Дмитр. Шостакович

Letter 18. *Shostakovich to Prokofiev.* Photocopy of the Original.

19.   *Prokofiev to Shostakovich*[65]

Moscow
14 Oct, 1952

[Dear Dmitri Dmitrievich,]

I was touched and deeply affected by your letter, dear Dmitri Dmitrievich. I have always valued your opinion. Thank you. I warmly embrace you.

Affectionately yours
Prokofiev

Notes

1.   Translated from a published version in *I.F. Stravinsky: Stat'i i materialy* [... Articles and materials], comp. L.S. Diachkova (Moscow, 1973), pp. 487-88.

2.   Massine=Míasin, Leonid Fyodorovich (1895-1979), a protégé of Sergei Diaghilev's and one of the principal dancers and choreographers with Diaghilev's Ballet Russe.

3.   Alexander Nikolaevich Scriabin=Skriabin (1871-1915) had died unexpectedly of massive blood poisoning from a boil on his lip on 14 April 1915 O.S.

4.   Viacheslav Gavrilovich Karatygin (1875-1925) was a music critic, composer, one of the participants in the important Evenings of Modern Music, and a friend of both Stravinsky's and Prokofiev's.

5.   The *Birzhevye Vedomosti* was one of St. Petersburg's leading newspapers.

6.   Prokofiev was not the author. See letter 2 above.

7.   "Our style" refers here to the Russian calendar (the Julian calendar) which lagged behind the Western or Gregorian calendar by thirteen days after the turn of the twentieth century.

8.   Translated from a photocopy of Prokofiev's original handwritten letter, kindly provided by Mr. Robert Craft. We take this opportunity to express appreciation to Mr. Craft, who made available in photocopies *all* of the letters included here from Prokofiev to Stravinsky. An English translation of the letter, differing in many details from this one, appears in Stravinsky's *Selected Correspondence,* Vol. 1, edited and with commentaries by Robert Craft (New York, 1982), pp. 67-68, n. 32. Published versions in Russian have appeared in *Sergei Prokofiev: Stat'i materialy* [... Articles and materials], comp. & ed. I.V. Nestyev and G.Ya. Edelman (2nd ed.; Moscow, 1965), pp. 320-21, and in *I.F. Stravinsky: Stat'i materialy,* p. 517, n. 1. In both Soviet publications, Prokofiev's bigoted sounding "to Jew down" *(zhidit')* has been replaced by an ellipsis.

9. Prokofiev's fondness for playing with words emerges here in his having taken the French "postale," spelled it in Russian transliteration in the original, and added a Russian suffix that makes it diminutive. Later in this same letter, he refers to the *Birzhevye Vedomosti* as the "Birzhovka," yet another diminutive, but in this instance, one that was also often used by others in familiar reference to the venerable newspaper.

10. Stravinsky's Symphony in E-flat, opus 1.

11. Nikolai Andreevich Malko (1883-1961), noted conductor and proponent of modern music who began his career at St. Petersburg's Maryinsky Theater. He was personally acquainted with both Stravinsky and Prokofiev and often programmed their music.

12. The ballet *Buffoon*, which Diaghilev had commissioned.

13. Stravinsky, who at that time was still the committed nationalist, had made the suggestion that Prokofiev look for inspiration in Russian folk sources.

14. Vladimir Vladimirovich Derzhanovsky (1881-1942), editor and publisher of the important journal *Muzyka* (1910-16). His correspondence with Stravinsky provides valuable insight into Russian music during the period immediately before World War I (See Stravinsky: *Selected Correspondence*, Vol. 1, pp. 43-69).

15. See n. 14 above. *Muzyka* was published in Moscow every week in the period 1910-16 and included reviews of music, books, and concerts, as well as theoretical and historical articles; thus, it was a major force in Russian musical life at the time.

16. The *Russkaia Muzykal'naia Gazeta* [The Russian Musical Gazette], edited by N.F. Findeizen, was published in St. Petersburg in the period 1894-1918; it, too, was a major if somewhat more conservative force in Russian musical life of the period, which accounts for Prokofiev's critical tone.

17. Alexander Nikolaevich Benois (1870-1960), renowned Russian painter, graphic artist, theatrical designer, and art historian; he was, along with Diaghilev, one of the principals in the organization of the Ballets Russes in Paris. Benois was co-author with Stravinsky of the scenario of *Petrushka*.

18. Walter Fyodorovich Nouvel, an associate with Diaghilev in the "World of Art" [*Mir iskusstva*] enterprise and one of the founders of St. Petersburg's Evenings of Modern Music, a circle of propagandists of contemporary music and sponsors of concerts devoted to it in the period 1900-12.

19. Alfred Pavlovich Nurok, like Nouvel, a Diaghilev associate and a founder of the Evenings of Modern Music.

20. Sergei Pavlovich Diaghilev (1872-1929).

21. Friends of Stravinsky and Diaghilev. Basil Khvotchinsky=Vasily Khvoshchinsky was attached to the Russian embassy in Rome; his attractive wife seems to have made Diaghilev jealous because of Massine's interest in her (Richard Buckle, *Diaghilev* [New York, 1979], p. 288).

22. The Russian Music Publishers=Rossiiskaia Muzykal'noe Izdatel'stvo=Editions Russes de Musique, the publishing house founded in 1908 in Moscow by S.A. and N.K. Koussevitzky=Kusevitsky.

23. Despite Russia's involvement in World War I.

24. Jurgenson was the music publishing house in Moscow that first published Prokofiev's works. In 1915, it was being run by the founder's son, Boris Petrovich (1868-1935).

25. See n. 8 above. Anti-Semitic expressions, such as *zhidit'*, "to Jew down" (from the vulgar *zhid*="yid"), were widely used in everyday Russian, frequently without attention to their unfortunate connotations.

26. Translated from a photocopy of Prokofiev's original handwritten postcard. The card is addressed to "Monsieur Igor Stravinsky, Clarens, Suisse," in Prokofiev's hand, but "Clarens" has been crossed through and "Morges" written by a different hand. Prokofiev was in Japan en route to the United States, after having received permission from the newly established Soviet authorities to leave Bolshevik Russia.

27. Translated from a photocopy of Prokofiev's original hand-written letter to Stravinsky. Another English translation of this letter has been published in Stravinsky and Craft, *Memories and Commentaries* (paperback ed.; Berkeley and Los Angeles, 1981), pp. 69-70.

28. Haensel & Jones were concert managers who represented Prokofiev in the United States during his career as a pianist.

29. Vera Janacopulos (1892-1955), a noted soprano of the period, arrived in the United States and made her first concert appearances here in 1918 at about the same time as Prokofiev. They became close friends, and it was Janacopulos who worked with him in preparing the French libretto of his opera, *The Love for Three Oranges.*

30. Fokine=Fókin, Mikhail Mikhailovich (1880-1942), Russian ballet dancer, ballet master, choreographer, and teacher associated with the Ballets Russes. It was he who worked out the scenario of *Firebird,* and after Stravinsky was asked to compose the music, Fokine worked closely with him in trying to obtain music that corresponded to Fokine's balletic conception.

31. We have chosen to translate the Russian folk saying as closely as possible, rather than trying to find an equivalent English one or merely giving its sense in English, which might be "he was unconcerned" or "he couldn't care less." The Russian expression is *"emú móre po koléno."*

32. Stravinsky's *Three Japanese Lyrics* of 1912-13.

33. The humor of the Russian derives both from the alliteration and from the absurdity of the full text: "the partridge dropped, vanished beneath the ice, and caught a priest, the son-of-a-priest, Pyotr Petrovich."

34. Translated from a photocopy of Prokofiev's original hand-written postcard. The card is addressed in Prokofiev's hand to "Monsieur Igor Stravinsky, Villa Bel-Respiro, Avenue Alphonse de Neuville, Garches, S. et O., France."

35. Another instance of Prokofiev's penchant for playing with words. He has taken the Russian word for "bake"—*pech'*—and created a passive verbal adjective, *pekomyi,* that does not exist in Russian usage.

36. Translated from a photocopy of Prokofiev's original handwritten and undated note. The character of the handwriting, especially the absence of abbreviations so common in Prokofiev's correspondernce after ca. 1930, has led us to assign this brief message to the 1920s.

37. Translated from a photocopy of Prokofiev's original handwritten and undated letter. The considerations mentioned in n. 36 above have led us to assign the letter to the 1920s, during which time Prokofiev lived at a number of different addresses in Paris. Another English translation of this letter, differing in some details, appears in Stravinsky's *Selected Correspondence,* Vol. 1, p. 396, n. 6 continued.

38.   Translated from a photocopy of Prokofiev's original handwritten note. Nicolas Nabokov remembers a *tour gastronomique* that he took with Prokofiev in 1930 or 1931, which he says was "enhanced by Prokofiev's abominable driving," and the recollections of other memoirists as well suggest that if Stravinsky provided Prokofiev with the needed address, Prokofiev either failed to follow through with lessons or did not benefit from them! (Cf. Nabokov, *Old Friends and New Music* [Boston, 1951], p. 157.)

39.   "Both" refers to Prokofiev and his wife, Lina Ivanovna, as she was known in Russian circles. Her maiden name was Carolina Codina (b. 1897). Madame Prokofiev's father was a Spanish national with the given name Juan, which was translated into the Russian Ivan to form the patronymic Ivanovna.

40.   Translated from a photocopy of a telegram. A postal stamp on the telegram shows its receipt at Voreppe (Isère) on 19 June 1932. Stravinsky and his family were living there in the Château de la Vironnière, where he would have celebrated his fiftieth birthday on 17 June 1932. Prokofiev's telegram must have been sent in honor of that occasion.

41.   Taken from Vera Stravinsky and Robert Craft, *Stravinsky in Pictures and Documents* (New York, 1978), p. 311. Prokofiev made a joke at Stravinsky's expense when he was given an autograph album to sign and discovered therein an outline of Stravinsky's hand with the latter's signature and identification as "pianist." Prokofiev, as the story was recounted by Gabriel Paitchadze, huffed and declared, "If that's all it takes, I'll draw a picture of my lungs and sign myself 'Prokofiev, singer'!" Stravinsky's holograph draft of this letter, which he kept on file, contrary to his usual practice, served as the basis for this English translation. The whereabouts of the original letter received by Prokofiev is unknown. We thank the Paul Sacher Foundation, present owner of the Stravinsky archive, for permission to republish the letter here. We also thank Mr. Hans Jörg Jans of the Paul Sacher Foundation, for his helpfulness in response to our inquiries.

42.   Translated from a photocopy of Prokofiev's original handwritten letter. A fragment of this letter in another English translation appears in *Stravinsky in Pictures and Documents*, p. 311.

43.   Translated from a photocopy of Prokofiev's original handwritten note.

44.   The Concerts Pasdeloup were an important forum for the performance of modern music in Paris during the 1920s and '30s.

45.   Prokofiev's *Symphonic Song=Simfonicheskaia pesn-=Chant symphonique* had been performed for the first time in Moscow on 14 April 1934; the first performance in Paris was indeed given on Saturday, 13 October 1934.

46.   Translated from a published version in "Vsegda dorozhu Vashim mneniem...." [I have always valued your opinion] (S.S. Prokofiev—D.D. Shostakovich. Correspondence), prepared for publication by M.G. Koslova in *Vstrechi s proshlym* [Meetings with the past], Installment 3 (Moscow, 1978), p. 255. Hereafter, *SSP-DDS*. The ellipsis appears in the published letter.

47.   Shostakovich's Fifth Symphony.

48.   Sokolniki is a park for culture and recreation located northeast of central Moscow where outdoor concerts have been held during warm weather since before the Russian revolutions.

49.   Abram Lvovich Stasevich (1907-71), a composer and well-known conductor noted for his devotion to works by contemporary Russian and Soviet composers.

50. Prokofiev is alluding here to the fact that Shostakovich had been sharply criticized in early 1936 by the guardians of Soviet cultural orthodoxy for his opera, *Lady Macbeth of the Mtsensk District*. He remained under a cloud until the first performance of the Fifth Symphony on 21 November 1937, when the symphony was immediately embraced as the "artist's creative answer to justified criticism." The enthisiastic, even exaggerated praise of the work reflected as much as anything else the enormous sense of relief Soviet musicians felt as a consequence of the official approval granted the work and its composer by Stalin's cultural watchdogs. Prokofiev's remark indicates that he felt the symphony would eventually prove its praiseworthiness not for symbolic reasons but for solid musical reasons.

51. Translated from *SSP-DDS*, pp. 255-56. The ellipsis appears in the published letter.

52. It did not receive a Stalin Prize.

53. Translated from *SSP-DDS*, p. 256. At the time this letter was written, Shostakovich was living in Kuibyshev, where the Soviet government had established a colony of illustrious evacuees from Moscow and Leningrad far-removed from the wartime threat of German attack. Prokofiev was in similar evacuation in Nalchik and in Tbilisi.

54. Prokofiev's opera *War and Peace* had only been completed in piano score on 13 April 1942. The composer's manuscript copy was immediately dispatched to Moscow, where a small jury representing the Committee on Art Affairs auditioned his first version of the opera in early May. Judging from his letter, Shostakovich did not attend this audition, but examined the score on his own.

55. Translated from *SSP-DDS*, pp. 256-58.

56. Semyon Isaakovich Shlifshtein (1903-75), Soviet musicologist who served in the period 1940-44 as a consultant to the Committee on Art Affairs of the Council of People's Commissars of the USSR.

57. Alexander Vasilievich Gauk (1893-1963), leading Soviet conductor and teacher of conducting, was principal conductor of the State Symphony Orchestra of the USSR in 1936-41; during the evacuation, 1941-43, he taught and conducted in Tbilisi at the State Conservatory.

58. The Committee on Art Affairs recommended that Prokofiev should strengthen the heroic-patriotic character of the opera as a whole, and in particular to emphasize the part of the Russian people in influencing the events of 1812. The Committee also urged Prokofiev to infuse the score with more lyricism.

59. Prokofiev relocated in Alma-Ata for the purpose of collaborating once again with the gifted film director Sergei Eisenstein, who was to produce an epic based on the life of Ivan the Terrible.

60. Nina Vasilievna Shostakovich, the composer's first wife.

61. Translated from *SSP-DDS*, p. 258. This was probably a telegram, to judge from its brevity and the character of its language. The occasion was the composer's fifty-seventh birthday.

62. Translated from *SSP-DDS*, p. 258. By the time of the first public performance of Prokofiev's Seventh Symphony—which was given on 11 October 1952, the day before Shotakovich's letter—Prokofiev's health was rapidly declining, to the immediate notice of anyone who saw him. Shostakovich was well aware of the fact when he wrote his letter of congratulation about the new symphony.

63. Samuil Abramovich Samosud (1884-1964), important Soviet conductor, gave the first public performances of Shostakovich's Seventh Symphony in Kuibyshev and Moscow (1942), conducted the stage première of the "peace" portion of Prokofiev's *War and Peace* (1946), and contributed significantly to Prokofiev's revisions of the opera's "war" scenes.

64. Mira Alexandrovna Mendelssohn-Prokofiev (d. 1968), the composer's second wife, according to Soviet accounts. There is no evidence, however, that Prokofiev ever instituted a legal process to divorce his first wife, Lina, whom he had married in Bavaria in 1923.

65. Translated from *SSP-DDS*, p. 259. This appears to have been a telegram, judging from its brevity and language.

Selected Bibliography of Works by Gerald Abraham

Nancy Basmajian

Gerald Abraham recalls that he published his first article, "Humour in Music," in *The Musical Mirror and Fanfare* at the age of 17, a precocious start to a prolific and versatile career that has now entered its seventh decade. The following bibliography represents only a selection from his formidable catalogue of works, which he has unfortunately never attempted to record. In his youth Professor Abraham contributed articles and columns regularly to several periodicals that receive, at best, token coverage here. Particularly for the first decade of his career, this list provides no more than a representative sampling of the more substantial articles, omitting many very brief though frequently provocative pieces from such periodicals as *The Musical Mirror and Fanfare, The Music Teacher,* and *Radio Times.*

Entries are arranged chronologically under five major categories: books, books edited and translated, articles and essays, entries in dictionaries and encyclopedias, and editions of music. The bibliography concludes with a brief summary of Professor Abraham's other editorial activities and an index to the numbered entries. This organization omits two categories: reviews of music and books. Professor Abraham's book reviews alone number well over 200, many of them multiple or comparative reviews, and the sheer volume becomes prohibitive. The majority have appeared in *Music and Letters* (since 1934) as "Reviews of Books," "Reviews of Music," and, in the early years, "Reviews of Periodicals"; in *The Listener* (mainly from 1940 to 1960) under "The Musician's Bookshelf" and other headings; in *The Music Review* (1942-62) as "Reviews of Music" and "Book Reviews"; and in *The Times Literary Supplement.* Professor Abraham has also contributed numerous reviews to such periodicals as *Tempo, The Musical Times, The Journal of the American Musicological Society,* and *The Saturday Review,* some of them quite substantial.

Several volumes of Professor Abraham's collected essays have been published, consisting mainly of pieces reprinted with minor revisions from periodicals. This bibliography does not provide individual listings of the contents of such collections, although the volumes themselves are indexed by title along with the other entries, and, in addition, the entries for the original articles supply cross-references to the volume in which they are reprinted.

I. Books

1. *Borodin: The Composer and His Music.* "A descriptive and critical analysis of his works and a study of his value as an art-force. With many References to the Russian Kouchka Circle of Five—Balakirev, Moussorgsky, César Cui and Rimsky-Korsakov with Borodin." London: William Reeves, [1927]. Reprint ed., New York: AMS Press, 1976. 2d ed., rev., 1935.

2. *This Modern Stuff.* "A fairly 'plaine and easie' introduction to contemporary music, by Gerald Abraham, with a preface by Sir Dan Godfrey." London: D. Archer, 1933. 2d ed. as "This modern stuff; an introduction to contemporary music, by Gerald Abraham, with a foreword by Sir Walford Davies." London: Duckworth, 1939. Reprint ed., London: Citadel Press, 1945. 3d ed., as *This Modern Music,* New York: Norton, 1952. Reprint eds., London: Duckworth, 1955; Boston: Crescendo Pub. Co., 1955.

3. *Nietzsche.* Great Lives series, no. 23. London: Duckworth, 1933; New York: Macmillan, 1933. Reprint ed., New York: Haskell House Publishers, 1974.

4. *Studies in Russian Music.* "Critical Essays on the most important of Rimsky-Korsakov's operas, Borodin's 'Prince Igor,' Dargomizhsky's 'Stone Guest,' etc.; with chapters on Glinka, Mussorgsky, Balakirev and Tchaikovsky." London: William Reeves, [1935]; New York: Scribner, 1936. Reprint eds., Freeport, New York: Books for Libraries Press, Essay Index Reprint Series, 1968; St. Clair Shores, Mich.: Scholarly Press, 1970. Facsimile ed., Salem, N.H.: Arno. German translation of selected chapters: see no. 11.

5. *Tolstoy.* Great Lives series, no. 47. London: Duckworth, [1935]. Reprint ed., New York: Haskell House Publishers, 1974.

6. *Dostoevsky.* Great Lives series, no. 69. London: Duckworth, [1936]. Reprint ed., New York: Haskell House Publishers, 1974.

7. With M.D. Calvocoressi. *Masters of Russian Music.* London: Duckworth, 1936; New York: Alfred A. Knopf, 1936. Reprint eds., New York: Tudor, 1944; New York: Johnson Reprint Corp., 1971.

8. *A Hundred Years of Music.* The Hundred Years Series. London: Duckworth, 1938; New York: Alfred A. Knopf, 1938. Reprint ed., Ann Arbor, Mich.: Xerox University Microfilms, 1974. 2d ed., London: Duckworth, 1949. 3d ed., London: Duckworth, 1964; Chicago: Aldine Publishing Co., 1964. 4th ed., London: Duckworth, 1974.

9. *Tchaïkovsky.* Novello's biographies of great musicians, gen. ed. William McNaught. London: Novello, 1938.

10. *Chopin's Musical Style.* London: Oxford University Press, 1939; reprinted with corrections, 1960. Reprint ed., Westport, Conn.: Greenwood Press, 1980.

11. *On Russian Music.* "Critical and Historical Studies of Glinka's Operas, Balakirev's Works, etc., with chapters dealing with Compositions by Borodin, Rimsky-Korsakov, Tchaikovsky, Mussorgsky, Glazunov, and various other aspects of Russian Music." London: William Reeves, 1939; New York: Scribner, 1939. Reprint eds., New York: Johnson Reprint Corp., 1970; Freeport, New York: Books for Libraries Press, 1970; New York: Irvington Pubs., Essay Index Reprint Series, 1982. German translation by Willi Reich, as *Über russische Musik* (selected essays, with others from *Studies in Russian Music* [no. 4], and a new essay, "Vom Musikschaffen in der Sowjetunion"), Basel: Amerbach-Verlag, 1947.

12. *Beethoven's Second-period Quartets.* The Musical Pilgrim series, no. 39. London: Oxford University Press, Humphrey Milford, 1942. Reprint ed., St. Clair Shores, Mich.: Scholarly Press, 1978.

13. *Eight Soviet Composers.* London: Oxford University Press, 1943. Reprint eds., Westport, Conn.: Greenwood Press, [1970]; Wilmington, Del.: International Academic Pub., 1979.

14. *Tchaïkovsky.* Great Lives series, no. 90. (Revised version of the biography originally published in *Masters of Russian Music;* see no. 7.) London: Duckworth, 1944. Reprint ed., as *Tchaïkovsky: A Short Biography,* Westport, Conn.: Hyperion Press, 1979. Hebrew translation, Music Library series, Tel Aviv: Masada, 1948.

15. *Rimsky-Korsakov.* Great Lives series, no. 91. (Previously published in *Masters of Russian Music;* see no. 7.) London: Duckworth, 1945. Reprint ed., as *Rimsky-Korsakov: A Short Biography,* New York: AMS Press, 1976.

16. *Mussorgsky: Boris Godunov (Rimsky-Korsakov Version).* Covent Garden Operas, edited by Anthony Gishford. London, New York: Boosey and Hawkes, 1948.

17. *Design in Music.* (Originally published as a series of articles in *Hallé;* see no. 124.) London: Oxford University Press, 1949.

18. *Slavonic and Romantic Music: Essays and Studies.* London: Faber and Faber, 1968; New York: St. Martin's Press, 1968.

19. *The Tradition of Western Music.* (The Ernest Bloch Lectures, April and May, 1969.) Berkeley and Los Angeles: University of California Press, 1974; London: Oxford University Press, 1974.

20. *The Concise Oxford History of Music.* London, New York: Oxford University Press, 1979. German translation in two parts by Karl L. Nicol, as *Geschichte der Musik,* vols. 9 and 10 of *Das grosse Lexikon der Musik. Komponisten, Interpreten, Sachbegriffe,* edited by Marc Honegger and Günther Massenkeil. Freiburg: Herder GmbH & Co. Verlag, 1983.

21. *Problems of Musical History.* Gwilym James Memorial Lecture of the University of Southampton, vol. 7. (Delivered at the University on 22 February 1980.) Southampton: University of Southampton, 1980.

21a. *Essays on Russian and East European Music.* London: Oxford University Press, 1984. This book was in press at the time of publication and therefore the contents are not individually listed.

II. Books Edited and Translated

22. Nicholas Kilburn. *Chamber Music and Its Masters in the Past and in the Present.* New ed., rev., and with additional chapters by G.E.H. Abraham. The Music Story Series. (Previously published under the title: *The Story of Chamber Music.*) London: William Reeves; New York: Scribner, [1932].

23. Werner Menke. *History of the Trumpet of Bach and Handel.* Translated by Gerald Abraham. London: William Reeves, [1934]. Reprint ed., St. Clair Shores, Mich.: Scholarly Press, [1974].

24.   Rudolf Kastner. *Beethoven's Sonatas and Artur Schnabel.* Translated by Gerald Abraham. London: William Reeves, 1935.

25.   *Tchaikovsky: A Symposium.* Music of the Masters series. London: Lindsay Drummond, [1945]. As *The Music of Tchaikovsky,* New York: Norton, 1946. Reprint eds., Port Washington, N.Y.: Kennikat Press, 1969; and The Norton Library reprint, with updated bibliography, of the 1969 ed. published by Kennikat Press, New York: Norton, 1974.

26.   M.D. Calvocoressi. *Mussorgsky.* Completed and edited by Gerald Abraham. The Master Musicians series. London: J.M. Dent and Sons, 1946; New York: E.P. Dutton and Co., 1946. Reprinted in the Great Composers series, New York: Collier Books, [1962]. 2d ed., revised and with additional material by Gerald Abraham, London: J.M. Dent and Sons, 1974; Totowa, N.J.: Littlefield, Adams, & Co., 1974.

27.   *Schubert: A Symposium.* Music of the Masters series. London: Lindsay Drummond, [1946]. Reprint ed., London: Oxford, [1952]. As *The Music of Schubert,* with the addition of the Preface and Chapter VII, New York: Norton, 1947. Reprint eds., Port Washington, N.Y.: Kennikat Press, [1969]; and Wilmington, Del.: International Academic Pub., 1979.

28.   *Sibelius: A Symposium.* Music of the Masters series. London: Lindsay Drummond, 1947. As *The Music of Sibelius,* New York: Norton, 1947. Reprint ed., New York: Da Capo Press, 1975.

29.   *Grieg: A Symposium.* Music of the Masters series. London: Lindsay Drummond, 1948. Reprint eds., Norman, Okla.: University of Oklahoma Press, 1950; London, New York: Oxford University Press, 1952; Westport, Conn.: Greenwood Press, [1971].

30.   *Schumann: A Symposium.* Music of the Masters series. London: Lindsay Drummond, 1952. Reprint ed., Westport, Conn.: Greenwood Press, 1977.

31.   General editor. *The History of Music in Sound.* 10 vols. London, New York: Oxford University Press, 1953-59. Including the following volumes edited by Gerald Abraham: vol. 8: *The Age of Beethoven, 1790-1830* (1958); vol. 9: *Romanticism, 1830-1890* (1958); vol. 10: *Modern Music, 1890-1950* (1959).

32.   *Handel: A Symposium.* Music of the Masters series. London: Oxford University Press, 1954. Reprint ed., Westport, Conn.: Greenwood Press, 1980.

33.   M.D. Calvocoressi. *Modest Mussorgsky: His Life and Works.* London: Rockliff, 1956; Fair Lawn, N.J.: Essential Books, 1956. Reprint ed., Boston: Crescendo Pub. Co., 1968. [Not to be confused with no. 26 above.]

34.   With Suzanne Clercx-Lejeune, Hellmut Federhofer, and Wilhelm Pfannkuch. *Bericht über den siebenten Internationalen Musikwissenschaftlichen Kongress, Köln, 1958.* Kassel, New York: Bärenreiter, 1959.

35.   With Dom Anselm Hughes. *The New Oxford History of Music.* Vol. 3: *Ars nova and the Renaissance, 1300-1540.* London: Oxford University Press, 1960.

36.   *The New Oxford History of Music.* Vol. 4: *The Age of Humanism, 1540-1630.* London: Oxford University Press, 1968. Italian translation by Francesco Bussi, as *L'Età del Rinascimento (1540-1630),* Milan: Feltrinelli, 1969.

37. *The New Oxford History of Music.* Vol. 8: *The Age of Beethoven, 1790-1830.* London: Oxford University Press, 1982.

III. Articles and Essays

38. "Haydn and the Scottish Folk-music." *The Scottish Musical Magazine* 4 (December 1922): 65-66.

39. "Burns and the Scottish Folk-Song." *Music and Letters* 4 (January 1923): 71-84.

40. "The Influence of Berlioz on Richard Wagner." *Music and Letters* 5 (July 1924): 239-46.

41. "The Leit-motif since Wagner." *Music and Letters* 6 (April 1925): 175-90.

42. "The Elements of Russian Music." *Music and Letters* 9 (January 1928): 51-58. Reprinted as "The Essence of Russian Music" in *Studies in Russian Music* (see no. 4).

43. "Glinka and His Achievement." *Music and Letters* 9 (July 1928): 255-64. Reprinted in *Studies in Russian Music* (see no. 4).

44. "Delius and His Literary Sources." *Music and Letters* 10 (April 1929): 182-88. Reprinted in *Slavonic and Romantic Music* (see no. 18).

45. "Borodin as a Symphonist." *Music and Letters* 11 (October 1930): 352-59. Reprinted in *Studies in Russian Music* (see no. 4).

46. "Prince Igor: An Experiment in Lyrical Opera." *The Musical Quarterly* 17 (January 1931): 74-83. Reprinted in *Studies in Russian Music* (see no. 4).

47. "Tolstoy and Moussorgsky: A Parallelism of Minds." *Music and Letters* 12 (January 1931): 54-59. Reprinted in *Studies in Russian Music* (see no. 4).

48. "'Sadko' and 'The Tsar's Bride.'" *The Monthly Musical Record* 61 (June 1931): 168-69.

49. "Rimsky-Korsakov's Gogol Operas." *Music and Letters* 12 (July 1931): 242-52. Reprinted in *Studies in Russian Music* (see no. 4).

50. "Genius and Inspiration." *The Musical Mirror and Fanfare* 11 (July 1931).

51. "Music of 'Sadko.'" *The Musical Standard* 37 (July, August 1931): 183-84; 197-98.

52. "A Basis for Scientific Criticism." *The Monthly Musical Record* 61 (September 1931): 270-71.

53. "The New David Club Discusses the Russians." *Musical Opinion* 54 (September 1931): 1028-29.

54. "Scriabin Reconsidered." *The Musical Standard* 37 (September 1931): 214-16.

55. "The New David Club Discusses Musical Criticism." *Musical Opinion* 55 (November 1931): 115-16.

56. "Nietzsche's Attitude to Wagner: A Fresh View." *Music and Letters* 13 (January 1932): 64-74. Reprinted in *Slavonic and Romantic Music* (see no. 18).

57.   "The Fertility Spot." *The Sackbut* 12 (April 1932): 147-50.

58.   "Haydn's Opus 1." *The Musical Standard* 38 (April 1932): 61.

59.   "The Unknown Rimsky-Korsakov." *The Musical Standard* 38 (September 1932): 153-54.

60.   "An Outline of Mahler." *Music and Letters* 13 (October 1932): 391-400. Reprinted in *Slavonic and Romantic Music* (see no. 18).

61.   "The Whole-Tone Scale in Russian Music." *The Musical Times* 74 (July 1933): 602-4. Reprinted in *On Russian Music* (see no. 11).

62.   "The Programme of 'Scheherazade.' "*The Monthly Musical Record* 62 (September 1933): 154-55. Reprinted in *On Russian Music* (see no. 11).

63.   "Balakirev's Symphonies." *Music and Letters* 14 (October 1933): 355-63. Reprinted in *On Russian Music* (see no. 11).

64.   "Psychological Peculiarities of Russian Creative Artists." *The Contemporary Review* 144 (November 1933): 606-12. Reprinted as "Some Psychological Peculiarities of Russian Creative Artists" in *On Russian Music* (see no. 11).

65.   "Weber as Novelist and Critic." *The Musical Quarterly* 20 (January 1934): 27-38. Reprinted in *Slavonic and Romantic Music* (see no. 18).

66.   "Liszt's Influence on the Russian Nationalists." *The Monthly Musical Record* 64 (March-April 1934): 57-58. Reprinted as "Liszt's Influence on the 'Mighty Handful'" in *On Russian Music* (see no. 11).

67.   "'Mlada,' a Curious Episode in Russian Musical History." *Musical Opinion* 57 (June, July, August 1934): 769-70; 866-67; 947-48. Reprinted as "The Collective 'Mlada'"in *On Russian Music* (see no. 11).

68.   "The Oriental Element in Russian Music." *The Monthly Musical Record* 64 (September 1934): 145-47. Reprinted as "Oriental Elements in Russian Music" in *On Russian Music* (see no. 11).

69.   "Borodin's Songs." *The Musical Times* 75 (November 1934): 983-85. Reprinted in *On Russian Music* (see no. 11).

70.   "Rimsky-Korsakov's *Mlada,* 1891." *Musical Opinion* 58 (November 1934): 118-19. Reprinted in *On Russian Music* (see no. 11).

71.   "'Eugene Onegin' and Tchaikovsky's Marriage." *The Monthly Musical Record* 64 (December 1934): 222-23. Reprinted in *On Russian Music* (see no. 11).

72.   "The History of 'Prince Igor.'" *Music and Letters* 16 (April 1935): 85-95. Reprinted in *On Russian Music* (see no. 11).

73.   "Shostakovich's 'Lady Macbeth of Mtsensk.'" *The Monthly Musical Record* 65 (July-August 1935): 121-23.

74.   "Handel's Clavier Music." *Music and Letters* 16 (October 1935): 278-85.

75.   "Balakirev's Piano Sonata." [G.A.] *The Listener,* 26 February 1936, p. 420.

76. *"A Life for the Tsar:* A Notable Centenary." *Musical Opinion* 59 (February, March 1936): 401-2; 497-98. Reprinted as "'A Life for the Tsar'" in *On Russian Music* (see no. 11).

77. "Balakirev's Music to 'King Lear.'" *The Monthly Musical Record* 66 (March-April 1936): 49-51. Reprinted in *On Russian Music* (see no. 11).

78. "Arensky's First Symphony." [G.A.] *The Listener,* 22 April 1936, p. 796.

79. "Grechaninov's Songs." [G.A.] *The Listener,* 29 April 1936, p. 848.

80. "Alexander Constantinovich Glazounov (1865-1936)." [Obituary] *The Monthly Musical Record* 66 (May 1936): 81-83.

81. "Early and Late Dvořák." [G.A.] *The Listener,* 22 July 1936, p. 189.

82. "Schubert's Piano Music." [G.A.] *The Listener,* 2 September 1936, p. 457.

83. "Tchaikovsky as a Song-Writer." [G.A.] *The Listener,* 21 October 1936, p. 788.

84. "Moussorgsky's 'Fair of Sorochintsy.'" *The Monthly Musical Record* 66 (November 1936): 195-96. Reprinted as "'The Fair of Sorochintsy' and Cherepnin's Completion of It" in *On Russian Music* (see no. 11).

85. "The Balakirev Centenary." *The Listener,* 23 December 1936, pp. 1211-12.

86. "The Foundation-Stone of Russian Music." *Music and Letters* 18 (January 1937): 50-62. Reprinted as "'Ruslan and Lyudmila'" in *On Russian Music* (see no. 11).

87. "Sorties into Musical By-Ways." *Musician* 42 (January 1937): 6-7.

88. "The Story of Russian Chamber Music." *Strad* 47 (February 1937): 445-46.

89. "Czech Music." *The Listener,* 3 March 1937, pp. 432-33.

90. "Dargomizhsky's Orchestral Pieces." *The Monthly Musical Record* 67 (May 1937): 73-75. Reprinted in *On Russian Music* (see no. 11).

91. "The Riddle of Tchaikovsky." *The Monthly Musical Record* 67 (July-August 1937): 129-31.

92. "Sibelius' Symphonic Methods." *Musical Opinion* 61 (October, December 1937; February, April, August 1938): 19-20; 211-12; 403-4; 598-99; 945-46; and *Musical Opinion* 62 (October 1938): 21-22.

93. "The Evolution of Russian Harmony: I. Glinka; II. Dargomizhsky and Moussorgsky; III. Borodin and Rimsky-Korsakov." *The Monthly Musical Record* 17 (December 1937): 225-26; and 18 (January, February 1938): 5-8; 37-40. Reprinted in *On Russian Music* (see no. 11).

94. "Reflections on Götterdämmerung." *The Listener,* 2 June 1938, p. 1204.

95. "Modeste Mussorgsky, 1839-1881." *The Listener,* 16 March 1939, p. 601.

96. "A Minor Master: Alexander Glazunov." *The Listener,* 1 June 1939, p. 1180.

97. "'The Flying Dutchman': Original Version." *Music and Letters* 20 (October 1939): 412-29. Conflated with "Wagner's Second Thoughts" (see no. 139) in *Slavonic and Romantic Music* (see no. 18).

98.   "The Three Scores of Schumann's D Minor Symphony." *The Musical Times* 81 (March 1940): 105-9. Reprinted in *Slavonic and Romantic Music* (see no. 18).

99.   "Tchaikovsky: Some Centennial Reflections." *Music and Letters* 21 (April 1940): 110-19. Reprinted in *Slavonic and Romantic Music* (see no. 18).

100. "Marschner and Wagner." *The Monthly Musical Record* 70 (June 1940): 99-104. Reprinted in *Slavonic and Romantic Music* (see no. 18).

101. "Dvorak's Musical Personality." In *Antonin Dvorak: His Achievement*, pp. 192-240. Edited by Viktor Fischl. London: Lindsay Drummond, [1942]. Reprinted in *Slavonic and Romantic Music* (see no. 18).

102. "The Carthaginian Element in 'Boris Godunov.'" *The Musical Times* 83 (January 1942): 9-12. Reprinted as "The Mediterranean Element in *Boris Godunov*" in *Slavonic and Romantic Music* (see no. 18).

103. "Soviet Composers." *The Monthly Musical Record* 72 (1942): "I. Aram Khachaturyan" (March-April): 56-61; "II. Lev Knipper" (May): 75-81; "III. Vissarion Shebalin" (June): 99-104; "IV. Dmitry Kabalevsky" (July-August): 129-34; "V. Yury Shaporin" (September): 148-54; "VI. Ivan Dzerzhinsky" (October): 177-83. Reprinted in *Eight Soviet Composers* (see no. 13).

104. "The Best of Spontini." *Music and Letters* 23 (April 1942): 163-71. Reprinted in *Slavonic and Romantic Music* (see no. 18).

105. "Hoffmann as Composer." *The Musical Times* 83 (August 1942): 233-35. Reprinted in *Slavonic and Romantic Music* (see no. 18).

106. "Shostakovich: A Study of Music and Politics." *Horizon* 6 (September 1942): 196-210. Reprinted in *Eight Soviet Composers* (see no. 13).

107. "Prokofiev as a Soviet Composer." *The Music Review* 3 (November 1942): 241-47. Reprinted in *Eight Soviet Composers* (see no. 13), and in German translation as "Prokofieff als "Sowjet"-Komponist" in *Serge Prokofieff*, pp. 35-40. Musik der Zeit: Eine Schriftenreihe zur zeitgenössischen Musik, edited by Heinrich Lindlar, Heft 5. Bonn: Boosey & Hawkes, 1953.

108. "M.D. Calvocoressi (1877-1944)." [Obituary] *The Musical Times* 85 (March 1944): 83-85.

109. "Rimsky-Korsakov's Songs." *The Monthly Musical Record* 74 (March-April 1944): 51-57. Reprinted in *Slavonic and Romantic Music* (see no. 18).

110. "Operas and Incidental Music" and "Religious and Other Choral Music." In *Tchaikovsky: A Symposium*, pp. 124-83; 230-35. Edited by Gerald Abraham (1945); see no. 25. Material from "Operas and Incidental Music" conflated with "Tchaikovsky's First Opera" (see no. 154) as "Tchaïkovsky's Operas" in *Slavonic and Romantic Music* (see no. 18).

111. "Mussorgsky's 'Boris' and Pushkin's." *Music and Letters* 26 (January 1945): 31-38. Reprinted in *Slavonic and Romantic Music* (see no. 18).

112. "Rimsky-Korsakov's Letters to a Publisher." *The Monthly Musical Record* 75 (June, September, October 1945): 105-8; 152-55; 182-85.

113. "The Art of Song Accompaniment." *Etude* 63 (August 1945): 435ff.

114. "Wagner's String Quartet: An Essay in Musical Speculation." *The Musical Times* 86 (August 1945): 233-34.

115. "Random Notes on Lyadov." *The Music Review* 6 (August 1945): 149-53. Reprinted in *Slavonic and Romantic Music* (see no. 18).

116. "The Bartók of the Quartets." *Music and Letters* 26 (October 1945): 185-94. Reprinted in *Slavonic and Romantic Music* (see no. 18).

117. "Anton Rubinstein: Russian Composer." *The Musical Times* 86 (December 1945): 361-65. Reprinted in *Slavonic and Romantic Music* (see no. 18).

118. "Gustav Holst." In *British Music of Our Time,* pp. 44-63. Edited by A.L. Bacharach. Middlesex: Harmondsworth, and New York: Pelican Books, 1946.

119. "Schumann's Opp. II and III." *The Monthly Musical Record* 76 (July-August, September 1946): 123-27; 162-64. Reprinted in *Slavonic and Romantic Music* (see no. 18). German translation by Gertrud Marbach as "Schumann's Werke II und III" in *Neue Zeitschrift für Musik* 117 (July-August 1956): 404-7.

120. "On a Dull Overture by Schumann." *The Monthly Musical Record* 76 (December 1946): 238-43. Reprinted in *Slavonic and Romantic Music* (see no. 18). German translation by Gertrud Marbach as "Schumanns Ouvertüre zu 'Hermann und Dorothea'" in *Neue Zeitschrift für Musik* 121 (June-July 1960): 196-98.

121. "The Symphonies." In *Sibelius: A Symposium,* pp. 14-37. Edited by Gerald Abraham (1947): see no. 28.

122. "The Genesis of 'The Bartered Bride.'" *Music and Letters* 28 (January 1947): 36-49. Reprinted in *Slavonic and Romantic Music* (see no. 18).

123. "Politics, Music and Shostakovich." *Hallé* No. 4 (February-March 1947): 8-11.

124. "Design in Music: I. The Nature of the Problem; II. Fugue and Some Related Methods; III. Variations; IV. The Sonata Principle; V. The Concerto Principle." *Hallé* Nos. 5 (June-July 1947): 6-8; 6 (August-September 1947): 16-18; 7 (October-November 1947): 14-17; 8 (January 1948): 13-16; and 9 (March 1948): 13-15. Reprinted in book form (1949); see no. 17.

125. "The Piano Concerto." In *Grieg: A Symposium,* pp. 26-31. Edited by Gerald Abraham (1948); see no. 29.

126. "Janáček and the Opera." *The Listener,* 17 June 1948, p. 985.

127. "What Is Musical Inspiration?" *Time and Tide* 28 (August 1948): 880-81.

128. "The Scores of Mendelssohn's 'Hebrides.'" *The Monthly Musical Record* 58 (September 1948): 172-76. Reprinted in *Slavonic and Romantic Music* (see no. 18).

129. "Personality in Music: I. What Is Musical Personality?; II. Mozart and Haydn; III. The Young Beethoven; IV. The Variation Test; V. Music and Man." *Hallé* Nos. 12 (September 1948): 1-4; 13 (November 1948): 12-14; 14 (January 1949): 16-18; 15 (March 1949): 8-11; 16 (May 1949): 11-15.

130. "Modern Research on Schumann." *Proceedings of the Royal Musical Association* 75 (1948-49): 65-75.

131. "Soviet Music and Russian Esthetics." *Saturday Review of Literature*, 30 April 1949, pp. 45ff.

132. "Schumann's *Jugendsinfonie* in G Minor." *The Musical Quarterly* 37 (January 1951): 45-60. Reprinted in *Slavonic and Romantic Music* (see no. 18).

133. "The Dramatic Music." In *Schumann: A Symposium*, pp. 260-82. Edited by Gerald Abraham (1952); see no. 30.

134. "Prokofieff als "Sowjet"-Komponist." In *Serge Prokofieff*, pp. 35-40. Musik der Zeit: Eine Schriftenreihe zur zeitgenössischen Musik, edited by Heinrich Lindlar, Heft 5. Bonn: Boosey & Hawkes, 1953. German translation of no. 107.

135. "Passion Music in the Fifteenth and Sixteenth Centuries." *The Monthly Musical Record* 83 (October, November 1953): 208-11; 235-41.

136. "Passion Music from Schütz to Bach." *The Monthly Musical Record* 84 (June, July/August, September 1954): 115-19; 152-56; 175-78.

137. Foreword to *A Guide to English Folk-song Collections, 1822-1952*, by Margaret Dean-Smith. Liverpool: University Press in association with the English Folk Dance and Song Society, 1954.

138. "Some Points of Style." In *Handel: A Symposium*, pp. 262-74. Edited by Gerald Abraham (1954); see no. 32.

139. "Wagner's Second Thoughts." In *Fanfare for Ernest Newman*, pp. 9-28. Edited by Herbert Van Thal. London: Arthur Barker, 1955. Reprinted, in a version conflated with "'The Flying Dutchman': Original Version" (no. 97), in *Slavonic and Romantic Music* (see no. 18).

140. "Anatoly Lyadov: 1855-1914." *The Listener*, 18 August 1955, p. 273.

141. "The Operas." In *The Mozart Companion*, pp. 283-323. Edited by H.C. Robbins Landon and Donald Mitchell. London: Rockliff, 1956; New York: Oxford University Press, 1956. Reprint eds., London: Faber and Faber, 1968; New York: Norton, The Norton Library, 1969; Westport, Conn.: Greenwood Press, 1981.

142. "Schumanns Werke II und III." *Neue Zeitschrift für Musik* 117 (July-August 1956): 404-7. Translation by Gertrud Marbach of no. 119.

143. "Pomp and Poetry: A Look at Sir Edward Elgar Across a Century." *High Fidelity* 7 (June 1957): 44ff.

144. "Frühe englische Mehrstimmigkeit." *Musica* 12 (July-August 1958): 385-89.

145. Foreword to *Franz Berwald*, by Robert Layton. London: Anthony Blond, 1959.

146. "Homage to Handel and Purcell." *The Listener*, 28 May 1959, p. 961.

147. "Czechoslovakia," "Poland," and "Russia." In *A History of Song*, pp. 181-93, 323-37, and 338-79. Edited by Denis Stevens. London: Hutchinson, 1960.

148. "A New Approach to Handel." *Score* 26 (January 1960): 46-51. (Edited version of a script broadcast in the B.B.C. Third Programme on 22 July 1959.)

149. "Schumanns Ouvertüre zu 'Hermann und Dorothea.'" *Neue Zeitschrift für Musik* 121 (June-July 1960): 196-98. Translation by Gertrud Marbach of no. 120.

150. "Slavonic Music and the Western World." *Proceedings of the Royal Musical Association* 87 (1960-61): 45-56. Reprinted in *Slavonic and Romantic Music* (see no. 18).

151. "Janáček Without Words." *The Listener,* 24 August 1961, p. 293.

152. "Bartók in England." *New Hungarian Quarterly* 2 (October-December 1961): 82-89. Reprinted in *Studia Musicologica* 5 (1963): 339-46, and in *Bartók Studies* (1976); see no. 191.

153. "Music in the World of Today." *International Music Educator* 4 (Autumn 1961): 137-38. Address delivered at the ISME convention in Vienna, June 1961. Reprinted in *Music Educators Journal* 48 (January 1962): 33-34; and in *Australian Journal of Music Education* 23 (October 1978): 3-5.

154. "Tchaikovsky's First Opera." In *Festchrift Karl Gustav Fellerer zum sechzigsten Geburtstag, am 7. Juli 1962,* pp. 12-19. Edited by Heinrich Hüschen. Regensburg: Gustav Bosse Verlag, 1962. Conflated with the chapter "Operas and Incidental Music" from *Tchaikovsky: A Symposium* (see no. 25) as "Tchaikovsky's Operas" in *Slavonic and Romantic Music* (see no. 18).

155. "The Worlds of Dmitry Shostakovich." *The Listener,* 19 July 1962, p. 115.

156. "Chopin and the Orchestra." In The Committee of the Chopin Year 1960, The Frederick Chopin Society, *The Book of the First International Musicological Congress Devoted to the Works of Frederick Chopin, Warszawa 16th-22nd February 1960,* pp. 85-87. Edited by Zofia Lissa. Warsaw: PWN—Polish Scientific Publishers, 1963.

157. "Rimsky-Korsakov as Self-Critic." In *Festschrift Friedrich Blume zum 70. Geburtstag,* pp. 16-21. Edited by Anna Amalie Abert and Wilhelm Pfannkuch. Kassel: Bärenreiter, 1963. Reprinted in *Slavonic and Romantic Music* (see no. 18).

158. "Bartók and England." *Studia Musicologica* 5 (1963): 339-46; reprint of no. 152.

159. "Rimsky-Korsakov's 'Mlada.'" *The Listener,* 12 March 1964, p. 448.

160. "Glazunov and the String Quartet." *Tempo* 73 (Summer 1965): 16-21. Reprinted in *Slavonic and Romantic Music* (see no. 18).

161. Foreword to *Antonín Dvořák: Musician and Craftsman,* by John Clapham. London: Faber and Faber, 1966; New York: St. Martin's Press, 1966.

162. "The Operas of Serov." In *Essays Presented to Egon Wellesz,* pp. 171-83. Edited by Jack Westrup. Oxford: Clarendon Press, 1966.

163. "The Poet of Fire." *The Listener,* 18 August 1966, p. 252.

164. "'The Queen of Spades.'" *The Listener,* 29 September 1966, p. 478.

165. "Musical Scholarship in the Twentieth Century." *Studies in Music* 1 (1967): 1-10.

166. "Lands Not Without Music." *Manchester Guardian,* 26 January 1967, p. 6. Extracts from a lecture delivered to the Royal Society of Arts, 25 January 1967.

167. "Creating a Musical Tradition." *Journal of the Royal Society for the Encouragement of Arts* 115 (May 1967): 417-29. Reprinted in *Music and Letters* 16 (September 1967): 14ff.

168. "Latin Church Music on the Continent—1: (e) Eastern Europe." In *The New Oxford History of Music,* vol. 4: *The Age of Humanism, 1540-1630,* pp. 301-11. Edited by Gerald Abraham (1968); see no. 36.

169. With Henry Coates. "Latin Church Music on the Continent—2: The Perfection of the *A Cappella* Style." In *The New Oxford History of Music,* vol. 4: *The Age of Humanism, 1540-1630,* pp. 312-71. Edited by Gerald Abraham (1968); see no. 36.

170. "V.V. Stasov: Man and Critic." In Vladimir Vasilevich Stasov, *Selected Essays on Music,* translated by Florence Jonas, pp. 1-13. London: Barrie & Rockliff, 1968; New York: Praeger, 1968.

171. "Pskovityanka: The Original Version of Rimsky-Korsakov's First Opera." *The Musical Quarterly* 54 (January 1968): 58-73.

172. "Verbal Inspiration in Dvořák's Instrumental Music." In *Bence Szabolcsi septuagenario,* pp. 27-34. Edited by Dénes Bartha. Fortdruck von *Studia Musicologica Academiae Scientiarum Hungaricae,* Bd. 11 (1969). Budapest: Akadémiai Kiadó, 1969; Kassel: Bärenreiter, 1969.

173. "18th-century Music and the Problems of Its History," in "18th-century Studies in Honor of Paul Henry Lang." *Current Musicology* 9 (1969): 49-51.

174. "A Lost Wagner Aria." *The Musical Times* 110 (September 1969): 927-29.

175. "'Prince Igor' and Its Publishers," in "Correspondence." *Music and Letters* 50 (October 1969): 553-54.

176. "Some Eighteenth-Century Polish Symphonies." In *Studies in Eighteenth-Century Music: A Tribute to Karl Geiringer on His Seventieth Birthday,* pp. 13-22. Edited by H.C. Robbins Landon in collaboration with Roger E. Chapman. London: Allen & Unwin, 1970; New York: Oxford University Press, 1970.

177. "Satire and Symbolism in 'The Golden Cockerel.'" *Music and Letters* 52 (January 1971): 46-54.

178. "Finishing the Unfinished." *The Musical Times* 112 (June 1971): 547-48.

179. "The 'Unfinished' in Russia," in "Letters to the Editor." *The Musical Times* 112 (November 1971): 1071.

180. "Scriabin: A Reassessment." *The Listener,* 6 April 1972, pp. 459-61.

181. "Heine, Queuille, and 'William Ratcliff.'" In *Festschrift Karl Gustav Fellerer zum 70. Geburtstag am 7. Juli 1972,* pp. 12-22. Edited by Heinrich Hüschen. Musicae scientiae collectanea, no. 12. Cologne: Volk, 1973.

182. "Opera in Other Countries: (c) Opera in Spain." In *The New Oxford History of Music,* vol. 7: *The Age of Enlightenment, 1745-1790,* pp. 281-87. Edited by Egon Wellesz and Frederick Sternfeld. London: Oxford University Press, 1973.

183. "The Slav Countries: From the Beginnings to 1600." In *A History of Western Music,* vol. 1: *Music from the Middle Ages to the Renaissance,* pp. 411-24. Edited by F.W. Sternfeld. New York: Praeger, 1973.

184. "Some Aspects of Chopin's Invention." In *Frédéric Chopin: Preludes, Op. 28: An Authoritative Score, Historical Background, Analysis, Views and Comments,* pp. 72-75. Edited by Thomas Higgins. Norton Critical Scores. New York: Norton, 1973. Excerpted from *Chopin's Musical Style* (1939): pp. 44-48, 72-73, 76-77, 94; see no. 10.

185. "The Apogee and Decline of Romanticism: 1890-1914"; "The Reaction against Romanticism: 1890-1914"; and "Music in the Soviet Union." In *The New Oxford History of Music,* vol. 10: *The Modern Age, 1890-1960,* pp. 1-79; 80-144; and 639-700. Edited by Martin Cooper. London: Oxford University Press, 1974.

186. "Church Music and Oratorio in Italy and Central and Eastern Europe: (d) Church Music in Central and Eastern Europe." In *The New Oxford History of Music,* vol. 5: *Opera and Church. Music, 1630-1750,* pp. 397-413. Edited by Anthony Lewis and Nigel Fortune. London: Oxford University Press, 1975.

187. "The Early Development of Opera in Poland." In *Essays on Opera and English Music: In Honour of Sir Jack Westrup,* pp. 148-65. Edited by F.W. Sternfeld, Nigel Fortune, and Edward Olleson. Oxford: Basil Blackwell, 1975.

188. "Our First Hundred Years." *Proceedings of the Royal Musical Association* 100 (1973-74): v-xi. Also as *Royal Musical Association Centenary Essays,* pp. vii-xiii. Edited by Edward Olleson. London: Royal Musical Association, 1975.

189. "Arab Melodies in Rimsky-Korsakov and Borodin." *Music and Letters* 56 (July-October 1975): 313-18.

190. "Musicology's Language Curtain." *The Musical Times* 116 (September 1975): 788-89.

191. "Bartók in England." In *Bartók Studies,* pp. 159-66. Compiled and edited by Todd Crow. Detroit Reprints in Music. Detroit, Mich.: Information Coordinators, 1976. Reprinted from no. 152.

192. "Music in the World Today." *Australian Journal of Music Education* 23 (October 1978): 3-5. See no. 153.

193. "Jack Allan Westrup, 1904-75." *Proceedings of the British Academy* 63 (1977): 471-82. Also published separately, London: British Academy, 1979.

194. "Acquaintance with Mozart." *Adam International Review* 41 (1980): 71-73.

195. "Musical Periodicals in 'Bourgeois Russia.'" In *Music and Bibliography: Essays in Honor of Alec Hyatt King,* pp. 193-205. Edited by Oliver Neighbour. London: Clive Bingley, 1980; Ridgewood, N.J.: K.G. Saur, 1980.

196. "Concise Errors?" in "Correspondence." *Early Music* 8 (October 1980): 575.

197. "On Writing Musical History." *The Listener,* 19 February 1981, pp. 236-37. Transcript of a discussion with Stanley Sadie, chaired by Michael Oliver, and broadcast by the B.B.C. on "Musick's Monument."

198. "The Artist of *Pictures from an Exhibition."* In *Musorgsky: In Memoriam 1881-1981,* pp. 229-36. Edited by Malcolm Hamrick Brown. Russian Music Studies, no. 3. Ann Arbor: UMI Research Press, 1982.

199. "Beethoven's Chamber Music"; "The Chamber Music of Beethoven's Contemporaries"; "Opera in Other Countries [Poland, Russia]"; and "Solo Song: (b) The Slav Lands, (d) England." In *The New Oxford History of Music,* vol. 8: *The Age of Beethoven, 1790-1830,* pp. 155-302; 303-24; 523-34; 572-83 and 591-92. Edited by Gerald Abraham (1982); see no. 37.

200. "Dostoevsky in Music." In *Russian and Soviet Music: Essays for Boris Schwarz.* Edited by Malcolm Hamrick Brown. Russian Music Studies. Ann Arbor: UMI Research Press, forthcoming.

IV. Entries in Dictionaries and Encyclopedias

201. H.C. Colles, ed. *Grove's Dictionary of Music and Musicians,* 4th ed., supplementary volume. London, New York: Macmillan, 1940.
  a. "Jazz." Pp. 302-3.

202. Friedrich Blume, ed. *Die Musik in Geschichte und Gegenwart.* 15 vols. plus supplement. Kassel and Basel: Bärenreiter, 1949-79.
  a. "Abraham, Gerald." Vol. 1, col. 43.
  b. "Ashton, Algernon Bennet Langton." (Tr. Herta Goos.) Vol. 1, cols. 749-50.
  c. "Bishop, Sir Henry Rowley." (Tr. Herta Goos.) Vol. 1, cols. 1863-66.
  d. "Bliss, Sir Arthur." (Tr. Herta Goos.) Vol. 1, cols. 1932-34.
  e. "Bridge, Frank." (Tr. Herta Goos.) Vol. 2, cols. 319-20.
  f. "Britten, Edward Benjamin." (Tr. Herta Goos.) Vol. 2, cols. 323-27.
  g. "Cavos, Catterino." (Tr. Herta Goos.) Vol. 2, cols. 938-41.
  h. "Cui, Cesar Antonowitsch." (Tr. Herta Goos.) Vol. 2, cols. 1818-22.
  i. "Fomin, Evstignei Ipatovič." (Tr. Friedrich Baake.) Vol. 3, cols. 490-92.
  j. "Glinka, Mikhail Iwanowič." (Tr. Friedrich Baake.) Vol. 4, cols. 261-67.
  k. "Gretschaninow, Alexander Tikhonowitsch." (Tr. Theodora Holm.) Vol. 4, cols. 835-40.
  l. "Ljadow, Anatolij Konstantinowitsch." (Tr. Wilhelm Pfannkuch.) Vol. 8, cols. 1059-62.
  m. "Ljapunow, Sergej Michailowitsch." (Tr. Wilhelm Pfannkuch.) Vol. 8, cols. 1062-63.
  n. "Lwow, Alexej Fedorowitsch." (Tr. Wilhelm Pfannkuch.) Vol. 8, cols. 1356-58.
  o. "Rachmaninow, Sergej Wassiljewitsch." (Tr. Wilhelm Pfannkuch.) Vol. 10, cols. 1839-44.
  p. "Rimski-Korssakow, Nikolai Andrejewitsch." (Tr. Christiane Blume.) Vol. 11, cols. 527-35.
  q. "Symphonie: C. Die Entwicklung der Symphonie im 19. und 20. Jahrhundert. IV. Slawische Länder." (Tr. Wilhelm Pfannkuch.) Vol. 12, cols. 1873-83.
  r. "Tanejew, Alexander Sergejewitsch." (Tr. Margarete Hoffmann-Erbrecht.) Vol. 13, col. 81.
  s. "Tanejew, Sergei Iwanowitsch." (Tr. Margarete Hoffmann-Erbrecht.) Vol. 13, cols. 81-85.

203. Eric Blom, ed. *Grove's Dictionary of Music and Musicians.* 5th ed. 9 vols., plus supplementary volume. London: Macmillan; New York: St. Martin's Press, 1954, 1961.
  a. "Balakirev, Mily Alexeyevich." Vol. 1, pp. 362-68.
  b. "Borodin, Alexander Porfirevich." Vol. 1, pp. 819-24.

      c. "Glinka, Mikhail Ivanovich." Bibliography and Catalogue of Works. Vol. 3, pp. 669-71.

      d. "Mussorgsky, Modest Petrovich." Vol. 5, pp. 1030-41.

      e. "Schumann, Robert (Alexander)." Vol. 7, pp. 602-40.

204.   Stanley Sadie, ed. *The New Grove Dictionary of Music and Musicians.* 20 vols. London: Macmillan, 1980.

      a. "Balakirev, Mily Alexeyevich." Reprinted from 5th ed., with work-list by Edward Garden. Vol. 2, pp. 47-56.

      b. "Borodin, Alexander Porfir'yevich: 1. Early Life; 2. Productive Years; 3. Final Decade; Bibliography." Reprinted from 5th ed.; remainder of text, and work-list, by David Lloyd-Jones. Vol. 3, pp. 54-57, 62.

      c. "Musorgsky, Modest Petrovich." Reprinted from 5th ed. Vol. 12, pp. 865-74.

      d. "Rimsky-Korsakov, Nikolay Andreyevich." Vol. 16, pp. 27-41.

      e. "Schumann, Robert." Reprinted from 5th ed., with new work-list and bibliography by Eric Sams.

      f. "Union of Soviet Socialist Republics: IX. Russian SFSR: 1. Russian Art Music: (i) Before 1730; (ii) 1730-1860; and (iii) 1860-1917." Vol. 19, pp. 380-84.

V. Editions of Music

205.   Schubert. Scherzo for the "Unfinished" Symphony in B Minor. Completed from Schubert's own material by Gerald Abraham. London: Oxford University Press, [1971].

206.   Wagner. String Quartet Movement in E on themes from *Siegfried.* (Reconstruction by Gerald Abraham.) London: Oxford University Press, 1947.

Forewords to the following Eulenberg miniature scores:

207.   Borodin. Overture to *Prince Igor.* Finished and orchestrated by Alexander Glazunov. (1950).

208.   Dvořák. Symphony No. 5 in F Major, Op. 76. (1965)

209.   Dvořák. Symphony No. 6 in D Major, Op. 60.

210.   Dvořák. Symphony No. 7 in D Minor, Op. 70.

211.   Dvořák. Symphony No. 8 in G Major, Op. 88.

212.   Dvořák. Symphony No. 9 in E Minor, Op. 95.

213.   Tchaikovsky. *Hamlet; ouverture-fantasie d'après Shakespeare,* Op. 67.

214.   Tchaikovsky. Suite No. 3 in G Major, Op. 55.

215.   Tchaikovsky. Symphony No. 2 in C Minor, Op. 17.

216.   Tchaikovsky. Symphony No. 3 in D Major, Op. 29.

VI. Other Editorial Activities

Gerald Abraham has served as editor or member of the editorial board for a number of periodicals and music series. Several of his editorial and directoral appointments have been with the British Broadcasting Corporation (BBC), which he first joined in 1935 as assistant editor of the *Radio*

Times. Continuing with the BBC as deputy editor of *The Listener* (1939-42), he subsequently held appointments as music editor of the same publication (until 1962) and editor of the BBC Music Guides, among other administrative posts. He has edited the periodicals *The Musical Standard* (ceased publication 1932) and *The Monthly Musical Record* (1945-60), as well as the series "Music of the Masters" (Lindsay Drummond, from 1945). In addition to his responsibilities as editor or co-editor of four volumes of *The New Oxford History of Music* (see nos. 35, 36, and 37, with vol. 9: *Romanticism,* in progress), Professor Abraham has acted as secretary of its editorial board and as general editor of the ten-volume supplement, *The History of Music in Sound* (see no. 31). He has been a member of the editorial committee for Musica Britannica since 1955 and of the committee supervising the series Early English Church Music for the British Academy since 1971, until 1980 as its chairman. He also served on the Advisory Board to *The New Grove Dictionary.*

Index to Bibliography Entries

(Note: Names appearing only as entries in *Die Musik in Geschichte und Gegenwart* [no. 202] are omitted from this index.)

Index